Hans-Georg Gadamer and African Hermeneutic Philosophy
(from interpretation to reality, knowledge and ethics)

Dr. Stanley Uche Anozie

CIP a Camerei Naționale a Cărții

Stanley Uche Anozie.

Hans-Georg Gadamer and African Hermeneutic Philosophy: from interpretation to reality, knowledge and ethics/Stanley Uche Anozie. – Chișinău: Generis Publishing, Online Marketing Group, 2020 (Print on demand). – 294 p.

Bibliography: p. 277-293.

ISBN: 978-9975-3402-8-1

1/14

S 78

Cover image: www.unsplash.com

Generis Publishing
Online Marketing Group SRL
MD-2068, Chisinau, Miron Costin 17/2, Of 519

Online orders: www.generis-publishing.com
Orders by email: info@generis-publishing.com

Table of Contents

General Introduction

I have been interested in Hans-Georg Gadamer and African Hermeneutic Philosophy for a long time. My earlier research in hermeneutic philosophy focused on: African Development: a philosophical interpretation. My subsequent hermeneutical philosophy projects was focused on: Contemporary African Concept of the Human Person: Martin Buber's *I* and *Thou* socio-philosophical interpretation (on intercultural understanding). I also made significant reference to African communitarian notion of person and the conditions for understanding International Human Rights (applied ethics and hermeneutics.) My current book therefore fits African Hermeneutic Philosophy in relation to Western culture /philosophy.

I developed interest in relating my Western philosophical studies to understanding African philosophical themes and the intercultural concerns in contemporary world through hermeneutics. I appreciate the challenge in understanding the demands of this intellectual undertaking, especially with regard to developing thoughts in African philosophy, African thought and literary theory as relatively new disciplines. In the light of the above, I align my research with the work of contemporary hermeneutic and intercultural scholar like Gadamer. I choose to name this project: Hans-Georg Gadamer's Philosophical Hermeneutics: the intercultural problem of language and hermeneutics (Chinua Achebe's *Things Fall Apart*: a casebook of African Thought.)

Gadamer provides for my research a philosophical framework, a platform and a meeting point to integrate Western and African philosophical thoughts/themes. As a hermeneutic project, it calls for a continual reflection and further intellectual inquiry for true meaning/understanding of African narrative and classical texts. My work is a contribution to African and Africana hermeneutical philosophy and some essential aspects of literary theory as part of the universality of hermeneutics (**leading to African Hermeneutics of Political Belongingness, another developing research topic associated with this project**).

Chinua Achebe's Hero-tragic *Things Fall Apart* serves as a casebook of Igbo African's worldviews and the text for the application of the universality of hermeneutics. His avoidance of a complete usage of an indigenous African language in his narrative has raised linguistic problems for hermeneutics and African philosophical thought, especially when it is a way of seeing Africa. For instance, the role of language in the communication of *communal* meaning of tragedy for the African, the notion of person and notion of *Chi* (fate or destiny) in the narrative, the misunderstanding of some philosophical values of the narrative proverbs and the relevant hermeneutical themes in African thought/philosophy etc. For this project, Gadamer's hermeneutical approach will provide a philosophical framework for the interpretation of Achebe's text and its specific African experience of the notion of tragedy which is a central theme in Achebe's narrative discourse. Gadamer addresses this intercultural problem of language and hermeneutics through his discourse on understanding and language.[1]

The hermeneutic approach is best suited to the intercultural problem of language in that hermeneutics aims at understanding (inter-comprehension or mutual comprehension) in the context of the worldviews, traditions and language of interlocutors. For Gadamer, hermeneutics may involve more than one truth and the strict use of scientific method. It requires using different perspectives, the "fusion of horizons" to come to a better understanding, since our horizon moves with us as we progress in understanding. For one to get at meaning, one needs to move from the whole to part, and back again. The 'whole' of a book is the text itself, while the words and sentences are the parts of the text (as whole.) Hermeneutics requires the understanding of language and the place of language in interpretation.[2] With language at the center of interpretation and understanding, Gadamerian hermeneutics claims to provide a solution of the intercultural problem of language. Through language and hermeneutics Gadamer moves us to a higher universality,[3] especially with regard to narratives/literature or texts. If this is the case, his approach would be

---

[1] Hans-Georg Gadamer, *Truth and Method*, trans. Joel Weinsheimer and Donald Marshall (London: Continuum, 2nd rev. ed., 2004), p. 402; Gadamer, *Truth and Method* (New York: The Seabury Press, 1975), p. 363.

[2] Hans-Georg Gadamer "Man and Language," *Philosophical Hermeneutics*, trans. and ed. David E. Linge (California: Berkeley University California Press, 1976), p. 66.

[3] David Ingram, "Hermeneutics and Truth," *Journal of the British Society for Phenomenology* 15, No. 1, January 1984, p. 70. There is an on-going dialogue through experience.

relevant to the problems present in *Things Fall Apart*. Hence the goal of this research is to apply this claim to universality to a hermeneutic text like Achebe's.

What will be the aim of this book?

This research considers the hermeneutical relevance of African thought and its understanding as part of the universality of hermeneutics. Achebe's narrative text, like the Greek texts, is an excellent work for the application of universal hermeneutics. However, I am not questioning the validity of the universality of hermeneutics, but rather expressing how significant Gadamer's approach is to understanding other people, cultural texts and worldviews if hermeneutics is universal. In other words, I am interested in the global significance of hermeneutical understanding. Gadamer provides the philosophical optimism and contemporary platform for African scholars in the interpretation and understanding of African cultural texts and being understood by other non-African cultures and philosophical persuasions. Hermeneutics considers every text or people's worldviews as interpretive or capable of communicating meaning despite being different, foreign or strange to us, yet they have some truths to tell us. The universality of hermeneutics at its best leads to a dialogic hermeneutics in a world of global understanding/peaceful co-existence.

What is new and the philosophical relevance of this book and the audience?

The target audiences for this book are: African scholars, graduate and undergraduate students in liberal arts/philosophy/humanities colleges and departments. This book will benefit non-Western scholars/students who are interested in dialoguing with other cultures/worldviews through interpretation and discourse on language. Many students (non-Western and Western/European students or scholars) in Comparative Philosophy, Philosophy of Diversity, Indigenous Philosophy or Multicultural Philosophy have longed to appreciate African worldviews through language or narrative philosophy as essential aspects of African Philosophical Thought or African Philosophical Studies.

The philosophical content of my book is that it discloses in a profound sense African hermeneutical/philosophical thought and worldviews. For instance, in Achebe's text, the *communal* aspect of Okonkwo's (the main character) tragedy is often missed by people of non-African cultural background because of their familiar understanding of Greek tragedy or Modern tragedy or Christian tragedy. For us to understand African tragedy narrative, the philosophical depths of Achebe's African insightful proverbs ought to be considered. The significances of these proverbs are not non-philosophical as some people may assume. African proverbs are rich with meanings. They are "the 'oil' with which Igbos eat their words (language)" (Igbo African saying.)[4] Another important philosophical relevance of my work is the use of the notion of *person* and notion of *chi* to articulate what *communal* tragedy means for Africans without misunderstanding it as a private individual tragedy. These philosophical contributions are better described in the words of a Gadamerian scholar, Prof. Fred Dallmayr, as "the hermeneutics of cross-cultural studies,"[5] a hermeneutic of intercultural dialogue and a part of the growing discipline of *"African Hermeneutic Philosophy."*

As contributions to *"African Hermeneutic Philosophy"* or, ethno-philosophy and hermeneutics, this book studies and identifies the relevant arguments presented to address the intercultural problem of language in hermeneutics. In what way did the claim to universality in hermeneutics satisfy hermeneutical and critical approaches to articulate the essence of interpretation or the ontology of understanding? I will use expository, hermeneutical and critical approaches to present *Things Fall Apart* as a "unit case" for the claim of universality of hermeneutics, by constructively identifying the language and hermeneutical problem present in one of Africans' literary narratives. Achebe's classic text/narrative stands out in contemporary philosophical and hermeneutical study of African worldviews and thought.

One of the reasons for choosing *Things Fall Apart* is that it was among the first African written books in response to mono-logical and unilateral

---

[4] Igbo people are known to eat their yams (staple food) with their sweet oil. Proverbs are the sweet oil for communicating in Igbo language (words.)

[5]   http://journals.sfu.ca/coaction/index.php/egp/article/viewArticle/1937/2187   (Accessed June 19, 2013.) Prof. Fred Dallmayr's article here is entitled: "Hermeneutics and intercultural dialog: linking theory and practice" 2009. Dallmayr suggests that Gadamer rejects a hermeneutics that is monological, unilateral and imperialistic in nature. Gadamer's approach urges engaging with any text and other cultures in a dialogue.

colonial narratives like Joseph Conrad's book entitled *Heart of Darkness*[6], which was, for most at Achebe's time, a poor representation of African world. Achebe's narrative aimed at addressing this one-dimensional or imperialistic representation of African worldviews and the consequent misrepresentation of his people at the university colleges and graduate schools. He wanted African narrative to be heard from an African voice. Prof. Tsenay Serequeberhan expressed it in a similar way: "hearken to what Africans have to say for themselves."[7]

Another reason for using Achebe's *Things Fall Apart* is that it is widely read by most African students and scholars, and many non-African scholars, with over ten million copies and translated in fifty languages (although not yet a complete translation in Igbo language.) I focus on language, hermeneutics and the African experience of the notion of tragedy in narrative aesthetics. Hence, this book makes use of available philosophical and hermeneutical information in respect to Achebe's *Things Fall Apart* as a casebook for applying Gadamer's hermeneutical contributions. Let me address the various chapters of this book.

Chapter one presents a brief historical survey of the development of hermeneutics with the aim of showing how it progressively claims to universality. Each historical period contributes to the general development of hermeneutics: *Ancient*, *Medieval*, and *Modern*. The various periods also have some distinct ways of understanding the concept of hermeneutics. There is no univocal definition of the term hermeneutics in the course of these historical periods but there is a clear influence of prior periods to later views on hermeneutics. At least the idea of the "inner" meaning or deeper meaning is vividly perceived in hermeneutics' historical development. This chapter also

---

[6] "Heart of Darkness" is a short colonial narrative by Joseph Conrad. It presents some of his experiences in Congo River of Central Africa in 1899 and some views on differences in civilizations and cultures. Achebe felt the book misrepresented African worldviews. I choose to focus on Achebe's text (*Things Fall Apart*) in order to carefully advance hermeneutical understanding with the claim of the universality of hermeneutics in Gadamer. According to Prof. Tsenay Serequeberhan, the reflective presentation of African philosophical thought (African philosophy) is connected to the "demise of European hegemony (colonialism and neocolonialism)." Tsenay Serequeberhan, ed., *African Philosophy: The Essential Readings* (New York: Paragon House, 1991), pp. 22-23.

[7] Tsenay Serequeberhan, ed., *African Philosophy: The Essential Readings* (New York: Paragon House, 1991.)

makes brief references to hermeneutics through "theater" (that communicates meaning through tragedy) and the intercultural encounter or situations in the ancient, medieval and modern periods.

The ancient and medieval philosophers influenced the views of modern hermeneutists.[8] I will limit my interests to important philosophers of these periods like *Plato, Aristotle, Saint Paul, Philo, Augustine, Schleiermacher, Dilthey, Husserl* and *Heidegger*. This is not because they are exhaustive of *all* the hermeneutists before Gadamer, but these provide the essential highlights in the development of Gadamer's universality of hermeneutics and the intercultural aspect of this book. They show a movement from local interpretation to a general method of hermeneutic universality. They also show how hermeneutics progressed from being a technique to a theory of understanding. Following the ancient to the modern period, one could also trace a form of inter-human or cross-cultural hermeneutics leading to what may be called *dialogic hermeneutics* or *intercultural dialogue* that has been associated with addressing an *intercultural problem of language in hermeneutics*. Hermeneutics has gradually moved from the interpretation of texts to the interpretation of philosophical perspectives, human cultural thoughts, lived experiences and conducts. It is not about a pure abstract theory. This hermeneutics now helps us focus our thoughts to the interpretation of texts on a people's worldviews and existential narrative literature as the main goal of this research.

Chapter two considers the significant issues of Gadamer's philosophical hermeneutical theory. The task of his hermeneutics is to address the fundamental importance of understanding and how "understanding manifests itself."[9] Philosophical hermeneutics explains the conditions of understanding and the art of understanding. Understanding is a way of getting at clear and inner meaning in a text. Gadamer's aim is to understand the structure of human thought and how we arrive at clear meaning. He is not only interested in dialoguing with a text, but also dialoguing with other people of different cultures. This is seen in each linguistic community, the literary art or literature,

---

[8] Kurt Mueller-Vollmer, ed., *The Hermeneutics Reader* (Oxford: Continuum, 1985), pp. ix-x.

[9] Hans-Georg Gadamer, *Philosophical Hermeneutics*, trans. and ed. David E. Linge (Los Angeles: University of California Press, 1976), pp. 18-19.

and the worldviews of societies. Philosophical hermeneutics is a science that is within the human sciences and social sciences.[10]

Gadamer hermeneutical theory is considered here because its claim of universality is based on ontological approach and on the dialogue with the other. There are other approaches in hermeneutics, but my aim is to test a philosophical theory that addresses the intercultural problem of language in hermeneutics. Gadamer is relevant because of his interest in dialoguing with narratives/traditions, written texts and literature. His approach is more precise to my main choice African literature (Achebe's *Things Fall Apart*) than Paul Ricoeur's. For instance, Ricoeur's work seems focused on philosophical anthropology, understanding of self, freedom and nature, freedom and its misuse, language and the role of metaphor, phonetics, lexical, syntactic and stylistic rules.

In this chapter I examine how hermeneutics becomes universal through its history. However, I choose to focus on the presentation of Gadamer's hermeneutical principles with regard to how they claim universality beginning with: the *Hermeneutical Circle* in which the whole determines the detail and the detail determines the whole in the understanding of texts;[11] the principle of *Temporal Distance* that separates traditions and contemporary interpretations; the role of *Prejudice* as part of the ontological conditions of understanding; the hermeneutical significance of the *Fusion of Horizons*; the *Hermeneutical Situation and Effective Historical Consciousness* as important in articulating the problem of understanding. His use of *Bildung* as culture and cultivation of capacities for universality will also be articulated here. The procedure is sufficient for our application of Gadamer's hermeneutics as a framework.

Hermeneutics is always mediated by language whenever we understand. One cannot do hermeneutics without language. Language is at the heart of Gadamer's hermeneutic project. There is the language we speak as our

---

[10] *Ibid.*

[11] Brice Wachterhauser, "Getting it Right: Relativism, Realism and Truth," *The Cambridge Companion to Gadamer,* Robert J. Dostal, ed (New York: Cambridge University Press, 2002), pp. 77-78, n. 4. See Tilottama Rajan, "Hermeneutics," *The Johns Hopkins Guide to Literary Theory and Criticism,* ed. Michael Groden and Martin Kreiswirth,[cited 26 November 2004]. Online:http://www.press.jhu.edu/books/hopkins_guideto_literary_theory/hermeneutics_1.ht ml.)

language and the language that emerges while we try to understand other cultures. Language and hermeneutics are two sides in the act of understanding. These influence the later discourse in chapter four on the problem of understanding as *one problem* with two sides: a) the intercultural *problem of language*, and b) the intercultural *problem of hermeneutics* present in written texts and literature. Then I look at Gadamer's brief essay on the relevance of Aristotle's concept of tragedy. This will be of specific value when relating Gadamer and Achebe's reflections on tragedy.

Chapter three focuses on Achebe's narrative: language and narrative of tragedy in Chinua Achebe's *Things Fall Apart* and contemporary Africa philosophical thought on the notion of person. It discusses the use of culture by Achebe and other African scholars in presenting African thought in a way that relates to Gadamer's *Bildung* (understood as culture.) In addition to a powerful story-line, Achebe's classic book articulates contemporary African ethno-philosophy and reality. For one to follow the discourse and be able to address some pertinent questions, it is necessary to take a look at the historical background[12] of Achebe's *Things Fall Apart*. I shall also summarily present Achebe's background as part of what influenced his method of narrative. Although Achebe's background story is not important to Gadamer's hermeneutical approach, it is only important for non-African or familiar readers of Achebe's text. As stated above, Achebe's narrative highlights his Hero-Tragedy character (Okonkwo) and the series of tragic events that culminate in his demise. This chapter looks at the various chapters of Achebe's text leading to his notion of African tragedy. I will thus inquire about the socio-philosophical notion of person and community that influenced Achebe's Hero-character. If a person in African thought is defined as relational "I am because we are," then the question of individual tragedy has to be hermeneutically understood as communal.

My task in this chapter is not to prove any distinction between the African notion of tragedy and the Western (Aristotelian) notion of tragedy, but to identify a subtle uniqueness implied in Achebe's tragedy narrative in light of the African notion of person. Tragedy is a common human phenomenon. Achebe himself accepts that there exist some relations between his cultural

---

[12] Mala Pandurang, "Chinua Achebe and the 'African Experience'," *Chinua Achebe Things Fall Apart (Authoritative Text, Contexts and Criticism)*, Francis Abiola Irele, ed (New York: W. W. Norton & Company, 2009), pp. 344ff.

views on tragedy and that of Aristotle.[13] Tragedy describes the context of Achebe's narrative of the tragic-hero: Okonkwo. In that line, I use tragedy and tragic-hero within the context of application and interpretation.

It would then seem that the specific cultural context of *Things Fall Apart* would pose a challenge to the universality of hermeneutics. How does the use of English affect the universality of Achebe's narrative? A section of this chapter addresses the prospects of English language used in expressing African worldviews in the book. Could it have caused some misunderstanding of African thought? Did Achebe's use of English language clearly express the truth of the reality of the Igbo (African) people in his work? Did he totally succeed without any critical interpretative implication, especially with regard to language? If language is universal and dynamic, could any African language have communicated African worldviews and life-world better than English language? Is there the possibility of a *continental African language* for philosophical literature? Finally, I analyze the mode of existence and the unfolding of history as it is the core implication of Achebe's book: *change* in the face of intercultural fusion of horizons or intercultural dialog. This chapter presents the one intercultural problem with two sides raised in Achebe's text (language and hermeneutics problem.)

Chapter four begins the intercultural dialog discourse by providing brief information on how we use the intercultural problem of language and hermeneutics in this research. The chapter also consists of the test of the universality of hermeneutics and argues that Gadamer's hermeneutical approach has a significant role in understanding Achebe's narrative literature about Igbo African people. Gadamer's hermeneutics is suitable for this research because it considers language as universal and not merely a tool for communication. It ontologically considers the universality of language from the perspective of the "inner" word or "inner" meaning relevant in hermeneutics. Language is the primary horizon of hermeneutics. Gadamer's theory of language/hermeneutics is that any language has the capacity to describe reality, but not the totality or the world as such. Every language

---

[13] See chapter three on Charles H. Rowell's interview with Achebe. Achebe in his interview with Rowell relates with Aristotle's idea of a superhuman or godlike individual going through tragic difficulties. Achebe describes his main character as a man who is larger than life. Certainly the simple nature of Achebe's world and how he presents Okonkwo may be a difficult in a multi-cultural parallel comparison of realities or worldviews.

communicates the worldviews of its people and is capable of communicating being through interpretation. Every language somehow imposes its perspective, horizon and culture on others. That means the languages (English and Igbo, in this case) need to function together in a fusion of hermeneutical horizons for a better interpretation.

Gadamer's hermeneutics as the theory of understanding of our human experience involves the literary art of a people, their tradition and culture. It deals with the truth of the world in which we live and experience one another as human beings. It is a new philosophical perspective that emphasizes consciousness of our linguistic communication with one another and our relation to the world. In Achebe's *Things Fall Apart* the new consciousness for language to communicate being and historical tradition is the object of hermeneutical application.

The primary goal is located under the theme in this chapter: the *Intercultural Problem of Language* as a critical aspect of Achebe's use of language in his African narrative literature and the advantages/gains/positive results as well as the disadvantages/loses/hindrances of using language. Achebe's narrative literature is important in my critical interpretive project on African philosophical thought and hermeneutical studies. Gadamer will address this problem of language through his ontological application of the *inner* word or *inner* meaning different from the political and post-colonial approach of some African scholars.

To evaluate the efficiency/pertinence of Gadamer's hermeneutics in interpreting *Things Fall Apart*, therefore epistemological procedure, my second main goal in this chapter is to develop further the universality of hermeneutics (as *dialogic hermeneutics*) through linguistic interpretation and understanding of African people, culture, tradition and their life-world within the context of Achebe's narrative (in terms of what is gained through the narrative or project.) This second section I refer as the *Intercultural Problem of Hermeneutics* which also uses Gadamer's hermeneutical framework to understand African worldviews. I think Achebe's *Things Fall Apart* (in English) presents a linguistic *misunderstanding* problem for African philosophical world. This misunderstanding of the *communal* tragedy will be addressed by Gadamer through the application of the hermeneutical good prejudices/fore-knowledge of the notions of *Chi* proverbs and the notion of *person*.

In other words, in attempt to advance understanding Achebe's African ethno-philosophy and narrative, I use Gadamer's universal hermeneutical framework and his ontological dialogue approach. This is especially pertinent with regard to Achebe's notion of tragedy in the narrative describing Igbo African thought through a Western/European language. Gadamer will help us address the two intrinsically related issues: a) the intercultural problem of language, and b) the intercultural problem of hermeneutics present in Achebe's *Things Fall Apart*. How does Gadamer address the language and hermeneutical difficulties in Achebe, especially considering the role of *English* language (instead of a continental African language) in his *African* tragedy narrative?

To help develop this thought, the African notion of *Chi* or Fate is also essential to this narrative. A look at the narrative style, the usage of proverbs would justify this interpretation of Achebe's work. Proverbs are essential to Igbo people's usage of their language in narratives. The use of the notion of *Chi* proverb (in chapter four) and notion of person (earlier discussed in chapter three) are brought in to bear on some hermeneutical themes derived from Achebe's text and necessary to justify a communal understanding of tragedy.

In conclusion, I claim that Achebe's English language hinders African linguistic communities from developing their languages.[14] It also fails to clearly portray the Igbo African narrative of tragedy through its linguistic aesthetic, thereby not advancing Achebe's primary purpose of his narrative, which is the true disclosure of his world against colonial misrepresentation. The epistemological test/application is weakened by Achebe's use of English to express African reality and experience. Although each language has the intellectual purity to communicate other peoples' thought and culture, but it is better and significant when the language of each people first does their own representation for them. The philosophical reality of each culture *should be* expressed through *its language*. Our language is part of who we are. Every

---

[14] Isidore Okpewho, "Introduction," *Chinua Achebe's Things Fall Apart: A Casebook* (Oxford: Oxford University Press, 2003), pp. 28-29.

language is capable of communicating[15] its people's worldviews. As Gadamer argues every language is "a life process"[16] in the understanding of other peoples' worldviews. His basic theory is: 'Being can be understood is language.' Language is the medium and horizon of understanding. Language and hermeneutics are the two essential aspects of understanding.

This understanding, I think, does not contradict Gadamer's hermeneutical framework: the principle of the universality of hermeneutics where he recommends focusing on the ontological aspect of language as inner word or meaning. Gadamer's recommendation is excellent in this regard, but there is the urge to use one's own language in narratives to avoid misunderstanding following colonial difficulties and the recognition of the intellectual purity of any language for its own world. This research advances Gadamer's intercultural dialog or dialogic hermeneutics in a contemporary world where the worldviews of others have some truths for us or meanings to give us. It also recognizes the place of African philosophical texts/narrative studies in the universality of hermeneutics as we address intercultural problem of language and hermeneutics. The importance of English language or a "world-wide language"[17] is not in dispute; however, Achebe's *first* use of English language for his narrative is disadvantageous to the development of African linguistic and philosophical narrative. He does use English language to raise some critical questions, especially the intercultural problem of language and hermeneutics. But his work is criticized for its neglect of the full role of language (indigenous language) in hermeneutics and narratives. Gadamer's approach will serve as a remarkable hermeneutical framework in this claim of universality of hermeneutics and understanding other cultural texts/narratives about reality.

---

[15] Jens Kertscher, "Gadamer's Ontology of Language Reconsidered," *Gadamer's Century: Essays in Honor of Hans-Georg Gadamer,* Jeff Malpas, Ulrich Arnswald and Jens Kertscher, eds (Cambridge, Massachusetts: The MIT Press, 2002), p. 143.
[16] Gadamer, *Truth and Method*, trans. Joel Weinsheimer and Donald G. Marshall, *op. cit.*, p. 443; Gadamer, *Truth and Method* (New York: The Seabury Press, 1975), p. 404.
[17] Okpewho, "Introduction," *Chinua Achebe's Things Fall Apart: A Casebook, op. cit.,* pp. 28-29.

CHAPTER 1

A General Survey of the Development of Western Hermeneutical Philosophy: From Plato to Gadamer

1.1 Ancient Philosophy and Hermeneutics

a. Plato

The ancient Greeks of Plato's time were struggling to appropriate the great texts of their tradition, i.e., the Homeric literature, which were written many centuries before them. Thus they required interpretation of these texts to get at the inner meaning. Hermeneutics has since become a discipline about meaning, understanding or explanation. I shall proceed with a general view on the development and understanding of the term hermeneutics to its particular use in Plato's time and the modern period.

Hermeneutics has developed to the point of claiming universality as a general theory of interpretation. Hermeneutics comes from the Greek word *"hermeneuein"* [ερμηνευειν] which means "to say," "to express," or "to explain." It also means "to translate." When one translates or explains the content of a text, one is applying hermeneutics. It is also means "to interpret" a text. According to *The Cambridge Dictionary of Philosophy*, hermeneutics is:

> the art or theory of interpretation as well as a type of philosophy that starts with questions of interpretation. Originally concerned more narrowly with interpreting sacred texts, the term acquired a much broader significance in its historical development and finally became a philosophical position in twentieth-century German philosophy.[18]

In ancient mythology, *hermeneia* [ερμηνεια] is attributed to the messenger-god called *Hermes*. According to some scholars, this etymology was proposed by Martin Heidegger but later been considered by Prof. Donald

---

[18] Robert Audi, ed. *The Cambridge Dictionary of Philosophy* (Cambridge: Cambridge University Press, 2nd ed., 1999), p. 377.

Ipperciel to be inaccurate. Hermes[19] has the duty to translate messages from the gods that are beyond human understanding.[20] Some hold that *Hermes* has only to repeat the same words that have been handed to him by the gods for humans.[21]

Following the discussion on hermeneutics above, as related to the understanding of words, message, meaning, information etc., Prof. Raphael O. Madu holds that hermeneutics is the process of acquiring meaning through the analysis of a text, an event or an assertion. In Richard E. Palmer's view hermeneutics is about the interpretation of data. He says that this

> analysis [of data] is interpretation…[it] is really not the primary interpretation but a derivative form. It has primarily set the stage with an essential and primary interpretation before it ever begins to work with the data. This is unfortunately as true as of the 'new analysis' that interprets the events of the day.[22]

It is common to associate hermeneutics with understanding, language and words. The idea common to all these concepts associated with *hermeneia* is the idea of the "process of bringing a thing or situation or text from unintelligibility to intelligibility. Thus, in Greek antiquity, hermeneutics dealt with the problem of the interpretation of the meaning of ancient mythologies and Homeric poems."[23] Hermeneutics includes interpreting a language, preaching, explaining texts, especially when the meaning contained in the text or message is not clear.[24] In fact hermeneutics means to explain or bring something to understanding. In other words, only where there is the problem of clarity that hermeneutics becomes necessary—*in claris non fit interpretatio.*[25]

For one to bring one's thoughts to clarity requires an expression through language. It means to translate one's thoughts thereby making them easy to understand by one's listener or interlocutor. Translation is the same as doing

---

[19] Maurizio Ferraris, *History of Hermeneutics*, trans. Luca Somigli (New Jersey: Humanities Press International, Inc., 1996), p. 1.
[20] Raphael Okechukwu Madu, *African Symbols, Proverbs and Myths: The Hermeneutics of Destiny* (New York: Peter Lang: 1996), p. 5.
[21] Hans- Georg Gadamer, *The Gadamer Reader: A Bouquet of the Later Writings*, Richard E. Palmer, ed (Evanston, Illinois: Northwestern University Press, 2007), p. 44.
[22] Richard E. Palmer, *Hermeneutics* (Evanston: Northwestern University Press, 1969), p. 23.
[23] Madu, *African Symbols, Proverbs and Myths: The Hermeneutics of Destiny, op. cit.*, p. 5.
[24] Gadamer, *The Gadamer Reader: A Bouquet of the Later Writings, op. cit.*, p. 44.
[25] Ferraris, *History of Hermeneutics, op. cit.*, p. 2.

hermeneutics. For instance, Grondin remarks that, "[T]he unitary function of ἑρμηνεία consists in meaning something through language, of translating thought into expression, of making oneself understood. The Greeks also used the word ἑρμηνεία to describe what we would call translation, and the ἑρμηνεύς also functioned as a 'translator,'"[26] For the Greeks the 'translator' is regarded as the 'interpreter.' Also in English, an interpreter orally translates between languages in order to understand the texts. Translation was not common to the Greeks. They rarely translated from any other language. The Latin word *translatio*—implies "to carry over on the other side."[27] It is best understood in terms of geographical location—to carry a unit of culture from one place to the other.[28] In this sense, hermeneutics is an art of translating foreign texts or something into "the language everybody speaks and understands."[29] It is this light that Maurizio Ferraris says that hermeneutics is a function of language[30] because our ability to understanding is mediated through language, whence the universality of hermeneutics.

These general views above lead us to the particular explanations of the individual philosophers (like Plato, Aristotle, Augustine, Heidegger etc.) One of the first dialogues of Plato that has a good connection to our discussion on the universality of hermeneutics is called *Ion*. The dialogue began with Plato's indicating that Socrates initiated a discourse with *Ion,* a professional rhapsode who teaches Homer's poetry and texts.

Plato in *Ion*[31] presents us with some aspects of the development of the idea of hermeneutics. The gods communicate their message to the community or people through their messengers. The messengers utter these words in their capacities as messengers and not their own words or message (*Ion* 534 b-d.) Socrates observes during his discussion with *Ion* that a proper definition of the

[26] Jean Grondin, *Sources of Hermeneutics* (Albany, New York: State University of New York Press, 1995), p. 25.
[27] Grondin, *Sources of Hermeneutics, op. cit.,* p. 26.
[28] *Ibid.,* p. 26. Grondin relates this notion of translation to the Middle Ages when science moved to the Arab and back again to the Latin world. (Grondin, *Ibid.,* p. 160.)
[29] Gadamer, *The Gadamer Reader: A Bouquet of the Later Writings, op. cit.,* p. 44.
[30] Ferraris, *History of Hermeneutics, op. cit.,* p. 1; See Karl Kerényi, "Hermeneia und Hermeneutike," *Griechische Grundbegriffe* (Rhein: Verlag Zürich, 1964), pp. 47-48. Gadamer relates hermeneutics with *sermo* or *verbum* (word or language). See Ferraris, *History of Hermeneutics, op. cit.,* p. 3.
[31] http://evans-experientialism.freewebspace.com/plato_ion.htm (Accessed November 30, 2012.)

rhapsode is important in describing his duty in the community which is interpreting accurately the different qualities of people as presented by the poet. A rhapsode displays the qualities of different people on stage. He speaks as the people he represents would have spoken. Socrates' claim is that the actor/rhapsode does not possess knowledge: theoretical (*epistémè*) or practical (*technè*) but is divinely inspired (536e-542a) rather than skilled in the art of interpreting the characters. He is inspired to communicate the message or meaning of Homer or any other Greek poet.

Plato used the term *hermeneutike* in *Politikos* 260 d 11, *Definitiones* 414 d 4, and *Epinomis* 975 c 6. He uses *hermeneutike* in terms of its religious function and the soothsaying duty (*mantike*) in relation to the gods in these two dialogues. The emphasis is not on the truth of statement but in assimilating the true meaning of a statement or utterance. Like in the ancient Greek mythology, Grondin affirms:

> *Hermeneutike* has a sacred or religious function in the *Politikos*. The *Epinomis* associates *hermeneutike* with *mantike*, or soothsaying, since both are kinds of knowledge that do not lead to Sophia because the interpreter understands only what is said as such (*to legomenon*), without knowing whether it is true (*alethes*). He comprehends a meaning, an utterance, though he cannot determine its truth—which is the first and foremost business of Sophia.[32]

In Plato's *Timaeus*, there is also a religious dimension to the idea of hermeneutics. It is the prophet (*prophetes*) who communicates the true meaning from the esoteric vision of the possessed. In *Timaeus* (71a-72b) those who are perceived as mad are not capable of interpreting the data presented in their experiences or the truth in the revelations they have received, which obviously are divinely inspired.[33] At the course of this inspiration, the person is not in full control of his/her actions and utterances. It is the prophet alone that is capable of communicating the truth present in the vision of the one possessed.

---

[32] Jean Grondin, *Introduction to Philosophical Hermeneutics*, trans. Joel Weinsheimer (New Haven: Yale University Press, 1994), p. 21.
[33] Grondin, *Introduction to Philosophical Hermeneutics, op. cit.,* pp. 21-22.

Plato describes something close to hermeneutics when he talks about the task of the *prophetes* to provide the meaning of the utterance through the observation of the seer. In this light, Hans-Georg Gadamer argues that it is the duty of the προφητης [*prophetes*] to present a convincing account of the meaning of the uttered words. During this process of divine inspiration, the seer is unable to give a clear evaluation of what has been revealed to him/her. It is the duty of the *prophetes* to assist the seer to disclosure the true meaning of what has been seen. Hermeneutics and divination or religious experience are connected.[34] A hermeneutist is a go-between of the seer and the rest of the people; the gods and mortals.

In *Techne hermeneia,* Plato uses hermeneutics to designate that act of shedding light or making something that lacks clarity to become meaningful. It is a process of moving from a hidden meaning to a disclosed meaning. Plato discusses other aspects of hermeneutics through his discourse on language. Language is the basis of hermeneutics. Language (spoken or written) is the home of hermeneutics and understanding. In the *Seventh Letter* and *Phaedrus*, Plato discusses written language and its difficulties, especially in difficulty of understanding the intention of the author in his/her absence. Written words present us with this problem whenever the question of intention is involved. One could understand Plato's concern about the misrepresentation of an author's intention in written words because of the practice of the Sophists at the time.[35] The Sophists were good at manipulating statements to win debates or for persuasions, while avoiding the truth of the statements. Plato recommends that word (written or oral) should be used for 'rememoration' of truth and communication of the whole meaning of what needs to be understood.

Some philosophers[36] are of the opinion that Plato's *Seventh Letter* is authentic and clearer than *Phaedrus*. The *Seventh Letter* briefly discusses the

---

[34] Leonardo Taran, *Academia: Plato, Philip of Opus, and the Pseudo-Platonic Epinomis* (American Philosophical Society, Philadelphia, 1975), p. 224.
[35] Chris Lawn, *Gadamer: A Guide for the Perplexed* (New York: Continuum International Publishing Group, 2006), p. 81.
[36] Gadamer holds the view that the *Seventh Letter* is authentic. Myles Burnyeat, Terence Irvin and Julia Annas think that the *Seventh Letter* is spurious. See Robert Gregg Bury, Prefatory note to "Epistle VII" in *Plato IX*, Loeb Classical Library (Cambridge, MA: Harvard University Press, 1929), pp. 463-475; See Terence Irvin, "The Intellectual Background," *The Cambridge Companion to Plato,* Richard Kraut, ed. (Cambridge: Cambridge University Press, 1992), pp. 78-79n4.

difference between written and oral language. Written language is not fixed because its meaning or truth could change. The oral word does not change and dialogue is the basis for true philosophical work. Metaphysical truth is not only in written word but in oral word. The essence of things lies in the oral. *Phaedrus* emphasizes the distinction between oral and written word. For Plato, the true meaning of a word lies in the soul. He states, "it is not something that can be put into words like other branches of learning; only after long partnership in a common life devoted to this very thing does truth flash upon the soul."[37] At this time in Greece the traditional way of education and understanding was through oral means of poetry and myth.[38] Philosophy and interpretation is not only about what is written down. Writing helps preserve spoken words. The spoken words express one's thoughts or thinking, which is the dialogue of the soul with itself. Plato prefers oral communication because it is direct, immediate and pure.

In *Phaedrus* 275 d, Plato admits writing is similar to painting. Written words are silent because they need to be read or questioned in order to get some answers. Plato affirms to Phaedrus (his interlocutor) that "[T]he painter's products stand before us as though they were alive: but if you question them, they maintain a most majestic silence. It is the same with written words: they seem to talk to you as though they were intelligent."[39] Plato again focuses on the problem of misunderstanding or misrepresenting written words rather than

---

[37] Plato, *The Seventh Letter* 341c-d; *Phaedrus and Letters VII and VIII,* trans. Walter Hamilton (London: Penguin, 1973), p. 136; See Rod Coltman, *The Language of Hermeneutics: Gadamer and Heidegger in Dialogue* (New York: State University of New York Press, 1998), p. 37.

[38] One could relate this to the later part of this thesis on African oral tradition, proverbs and names. See Coltman, *The Language of Hermeneutics: Gadamer and Heidegger in Dialogue, op. cit.,* p. 46. See discussions on the emergence of written culture in the oral culture of ancient Greece (about 750 BC) by Eric Alfred Havelock, *The Literate Revolution and its Cultural Consequences* (Princeton: Princeton University Press, 1982), pp. 122-125; Arthur Adkins, "Orality and Philosophy," *Language and Thought in Early Greek Philosophy,* Kevin Robb, ed. (LaSalle: Hegeler Institute, 1983), pp. 207-227; Joseph Margolis, "The Emergence of Philosophy," *Language and Thought in Early Greek Philosophy*, Kevin Robb, ed. (LaSalle: Hegeler Institute, 1983), pp. 228-242; Henri Irénée Marrou, *A History of Education in Antiquity,* trans. George Lamb (New York: Mentor, 1964), pp. 31ff.

[39] Plato, *The Collected Dialogues of Plato,* eds. Edith Hamilton and Huntington Cairns (Princeton, New Jersey, 1961); *Phaedrus* 275d; See also David Dawson, "Plato's Soul and the Body of the Text in Philo and Origen," *Interpretation and Allegory: Antiquity to the Modern Period,* ed., with introductory essay by Jon Whitman (Leiden: Koninklijke Brill NV, 2000), p. 95.

oral or spoken words through genuine conversation. To understand something is to understand the soul of what is said. Plato accepts that there has to be the inner meaning of what is uttered.

In *Cratylus*, Plato talks about dialectic and dialogue (*Cratylus* 390c.)[40] These are ways of enunciation or explanation of statements or getting at meanings. Dialectics or dialogue involves working back and forth with the statement or text. The nature of language is important in *Cratylus*. Is language conventional or natural? Plato's *Cratylus*, presents the argument by Cratylus that language is conventional and natural in communicating meaning. In *Epinomis*, the duty of the hermeneutist is to understand what something means or signifies. Hermeneutics concerns itself with what the interpreter considers as the meaning of what has been revealed and does not determine what the truth of the meaning is. Hermeneutics makes it possible for one to understand what is asserted by an author, what he really means. What an author says or means does not need to be logically sound or valid.

In this section I will like to bring in some intercultural encounters of Plato in the communication of meaning and ideas with people of other cultural perspectives. These intercultural encounters of Plato include his many travelling to Syracuse in Sicily and other places. In 326-328d, Plato first visits Sicily during the reign of Dionysios the elder. It did not take long before Dionysios the elder dies and Plato returns home. When Plato meets Dion (a military officer and relative of Dionysios), he exchanges with him some ideas on political philosophy and on the virtues of leaders. Plato teaches him and expresses support for Dion's political wishes for Syracuse citizens' happiness and peace.

At Plato's second visit to Sicily, Dion invites him to help his young nephew (Dionysios son of Dionysios the elder) be able to rule in an orderly manner for peace and happiness in the city-states. He wants Dionysios the younger to be educated by Plato in order to become a philosopher-king rather than a tyrant. Dion expects Dionysios the younger to overcome the political difficulties of his own father Dionysios. Dion was a good student of Plato's teaching. He was more than any of the majority of the Italian and Sicilian Greeks. He likes virtues, rather than a life of self-indulgence and pleasure.

---

[40] Coltman, *The Language of Hermeneutics: Gadamer and Heidegger in Dialogue, op. cit.*, p. 45.

Dion recommends genuine happiness for all Syracuseans and a life of nobility as the best life. Plato accepts to teach the younger Dionysios but it did not work out well. It was not long the beneficiaries of Dionysios' excesses accuse Dion of having interest in taking over the leadership of the city-states. Plato also was accused of working with Dion to accomplish this ignominy. But Dionysios reassures Plato to stay in Syracuse as he did not want to lose Plato's services which make him appear as a good leader. Meanwhile, Plato regrets counseling people like Dionysios who are not ready to learn about leadership and life of virtue. Plato leaves Sicily after his second visit because of the war going on. He leaves disappointed, although Dionysios asks Plato to return after the war.

For the third time Plato returns to Sicily in order to make philosophy survive in the service of the common good. Plato reassures himself that by transforming a philosopher-king, he might as well have done the best for the common good of the community. At this visit, Plato now tests Dionysios genuine interest in philosophy by asking him to take some non-interesting philosophical studies. Unfortunately, Dionysios turns out a bad ruler who claims that he has written a metaphysical treatise. But for Plato the deepest truths of metaphysics one attains through the *logos*, *episteme*, not through writing.

The intercultural aspect of these visits by Plato, which is another basis of our reading of the *Seventh Letter* of Plato, is that although all these city-states were under one ruler as an Empire, they were different city-states with different cultural practices. There are the Italian Greeks and the Sicilian Greeks. During Plato's visits to Sicily he notices a new cultural perspective on the life of happiness. It is a life at banquets and of debauchery among the Syracuseans. Plato disapproves of their manner of life. For him, a life of debauchery and life of wisdom are not a good combination. He becomes worried of the immanent political danger in the city-states because of the culture of squander and idleness. Plato hopes to use education and philosophy to transform the people. The inner meanings of the principles and manner of life Plato describes as ways to re-direct the moral difficulties of Syracuse people. He reassures himself that if he succeeds in transforming one man, he has accomplished enough for the idea of a philosopher-king. One could see the connection to Plato's *Politics* because there were in Sicily the bad constitutions of tyrannies, oligarchies and democracies. After Dion's death in the hands of his Athenian friends, Plato on one occasion advises Dionysios to abolish despotism in Sicily and establish a constitutional government with the rule of laws. Although Plato did not succeed with Dionysios, he admonishes his followers to avoid partisan strife, live moderately and prudently. When the ideal of having a philosopher-king is impossible, the second-best option for the people is the rule of law. Let us now take a brief look at Plato's *Politics* with regard to some intercultural elements in constitutions or political practices of these different cultures in Plato's time.

Plato's *Politics* is about the constitutions of men and leadership in the city-states. Plato describes the different kinds of government practiced in the different city-states and countries. Some use the 'bad' constitutions of tyranny, oligarchy, democracy etc. Some also use the 'good' ones like, monarchy, aristocracy, constitutional government etc. Plato is suggesting that different kinds of cultures and people choose different kinds of constitutions to govern them. During his travels, he tries to suggest a leadership that is at the best interest of the people to be formed and sustained. He, like in the *Seventh Letter*, advocates for the rise of a philosopher-king or a statesman who will become a philosopher in order to rule for the common good. The intercultural aspect here is the cross-cultural opportunities of exchanging socio-economic and philosophical ideas among the Empire and the then Greek world. In Plato's *Statesman* the elements of cultural differences and divisions of human beings were sparsely mentioned. It is only in a very broad sense that intercultural encounter is applied below.

Plato's *Statesman* (262) provides us with some information on the intercultural relationship between people of different cultural perspectives during the time of Socrates and Plato. For him human beings are the source of divisions between the Hellenes and Barbarians. The Phrygians equally divides humanity into Phrygians and Barbarians. There is same division between kings and slave or servants. It is likely that other animals could do the same by classifying their kind. In the absence of these divisions, the dialogue or the discourse we have about other people of different culture is all on the improvement of our lives and that of others. The relevant part of this dialogue is on the idea of the differences in cultures, divisions in thought and perspectives, and not necessarily on the kind (human beings.) One has to bear in mind that the usage of intercultural encounter or relationship is better or clearly seen in the medieval and modern period. In the ancient the divisive approach considers other cultures and peoples in not so positive perspective. There are a few other examples of intercultural encounters in Plato but for lack of space we shall consider the above as adequate.

In summary, Plato presents a limited understanding of hermeneutics from a religious dimension. Hermeneutics is about the communication of true meaning. Through hermeneutics one moves from what is unclear to what is clear and arrives at the meaning of utterances. Language is important in understanding, but written language is not better than oral language when it comes to understanding. However, recent understanding makes written language the primary object of hermeneutics. Ancient Greeks had a common understanding of the role of theater in teaching the people and for entertainment. The intercultural encounters of the peoples and cultures of the Greek and Roman city-states happened in main cities, trader centers, philosophical schools and capitals of some provinces. Each of the cultures learned something from the other as time went on.

To conclude this section, I have only chosen to trace the history of universal hermeneutics through some of Plato's *Dialogues* because of his influence on Gadamer's philosophical hermeneutics and Gadamer's concern in addressing the problem of language/hermeneutics as a problem of understanding. Plato's contributions are understood in the interpretation of text and oral interpretive dialogues with other people and cultures (broadly understood as the intercultural problem of understanding.) Later in chapters two and four I will be using Gadamer's theory of hermeneutics and language to discuss the intercultural aspects of my book.

To further understand ancient hermeneutics we proceed to Aristotle. It is a common philosophical stand- in the heideggerian tradition- that Aristotle opened the way to understanding Plato[41] and linked classical hermeneutics to

---

[41] Martin Heidegger, *Platon; Sophistes*, Gesamtausgabe volume 19 (Frankfurt: Vittorio Klostermann, 1992), p. 11; See also Martin Heidegger, *Plato's Sophist*, trans. Richard Rojcewicz and Andre Schuwer (Bloomington: Indiana University Press, 1997), p. 11; See Coltman, *The Language of Hermeneutics: Gadamer and Heidegger in Dialogue, op. cit.*, p. 37; See Gadamer, "Heidegger und die Griechen," Alexander von Humbolt Stiftung: Mitteilungen 55 (August 1990), pp. 29-38; Gadamer, *Neuere Philosophie I: Hegel Husserl Heidegger, Gesammelte Werke* volume 3 (Tübingen: J. C. B. Mohr, 1990), pp. 238-248; See Gadamer, *Heidegger's Way* (Albany: State University of New York Press, 1994.) Rod Coltman in *The Language of Hermeneutics: Gadamer and Heidegger in Dialogue, op. cit.*, p. 37 argues in line with the later part of this book (On Achebe and African thought.) He

the modern time. The Latin word used for this art of understanding is *hermeneutica* which was first used around the 17th Century. It was probably drawn from Aristotle's *Peri hermeneias* (*De interpretatione*) by Johann Dannhauer (a theologian from Strasbourg) who gave much credit to Aristotle in his work on hermeneutics. [42]

b. Aristotle

Aristotle, in *Perì hermenéias*, uses the word hermeneutics to designate "the concept of interpretation" like in presenting meanings of something or to enunciate something. Thus to interpret is to outline the meaning of something.[43] Every uttered language is the interpretation of thought. It is the translation of thought to word or language. There is a mediation or go-between of thoughts and the interpreter or reader. The Latin word for *hermeneia* is interpretation. Like Aristotle, another philosopher, for instance, Demetrius,[44] a Peripatetic, wrote a *Peri hermeneias*. Meanwhile, some scholars have argued that Aristotle's *Perì hermenéias* is not suitable to be referred to as a text on hermeneutics. Among these scholars is Gadamer who observes that "Aristotle's *Perì hermenéia[s]*...is not a hermeneutics, but a part of logical grammar concerned with the structures of *apophantic logos*, and of all the other parts of *logos* in which truth is not yet in question."[45] Making statements provides us with the truth or falsity in a statement, an object, or a decision. He

writes in regard to the time of Plato and hermeneutics: "By this I mean such factors as the social and political situation of fifth-century Athens, the dramatic settings of the dialogues, and the constant religious and mythological allusions that suffuse Plato's writing all of which one would perhaps expect of a truly Heideggerian interpretation and which Gadamer, as we shall see, takes great pains to develop." (*Ibid.*, p. 37.)

[42] See Hasso Jaeger, "Studien zur Frühgeschichte der Hermeneutik," *Archiv für Begriffsgeschichte*, 18, (1974), pp. 35-84. For the relation between the Renaissance and hermeneutics, see Claus von Bormann's, article "*Hermeneutik*," *Theologische Realenzylopaedie*, vol. XV (New York/Berlin: de Gruyter, 1986), pp. 131-137.

[43] See Jean Pepin, "Hermeneutik," *Reallexikon für Antike und Christentum* 14: 724. According to Aristotle's commentator, Ammonios (*Comm. in Aristotle* GR. 4, 5, 5, 17/23.)

[44] See Karl Kerényi, "Hermeneia und Hermeneutike," *Griechische Grundbegriffe* (Rhein: Verlag Zürich, 1964), p. 48; See also Ferraris, *History of Hermeneutics, op. cit.*, p. 5.

[45] Hans-Georg Gadamer, "Hermeneutik," *Historisches Wörterbuch der Philosophie*, Joachim Ritter ed. (Basel-Stuttgart: Schwabe, 1974, 3 vols), p. 1062. Karl Kerényi thinks that *Perì hermenéias* was not the correct translation for the Latin *De interpretatione*. *Perì hermenéias* focused on sentence as linguistic expression. It could be understood as *hermeneía*. See Kerényi, "Hermeneia und Hermeneutike," *Griechische Grundbegriffe, op. cit.*, p. 48.

argues that Aristotle uses the terms *hermeneias* strictly in the logical sense of a true or false statement. In that sense, Aristotle is concerned only with *logos apophantikos*. This makes Aristotle's project cognitive, such that "the term *hermeneia* and *hermeneus* came in later Greek culture to mean one who makes a 'learned explanation' and an 'explainer' or 'translator'"[46] In Aristotle's position, there is an individual who explains or translates the message of another, who may be a higher being. Nonetheless, the religious aspect in hermeneutics is still present in Aristotle's view on hermeneutics.[47]

In *Perì hermenéias*, Aristotle argues that written signs are symbols for spoken words.[48] What is written down helps us to recall the spoken words. However, the written word could cause some misunderstanding. It is only a medium to proper understanding. In recent hermeneutics, following Aristotle's influence, the full meaning of the word is recognized in a written text. Hermeneutics basically means understanding the uttered word in a text or a dialogue, a question or in a descriptive comment. Whenever a word is uttered or spoken, the task of hermeneutics is required to understand it. Hermeneutics now includes all forms of communication of truth or falsity, and other means of communicating or interpreting.

Aristotle's views in *Rhetoric* and *Poetics* contain some important aspects of interpretation, although they are not primarily concerned with truth and falsity but with persuasion and emotions respectively. As Friedrich Schleiermacher wrote, "hermeneutics and rhetoric are intimately related in that every act of understanding is the reverse side of an act of speaking."[49] So there is a kind of connection between them. Following Schleiermacher's comment, let me give a brief reflection on Aristotle's use of rhetoric for the purpose of this book.

According to Aristotle, rhetoric is defined as:

---

[46] Gadamer, *The Gadamer Reader: A Bouquet of the Later Writings, op. cit.*, p. 45.
[47] Gerhard Ebeling, "Hermeneutik," *Die Religion in Geschichte und Gegenwart*, 3rd edition done in collaboration with Hans von Campenhausen, Erich Dinkler, Gerhard Gloege, and Knud E. Løgstrup, ed. Kurt Galling, (H-Kon), columns 242-62.
[48] *De interpretatione*, 16 a 4 ; See Heinz-Gerd Schmitz, "Die Eröffnung des sprachphilosophischen Feldes. Überlegungen zu Platons Kratylos," *Hermes. Zeitschrift für klassische Philologie*, 119 (1991), 43-60, (46 ff.)
[49] Friedrich Daniel Ernst Schleiermacher, *Hermeneutics: The Handwritten Manuscripts*, ed. Heinz Himmerle (Missoula, Montana: Scholars Press, 1977), Ms. 3, p. 97; See Madu, *African Symbols, Proverbs and Myths: The Hermeneutics of Destiny, op. cit.*, p. 4.

the faculty of observing in any given case the available means of persuasion.... But rhetoric we look upon as the power of observing the means of persuasion on almost any subject presented to us; and that is why we say that, in its technical character, it is not concerned with any special or definite class of subjects[50] (1355b25-36).

The quotation provides a clear perspective that rhetoric is more general than any other science in convincing or persuading people. On the technical aspect, Aristotle further notes that there are three modes or three kinds of persuasion: "The first kind depends on the personal character of the speaker; the second on putting the audience into a certain frame of mind; the third on the proof, or apparent proof, provided by the words of the speech itself." [51]

The first is based on *ethos*, the second is *pathos*, and the third is *logos*. We effectively persuade other people through these three kinds. The speaker's personal character speaks louder than his/her words, especially before even he/she speaks. The character of a person makes people think the person is credible. We readily believe good people or apparently good people. Aristotle argues that this kind of persuasion "should be achieved by what the speaker says, not by what people think of his character before he begins to speak... his character may almost be called most effective means of persuasion he possesses."[52] According to some writers at the time of Aristotle, the personal good quality or character revealed by the speaker adds nothing to his power of persuasion. But the development of rhetoric has proved this wrong. Good character is a good tool to effective persuasion.

The second is *pathos* or emotion. We respond differently to different situations. Friendly people we listen to as friends. Cheerfully communicated information is easily appreciated than sternly communicated information. For Aristotle it is an important way to persuade others but not the most important. He observes, "[I]t is towards producing these effects, as we maintain, that

---

[50] Aristotle, *The Basic Works of Aristotle* (New York: Random House, 1941.)
[51] *Rhetoric,* (1356a1-22.)
[52] *Ibid.*

present-day writers on rhetoric direct the whole of their effort."[53] To make the point, Aristotle defines emotions as "all those feelings that so change men as to affect their judgments, and that are also attended by pain and pleasure. Such are anger, pity, fear and the like, with their opposites" (1378a20-23.) The third is persuasion effected "through the speech itself when we have proved a truth or an apparent truth by means of the persuasive arguments suitable to the case in question"[54] (1356a1-22). The latter aspect is often regarded as the most important following Aristotle's attempt at bringing rhetoric to its best forms in terms of arguments. William David Ross affirms that the third species of persuasion "is the rhetorical method par excellence, 'the body of persuasion.' 'Arguments by example are no less persuasive, but enthymemes win more applause.'"[55] Aristotle also proceeds to list the three branches of rhetoric based on the hearer: (a) the politician or counselor that focuses on the future and important decisions, (b) the judge or advocate that focuses on the past and acts that are legal or illegal, and (c) the epideictic--focuses on praise and censure. It is about the present situation. This forms the core view of Aristotle on rhetoric. But the question is: how does one understand the relation between Aristotle's view on rhetoric and to hermeneutics (interpretation)?

Hermeneutics or interpretation, in a broad sense, is concerned with the formulation of meaningful statements, the communication of meaning and persuasion. Persuasion or the art of speaking is also an important aspect of hermeneutics and a means of evoking understanding. In fact the art of speaking (rhetoric) and the art of understanding (hermeneutics) are closely related because both are about the communication of meaning or understanding. Whatever that is communicated through "the art of speaking" (rhetoric), ought to communicate meaning and understanding (the art of hermeneutics.) Rhetoric focuses on persuasion but we cannot persuade the other person without being effective in communicating meaning. Rhetoric and hermeneutics do not emphasize the communication of truth but whatever that could be understood

---

[53] *Rhetoric,* (1356a1-22.) Robert N. Gaines describes emotion as "mental contexts wherein different arguments seem reasonable." p. 9. Otfried Höffe has a more negative description for rhetoric, as "nothing more than the art of well-formulated speech, occasionally even a mere technique of persuasion, which uses irrelevant arguments or a cynical manipulation of emotions." p. 38; Otfried Höffe, Aristotle, trans. Christine Salazar (New York: State University of New York Press, 2003), p. 38.

[54] *Ibid.*

[55] William David Ross, *Aristotle* (London: Methuen & Co. LTD, Third Edition, 1937), p. 271. See *Rhetoric,* (1356 b22.)

or expressed as a clear meaning. Let us briefly see how Paul Ricoeur[56] interprets Aristotle in this case, since he had a renewal of interest in Aristotle's *Rhetoric.*

Ricoeur describes rhetoric as a theoretical discipline, without a determinate theme-it could take any form or topic; it has a neutral criterion of *pithanon,* of 'the persuasive as such.' In other words, rhetoric is about persuasion but when we say 'persuasive as such' it implies that "it expresses rhetoric's movement towards a technique of arguments or proof."[57] One can hold that what we employ in persuasion will depend on the capabilities of our hearers. Rhetoric is about the dynamics of persuasion[58] and argument in terms of the "stuff of proof"[59] and the "appearance." It is the way in which a thing is said and is about persuading or convincing another person or people. It implies that 'the way in which a thing is said does affect its intelligibility [pros to dêlôsai]'(1404 a 9-10)."[60]

Aristotle tries to clean rhetoric from focusing only on emotions and considers also argumentation, style, and "a comprehensive treatment of the subject."[61] Rhetoric serves the purpose of effecting understanding in the

---

[56] Robert N. Gaines is of the opinion that Ricoeur is among the philosophers who interpret Aristotle within a socio-historical context. See Robert N. Gaines, "Aristotle's Rhetoric and the Contemporary Arts of Practical Discourse," *Rereading Aristotle's Rhetoric*, Alan G. Gross and Arthur E. Walzer, eds (Illinois: Southern Illinois University Press, 2000), pp. 20, 23; Alan G. Gross includes Jacques Derrida and Michel Foucault in that approach (p. 25). See Alan G. Gross, 'What Aristotle Meant by Rhetoric," *Rereading Aristotle's Rhetoric, op. cit.,* p. 25. Gross includes Eugene Garver as using his own approach to construct Aristotle's rhetoric. p. 35. Garver accepts his not quoting exactly and conclusively from Aristotle. See Eugene Garver, *Aristotle's Rhetoric: An Art of Character* (Chicago: The University of Chicago Press, 1994), p. 45.

[57] Paul Ricoeur, *The Rule of Metaphor*, trans. Robert Czerny, Kathleen Mclaughlin and John Costello (Toronto: University of Toronto Press, 1977), p. 30.

[58] According to Joseph Owens, Rhetoric "studies persuasive arguments and how they are to be used in literary composition (111, 8) and in speeches." See John R. Catan (ed), Aristotle: *The Collected Papers of Joseph Owens* (Albany: State University of New York, 1981), p. 12. Fred D. Miller agrees on the role of persuasion. Like in persuading those who possess political powers to co-operate and respect the rights of others. Like Aristotle, "it is a problem of rhetoric." (Rhetoric 1355b26-27.) See Fred D. Miller, Jr. *Nature, Justice, and Rights in Aristotle's Politics* (Oxford: Clarendon Press, 1995), p. 294.

[59] Ricoeur, *op. cit.,* p. 31.

[60] *Ibid.*

[61] Abraham Edel, *Aristotle and His Philosophy* (Chapel Hill: The University of North Carolina Press, 1982), p. 341; Gaines, *op. cit.,* p. 9. Gaines explains, "since ethos and pathos both involve feelings and emotions… then there is an "inherent involvement of ethos and

hearer. According to Ricoeur, Aristotle's contribution to hermeneutics is more general than other ancient philosophers. For him, Aristotle's scope of hermeneutics extends to meaningful discourse which interprets reality "precisely to the degree that it says 'something of something,'"[62] especially in light of the subject matter or text, time, and experience.

According to Robert N. Gaines, while considering Aristotle's *Rhetoric* and Ricoeur's commentary, notes, "[T]he object here is for the historically situated reader to understand the significance of the *Rhetoric*....like any other text, the *Rhetoric* is subject to a multitude of legitimate interpretations. The reader then encounters the work, conceiving it as a reply to a question of relevance to the reader's time, place, and experiences."[63] Any text continually provides us with contents to be understood. Gaines recommends "a fresh return to the text of the Rhetoric."[64] He places Ricoeur's approach under phenomenological hermeneutic (understand the significance of the Rhetoric) and the other is philological hermeneutic (understand the meaning intended by Aristotle as a 4th Century BCE work.)

I shall now take a look at another aspect of this general development of hermeneutics which is on the ancient period's use of "theater" or drama in relation to tragedy. Some aspects of Aristotle's discussions on "theater" and tragedy relate to an aspect of my book, especially because of his influence on Gadamer and on Western understanding of personal tragedy. In ancient philosophy hermeneutics uses the interpretation of poetry. However, it did also apply to the interpretation of art, sculpture, dance, drama etc. Hermeneutics was not univocally conceived. Hermeneutics has been used within the field of aesthetics to provide interpretation of works of representation. The resources of hermeneutics include tragedy, comedy, myth, theater have been used in the understanding of the universality of hermeneutics. This book will use the claim of universality of hermeneutics in light of applying Gadamer's hermeneutics in chapter four on a slightly different text with a notion of

---

pathos with enthymemes," p. 8. Fisher (1964), Miller and Bee (1972) agree with this interpretation.

[62] Paul Ricoeur, *The Conflict of Interpretations*, ed. Don Ihde (Evanston, Illinois: Northwestern University Press, 1974), p. 4; See Madu, *African Symbols, Proverbs and Myths: The Hermeneutics of Destiny, op. cit.*, p. 5.

[63] Robert N. Gaines, "Aristotle's Rhetoric and the Contemporary Arts of Practical Discourse," *Rereading Aristotle's Rhetoric*, Alan G. Gross and Arthur E. Walzer, eds (Illinois: Southern Illinois University Press, 2000), p. 20.

[64] *Ibid.*, p. 19.

tragedy that is not individual but *communal*, if we are to truly understand Chinua Achebe's *Things Fall Apart* tragic-hero text.

Aristotle is an important philosopher in the discourse of Greek dramatic criticisms, analysis of plays in the centuries before him (5th Century) and for setting the foundation for the construction of tragedy. His views on the structure and purpose of theater were set from Greek tragedy with some modifications and influences. For the structure of tragic drama, he includes plot, character, theme, drama, melody and spectacle. Aristotle recognizes tragedies by Aeschylus, Euripides and Sophocles as models for tragedy.[65] *Oedipus the King* by Sophocles was chosen because of its plot, use of language and clarity of idea. Greek theater or drama considers plot to be more important than character. Plot tests the character as the drama plays out or works out. These are used in aesthetics in the representation of poetic drama and arts during Greek festivities. Theater is a means to communicate the worldviews and ethical values of those in the position of authority. The language and symbols used in the dramas were associated to authority, while the audience had a passive role. The life of the ruling class and their values were objects of excellent theater. 'Good' is represented with a particular form of face (mask), likewise 'courage' and other concepts. The actors use masks, songs, dance, rituals etc., to which the audience /community participate because it is an open-air production. It is called a people's theater or a community activity.[66] Language is not considered a barrier, communication was through symbolic meaning, and it was open interpretation. Aristotle uses hermeneutics to explain the representation of human action in theater and not just arts. He defines tragedy as "a representation of an action that is heroic and complete and of a certain magnitude."[67] For him this representation is not in the form of narrative but something that is acted out in "theater" so as to evoke some emotional responses from the viewers/audience. In the *Poetics* Aristotle mentions some important aspects of this 'theater' for the representation of actions and communication of meaning.

---

[65] Martha Fletcher Bellinger, *A Short History of the Drama* (New York: Henry Holt and Company, 1927), pp. 61-67. Euripides tragedy was Helena—known for its complicated plot and most tragic.

[66] See Richard Southern, *The Seven Ages of the Theater* (New York: Hill and Wang, 1961.) Augusto Boal, *Theater of the Oppressed*, trans. C.A. and M.O.L McBride (New York: Urizen Book Inc., 1979, original work published in 1974.)

[67] Aristotle, *Poetics*, trans. William Hamilton Fyfe (London, William Heinemann Ltd. 1932.)

There is also an intercultural aspect to this theater in that the heroes of the Romantic theater are different from the Greeks. The Greek heroes relate to the human situations of the audience or spectators but still have some higher human qualities.[68] The heroes possess a mixed nature. This causes their misfortune to appeal and evoke human sympathy, pity and fear in the people. Although tragedy purges the audience through sympathies, pity or fear, but it also gives pleasure. Comedy does purge the audience through laughter or mirth. I will further discuss Gadamer's views on Aristotle's tragedy (in theatrical form and aesthetic context) in chapter two of this book.

To conclude this section, the development of the concept of hermeneutics has been a gradual process with different emphasis at each stage. From ancient philosophy hermeneutics has been used in the understanding of Homeric poetry and texts. It has also been used in translation of divinations in Greek religious practices. Part of its development in ancient period is in Aristotle's contribution through his *Perì hermenéias* and other significant comments in *Rhetoric* (as Schleiermacher highlighted above.)[69] His works present us with the role of language in grammar and logical statement. We learn of his hermeneutics as being concerned with explanation, translation and communication of persuasive meaning. His views above could be considered as an interpersonal aspect of intercultural understanding and the interpretation of Greek texts/narratives.

I have to mention that there is another important source of hermeneutics in the ancient period. This is associated with medicine, for instance, the understanding of "symptoms" of sickness or illness that needs interpretation. For the scope of my task, the more common aspect of hermeneutics is that it is the act of explanation, understanding and communication. Even with the rise of Christianity, the school of Alexandria, Philo and others the notion of hermeneutics has continued to develop. Let us now focus on Saint Paul, Philo and Augustine since Aristotle and others influenced their hermeneutics and the role of language in understanding. Philo and Augustine's hermeneutics are linked to the universality of allegory and the universality of hermeneutic

---

[68] Alice Lovelace, "A Brief History of Theater Forms," *Motion Magazine*, February 15, 1996.
[69] Aristotle's *Perì hermenéias* has been described in German as Aristotle's *Hermeneutik*. See Hellmut Flashar, "Aristoteles," *Überweg- Praechter, Grundriss der Geschichte der Philosophie: Die Philosophie der Antike*, 3 (Basel/Stuttgart: Schwabe, 1983), pp. 203, 237.

because understandability is mediated by language. They also made use of allegory in the interpretation of Christian message.

1.2 Early Christian and Medieval Period of Hermeneutics

a. Saint Paul

In AD 5 Paul was born in Tarsus, Cilicia.[70] Tarsus was one of the largest trading communities of the Mediterranean coast with its seaport.[71] Several years before Paul's birth, Alexander the Great is said to have brought Hellenistic culture, custom and thought to Tarsus when he conquered it and other parts of Asia Minor. It becomes a Greek city-state in 170 BCE. Following conquer of Tarsus by the Romans; it ceases to be a Greek city-state and becomes a Roman city-state in 64 BCE (part of the Roman Empire.) It soon becomes the capital city of Roman province of Cilicia and enjoys the privilege of a city-state as it was during the Seleucidic dynasty.[72] Some citizens of Tarsus were also regarded as citizens of Rome. Paul has his Roman citizenship through his grandfather.[73] Tarsus becomes a city of commerce and has a university city in Paul's time. It is also a centre of intercultural/multicultural ideas and education. Educators from around the then world of Roman Empire come to teach at the schools in Tarsus. Some of the instructors were Grecian, Romans, Egyptians, and Africans.[74]

Paul had a Jewish-theological education but the Hellenistic–Roman world also did influence him.[75] In his youth, he learns Greek and reads the bible in Greek language. He also speaks *Koine* Greek, common in Tarsus, and Classical Greek. As is obvious, language communicates ideas and so through

---

[70] George. T. Montague, *The Living Thought of St. Paul* (Milwaukee: Bruce Publishing Co., 1966), p. 1.

[71] http://www.biblicaltheology.com/Research/WallaceQ01.html (Accessed July 20, 2013.) See Quency E. Wallace, *The American Journal of Biblical Theology*, 2002 (online.)

[72] Robert Picirilli, *Paul the Apostle* (Chicago: Moody Press, 1986), p. 3.

[73] John Pollock, *The Apostle* (Wheaton, III: Victor Publishing, 1972), p. 5; See George. T. Montague, *The Living Thought of St. Paul, op. cit.,* p. 2; Ernest G. Wright, *Great People of the Bible and How They Lived* (Pleasantville, New York: The Reader's Digest Association, Inc., 1974), p. 404.

[74] http://www.biblicaltheology.com/Research/WallaceQ01.html (Accessed July 20, 2013.) See Quency E. Wallace, *The American Journal of Biblical Theology*, 2002 (online.)

[75] Frederick Clifton Grant, "St. Paul and Stoicism," *The Biblical World* (Chicago: The University of Chicago, Press, May, 1915), Vol. 45, No. 5, p. 274.

Greek language he learned Greek ideas. At this time stoicism was very prominent. Some refer to the stoic philosophers as "messengers of Truth". Stoicism is like a religion of thought practiced by the progressive elements of the Greco-Roman community. It is likely that the philosophical thought and culture of this time did influence Paul as stoicism contributed to the language used in daily life. Paul uses some of the stoic forms of speaking and use of metaphors to communicate the meaning/message of salvation to the new converts in Christianity. He begins with what was familiar or common to his listeners (Greek thought) and eventually ends up with the meaning of the resurrection of Christ. For instance, some of his teachings relate to stoical usage. They are: Romans 1:20; Roman 7:23-25; 1 Corinthians 11:14; 1 Corinthians 7: 35. Paul was also said to have used terms or concepts like "syneidesis"—conscience, logos, virtue, spirit etc., developed by the stoics. Through his teaching or instruction approach, he is able to associate Greek thoughts/culture and Christian thought/culture where they connect, and also he uses Christianity to address what he considers as erroneous teachings of the stoics or other worldviews contrary to Christianity.

The intercultural aspect of Paul is that he meets people of other cultures "where they are" so as to convince them about the meaning of Christianity. This is like in hermeneutics to avoid misunderstanding and facilitate understanding of the truth of Christianity through the didactic process, and assist his Gentile audience. Paul also uses the stoic type of teaching which was like preaching to the common people in the streets and market places. He teaches the people about the inner unity of the ideas and meanings in the Old Testament and the New Testament. Paul is likely to have been aware of ancient Greek and Roman theaters on tragedy and the Christian approach in the use of Christ's death or tragedy in teaching new members. A little more on Christian theater will be presented at the end of this subsection (following Augustine.)

Paul is closer to Philo of Alexandria as a contemporary in the Wisdom school. Both were Hellenists, and depend on the Haggadic interpretation of the Scripture. They serve the various communities of the Diaspora[76] by instructing the people on how to understand the (inner) meaning of God's Word. To show the intercultural language situation of this time, both Paul and Philo are said to

---

[76] Grant, *op. cit.*, p. 280.

be "thinking Hebrew, speaking Greek." The cultures of this time come from a mixture of various cultures of peoples that come to Tarsus and Alexandria.

b. Philo of Alexandria

Philo (c. [20] 25 BC—c.50 AD)[77] was born in Alexandria, Egypt. He was a leader of the

Alexandrian Jewry and was inclined to life of religious contemplation and speculative philosophical thought. He interprets the Old Testament in light of Greek philosophy[78] and the Stoics. Mircea Eliade classifies[79] Philo's writings into: *Historical and Apologetic*; *Philosophical* (On the Eternity of the world, On Alexandria etc); *Legislative* (On the Decalogue, On the Special Laws, On the Virtues etc)[80], and *Expository on the Pentateuch* (the creation of the world, On Abraham, the Allegorical interpretation etc.)

Philo's influence comes from the Greek philosophy of the Platonic schools and he uses allegories to transmit the ideas and traditions to his community. In using this allegorical method, he applies a form of intercultural synthesis between different religions, cultures and Greek philosophy.[81] At one time philosophy was predominantly Platonic. Plato has the notion of the sensible world (*kosmos aesthetikos*) and the intelligible world (*kosmos noëtos.*)[82] There is the dualism of matter and form (idea-'*eidos*'): material world are imitations of the world of forms. Matter is sensible and evil, while form is immaterial and good. But Philo prefers to focus on a constitutive world

---

[77] David Dawson, *Allegorical Readers and Cultural Revision in Ancient Alexandria* (California: University of California Press, 1992), p. 73.

[78] T. E. Page, Edward Capps, William Henry Denham Rouse, eds., *The Loeb Classical Library ---Philo* (London: William Heinemann Ltd, MCMXXIX), Vol. 1, p. xv (Introduction.)

[79] Mircea Eliade, ed., *The Encyclopedia of Religion* (New York: Macmillan Publication Co, 1987), Vol. 11, p. 287.

[80] Samuel Sandmel, *Philo of Alexandria* (New York: Oxford University Press, 1979), pp. 29-49.

[81] Seyyed Hossein Nasr, *Islam: Religion, History, and Civilization* (New York: HarperSanFrancisco, 2003), p. 164. Seyyed Hossein Nasr is a prominent professor of Islamic studies at the George Washington University in Washington, D.C.; See Manlio Simonetti, *Biblical Interpretation*, trans. John A. Hughes (Edinburgh: T&T Clark Ltd, 1994), p. 6.

[82] Sandmel, *op. cit.*, p. 25.

as his approach to interpreting reality which he inherited from his Hellenistic socio-philosophical world.[83] He develops his thought through "the Platonic tradition and saw it as…deepening his understanding of the God of Moses."[84] Greek philosophical thought and culture were used in his interpretation of his religious experiences and the use of allegories for didactic purposes.

The Greek word *logos* means *account, definition, or reason*. Plato uses *logos* to mean *'a true analytical account.'* In Plato's *Phaedo 76b, logos* is the capacity to provide an account of what we know. Stoic distinguishes between 'interior *logos*' (thought) and 'exterior *logos*' (speech.) Samuel Sandmel attests, "[A]t no time does Philo…ever define Logos for us. What we can do here is to assemble some of what Philo tells us."[85] For Philo, *logos* means "account" or "reason,"[86] or a creative force in the universe. Philo uses the logos as the source of what we know "about God and his functions."[87] His *logos* has a distinctive role in the creation of the world. The *logos* or the *Divine Logos* is in-between the *To ontos on* (*that which existingly exists*) and the sensible world. Philo interprets the *logos* to be like the Christian *'Christ,'* sent by the Father (God) and reveals Him. In fact, his interpretations of the Sacred Scriptures are carried out in view of the deeper meanings communicated through allegories.

In the Christian New Testament, the "logos" is "the *Word"* from the beginning in John's gospel. The *logos* is significant today "because of the similarity and dissimilarity—of Philo's conception to that of the Prologue of the Fourth Gospel."[88] Philo may have borrowed the notion that *logos* is *"the vivifying power"* from Heraclitus and Stoicism. The *logos* is the *"force*

---

[83] *Ibid.*, p. 143. See Erwin Ramsdell Goodenough, *By Light, Light: The Mystical Gospel of Hellenistic Judaism* (London: H. Milford, Oxford University Press, 1935), pp. 184-207.
[84] Philo Judaeus, *The Works of Philo*, trans. Charles Duke Yonge (Massachusetts: Hendrickson Publishers, 1993), Forward, p. xiii. Some say that Philo represents Middle Platonism (the Platonic tradition between Plato's immediate successors and the rise of the 3rd Century AD Neoplatonism.)
[85] *Ibid.*
[86] Hans-Georg Gadamer, *Plato's Dialectical Ethics*, trans. Robert M. Wallace (New Haven: Yale University Press, 1991), p. 8. Gadamer uses "logos ousias" meaning 'word or reason of being.'
[87] Sandmel, *op. cit.*, p. 94.
[88] T. E. Page, Edward Capps, William Henry Denham Rouse, eds., *The Loeb Classical Library ---Philo, op. cit.*, p. xx.

vitale"[89] or Divine Reason. [90] The Divine reason is mind for Philo and he uses synonyms like *'nous,' 'dianoia'* and *'logos'* to describe the higher mind. In Plato the cosmic *'nous'* or reason is *"the maker."* It is described as *divine* (*Timaeus* 30*b*), *rules* (*Laws 875c—d*), and *orders* (*Laws 966e.*) This shows the influence of Plato's Greek culture and thought in Philonic *logos*.[91] How did Philo harmonize Greek philosophical views and Judaism through allegorical interpretation? He involves the application of non-literal interpretation, which means that in the use of allegory the texts having inner meanings beyond the literal understanding. The spoken *logos* is a pointer to another invisible *logos*. Human *logos* or language/word communicates different allegorical meanings. Allegorical interpretation was used in the rabbinical school.[92] It makes available the truth of anything religious or faith to simple people, i.e. as a means of providing meaning and teaching the uneducated members of the community, especially the deeper meanings in the Scriptures.

In the Genesis account (Old Testament) (in *Legum Allegoriae*, iii 222-225)[93], for instance, the *serpent* is used to explain *desire*; *the man* is the *mind* and *the woman* is the *sense*. A literal interpretation of these concepts makes understanding difficult. Sandmel explains Philo's 'man' allegory to mean that "Man's higher mind... can so regiment the senses and passions that the soul can be freed from bodily domination."[94] Philo's Jewish tradition is male-dominated and its influence could be seen in his allegorical interpretations. The sensitive nature of these interpretation carried out by Philo has been describes

---

[89]Tempels Placide, *Bantu Philosophy* (Paris: Presence Africains, 1959.) *The 'logos' and the "force vitale"*- *"vital force"* may not totally be same but there is that ontological 'similarity' with Bantu-East African ethno-philosophy and cosmogony. See William Sweet, ed., *Philosophy, Culture and Pluralism* (Quebec: Editions du Scribe, 2002), p. 89.

[90] Philo, *Allegorical Interpretation*, trans. F. H. Colson and G.H. Whitaker (London: William Heinemann Ltd, MCMXXIX), Vol. 1, pp. xix-xx. It uses powers or potencies, which is same with reason.

[91] Hans-Georg Gadamer, *Hermeneutics, Religion and Ethics*, trans. Joel Weinsheimer (New Haven: Yale University Press, 1999), p. xi. Joel Weinsheimer uses this to describe the *logos*. This is my interpretation with respect to Philo, Logos and Religion.

[92] Sandmel observes that the volume 1 of the Loeb edition provides a brief list of biblical names and the allegorical meaning Philo gives to them. Vol. X of the Loeb edition (pp. 269-433) has a longer list, explanations and other details. See Basil Mitchell Lucas et al., *An Engagement with Plato's Republic: A Companion to the Republic* (England: Ashgate Publishing Limited, 2003), pp. 15-116; See Nicholas Pappas, *Plato and the Republic* (New York: Routledge Taylor & Francis Group, 2003, Second edition), pp. 50-57.

[93] Philo Judaeus, *The Works of Philo, op. cit.*, pp. 222-225.

[94] Sandmel, *op. cit.*, p. 25.

as a "revisionary interpretation of culture."[95] Some scholars interpret Philo revisionary approach as suggesting a form of complex community or an intercultural community dealing with different symbols and thought or meanings behind these symbols. The fact is: Philo uses allegory in "scriptural passages which on the surface seem to be irrational, or illogical…that can be troubling to a rationalistic mind."[96] The allegorical interpretation helps to unveil or reveal the hidden or spiritual meanings relevant to the community. There is a connection between the visible and the invisible world of understanding and meanings. His allegories are well structured on issues important to his community as a community influenced by other cultures around (intercultural situation and society.)

Philo's notion of society is *"politeuma"*---specifically focuses on the Jews of the Alexandrian community. The philosopher-king directs the community. The true philosopher-king is Moses: lawgiver, priest, and prophet. Moses is the embodiment of the divine laws (nomos empsychos koi logikos)[97] that guide people. Philo's *megalopolis* is an intercultural community of universal peace, with religious and moral responsibilities. He makes some contributions to Hellenic philosophy and the use of the universality of allegory for the interpretation between the Jewish culture and Greek philosophy/culture. He prefigures the development of the universal claim of hermeneutics and the communication of meanings between people of different cultural influences (Judaic interpretation of the Torah and Greek thought.) His approach also universalizes the literal and the allegorical meanings in hermeneutics and use of language (*logos* or word.) Later I shall briefly present the understanding of 'theater' and tragedy at this period after discussing Augustine. Generally, the early Christian period and medieval time had same attitude to the use of theater and understanding of tragedy as a didactic drama.

c. Augustine

Augustine has been described as one of the scholars that made use of hermeneutics in theological discourse. In theological studies hermeneutics

---

[95] Dawson, *Allegorical Readers and Cultural Revision in Ancient Alexandria, op. cit.*, p. 74.
[96] Sandmel, *op. cit.*, p. 18.
[97] *Ibid.*, p. 104.

designates "the art of rightly interpreting the holy [Holy] scriptures [Scriptures], which in itself is an ancient art."[98]

In the time of the Church fathers, hermeneutics, as portrayed in Augustine involves, amongst other elements and strategies- the use of allegories or allegorical interpretation. Gadamer affirms that "it was systematized in the Middle Ages…[the] method of the fourfold sense [the literal, allegorical, moral, and anagogical meanings] of scripture."[99] Allegory was an ancient form of interpretation that involved another meaning outside the literal meaning that an object possesses. Sandmel explains that "allegory is the assertion that such texts are not saying what they are saying, but saying something different."[100] It means *an appeal to imagination* and applies a special meaning that is not present on the surface.[101] The Greek term associated with it is *hyponoia* –that is, the meaning behind the literal meaning. There were gradual changes in ancient Greece on allegories until the "allegorical interpretation of Homer developed into a universal method, especially in the Stoics."[102]

Augustine applies the role of rhetoric in the understanding of Scriptures and for the effective communication of meaning and the truth of God. Prior to the Christian period, rhetoric has been used in classical studies. Augustine uses his *De doctrina Christiana*[103](DDC) as a way of introducing rhetoric in the interpretation of the Scriptures (DDC 4.28.61.) Let us take a close look at the parts of his work.

In Parts I-II[104] of the *De doctrina Christiana* Augustine talks about terms like interpretation, use, enjoyment and their relation to the Christian faith. We ought to enjoy God as the truest Being (*Confessiones* 7.9.13ff; *De civitate Dei*

---

[98] Gadamer, *The Gadamer Reader: A Bouquet of the Later Writings, op. cit.*, p. 46.
[99] *Ibid.*
[100] Sandmel, *Philo of Alexandria, op. cit.*, p. 17.
[101] *Ibid.*, p. 18; See Basil Mitchell Lucas et al., *An Engagement with Plato's Republic: A Companion to the Republic* (England: Ashgate Publishing Limited, 2003), pp. 15-116; See Nicholas Pappas, *Plato and the Republic* (New York: Routledge Taylor & Francis Group, 2003, Second edition), pp. 50-57.
[102] *Ibid.*
[103] Edward D. English, *Reading and Wisdom of the De Doctrina Christiana of Augustine in the Middle Ages* (Notre Dame and London: University of Notre Dame Press, 1995.); http://www.franciscan-archive.org/lombardusll-Sent.html (Accessed September 25, 2013.)
[104] This could also be called books. There are four books of *De doctrina Christiana*.

12.2; *De libero arbitrio* 2.14-15; DDC *Prooem.* 7, 1.32.35) and use things. These parts also discuss on how we understand the meaningfulness of thing (res) used for others different from the whole or fullness of thing (thing enjoyed for itself or good in itself). This section includes the discovery of what deserves to be understood and how to communicate or teach what has been discovered (DDC 2.40.60-2.42.63—God's truth.) For Augustine, a true understanding of the Scriptures ought to lead one to Christian charity/love (DDC 2.42.63; DDC 1.33.37; 3.10.16—on the love of *oneself* and one's *neighbour*.) In interpretation truth is more desirable than logic. Language is important in understanding Scriptures since there are many unknown and figurative signs used in the Scriptures.

In Part III, Augustine brings to light the mode of writing which helps present meaning. This includes the interpretation of complicated words or meanings, especially literal and figurative expressions (DDC 3.10.14-3.23.33). Also signs and figurative symbolism could imply a profound meaning. For instance, a dove is easily seen as figure for peace or peacefulness. It could also simply means a bird in a literal context.

In Part IV, Augustine shows the influence of the contributions of classic rhetoric that was brought in through the use of Cicero's rhetorical theory. Augustine discusses the relationship between Christian truth (DDC 2.40.60-2.42.63) and role of the use of rhetoric by the preacher of the Word. The preacher carries out this active inquiry with humility (DDC 2.41.62.) Augustine concentrates on the proper use and the suitability of rhetoric by Christian teachers. The role of rhetoric serves as the main focus of this work because Augustine responds to the change of the time when Christianity became the determining religion and so required rhetoric in light of the communication of truth or interpretation of Scriptures (DDC 4.1.1-4.56.10.) Rhetoric, he says, is not good in itself but only for use in interpretation. Preachers are not required to be rhetoric but should be people of wisdom. The use of different kinds of style is important to communicate accurately. Augustine also synthesizes the written and oral aspects of meaning and how this meaning relates to the inner word (*verbum interius.*)

In brief, the use of rhetoric is to make the communication of understanding become universal. With rhetoric the preacher is able to get at the universal message of the Scriptures. The truth of the Scriptures is properly interpreted and translated. This also helps with the allegorical interpretation of the historical and cultural situations of those who were inspired to write the Scriptures. Rhetoric should not be desired for itself but for the universality of meaning. Clarity of meaning is more important to the Christian teacher rather than the skill of rhetoric is to interpretation (DDC 4.7.14-15.)

According to Gadamer, Augustine in *De doctrina Christiana*[105] uses interpretation as a methodical process of consciousness. Gadamer further explains:

> The task of Christian dogmatics in early times was shaped by the tension between the particular history of the Jewish people and the universal proclamation Jesus put forward in the New Testament. Here methodical reflection is called on to help create solutions to this problem. With the help of notions from Plotinus, Augustine in *De doctrina Christiana* [106]described the ascent of the spirit from the literal sense of a text to the moral meaning, and then further upward to the spiritual meaning. In this way he solved a doctrinal problem by integrating the ancient hermeneutical heritage into a single, unified standpoint.[107]

Augustine also distinguishes between what the predicative statement is (*actus signatus*) and what its completion is (*actus exercitus*) which comes from an understanding person. Everyone desires full or complete meaning accomplished through understanding. Augustine's message is that we have to go beyond signs to full meaning if we want to understand linguistic comments or statements. Signs are not adequate for fullness of meaning. There has to be a completion of meaning in hermeneutics, including spiritual and moral meanings that are beyond the literal meaning (DDC 3.10.14-3.23.33.)

Plato influenced Augustine, especially on the written word that is from the "inner Word." The inner *Word* is the word of the soul. We remember Plato

---

[105] Gerhard Ebeling, "Hermeneutik," *Religion in Geschichte und Gegenwart* (1959, Band III), p. 249.
[106] *Ibid.*
[107] Gadamer, *The Gadamer Reader: A Bouquet of the Later Writings, op. cit.,* p. 46; Paula Fredriksen, "Allegory and Reading God's Book: Paul and Augustine on the Destiny of Israel," *Interpretation and Allegory: Antiquity to the Modern Period,* ed., with introductory essay by Jon Whitman (Leiden: Koninklijke Brill NV, 2000), pp. 125-149. There are some information on Augustine's views about exegesis and allegorical interpretations.

calls thinking the "the dialogue of the soul with itself."[108] The inner word of the soul is the true object of hermeneutics when we seek to understand— understand the inner meaning. The meaning is what is present in a language and conveyed through a language. There is a difference between the spoken word and its true being. This difference could lead to misunderstanding because "what comes into language is something different from the spoken word itself. But the word is a word only because of what comes into language in it. Its own physical being exists only in order to disappear into [inner meaning or true being of] what is said."[109] The dualism in Plato's philosophy influenced Augustine, especially Plato's ontology in which there are the sensible and intelligible, the physical and the spiritual worlds. Augustine seems to have used this idea in his ranking of nature/ understanding of existence and meaning (DDC 1.23.22; 2.23-35.)[110]

Augustine makes some contributions to the study of hermeneutics through his distinction between internal and external words. He argues that the difference between the *logos prophorikos* (external word) and the *logos endiathetos* (the internal word) is that the internal word of the soul has much depth of meaning that are never properly communicated or expressed in an exhaustive manner. This is why the task of hermeneutics is ongoing in order to capture this deep meaning. We understand properly by understanding deeply the fullness of meaning that lies in the inner word. The external word does not have the depth of meaning as the internal word.

He uses the distinction between the λόγος προφορικός (*logos prophorikos*) and λόγος ἐνδιάθετος (*logos endiathetos*) to give a theological understanding to incarnation. The incarnation (the Word of God that became human)[111] is one of the mysteries of the Christian message. This distinction between the external word and the internal word by Augustine is important in interpreting the nature of the Word that became human. The λόγος is the 'Wisdom' of God that came among humans. Augustine discusses the theory of

---

[108] *Theatetus* 184; *Sophiste* 263e, 264 a.; Grondin, *Sources of Hermeneutics, op. cit.*, p. 28. Aristotle has something similar to this. See Aristotle, *Categories and De Interpretatione*, trans. John Lloyd Ackrill (Oxford: Clarendon Aristotle Series, 1963), p. 43.
[109] Gadamer, *Truth and Method*, trans., rev. Joel Weinsheimer and Donald G. Marshall, *op. cit.*, p. 470. Relate to Gadamer, *Truth and Method*, trans., rev. Joel Weinsheimer and Donald G. Marshall (New York: Crossroad, 2nd rev. ed, 1991), p. 482.
[110] See also Augustine's Confessions VII.X.16.
[111] Jesus Christ –the Word made flesh.

word (*Verbumslehre*) and the incarnate word, which is recognized as his way of establishing the non complete project of the forgetfulness of language in Western thought.

To understand the true meaning of a statement, we have to go beyond the outer to the inner word. We have to transcend the physical, uttered word to reach the true *verbum*.[112] Uttered words could easily be perceived as physical but the inner word has to be translated from the concrete language. Etienne Gilson clarifies:

> Correctly understanding words whose meaning is known means, in principle, knowing the thought of the person who spoke them…Since a certain disconnection between language and thought has been noticed in some cases, it is possible that in other cases their union may not be as secure as one might think.[113]

In Augustine's hermeneutics, the distinction between the outer and inner word is in the fact that the word we wish to understand is not that which we just listen to but the one that is originally intended. That is the "the word of reason in its universality."[114] Augustine's notion of the inner word raises the question that will come up again in Schleiermacher's hermeneutics: Is the inner word about psychological interpretation or mental language? Some scholars have argued that the commentary about the inner word belongs to Jean Grondin's perspective, and not necessarily Augustine's or Schleiermacher's. Meanwhile, my interest at this point is to focus on Augustine's contributions to hermeneutics following the influence of Plato and the ancient Greek philosophy.

For Augustine, there is something more important outside the signs that come from the word (uttered words). That means the inner word (belonging to the soul) does not apply to a particular language but to language as thought about the subject matter (*forma excognitata.*)[115] The process described above is the process by which words are seeds of understanding or words search for understanding. As Augustine puts it, "[E]very doctrine is of things, or signs.

---

[112] Saint Augustine, *De trintiate*, XV, chapter X, 19; XV, chapter XI, 20.

[113] Etienne Gilson, *Introduction à l'étude de Saint Augustin* (Paris: Librairie Philosophique J. Vrin, 1982), p. 91.

[114] Grondin, *Sources of Hermeneutics, op. cit.*, p. 105; See also *De trinitate*, XV, chapter XV, 25.

[115] See Grondin, *Sources of Hermeneutics, op. cit.*, p. 105.

But even things are learned through signs. But those are properly named things, which are not employed to signify anything; but signs, those whose use is in signifying."[116] In this case, words are signs—signifying—thoughts or meanings. With words we have access to understanding thoughts. There has to be a complete process of moving from *actus signatus* (statements as signs) to *actus exercitus* (the subject matter as completion or thought to the end.)

Words are important in propositions and they are reflected in the responses or answers we give to proposition as questions. In this process of words formulating propositions and words used in providing answers we have the universality of language which is present in the dialectic of question and answer. This process influenced later modern and contemporary hermeneutics. Words as propositions do not give truth in themselves. The truth is in the wholeness of communication, e.g. the inner meaning. There are propositions that do not bear the truth directly. Their truth could only be discerned through the inner word which is where we locate the universality of language. Why is this universality of language for Augustine? It is because language mediates understanding and language in its real hermeneutical sense is language in its universality as 'inner' word. Our understanding is constitutively linguistic. It is not as in a particular or spoken language. However, each 'external' or concrete language does have its own importance in hermeneutics.

Words do not exhaust what we have in our thoughts or "in mind." We are closely connected to other people in dialogue through the inner words. The inner word brings out the intimate aspect of language during our inquiries. Augustine and Plato agree in this regard because for Plato the *verbum interius* which is the soul of the word or the inner word is where the true meaning of the word uttered is found. Augustine further develops this view and helps form a hermeneutical theory of language through his universality of the inner *logos* and that hermeneutics is in a universal sense bound to language.

Before we go to the modern period of hermeneutics, following the influence of ancient and medieval times, one thing to remember is that

---

[116] The source of this translation is from Alexis Bugnolo (with minor modification of the English translation according to B. Hoon Woo.) See B. Hoon Woo, "Augustine's Hermeneutics and Homiletics in *De doctrina Christiana*: Humiliation, Love, Sign, and Discipline," *Journal of Christian Philosophy* 17 (2013), pp. 97-117. See http://www.franciscan-archive.org/lombardusII-Sent.html (Accessed 25 September 2013.)

Augustine carefully presents the universality of language, hermeneutics and the condition for the possibility of understanding as seen in the notion of the 'inner word' for interpreting and communicating of meaning of the passages of the Scriptures. He also provides us with a theory of language. There is a good introductory look into the intercultural problem of hermeneutics and language because of his focus on rhetoric, use of allegory and use of the texts of the Scriptures (as coming from different cultural heritages of his time.) I shall relate the intercultural issue in the medieval time to the use of theater to communicate Christian meaning to the peoples of various cultures so that they understand the truth of Christian message.

In this section on medieval contributions to hermeneutics, I will like to briefly discuss the notion of theater in light of tragedy and hermeneutics. This helps us to focus our attention on the primary issues of this book. According to Richard Southern, there is the ancient people's theater of tragedy and the Christian theater of tragedy.[117] The people's theater we have discussed earlier under ancient period and Aristotle. The Christian theater focuses on the actor rather than on the plot. It also emphasized spectacle, stage direction and use of vernacular because of larger audience. We could also relate this larger audience to the intercultural needs of different cultures. The audience or the community are mere observers and so passive. It is unlike Aristotle's people's theater where the people determine the drama following their interests and needs. Theater at this medieval period is an in-door activity and words with specific meanings are the focus of attention. What is communicated and interpreted is structured to have specific meaning for the people. There are music, dance, costume etc., but theater at this time becomes a monologue than a dialogue with the people.

The Christian period sees a rejection of the ancient Aristotelian view of theater and tragedy. Ancient theater and tragedy are seen as devilish and immoral. Liturgical drama and morality plays (as didactic allegories) were prevalent as this time. It is likely that Philo, Tertullian and Augustine did adopt theater/drama in teaching religious themes, general Christian doctrine, and the evangelization of the people through allegories. The early Christian and medieval time saw the rapid use of theater in the communication of the

---

[117] See Richard Southern, *The Seven Ages of the Theater* (New York: Hill and Wang, 1961); See also Alice Lovelace, "A Brief History of Theater Forms," *Motion Magazine*, February 15, 1996.

meaning of Christ acts of redemption, suffering and resurrection. There was the dramatizing of biblical traditions at specific occasions. For instance, the Good Friday passion (like a tragedy narrative) and the Christmas Nativity narratives are as a result of Christian approach to theater at this period and serve as means to transmit the Christian meaning of salvation to a large number of illiterate population. Theater becomes the means to teach the people and emphasize religious faith and orthodoxy. In the modern and contemporary time, one could allude to Christian theater's influence in Oberammergau Passion play in Oberammergau, Bavaria, Germany. There are many rich medieval and reformation traditions of hermeneutics but for lack of space and the specific purpose of the book, I shall now focus on the progress of hermeneutics in the modern period. [118]

1.3 The Progress of Hermeneutics in the Modern Period

a. Friedrich Schleiermacher

The debate about *Hermeneutik* started in Germany in the 18th Century. It arose during the debate over the problem of biblical exegesis and study of secular classical texts (philology.) It also included the development of the historical sciences during the close of the 19th Century. The central concept of the debate was *Verstehen* (Understanding.) Understanding the Scriptures was a major issue of Protestant critics. Hermeneutics in the modern period focused on the vernacular translation of the Bible. Understanding or hermeneutics started with the influence of Protestantism in the early period of Martin Luther's doctrine of the *sola scriptura.* Among Protestants there was no canon of interpretation. The Protestant critics in Europe, especially in Germany, searched to develop canons or standards for interpreting the Sacred Scriptures. According to Madu, "[T]he new movement recognized no hierarchy whatsoever pre-existing its own interpretation, and between 1720 and 1820, hardly a year passed without the appearance of some new hermeneutical manual to aid Protestant ministers."[119]

---

[118] Gadamer, *The Gadamer Reader: A Bouquet of the Later Writings, op. cit.,* p. 49.
[119] Madu, *African Symbols, Proverbs and Myths: The Hermeneutics of Destiny, op. cit.,* p. 7; See Palmer, *Hermeneutics, op. cit.* p. 34.

The pace or progress of hermeneutics reflects the various approaches adopted in different periods in history. Richard E. Palmer mentions the six different approaches associated with hermeneutics and they go beyond the modern time. He notes:

> (1) The theory of biblical exegesis; (2) general philological methodology; (3) the science of all linguistic understanding; (4) the methodological foundation of *Geisteswissenschaften*; (5) phenomenology of existence and of existential understanding; and (6) the systems of interpretation both collective and iconoclastic, used by man to reach the meaning behind myths and symbols.[120]

Although Palmer mentioned some approaches that are beyond our period of discussion (modern), it goes to show the changing nature of what hermeneutics has been. We have had biblical hermeneutics, philological hermeneutics, existential hermeneutics, cultural hermeneutics, philosophical hermeneutics (Gadamer's form of hermeneutics.) Philosophers, like Madu, Ricoeur argue that there is no one hermeneutics. Ricoeur says: "[T]here does not exist a general hermeneutics, that is, a general theory of interpretation, a general canon of exegesis, there are only various separate and contrasting hermeneutic theories."[121]

Schleiermacher defines hermeneutics as the art of interpretation or the theory of methods of interpretation or understanding. As an art of understanding, hermeneutics in Schleiermacher's view is beyond one aspect of hermeneutics like philology. His interest is in formulating a general hermeneutics that serves all kinds of text interpretation. According to Madu:

> He (Schleiermacher) set out to explore what may be regarded as the fundamental act of all hermeneutics. This marked the beginning of the conception of hermeneutics as the science which described the conditions of understanding. For the first time hermeneutics was defined as the doctrine of the act of understanding (*Verstehen*) itself. It is related to the concrete,

---

[120] Palmer, *Hermeneutics, op. cit.*, p. 33.
[121] Ricoeur, *The Conflict of Interpretations, op. cit.*, p. 317.

existing and acting human being in the process of understanding dialogue."[122]

Schleiermacher's hermeneutics includes both psychological and grammatical interpretations. The psychological interpretation imperatively requires putting oneself in the mind of the author. The grammatical interpretation focuses on human speech, texts and grammar.[123] According to Manfred Frank, it is difficult to depend on what Schleiermacher says on each of these forms of interpretation to judge which is more important to him. He notes that Schleiermacher did less with the psychological interpretation because he has better command of the information in grammatical interpretation.[124] However, other documents show that Schleiermacher recognizes the stages of interpretation since "only when one has obtained certainty about an author through language, can the other, psychological task [of interpretation] begin."[125] There is interdependence between these two interpretations, especially through his dialectical approach[126] and their relation is infinite. Language has an infinite domain and these two interpretations share this infinite quality.[127] The level of this relation between psychological and grammatical is thus: "If interpretation is concerned with fully understanding the point of view of the other it must be psychological according to Schleiermacher, but to the extent that interpreted meaning is to remain applicable to the self it must be grammatical."[128]

The subjective aspect of interpretation is not all covered by the psychological interpretation. Schleiermacher introduces the technical interpretation to balance the psychological through which the author shows his thoughts moving from meditation to composition. The technical interpretation

---

[122] Madu, *African Symbols, Proverbs and Myths: The Hermeneutics of Destiny, op. cit.*, p. 7; See Palmer, *Hermeneutics, op. cit.*, p. 9.

[123] Some consider these as psychological (subjective) and grammatical (objective) aspects of hermeneutics. Wilhelm Dilthey, *Selected Works, Volume IV: Hermeneutics and the Study of History*, ed., with an introduction, by Rudolf A. Makkreel and Frithjof Rodi (New Jersey: Princeton University Press, 1996), p. 7.

[124] Manfred Frank's introduction to Friedrich Schleiermacher, *Hermeneutik und Kritik* (Frankfurt am Maim: Suhrkamp, 1977), p. 60ff.

[125] Friedrich Schleiermacher, *Hermeneutik und Kritik* (Frankfurt am Maim: Suhrkamp, 1977), p. 80.

[126]Dilthey, *Selected Works, Volume IV: Hermeneutics and the Study of History, op. cit.*, p. 7.

[127] Schleiermacher, *Hermeneutik und Kritik, op. cit.*, p. 80.

[128] Dilthey, *Selected Works, Volume IV: Hermeneutics and the Study of History, op. cit.*, p. 8.

provides the balance and the form that guides the author in meditation and composition or the rules of how the author works.[129] The historical, cultural and linguistic environs or milieu of the writer must be considered or understood. Also "the distinctive thought and experience of the author"[130] and other individual details have to be understood (the personal dimension or part.)

The psychological aspect of Schleiermacher's hermeneutics calls for historical identity with the text's author. This is a call to forsake the interpreter's world for the world of the author; it is, in a sense, an attempt to *be* the author in there production of the text. Further, it is an attempt to avoid all prejudices in approaching the text. Indeed, understanding inevitably involves prejudice and one of the prejudices Schleiermacher wishes to get rid of is the temporal distance.

The art of interpretation involves a temporal distance between the author, the texts and the interpreter. This distance makes it difficult to accomplish full understanding if one has to identify with the historical and social conditions of the author. For Schleiermacher, the temporal distance is something that must be overcome (i.e., by entering in to the world of the author.) This is seen to be rather a difficult task that "we must transpose ourselves into the spirit of the age, think[ing] with its ideas and its thoughts, not with our own, and thus advanc[ing] toward historical objectivity," [and we must acknowledge that] "the important thing is to recognize the distance in time as a positive and productive condition enabling understanding."[131] Schleiermacher's "subjective interpretation" accepts that the temporal distance must be transposed for us to have access to the intentions of the author. But some others argue that when we wish to understand the meaning in a text, we do not need to recapture the writer's attitude of mind. Canonical-compositional hermeneutics is not concerned with establishing a writer's attitude of mind or a psychological dimension of the hermeneutical process. The issue is the text itself, not the author of the text. We can gain the perspective within which the author formed his views, but we can do this only by reading the text itself. Schleiermacher's position could be explained through the "divinatory method"

---

[129] Schleiermacher, *Hermeneutik und Kritik, op. cit.*, p. 184.
[130]Anthony C. Thiselton, *New Horizons in Hermeneutics: The Theory and Practice of Transforming Biblical Reading* (Grand Rapids, Michigan: Zondervan Publishing House, 1992), p. 221.
[131] Gadamer, *Truth and Method*, trans. Joel Weinsheimer and Donald G. Marshall, *op. cit.*, p. 297.

as a way of getting access to the intentions of the author (mentis auctoris.) Ryan Mcgivern confirms that "Schleiermacher's assertion that the hermeneutical undertaking is completed by the 'divinatory method' by which the interpreter places themselves into the mind of the author."[132] In this way, the interpreter is able to understand the author better than he understands himself.

Schleiermacher also formulates the hermeneutical circle which involves that parts are understood as essential aspect of the whole and vice versa. This hermeneutical circle dialectically explains the original constructive act which grasps the unity from individual parts to whole of a text. This theory urges that we understand the text's linguistic parts and structure by understanding in the context of the whole and then through the part, which is in coherence with the whole. The context (i.e., the whole) determines the meaning of the part. It means understanding every structure of thought in the whole (historical condition) context of human being. This includes psychological understanding. The hermeneutical circle is historical because it moves between the text and ancient history. The purpose is to understand the text and the author or writer better, even better than he/she understood himself/herself.

Schleiermacher aims at developing a free hermeneutics that is not dogmatic but is perceived "as a universal [*allgemeine*] doctrine of understanding and interpretation."[133]As a universal doctrine of understanding hermeneutics involves literal, philological and biblical texts. The biblical texts were important to Schleiermacher.

> In Schleiermacher the occasional, disciplinary elements arise only in a supplementary way; in turning to the biblical text, of course, they are given their due. With his hermeneutical theory, Schleiermacher could defend the scientific character of theology, especially against inspiration-based theologies. These theologies had fundamentally put in question the validity of understanding

---

[132] Hans-Georg Gadamer *"The* Problem of Historical Consciousness" *Interpretive Social Science: A Reader,* Paul Rabinow and William M. Sullivan, eds. (Berkeley: University of California Press, 1979), p. 147.

[133] Gadamer, *The Gadamer Reader: A Bouquet of the Later Writings, op. cit.,* p. 50. Friedrich Schlegel influenced Schleiermacher in terms of getting a universal doctrine of understanding.

the holy scriptures [Holy Scriptures] by means of textual exegesis, historical theology, philology, and so on.[134]

His hermeneutical view argues that to understand involves "a reproductive repetition of the original intellectual act of the author's production of the meaning on the basis of the congeniality of spirit."[135] That means one can, from a gadamerian perspective, interpret Schleiermacher as grounding understanding on a specific form of dialogue, repetition and on interhuman relationship. By so doing he establishes a solid foundation—a deeper foundation for hermeneutic than was the case earlier. In this way hermeneutics becomes scientific and scholarly, while focusing not only on theology but on other human sciences.

For Schleiermacher, the art of understanding or hermeneutics also includes the art of avoiding whatever brings misunderstanding and overcoming misunderstanding. His hermeneutics shows us how to

exclude by controlled, methodical consideration whatever is alien and leads to misunderstanding—misunderstanding suggested to us by distance in time, change in linguistic usages, or in the meanings of words and modes of thinking—that is certainly far from an absurd description of the hermeneutical endeavor.[136]

Schleiermacher institutes a form of revolution in the notion of hermeneutics. Hermeneutics is important because of the lack of understanding of the text. When what is stated in a text is difficult to understand because of some impending reasons, hermeneutics starts from there. What we do to overcome misunderstanding and accomplish genuine meaning is hermeneutics. In other words, hermeneutics begins with the natural priority of avoiding *mis*understanding. Schleiermacher declares that the more lax practice of hermeneutics or the art of understanding, the more it "proceeds on the assumption that understanding arises naturally... The more rigorous practice proceeds on the assumption that misunderstanding arises naturally, and that

---

[134] *Ibid.*

[135] *Ibid.*

[136]Gadamer, *Philosophical Hermeneutics*, trans. and ed. David E. Linge (Los Angeles: University of California Press, 1976), p. 7.

understanding must be intended and sought at each point."[137] As an aspect of avoiding misunderstanding, Schleiermacher has also been credited to have used hermeneutics in the understanding of other cultures (intercultural understanding.) One should not take the meanings in other cultures for granted. Hermeneutics requires being open to the rational and coherent aspects of understanding other cultures, even when they are unfamiliar to us. One has to avoid the use of prejudices that come from one's cultural, theological or philosophical background in the evaluation of others. This is done by critically looking at our hermeneutic prejudices. Schleiermacher moved from a technique approach to a universal theory of hermeneutics. A universal theory of hermeneutics is useful for all situations, disciplines, texts and cultures.

In summary, the temporal distance, changes in word meanings, current perspectives of authors and so on may create a huge gap between the author and the interpreter. All these intervening socio-historical developments/conditions could hinder the clear process of "understanding unless their effects are neutralized."[138] Hermeneutics for Schleiermacher truly involves the reconstruction of the grasp of reality through our mind and the application of the hermeneutic rules of parts and whole; distinctiveness and identity.[139] He receives the credit for bringing under critical analysis the reconstruction of the historical situation or the life-context. The author's meaning to us could only be revealed under this critical and methodically determined form of interpretation. Schleiermacher develops a more 'general hermeneutics' that sees understanding itself as the interpreter's personal "reconstruction of the creative consciousness from which the text emerges."[140] Understanding other cultures is part of his intercultural contribution in hermeneutics and language.

---

[137] Schleiermacher, *Hermeneutik,* trans. Heinz Kimmerle (Heidelberg: Karl Winter, 1959), p. 86.

[138] Gadamer, *Philosophical Hermeneutics, op. cit.,* pp. xii-xiii.

[139] Dilthey, *Selected Works, Volume IV: Hermeneutics and the Study of History, op. cit.,* p. 9.

[140]Jon Whitman, "A Retrospective Forward: Interpretation, Allegory, and Historical Change," *Interpretation and Allegory: Antiquity to the Modern Period,* ed., with introductory essay by Jon Whitman (Leiden: Koninklijke Brill NV, 2000), p. 13.

b. Wilhelm Dilthey

There have been different conceptions of hermeneutics in history. In an attempt to attain a universal concept of hermeneutics, Wihelm Dilthey addresses the most pertinent project in arriving at the fundamental importance of understanding. This "is necessary to determine the attainable degree of universality that is possible for each kind of understanding beginning with its logical forms."[141]

Dilthey rarely uses the term hermeneutics because it depicts narrowly the art of providing rules for textual exegesis. As a student of theology, he was influenced by the narrow application of hermeneutics by August Boeckh in philological hermeneutics.[142] However, Dilthey's concern is ensuring that hermeneutics becomes part of the epistemological foundation of the sciences. He is also reacting to the rise of positivism and scientism. He focuses on developing an empirical theory of history that is founded on the opposition between the natural sciences (concerned with the explanation of things) and the human sciences (concerned with the understanding of things.)[143] He argues that the human sciences, especially psychology, proceed from understanding rather than explanation. As he often says we explain nature and causes, but we understand human mental life.[144] The mental phenomena are easily intelligible because of the nature of inner experience. They are unlike the external experience that goes through the senses. This means we cannot have them as they are (the external experience.) Dilthey was influenced by Johann Gustav Droysen's[145] work entitled: *Historik.* The two main works of Dilthey are: *Introduction to the Human Sciences* and *Formation of the Historical World in the Human Sciences.*

He has interest in the domain of the human sciences and understanding individuality. He agrees with developing a hermeneutics that includes the

---

[141] Wilhelm Dilthey, *Gesammelte Schriften*, VII, 217-218; See Dilthey, *Selected Works, Volume IV: Hermeneutics and the Study of History, op. cit.*, p. 6.

[142] Dilthey, *Selected Works, Volume IV: Hermeneutics and the Study of History, op. cit.*, p. 4.

[143] *Ibid.*, p. 6.

[144] Dilthey, *Gesammelte Schriften* 5 (Göttingen, 1966), p. 144. Dilthey was not successful in making psychology the foundation of human sciences. His project was criticized. See Grondin, *Introduction to Philosophical Hermeneutics, op. cit.*, pp. 86-87.

[145] Dilthey *Jahrbuch 3* (1985), p. 200.

understanding of history which is clearly guided by philosophical insight. Only this could provide the genuine background for a general hermeneutics.[146] He seeks to free the human sciences from being placed under the natural sciences. This is his way of seeking a solid foundation[147] that bears signs of his scientific interest. Dilthey felt that the interest in hermeneutics is fading. He tried to revive it through broadening the scope of understanding by including the important aspects of the human sciences and the natural sciences.[148] In developing from technique to theory of hermeneutics, Dilthey introduces a different approach to hermeneutics. His approach is to give to human sciences the same scientific explanation we find in the natural sciences. His main task is to make hermeneutics provide the universal methodological basis of the *Geisteswissenschaften* (human sciences): "Insofar as they adhered to the guidelines of methodical interpretation, the human studies could lay claim to a knowledge of the human world... as rigorous as the natural sciences' knowledge of nature." [149]

Following Schleiermacher's example, Dilthey relates hermeneutics to the meaning of the subjective intention of its author (mentis auctoris.) The understanding of the intention of the author requires focusing on the documentations, actions, objects or artifacts that have the significance of the historical world. It includes understanding the author as a historical agent and his original life-world. This understanding is one that is about "self-transposition or imaginative projection whereby the knower negates the temporal distance that separates him from his object and becomes contemporaneous with it."[150] For Dilthey, the author's intention or his original life-world can have only a negative implication, especially in the light of distortions and prejudices. But the presence of prejudice does not necessarily mean a total loss of true understanding. It has to be transcended, even though not completely. This is because it is essentially part of human finitude and the historicity of our understanding. The historical understanding is the "action of subjectivity purged of all prejudices, and it is achieved in direct proportion to the knower's ability to set aside his own horizons by means of an effective

[146] Dilthey, *Selected Works, Volume IV: Hermeneutics and the Study of History, op. cit.*, p. 4.
[147] Grondin, *Introduction to Philosophical Hermeneutics, op. cit.*, p. 84.
[148] Dilthey, *Selected Works, Volume IV: Hermeneutics and the Study of History, op. cit.*, p. 15.
[149] Gadamer, *Philosophical Hermeneutics, op. cit.*, pp. xiii-xiv.
[150] *Ibid.*

historical method."[151] Dilthey finds the conditions of validity and objectivity in the inner experience.[152] Understanding in the human sciences involves the return from outside experience to the inside experience where there is objectivity. It is like the natural science that finds its objective foundation on the principle of explanation. The central task of all human sciences is to understand. Dilthey holds that the validity of experience is from the structuring of pure human consciousness.[153] The emphasis on the structure or conditions of consciousness influences him to accept that "only reflection on the psychological foundations of the human sciences would be capable of grounding the objectivity of their knowledge."[154]

Hermeneutics for Dilthey is related to historical consciousness and the interpretation of all historical objectifications.[155] Understanding involves the concrete aspect it has in relation to one's present experience. Dilthey considers Protestantism to have made use of historical consciousness/life experience in hermeneutics, especially following Luther's *sola scriptura* approach. In his own way, Dilthey influences the new perspective in hermeneutics by his analysis of the concept of *Erlebnis*, which is the psychological basis of hermeneutics. *Erlebnis* is our life experience. Life experience provides us with meaning. Life experience is common to all but may not be exactly the same for everyone. Human nature is always the same. This is the point of universality. Dilthey opines, "[A] universal human nature and a trend toward an order of individuation are coordinated and firmly related of life and reality; and, reality is everywhere and forever the same, and life always reveals the same aspects."[156] His form of hermeneutics involves history because its goal is to understand the past. The historical aspect of hermeneutics in this case would involve three distinguished levels. They are a) the chronicler with an epic

---

[151] *Ibid.* p. xiv.

[152] Dilthey, *Dilthey's Philosophy of Existence: Introduction to Weltanschauungslehre*, translation of an Essay with Introduction by William Kluback and Martin Weinbaum (Westport, Connecticut: Greenwood Press, Publishers, 1978), p. 39. Dilthey focuses on inner experience which is what is common to all in its objectivity. This experience is also the individual *Erlebnis* that is extended to all individuals. (*Ibid.* 8.)

[153] See Dilthey, *Gesammelte Schriften* (Göttingen, 1966), p. xvii.

[154] Grondin, *Introduction to Philosophical Hermeneutics, op. cit.*, p. 85. The time frame was from 1880 and following, human sciences used methodological research which is guided by the universal principle of phenomenality.

[155] Dilthey, *Selected Works, Volume IV: Hermeneutics and the Study of History, op. cit.*, p. 12.

[156] Dilthey, *Dilthey's Philosophy of Existence: Introduction to Weltanschauungslehre, op. cit.*, p. 28.

interest; b) the pragmatic historian with a political interest; c) the universal historian with the interest and the task of reconstructing our inner life, thereby leading to another self-consciousness of history. Related to this is his view that the inner movement of the mind is the foundation of life. Dilthey adopts the principle of hermeneutics which maintains that genuine understanding requires the articulation of the historical particulars or parts and the whole, and vice versa. He affirms it as "the great movement of German culture, which apprehends structure and the articulation and distinction of parts on the basis of a whole."[157] Dilthey holds that hermeneutical task as understanding involves the whole of a text. He further argues that the whole has to be understood on the basis of the particular or the detail and the detail on the basis of the whole. Also, when he says that understanding involves the whole of a text, it is essentially about language. This is because language is the means of expressing and representing all that we see, perceive or experience.

In conclusion, Dilthey states:
If understanding is basic for the human sciences…the epistemological, logical, and methodological analysis of understanding is one of the main tasks for the foundation of the human sciences. The importance of this task only becomes fully apparent when one makes explicit the difficulties contained in the nature of understanding with reference to the practice of a universally valid science.[158]

Dilthey's project is that understanding and explanation could at some point mean the same thing. Hermeneutics is understood in relation to universal history which is a study that involves every aspects of life within a certain time gap. For him, every experience is a perspective of the world to us. From these particular experiences we develop a universal interpretation through which the "universal attitude are begotten."[159] Hermeneutics becomes the foundation of human science rather than psychology. Psychology retains its foundational function to the human sciences.[160] Dilthey also maintains the classical

---

[157] Dilthey, *Selected Works, Volume IV: Hermeneutics and the Study of History, op. cit.*, p. 6; See Dilthey, *Gesammelte Schriften*, XIII, pp. 183-207.
[158] *Ibid.*, pp. 252-253.
[159] Dilthey, *Dilthey's Philosophy of Existence: Introduction to Weltanschauungslehre, op. cit.*, p. 24.
[160] Michael Ermarth, *Wilhelm Dilthey: The Critique of Historical Reason* (Chicago, 1978), p. 235.

understanding of hermeneutics which is to demonstrate the possibility of knowledge from the historical world. The interpreter is able to overcome prejudice and the negative effects of his/her historicalness or historical situation.

c. Edmund Husserl

Husserl's interest in transcendental phenomenology focuses on the essence of objects and their modes of appearance.[161] His concern is not in the interpretation of phenomena but on what phenomena are in themselves, and allowing things to speak for themselves. Thus, interpretation is only necessary for getting at things-in-themselves or the essence of things. The essence is that which is behind that which exists or which is seen, behind the word we listen to. For Husserl, hermeneutics could present one with different interpretive approaches to phenomena which are part of getting at the essence of things. How do we get at things-in-themselves without being distracted by theories or methods of interpretations? Husserl recommends the combination of a number of interpretations in order to access the essence of things or what phenomena are in themselves.

Husserl approaches phenomenology as a philosophical activity that anyone could undertake. Phenomenology is a personal inquiry[162] that one could take on reality. It is not the only means to the truth of reality. He did encourage his students through his liberal approach to phenomenology to undertake this project. Husserl's second main work was the *Ideen* (*Ideas*) after the *Logical Investigation*. In *Ideen* Husserl argues that the principle of all principles is: "all originally-given intuition functions as an original source of knowledge."[163] The intuition provides the hermeneutic probity that is essential in philosophy or the task of philosophy (as the first science.) In other words, philosophy has to start from the intuitive, i.e., as things present themselves intuitively. Rigorous philosophy must be based on the intuition and what the intuition "gives".

---

[161] John B. Thompson, *Critical Hermeneutics: A Study in the Thoughts of Paul Ricoeur and Jürgen Habermas* (Cambridge: Cambridge University Press, 1981), p. 36.
[162] Gadamer, "The Phenomenological Movement," *Philosophical Hermeneutics* Hans-Georg Gadamer (Berkeley: University of California Press, 1976), p. 143; See Martin Heidegger, *Platon: Sophistes, Gesamtausgabe* vol. 19 (Frankfurt: V. Klostermann, 1992), p. 9.
[163] *Husserliana* III, 51. See also paragraph 24.

Husserl did also some philosophical reflections on the *Meditations* of Descartes.[164] Like Descartes, he seeks to develop a method that begins with the rejection of presuppositions. Husserl's effort to get at a 'presuppositionless' view would lead to having access to transcendental subjectivity (the human consciousness.) This access to things themselves requires in Husserl's terms a 'putting in brackets' of our pre-conceptions. This "includes respecting the nature of Being: this entire natural world *therefore* which is continually 'there for us,' 'present to our hand,' and will ever remain there, is a 'fact world' of which we continue to be conscious."[165] The question is: how possible is it to analyze anything without any prior knowledge or presupposition? This is one of the problems facing understanding in Husserl. Husserl later published *Krisis*, focusing attention on presenting his phenomenological thoughts which is his way to the things themselves through words. As he affirms, it is "from simple words (...) to the things themselves."[166] His hermeneutical approach presented through his phenomenology is the "return from the spoken word to the meaning that animates it. In other words, understanding involves discerning the question that motivates the exterior word."[167]

Husserl was known to have provided his students with opportunities to get involved with hermeneutics and the publication of some of his thoughts. He did influence later philosophers, including Heidegger.[168] This influence on Heidegger (and later Gadamer) is noticeable in the hermeneutical application of phenomenological principles. The way to get at things themselves is through the interpretation of what constitutes, for instance, *Dasein*, which is a return to the essence of *Dasein*. Husserl's acceptance of discourse as a way to the

---

[164] Eugen Fink, *VI. Cartesianische Meditation*, ed. Ebeling, J. Holl and Kerckhoven (2 Volumes) (Dordrecht: Kluwer Academic Publisher, 1988.)

[165] Edmund Husserl, *Ideas: General Introduction to Pure Phenomenology*, trans. William Ralph Boyce Gibson (London: George Allen and Unwin, 1931, 1976), p. 110; See also Madu, *African Symbols, Proverbs and Myths: The Hermeneutics of Destiny, op. cit.*, p. 15.

[166] Edmund Husserl, *Logische Untersuchungen, Husserliana XIX/I*, paragraphs 2, 10; See also Herbert Spiegelberg, *The Phenomenological Movement: A Historical Introduction* (The Hague: Martinus Nijhoff, 3rd ed., 1982), p. 109.

[167] Grondin, *Sources of Hermeneutics, op. cit.*, pp. 37-38.

[168] Otto Pöggeler, "Die Krise des phänomenologischen Philosophiebegriffs (1929)," *Phänomenologie im Widerstreit*, ed. Christoph Jamme and Otto Pöggeler (Frankfurt: Suhrkamp, 1989), pp. 225-276. Heidegger describes his relationship with Husserl his teacher (paragraph 7.)

'things themselves' inspires Heidegger's return to language. We return to things themselves through discourse and words.

The notion of the horizon is also an element of Husserl's theory that will be put to use by later phenomenology and hermeneutics. The horizon of the life-world is the perspective of revelation of phenomenon. The horizon is also the world of life (*Lebenswelt*) in which we are thrown. The horizon of the question and answer is important in interpretation's guideline and getting through to the things themselves through discourse. Language or word is not the thing itself. There is a gap between the thing one sees and the language one uses to describe it. To get to the meaning of a thing, we have to get to the thing itself. There could be many words for one thing or the meaning of one thing. There has to be a sense of correspondence between the two sides: a) the meaning of a thing, and b) the thing in-itself. In phenomenology truth is by adequation. This is also part of the return that Husserl craves for.

Husserl's return to the things themselves is a rejection of the falsely established scientific theorization; it is a rejection of the inadequacies of scientific abstraction when applied to the type of phenomenon he is considering. His critique of abstractions while going after the things themselves is present in his *Logical Investigations* and the *Krisis*. He tries to get away from the theoretical aspect of science. His focus is on what brings us to the things themselves. In Husserl's own words, this return to the things themselves is the way of "an authentique consciousness, of an authentique science, of an authentique method. The logical ideas are from the start ideas of authenticity (*Echtheit.*)"[169] This is the focus of reason that involves the use of the notion of phenomenological reduction, which is a call for a "re-direction." It means we redirect or detach what is thought to be around us to rather that which is around the world as it presents itself. It is a reduction that is akin to research as exploring phenomena. In hermeneutics, we understand by taking a distance in order to access the true meaning of something. Husserl influenced later hermeneutists through the concept of intentionality. Intentionality, for Husserl, is the fundamental property of consciousness. It is the characteristic feature of our conscious or mental state and experiences. Some simply refer to it in words like "conscious" or "aware."[170] Intentionality comes from the Latin

---

[169] Husserl, *Formale und transzendentale Logik, Husserliana XVII*, 32.
[170] See Ronald McIntyre and David Woodruff Smith, "Theory of Intentionality," *Husserl's Phenomenology: A Textbook*, eds. J. N. Mohanty and William R. McKenna (Washington,

word '*intendere*' meaning 'to point to' or 'to aim at'. In other words, it means "directed toward something." It is the nature of thought to be 'directed toward something' or 'about' an object. It connects the psychical and the natural object through experience. However, not everything is representational or 'directed toward' some object.

Following the influence of medieval scholastics and Brentano, Husserl considers intentionality to mean the characteristics of the mental phenomenon which differentiates it from physical phenomenon. We have the object that exists in understanding and the object that exists in reality. Each mental phenomenon has an intentional content –i.e., object. For instance, every desire has something to which it is all about (an external object), an object of thought. Every belief has something outside to which it is about. To make a judgment of something is to affirm or deny something outside.

Like the aspects of psychical and natural phenomena, Husserl's intentionality has two aspects a) intentional act (*noesis*), and b) the act-matter (*noemata*) graspable objects. There is a correlation that exists between the act-matter (*noema*) and the intentional acts (*noesis*.) When one intends something, he/she intentionally states what the word means for him/her, but this does not prevent the possibility of miscommunication. When one utters something, he/she communicates the ideal meaning. There is the intimate aspect to the person one is at dialogue with because of certain mental states or experiences.

Husserl also identifies intentionality with the nature of act. For me to understand anything, it requires that I intend something. It is how one thinks of an object as an 'object' with an identity and how it appears to the person or how one comprehends it. When one becomes conscious of something, it is because one is conscious of the object as an 'identity' of its own and not the creation of the mind. It is not what the mind presents it as 'being.' Here the content or *noemata* are correlated with this object of thought.

The correlative relationship that exist between one that is conscious of a thing and the thing affects one in return. One is conscious of everything that

D.C.: Center for Advanced Research in Phenomenology and University Press of America, 1989), pp. 147-79; See Ronald McIntyre and David Woodruff Smith, *Husserl and Intentionality: A Study of Mind, Meaning, and Language* (Dordrecht and Boston: D. Reidel, 1982.)

one brings before the mind. For Husserl, every aspect of our mental life is involved. For instance, perceptions, thoughts, beliefs, hopes etc., have the feature of being 'about' something. For instance, I have a perception of my car. This connects to our discussion above about Plato's inner word and outer word. The mental state or experience is in a way a representation of something rather than itself like the outer word points to an object or meaning outside itself. This character of the mind or consciousness 'to represent' something is what is meant by intentionality. This is how Husserl addresses the extreme aspect of psychologism in Dilthey's hermeneutics. Psychologism is referred to as an assumption that language is mainly to be understood as an outward expression of what is internal. The outer expression communicates the inner psychic life. We arrive at meaning through a reverse process of working back from the outer expression to the inner experience. Psychologism involves reconstructing and reliving the inner psychic experiences.

For Husserl language is representational as in 'representing things.' The things represented possess meaning or have interpretations given them by individuals or creatures that possess mental power. Intentionality or representationality of one's experience involves the person who experiences and the external object of experience. Meanwhile, not all intentional objects are actually true existing external object. Unicorns are not actual and true existing things. His theory of intentionality has been used for clarifying and founding other aspects of philosophy, e.g., theory of consciousness, logic, philosophy of language, philosophy of action and value.

His effort in bracketing issues of existence in his methodology had some effects on understanding the nature of *noesis*, *noema* and intentional object. He has been accused to have left some of these issues unexplained. Heidegger himself referred to intentionality as care (*Sorge*) in his philosophy of existence. Intentionality as care is same as existentiality or facticity with ontological significance.

d. Martin Heidegger

There was a very limited publication of the hermeneutical contributions of the nineteenth century. It was only later after the death of hermeneutists like Boeckh, Schleiermacher, Droysen, and Dilthey that their students took up the responsibility of disseminating their thoughts in reviews, short publications, and fragments.

The situation did change with Martin Heidegger (1889-1976.) One of Heidegger's important contributions to hermeneutics is through his lecture entitled: "Hermeneutics of Facticity." His concern is more with interpretation as the self-interpretation of *Dasein* more than on the theory of interpretation. For him, interpretation is the subject matter of hermeneutics which is about the self-transparency of Dasein as an understanding being who is always involved in this hermeneutical process. And because Dasein is always involved in the act of interpretation (as an act of philosophical clarification), he has to reveal himself in a continued manner.[171]

Heidegger's book- *Being and Time* contains an important development of his hermeneutics. He focuses on the hermeneutics which he sees at the background of all human judgment and care. Paragraphs 31-33 of *Being and Time* reflect some of Heidegger's hermeneutical views. Heidegger entitled the final paragraphs of that section "Assertion as a Derivative Mode of Interpretation." The interpretive tendency is a basic character of the human Dasein. This tendency has been considered as Heidegger's hermeneutics of facticity or existence. It involves the interpretation of Dasein's care structure as perceived in utterances or expressions which come to us through understanding.

Heidegger's other contribution to hermeneutics is his notion of the *ontological* significance of understanding. He deals with the understanding of being in the context of Dasein's situatedness or historicity. Heidegger's view involves Dasein, its projections into the future and its relation to the interpreter. There is an interaction between a text and its interpreter. Interpretation is part of the limited and situated nature of all forms of human knowledge or act of understanding. Hermeneutics is not a method but a universal or an ontological activity. Heidegger's project occupies Gadamer, whose work could be regarded as an attempt to work out the implications of

---

[171] See Carl Friedrich Gethmann, *Verstehen und Auslegung: Das Methodenproblem in der Philosophie Martin Heideggers* (Bonn, 1974), p. 117; See Rainer Thurnher, "Hermeneutik und Verstehen in Heideggers 'Sein und Zeit'," *Salzburger Jahrbuch für Philosophie* 28-29 (1984-1985), p. 107.

Heidegger's ontological significance of understanding. In *Philosophical Hermeneutics*, the editor argues that:

> All deliberate interpretation takes place on the basis of *Dasein*'s historicity, that is, on the basis of a prereflective understanding of being from within a concrete situation that has intrinsic relation to the interpreter's past and future. It is the meaning of Heidegger's description of *Dasein* as "thrown projection"....As projective, understanding is intrinsically related to the future into which Dasein continually projects itself. Similarly, understanding is thrown, that, situated by the past as a heritage of founded meanings that Dasein takes over from its community. Thus Heidegger shows that every interpretation—even scientific interpretation—is governed by the concrete situation of the interpreter. There is no presuppositionless, "prejudiceless" interpretation, for while the interpreter may free himself from this or that situation, he cannot free himself from his own facticity, from the *ontological* condition of always already having a finite temporal situation as the horizon within which the beings he understands have their initial meaning for him.[172]

As opposed to Husserl (his teacher), Heidegger has problems with objective 'presuppositionless' interpretation. For him, understanding has its own fundamental structure referred to as the fore-structures of understanding. Interpretation or understanding is "never a 'presuppositionless' grasping of something given in advance."[173] Dasein's thrownness is not a choice. Thrownness is the individual's existence in the world. It is about the interactions of the subject (in his finitude) with his surrounding or environment. We are always involved with our environment and the world. This is also what Heidegger describes as Dasein *being* eventful[174] and involved. This involvement and thrownness is the meaning of our "facticity."[175]

---

[172] Gadamer, *Philosophical Hermeneutics, op. cit.,* pp. xlvii-xlviii.
[173] Heidegger, *Being and Time,* trans. Joan Stambaugh (Albany, New York: State University of New York, 1996), pp. 141-142.
[174] Gadamer, *Philosophical Hermeneutics, op. cit.,* p. liv.
[175] Grondin, *Introduction to Philosophical Hermeneutics, op. cit.,* p. 95.

The fore-structure of understanding is the thematic framework of every interpretation. It is always there at each particular existential situation. Every interpretation is to be aware of one's own fore-structure. The interpretation of a text requires the understanding the fore-structure and the text. This helps avoid the "monologue" of interpreting one's own fore-understanding. To interpret a text we need to make our position transparent so as to have a true experience of the other or the other as text. Thus our prejudices do not hinder the disclosure of the other or the text against the background of our fore-structure of understanding. The fore-structure of understanding are: *Vorhaben* (already present or what we have); *Vorsicht* (perceptible or what is already grasped); and *Vorgriff* (what we already conceive as concept or *Vormeinung.*) With these Heidegger provides an answer to the epistemological inquiry on the nature of what makes knowledge possible. Understanding and interpretation are essential modes of Dasein. Dasein remains at the centre of hermeneutics. Heidegger argues:

> [T]he logos of a phenomenology of Dasein has the character of *hermeneuein* (to interpret) through which are made known to Dasein the structure of his own Being and the authentic meaning of being in his (preconscious) understanding of being. Phenomenology of Dasein is hermeneutics in the original sense of the word, which designated the business of interpretation.[176]

Heidegger's idea of interpretation or hermeneutics associates with the ontology of the nature or conditions of understanding. He sees understanding as fundamental in human existence. It is a fundamental mode of the being of Dasein because it is always there as a fore-structure of the being of Dasein. As Heidegger argues, "[U]nderstanding is the existential being of the ownmost potentiality of being of Dasein in such a way that this being discloses in itself what its very being is about."[177] Understanding is not same as 'explanation'[178] Understanding is part of being the being that is there. The Dasein is the being or the subject in the World. This being, as an individual subject, in the World is involved in a continued process of awareness of self and self-understanding.[179] Understanding of self is about disclosing to oneself how one exists and one's possibilities. When one understands, it means being aware of

---

[176] Heidegger, *Being and Time*, trans. Joan Stambaugh, *op. cit.*, p. 33.
[177] *Ibid.*, p. 135.
[178] *Ibid.*, p. 134.
[179] *Ibid.*

what one is up to or capable of doing. It is an understanding that involves practice. It is part of our practical life, even with no clear knowledge. This is why it is also called "practical" understanding. It is to master something; it is an "art". It means to know one's way around and exist in a world or find one's way in the world (*Sichauskennen.*) Because understanding is common to all and part of our existence it is called universal. Grondin argues:

> It is extraordinarily significant that Heidegger applies precisely the concept of "hermeneutics" to pre-predicative understanding. This is consonant with the fundamental effort of hermeneutics to reach what is be-fore (or better, in and behind) statements-in brief, the mind and soul that expresses itself in the word. There can be no doubt that Heidegger appropriates the notion of hermeneutic understanding in order to radicalize it by demonstrating its universal embeddedness in the care structure of *Dasein.*[180]

Care is the fundamental basis of being in the world which makes understanding what it is as part of *Dasein's* concern for itself. Dasein's care means being concerned about its mode of being in the world and looking after itself. It means projecting its own possibilities/undertakings and that of other beings. Dasein understands things around it through caring about them. Understanding is thus a potentiality of discloseness that makes it possible for seeing things.[181] It is about the whole fundamental constitution of being-in-the-world with others. The understanding of existence is the understanding of the world. We understand what is out there and what is out there is part of the world that is.[182] Understanding or hermeneutics involves interpretation. Heidegger distinguishes between understanding and interpretation. He explains:

> We shall call the development of understanding *interpretation*. In interpretation understanding appropriates what it has understood in an understanding way. In interpretation understanding does not become something different, but rather itself. Interpretation is existentially based in understanding, and not the other way around. Interpretation is not the acknowledgment of what has

---

[180] Grondin, *Introduction to Philosophical Hermeneutics, op. cit.*, p. 94.
[181] Heidegger, *Being and Time*, trans. Joan Stambaugh, *op. cit.*, p. 135.
[182] *Ibid.*, p. 137.

been understood, but rather the development of possibilities projected in understanding.[183]

Understanding is the first and primary thing that is made explicit through interpretation. Interpretation could be referred to as the cultivation [*Ausbildung*] or extension of understanding.[184] Another word for understanding is "self-elucidation," "unfolding," that flows from the prime or first understanding. Understanding is a continual process. This is also part of the transparency in understanding of *Dasein*.[185] Understanding is about the existential nature of *Dasein* and its potency.[186] The potency or potentiality for *Dasein* is that of being understood that involves a form of circularity. How does Heidegger explain this form of circularity?

Heidegger is of the view that understanding involves a circle. The importance of this circle lies in getting into it in the right manner. This circle is also part of the essential fore-structure of *Dasein*.[187] Heidegger adds that the circle is not to be understood as a vicious circle. Rather in the

> circle is hidden a positive possibility of the most primordial kind of knowing. To be sure, we genuinely take hold of this possibility only when, in our interpretation, we have understood that our first, last, and constant task is never to allow our fore-having, fore-sight and fore-conception to be presented to us by fancies and popular conceptions, but rather to make the scientific theme secure by working out these fore-structures in terms of the things themselves.[188]

The hermeneutical circle is also part of the care-structure and the fore-structure of *Dasein*. The grounding or foregrounding of the development fore-structure is needed to involve truly in the process of interpretation. The disclosure of this fore-structure of understanding is what Heidegger sees as

---

[183] *Ibid.*, p. 139.

[184] Grondin, *Introduction to Philosophical Hermeneutics, op. cit.,* p. 96.

[185] For a discussion on Heidegger's "*Durchsichtigmachen*" (making transparent), see Gadamer, "Heidegger's 'theologische' Jugendschrift," Dilthey, *Jahrbuch 6* (1989), p. 232.

[186] Heidegger, *Being and Time*, trans. John Macquarrie and Edward Robinson, *op. cit.*, p. 184; pp. 188-189.

[187] Heidegger, *Being and Time*, trans. Joan Stambaugh, *op. cit.*, p. 143; See Heidegger, *Being and Time*, trans. John Macquarrie and Edward Robinson (New York, 1962), p. 153.

[188] Heidegger, *Being and Time*, trans. John Macquarrie and Edward Robinson (Southampton: Camelot Press, 1980), p. 195.

interpretation. It opens the dialogue that exists between the subject matter and the unfamiliar other.[189] This dialogue is the process of Dasein's expression of oneself through language.

Heidegger recognizes the place of language in Dasein's expression of oneself. Language is part of the essential existence of human beings. It is what Dasein listens to and through it reveals its initiative. We express our being and initiatives in language and by way of language. In *Philosophical Hermeneutics*, the editor explains, "the language of a time is not so much chosen by the persons who use it as it is their historical fate the way being has revealed itself to and concealed itself from them as their starting point... As Heidegger has said, we are therefore always "on the way to language." [190] Dasein's self-interpretation must be understood within language. Every spoken word is heard as part of Dasein's care and self-disclosure.[191] Language is at the base of Dasein's care. Discourse (*Rede*) is the self-interpretation of Dasein by using language. There is for Heidegger the hermeneutic character of language which has to be preserved, even in the struggle to express oneself with the right words. For him language is not first and foremost a means of communication or for calculating or expressing things.[192] It is truly discloses being itself.

In Heidegger's *On the Way to Language* (1959), he recalls Schleiermacher's definition of hermeneutics as, "the art of understanding rightly another man's language, particularly his written language."[193] This does not totally explain language in the context of hermeneutics. Heidegger believes hermeneutic is enigmatic and that language is hermeneutics and the study of hermeneutic is the study of language. Despite the lack of precise definition of hermeneutics, Heidegger defines it as "the exposition which brings tidings because it can listen to a message."[194] The 'tidings' that is brought is through language or communicated through language. Hermeneutical question is a language question. As Madu puts it, "he emphasizes the role of language in the

---

[189] Grondin, *Introduction to Philosophical Hermeneutics, op. cit.,* p. 97.
[190] Gadamer, *Philosophical Hermeneutics, op. cit.,* pp. lv-lvi.
[191] Grondin, *Introduction to Philosophical Hermeneutics, op. cit.,* p. 100.
[192] *Ibid.,* p. 103.
[193] Heidegger, *On the Way to Language,* trans. Peter D. Hertz (New York, 1971), p. 11.
[194] *Ibid.,* p. 29.

understanding of Being. Being comes to light in language."[195] In Heidegger's own word, language is essentially part of our being and being comes to be known in and through language.[196]

In summary, philosophers have moved from using hermeneutic techniques to considering hermeneutics as a theory of understanding of words or discourses. Hermeneutics implies explaining, interpreting, and translating. The ancient philosophers were focusing on the relationship between understanding the spoken word and the written word. Their concern was the understanding of the true meaning in a message, and a text; the difference between the outer word (spoken) and inner word. Ancient hermeneutics associates with the interpretation or communication of the true meaning of a divine message by the messenger. Hermeneutics is about intelligibility and clarity of meaning. The use of theater and tragic drama were ways of communicating meaning with other cultures of the time. There were Greek heroes and Roman heroes depicted in drama and poetry.

The early Christian and medieval period applies hermeneutics to the interpretation of the Holy Scriptures or sacred texts. Philo and Augustine provide a good introduction into understanding the task of hermeneutics at this time through the use of allegories. Their influences come from the contributions of Plato, Aristotle and others. The main aspect of hermeneutics in the medieval time was the focus on theological studies and how the method of hermeneutics is relevant to the Christian message. The issue bears on the importance of word or language in understanding reality, especially the reality of the salvation message, the Incarnation, Good Friday Passion etc. The messages of salvation were also put in plays and dramas. There were liturgical and morality plays to teach the new converts who came from different cultural background (Greeks, Romans and Jews) about Christianity. Theater serves intercultural needs. The notion of theater was devoid of what they considered as the satanic theatricals of the ancient Greek period. It now focuses on spectacle (not plot), passive audience and specific meaning.

---

[195] Madu, *African Symbols, Proverbs and Myths: The Hermeneutics of Destiny, op. cit.*, p. 17.
[196] Heidegger, *An Introduction to Metaphysics*, trans. Ralph Manheim (New Haven: Yale University Press, 1959), p. 82.

The modern period notes a significant development in the use of the term hermeneutics. Some philosophers like Schleiermacher, Dilthey consider hermeneutics began as a result of the eighteenth-century movement on understanding philosophical and theological texts. It was a period when most philosophers were involved in the art of understanding of texts. For the scope of this research the important philosophers of this period include: Schleiermacher, Dilthey, Husserl, Heidegger and Gadamer. The modern period experiences the dominance of the natural sciences which emphasize rational and methodical explanation. However, some other philosophers designate as hermeneutics those disciplines in the social and human sciences[197] that make use of interpretation. Human science accepts that there are other ways to truth different from the methodological approach of natural sciences. Hermeneutics[198] is at the basis of human science and not a natural science. It is a human science found on disclosing the true meanings or making known hidden meanings.[199] It is at the basis of literary, philological and philosophical interpretations. The main focus of the human sciences is the dynamic nature of the human world and experiences. We can understand the human world without the monopoly of the method of the natural sciences. The human sciences use hermeneutics to access other truths that cannot be totally accessed by the natural sciences.

This historical survey of the development of hermeneutics serves as a background to understanding Gadamer's philosophical hermeneutics and the claim of the universality of hermeneutics. One of the main issues of interculturality which is language was recognized as being at the center of hermeneutics and understanding. As a way of communicating meaning and understanding the use of theater and tragedy in the ancient and medieval periods were introduced, especially for aesthetic and didactic purposes. Theater serves as means to teach and communicate meaning to people. Modern hermeneutics focuses on the avoidance of misunderstanding and to ensure clear understanding of oral communication and written texts. Although the advent of the modern period did see the end of Christian form of theater and

---

[197] Mueller-Vollmer, ed., *The Hermeneutics Reader, op. cit.*, p. x.
[198] Prof. Donald Ipperciel explains that hermeneutics is not a science (human or natural). It is a theory that takes on different forms depending on the approach. However, it is at the basis of human science. I agree with this insightful view on hermeneutics.
[199] Palmer, *Hermeneutics, op. cit.*, p. 43; See Madu, *African Symbols, Proverbs and Myths: The Hermeneutics of Destiny, op. cit.*, pp. 4ff.

understanding tragedy, it also introduces the use of farce to criticize and make fun of religious institutions or superior authorities.

Modern theater is shaped by the socio-political situation and the scientific cum technological developments of this age. The challenges of our societies become subjects of modern theater representation and quest for understanding. Human conditions and experiences are now dramatized to effect social change or create awareness. The use of symbolisms and metaphors in languages are means to understanding philosophical and hermeneutical truths. Modern satires and comics are part of the theater of this period used as instruments for social change, representation of human actions and to truly understand human experiences. It is the realism of modern theater to represent reality in its truthfulness through art.

1.4 Conclusion

In the above, I have traced the historical development of hermeneutics and the aspect of intercultural encounter from the ancient to modern period. The encounter between cultures and peoples gave rise to means and ways of communicating the inner meanings of our thoughts for clear understanding. Although the various periods of hermeneutics development had different points of emphasis, word and language are central in understanding the main task of hermeneutics. Grondin concludes, "[T]he task of hermeneutics, from Plato to our times, is to preserve this true meaning of the word, the written or spoken word, by relating it back to its intent, original meaning, scope, and context."[200] Modern theater is an essential part of the communication of meaning and understanding. There is a revival of interest in the study of Aristotle's theory of tragedy and some aspects of the medieval theater approach to tragedy. This will be seen in Gadamer's treatment of Aristotle's tragedy from an aesthetic perspective and the recognition of the different types of tragedy. Tragedy used in aesthetic serves the purpose of understanding of art or drama and shows the role of language in understanding.

I shall now turn to Gadamer who has been credited with developing a philosophical hermeneutics following the influence of Plato, Aristotle, Philo, Augustine, Schleiermacher, Heidegger, and others. I shall focus a little more on Gadamer's criticism of Schleiermacher's contributions as he develops his

---

[200] Grondin, *Sources of Hermeneutics, op. cit.*, p. 33.

own philosophical hermeneutical theory. Schleiermacher's view seems most appropriate because of its unique influence on others and Gadamer. This discourse will lead us to Gadamer's claim of the universality of hermeneutics that applies to all cultures and texts. Gadamer does provide us with the hermeneutical framework to address intercultural problems of understanding in an African text – as an essential part of this books' claim on the universality of hermeneutics.

CHAPTER 2

Gadamer's Philosophical Hermeneutics Theory

2. 1 Gadamer's Development of the Hermeneutical Theory and an Overview of the Essential Thesis

Gadamer's hermeneutics is about the encounter of meaning and understanding. Hermeneutics is *what* happens when we engage in interaction or conversation with other people and texts.[201] It is not about the method of understanding. His main concern is to put across in the clearest form the conditions of understanding and how it takes place in human experience of knowledge and truth. Understanding involves apprehending the content of knowledge and bearing in mind the historical situations, as Gadamer affirms.[202]

Philosophical hermeneutics deals with the phenomenon of understanding and not with the problem of methodology in relation to the human sciences. It does not focus on a scientific method for its justification. It seeks the experience of truth that transcends the arena of scientific method and its control through a set of rules. Gadamer's philosophical hermeneutics provides an account of this other proper ground for understanding; he insists on the limited role of method, but he does not reject the importance of methodological concerns. His hermeneutic approach is peculiar to human sciences like philosophy, art, and history because they are not restricted to the specific method of the natural sciences. Human science addressed the question of the modes of experience which are completely outside the experimental approach and determined results of the natural sciences. Certainly there are different modes of experience of truth, but truth does not always need the verifiability method of the natural sciences. The understanding of experiences of art, history and philosophy challenge the method of scientific consciousness to acknowledge its own limits. Joel Weinsheimer, a Gadamer expert and translator argues:

---

[201] Gadamer, *Philosophical Hermeneutics*, *op. cit.*, p. xii.
[202] Gadamer, *Truth and Method*, trans. Joel Weinsheimer and Donald G. Marshall, *op. cit.*, p. 294.

In regard to the historical tradition of philosophy, understanding occurs to us as a superior experience enabling us easily to see through the illusion of historical method characteristic of research in the history of philosophy. It is part of the elementary experience of philosophy that when we try to understand the classics of philosophical thought, they of themselves make a claim to truth that the consciousness of later times can neither reject nor transcend.[203]

In *Truth and Method*, the starting point for Gadamer is the experience of art and of historical tradition which is part of philosophical thinking. The human sciences provide us with another option in the interpretation of the totality of experience and attempt to present the experience of reality in its full context. Truth is a totality that we come to understand in different ways or modes of experience. The experience of truth does not solely need to be experimented in order to be justified as being rational. In fact, any other mode of experience of truth is equally a mode of philosophizing or thinking. That the claim to truth is not suitable to the natural sciences does not mean that they are inadequate. It only confirms that there are other ways of experiencing the truth of our historical world.

Gadamer's hermeneutic approach incorporates the relevant contributions of philosophers before him, while adapting views that are important to philosophical knowledge. Gadamer avoids the limitations of other hermeneutists, especially Schleiermacher, Droysen and Dilthey, in order to advance his notion of philosophical hermeneutics. I choose to briefly focus on Schleiermacher because of his unique influence on these other hermeneutists and on Gadamer. As we have seen, Schleiermacher views hermeneutics essentially as an art of avoiding misunderstanding and seeking clarity. The hermeneutic arguments that have stood the test of time in philosophy have been shared by some of the philosophers discussed in chapter one despite the fact of differing historical situations. Thus, as Alasdair MacIntyre observes about Gadamer:

we learn to identify standards, independent of any particular historical perspective, that are indispensable to philosophical inquiry. But in so learning it seems undeniable that we have made

---

[203] *Ibid.*, p. xxi.

philosophical progress, the same kind of progress that is both recorded and extended in Gadamer's narrative in *Wahrheit und Methode* of the development of hermeneutics from Schleiermacher through Droysen, Dilthey and Heidegger, up to his own work, work that embodies the insights of earlier approaches but avoids their errors and overcomes some of their limitations.[204]

Gadamer's view of the hermeneutical rule[205] holds that the process of understanding and acquiring meaning normally moves "from the whole to the part and back to the whole."[206] This hermeneutical rule involves the whole which determines the detail and the detail that determines the whole. Understanding occurs when the details agree with the whole and vice versa. Schleiermacher's influence on Gadamer is obvious in this respect. This hermeneutical rule requires understanding our structure of thought as part of the total context of our life. The total context and the details are part of the general reality that gives meaning and understanding.

Gadamer's process of developing his hermeneutics starts with criticizing Schleiermacher's hermeneutical approach. He regards Schleiermacher's approach to transpose oneself into the writer's mind[207] as subjective or mainly a psychological interpretation of understanding. Schleiermacher's psychological interpretation does emphasize the author's role in the understanding of his composition.[208] He recommends that the interpreter personally reconstructs the "creative consciousness from which the text emerges."[209] According to Gadamer,[210] Schleiermacher through his objectivity

---

[204] Alasdair MacIntyre, "On Not Having the Last Word: Thought on Our Debt to Gadamer," *Gadamer's Century: Essays in Honor of Hans-Georg Gadamer,* Jeff Malpas, Ulrich Arnswald and Jens Kertscher , eds (Cambridge, Massachusetts: The MIT Press, 2002), pp. 166-167.

[205] Gadamer, *Truth and Method,* trans. Joel Weinsheimer and Donald G. Marshall, *op. cit.,* p. 291; Gadamer, *Truth and Method* (New York: The Seabury Press, 1975), pp. 258-259.

[206] *Ibid.* See Gadamer, *Truth and Method* (New York: The Seabury Press, 1975), pp. 258-259.

[207] Gadamer, *Truth and Method,* trans. Joel Weinsheimer and Donald G. Marshall, *op. cit.,* p. 292.

[208] Friedrich Schleiermacher, *Hermeneutik und Kritik* (Frankfurt am Maim: Suhrkamp, 1977), p. 184.

[209] Jon Whitman, "A Retrospective Forward: Interpretation, Allegory, and Historical Change," *Interpretation and Allegory: Antiquity to the Modern Period*, ed, with introductory essay by Jon Whitman (Leiden: Koninklijke Brill NV, 2000), p. 13.

underestimates the role of historical consciousness in hermeneutical theory. Gadamer argues that through such approach the reflexive aspect of understanding has been overlooked by the "'science of hermeneutics' during the last century."[211]

Understanding brings together the movement of tradition and that of the hermeneutist. The natural sciences are easily involved with the distinction between the subjective and objective aspects of understanding, but Gadamer's view of hermeneutics is set within the human sciences. His hermeneutical theory requires that the interpreter be objectively and subjectively involved. Understanding does not have to be subjective or objective; it is rather the "sharing in a common meaning."[212] How one arrives at understanding. That is the main question of Gadamer's hermeneutics. He does not subscribe to fixed "methodological" approach to understanding. His hermeneutical approach rather deals with the "ontological structure of understanding."[213]

The objective interpretation is not adequately considered by Schleiermacher. In some analysis, Schleiermacher's universalizing of historical consciousness denies any validity in tradition as a basis for hermeneutical activity, since he tries to relate objectivity in interpretation to the natural sciences, but he fails to identify or he overlooks the "concretion of historical consciousness in hermeneutical theory."[214] For Gadamer, tradition provides us with a basis and the resources for hermeneutical activity. His hermeneutics does not depend on a one-sided interpretation approach. It is not subjective or objective. There is always something brought to the text in "anticipation of meaning that proceeds from common tradition; this is not subjectivity."[215]

Gadamer's hermeneutics describes understanding as content-based, not author-oriented. It is a content-oriented project because the content of the text

---

[210] Daniel L. Segrave, "Gadamer's Hermeneutical Circle, Canonical-Composition Hermeneutics and Paul's 'Mystery of Christ'," Paper presented at the Annual Symposium Urshan Graduate School of Theology, Florissant Mo. November 6-7, 2008.

[211] Gadamer, *Philosophical Hermeneutics*, *op. cit.*, p. xii.

[212] Gadamer, *Truth and Method,* trans. Joel Weinsheimer and Donald G. Marshall, *op. cit.*, p. 292.

[213] *Ibid.*, p. 293.

[214] *Ibid.*

[215] Segrave, *op. cit.*

is at the center of attention and it is the horizon of the task of hermeneutics. In this way he avoids the emphasis on the subjective, he goes beyond the author's mind, and focuses on the subject matter of the text. One of the impossible tasks, as Gadamer affirms, is to "transpose ourselves into the author's mind."[216] He requires that we transpose ourselves into the perspective within which the author formulated his views. In another translation it states, "we try to understand a text, we do not try to recapture the author's attitude of mind."[217] We rather focus on recapturing the perspective within which the author formulated his views.[218] In Gadamer's view, hermeneutics should not be concerned with establishing a psychological dimension to understanding. The perspective within which the author formed his views is what concerns us most in understanding, which is available to us by reading the text itself without necessarily focusing on the author.[219] It is similarly impossible to be in the situation of a contemporary [original] reader during the process of hermeneutics. This transposition of our perspective within the perspective of the author or writer is because hermeneutics is content-based and the meanings are developed also based on context. The process of the development of a text includes a full grasp of meaning through the fusion of the parts with the greater whole and the context of writer. There is more than one factor involved in understanding a text even when we have limited available information. Gadamer adds that to understand one does not need to forget about himself and his hermeneutical situation. The text and his situation must be together considered to understand the text.

Gadamer's contributions above mean that Schleiermacher's notion of "divinatory method"-the way by which one gains immediate access to the mind of the writer or author, discussed in chapter one, is not the main issue of

---

[216]Gadamer, *Truth and Method,* trans. Joel Weinsheimer and Donald G. Marshall, *op. cit.*, p. 292; Gadamer, *Truth and Method* (New York: The Seabury Press, 1975), p. 259.

[217] See Segrave's copy of Gadamer, *Truth and Method* (New York: The Seabury Press, 1975), p. 259. In Segrave's essay, there is a new form of analysis called Canonical-compositional hermeneutics. It is not concerned with establishing a psychological dimension of the hermeneutical circle. The issue is the text itself, not the author of the text. We can gain the perspective within which the author formed his views, but we can do this only by reading the text itself.

[218] Segrave, *op. cit.* See Gadamer, *Truth and Method* (New York: The Seabury Press, 1975), p. 259; Gadamer, *Truth and Method*, trans. Joel Weinsheimer and Donald G. Marshall (London: Continuum, 2nd rev. ed., 2004), p. 292. One of the differences in the translation is 'transpose' (2004 edition) and 'recapture' (1975 edition.)

[219] Gadamer, *Truth and Method*, trans. Joel Weinsheimer and Donald G. Marshall, *op. cit.*, p. 292; Gadamer, *Truth and Method* (New York: The Seabury Press, 1975), p. 259.

hermeneutics. Accepting this divinatory method means to support Schleiermacher's position that an interpreter could understand the author better than he understand himself. Gadamer avers that the task of interpretation is not merely penetrating the spiritual and mental activities of the author, but "it is simply a question of grasping the meaning, significance, and aim of what is transmitted to us."[220] It is possible to understand an author better than he understands himself but this is only done through the texts.

The historical, cultural and linguistic milieus of the writer have to be considered and understood.[221] The focus on the text shows the objectivity of understanding and the importance of language to understanding. The focus on the text draws attention to the subject matter which communicates "a certain 'ideality of meaning'"[222] that is not determined by the subjectivity and psychological conditions of the author of the text.

In the above, I have presented a preliminary discussion that leads us to some of the main principles involved in Gadamer's hermeneutical theory. In this section below there is no particular order observed in treating these principles since each of these principles is significant and equally relates to other hermeneutic principles in an integrated act of understanding. The hermeneutical principles are not mutually exclusive of each other but rather are interrelated in a manner that leads systemically to better understanding a text or other people. The hermeneutical circle relates to the fusion of horizons in the same way as the notion of prejudice relates or integrates the understanding of the fusion of horizons or the effect of history to human understanding. In discussing the fusion of horizons one is influenced by the good prejudices of one's historical conditions. The effect of history relates to the hermeneutical situation in an intrinsic way. The principles as conditions of understanding are not "either-or" principles of understanding. Gadamer's hermeneutic principles prepare us in interpretation or application to Chinua Achebe's text in chapter three. Later, the discussion on *"Bildung"* –'culture' or 'formation' gradually

---

[220] Gadamer "The Problem of Historical Consciousness," *Interpretive Social Science: A Reader,* Paul Rabinow and William M. Sullivan, eds (Berkeley: University of California Press. 1979), p. 147.
[221] Anthony C. Thiselton, *New Horizons in Hermeneutics: The Theory and Practice of Transforming Biblical Reading* (Grand Rapids, Michigan: Zondervan Publishing House, 1992), p. 221.
[222] Gadamer, *Philosophical Hermeneutics, op. cit.,* p. xx.

leads us to the discourse on Achebe's African cultural narrative and African philosophical thought. Let us discuss the principle of hermeneutical circle.

2.1.1 Hermeneutical Circle

Gadamer's hermeneutical theory requires that the movement of understanding constantly goes in full circle from the whole to the part and back to the whole.[223] This process has been part of ancient rhetoric and adopted by modern/contemporary hermeneutics as part of the art of understanding. Heidegger and Gadamer advanced this notion of hermeneutic circle as part of the knowing process. It is an essential aspect of the nature of human knowledge. According to Heidegger and Gadamer, this circularity does not lead to a vicious circle but an ontological condition for understanding. It is really a circular interaction in the general process of understanding, such that "[T]he anticipation of meaning in which the whole is envisaged becomes actual understanding when the parts that are determined by the whole themselves also determine this whole."[224] True understanding is achieved when all details harmonize with the whole and the whole harmonizes with the different parts of the text. This process of moving from whole to parts, going backward and forward only comes to an end when we arrive at understanding. It is important for the part and whole to be clearly understood in the circular movement of understanding.

Understanding always occurs in a temporal and historical context. Hence the hermeneutical circle considers understanding to involve tradition and the interpreter. Tradition is part of the interpretational process in various communities. Each tradition influences the prejudices that we bring to the text when interpreting. One draws on tradition as the interpreter tries to understand or make meaning out of the text, especially when both come from different times in history. Each interpreter's understanding of a text continues to improve during the interpretational process and he/she becomes more fully aware of meaning despite the lapse in time between a written text and the interpreter. This introduces us to the principle of temporal distance and the role

---

[223] Gadamer, *Truth and Method*, trans. Joel Weinsheimer and Donald G. Marshall, *op. cit.*, p. 291; Gadamer, *Truth and Method* (New York: The Seabury Press, 1975), p. 259.
[224] *Ibid.*

of time as a condition of understanding or as a factor involved in our acquisition of knowledge.

2.1.2 Temporal Distance

Gadamer identifies the notion of temporal distance to have a significant place in his hermeneutics. Our on-going experience of reality is affected by time or temporality. There is a lapse in time between the written texts and their interpreters. In hermeneutics we consider the place of temporal distance in the understanding of a text or an author as not necessarily a problem but part of the productive conditions of understanding. Each text has its own context and period in which it was written. Each author is influenced by a particular temporal circumstance different from the time of interpretation.

One may believe that the proper thing to do in order to gain understanding is to overcome the temporal distance between a text and an interpreter.[225] For Gadamer, however, it is counterproductive to view temporal distance as something to be overcome. Moreover, he argues that the idea that temporal distance is something that must be overcome (i.e., by "entering" into the world of the author) is "the naïve assumption of historicism."[226] Temporal distance does not cause any hindrance in the understanding a text. And as Gadamer opines, rather than thinking that "we must transpose ourselves into the spirit of the age, think[ing] with its ideas and its thoughts, not with our own, and thus advanc[ing] toward historical objectivity,"[227] the most important thing is to recognize and accept that temporal distance is a productive condition that enables understanding rather than hinders it.[228] There are many factors involved in the interpretation of a transmitted text. Every written text as the real object of the hermeneutical task is a part of a whole tradition that arouses the interest for a historical period. Understanding a transmitted text requires understanding how it relates or speaks to the interpreter. Temporal distance is "always co-determined also by the historical situation of the interpreter and hence by the totality of the objective course of history."[229]

---

[225] Gadamer, *Truth and Method,* trans. Joel Weinsheimer and Donald G. Marshall, *op. cit.*, p. 297.
[226] *Ibid*. Gadamer, *Truth and Method* (New York: The Seabury Press, 1975), p. 264.
[227] *Ibid*.
[228] *Ibid*.
[229] *Ibid.*, p. 296.

Hermeneutics relates (as a theory of real experience) to the literary art of a people, its tradition and culture. It is also about the truth of the world in which we exist as rational and hermeneutical beings. It expresses itself in the way we experience the world, experience one another, our historical traditions, and these constitute our hermeneutic universe that is open to us. This new understanding of the historical and philosophical world has encouraged this movement in hermeneutics. Gadamer observes that his primary concern is about responsible thinking that encourages the use of a new form of critical and constructive consciousness. The values of thinking and the ability to communicate through language are part of our normal human life. We use what is part of our existence to review our experiences in the context our historical tradition.

As earlier discussed under 'author's intention', Gadamer's form of hermeneutics requires that interpreters do not concentrate solely on the occasional context of the writer. For Gadamer, the aim of contemporary philosophical hermeneutics is to achieve clarity of understanding and each historical people have to accomplish this clarity in its own way. There is "no canonical interpretation of a text... rather, [it] stand[s] open to ever new comprehensions."[230] This openness to new understanding is an indication of the productive role of interpretation since people at different times understand the same text differently. Hermeneutics could provide us with meanings surpassing that of the initial meaning of a writer. Moreover, Gadamer explains that there is always this initial relationship between a transmitted text and the present reader or interpreter. Every generation of interpreters works in a different way with the handed text. Each generation could have different interests with which it seeks understanding from the text and this text is also influenced by the historical situation of the reader and the course of history. All these factors help guarantee a productive hermeneutical project in which our understandings vary despite having same transmitted text given to us.[231] In another passage, discussing that people differently understand the same text, Gadamer notes:

> [B]ut this statement does not mean that it involves no task of understanding, or that we do not find its historical heritage within it.....In all the openness and all the richness of its possibilities for

---

[230] Gadamer, *Philosophical Hermeneutics*, *op. cit.*, pp. xxv-xxvi.
[231] See Gadamer, *Truth and Method*, trans. Joel Weinsheimer and Donald G. Marshall, *op. cit.*, p. 296.

comprehension, it permits–indeed even requires-the application of a standard of appropriateness of comprehension raised at any particular time is correct.[232]

Any understanding which surpasses its author is a form of an extension of perspectives or understanding. Every linguistic interpretation adapts to the hermeneutical situation of its time. The historico-hermeneutical situations of the interpreter and those interpreting him/her ought to be considered in the process of understanding. As we recall, for philosophical hermeneutics, temporal distance is not a hermeneutical problem to be overcome. This applies also to the concept of prejudice. Prejudice and temporal distance are necessarily parts of our horizons. We do not overcome temporal distance and prejudices while analyzing a text for meaning and understanding. Let us look at prejudice as another important principle of hermeneutics.

2.1.3 Prejudice

Gadamer rehabilitated the notion of prejudice which was seen in a negative light, especially during the Enlightenment period. Prejudice comes from the Latin word 'praejudicium'-meaning-"adverse effect," "disadvantage," The French 'préjugé' and German 'Vorurteil' mean an "unfounded judgment" or "a non fact-based judgment." Gadamer describes it as "a judgment that is rendered before all the elements that determine a situation have been finally examined."[233] This is the negative aspect of looking at prejudice. However, prejudice is part of the conditions of understanding or what Heidegger refers to as the fore-structure of understanding.[234] Prejudice is ontologically present in every act of interpretation. We interpret with prior or past known information. It is always part of our thinking to interpret with our own preconceptions. It does not mean a defective factor in our experience of truth. In fact prejudice constitutes the "initial directedness of our whole ability to experience." [235] It constitutes our being and our openness to the world. It is part of the conditions in which we experience or encounter something new. It is not a sign of being enclosed within one's biases.

---

[232] Gadamer, *Philosophical Hermeneutics, op. cit.*, p. 96.
[233] Gadamer, *Truth and Method*, trans. Joel Weinsheimer and Donald Marshall, *op. cit.*, p. 273.
[234] *Ibid.*, p. 272.
[235] Gadamer, *Philosophical Hermeneutics, op. cit.*, p. 9.

Gadamer explains that interpretation requires using one's preconceptions or prejudices in a positive way. We do not have "prejudiceless" interpretation. We can only free ourselves from our circumstances and situations, but not free from who we are, what we have known earlier or our own facticity. Temporality or temporal situation is part of the ontological conditions of understanding.[236] It is impossible to overcome *all* our prejudices or preconceptions during interpretation. He argues:

> [T]o try to escape from one's own concepts in interpretation is not only impossible but manifestly absurd. To interpret means precisely to use one's own preconceptions into play so that the text's meaning can really be made to speak for us.[237]

Prejudice is not inherently problematic. However, some should be avoided while interpreting a text. Indeed, all our understandings do involve some prejudices. There are legitimate prejudices or good prejudices and blind prejudices. Even the Enlightenment's criticism of prejudice is itself based on the prejudice of the Enlightenment period. It assumes that reason is the only reliable source of knowledge. Enlightenment's criticism of the term 'prejudice' is problematic because of its own presupposition-that reason is the only true source of knowledge and understanding. This is what Gadamer describes as "the prejudice against prejudices" that denies tradition its place and power.[238] In so doing, he is not rejecting the role of reason and scientific method but is making sure that nothing is left out in understanding. Whatever is necessary for understanding, including prejudices for hermeneutics, should not be rejected. Tradition is a source of knowledge and judgment. Prejudice is part of the historical reality of an individual.

Prejudices mark out our hermeneutical situation as is given to us by the very movement of tradition and constitute our immediate participation in this effective history. Gadamer's prejudices function as the power of self-consciousness: "It is not so much our judgments as it is our prejudgments that constitute our being."[239] The difficulty with prejudices is that as inherited views they may be used in a negative way rather than in a positive way as is

---

[236] *Ibid.*, pp. xlvii-xlviii.

[237] Gadamer, *Truth and Method*, trans. Joel Weinsheimer and Donald Marshall, *op. cit.*, p. 398; Gadamer, *Truth and Method* (New York: The Seabury Press, 1975), p. 358.

[238] *Ibid.*, p. 274.

[239] Gadamer, *Philosophical Hermeneutics*, *op. cit.*, p. xvii; See Gadamer, *Wahrheit und Methode: Grundzüge einer philosophischen Hermeneutik* (Tübingen: Mohr, 1960), p. 261.

the case in the use of good prejudices.[240] We bring in our prejudices in interpretation because they are part of the fore-structure of human understanding. Whatever is part of the fore-structure of our understanding is also constitutive of our range of vision or horizon.

2.1.4 Significance of the Fusion of Horizons

Gadamer's view of hermeneutics has been related to Hegel's concept of universal history. Universal history is as central to understanding as the notion of the fusion of horizons. Each horizon is a particular expression of meaning or perspective of an individual that fuses with the horizon of another in leading to a higher horizon of understanding. Gadamer recalls:

> The well-known young theologian Wolfhart Pannenberg has presented a highly useful discussion of my book in his article 'Hermeneutics and Universal History,' which relates...more particularly to the question of whether my philosophical hermeneutics necessarily but unconsciously rehabilitates the Hegelian concept of universal history (such as in the concept of fusion of horizons, where the ultimate horizon is, says Pannenberg implied or presupposed in the direction of every individual event of fusion).[241]

Gadamer's idea of the fusion of horizons[242] means that each person's horizon is the range of vision of that person. We require the combination of other horizons for a better standpoint of observation. The awareness of a limited nature of our horizon pushes us to inquire beyond our range of vision. Each individual horizon determines the range of a person's hermeneutical involvement. One's horizon does not limit one's vision to what is nearby.[243] It is only someone without a horizon that does not see much beyond. He explains that the finiteness of horizon is part of its nature. This is not a negative

---

[240] MacIntyre, *op. cit.*, p. 169. MacIntyre argues, "We all of course, virtuous and vicious interpreters alike, as Gadamer has emphasized, bring to our reading of text the prejudices, the prejudgments, that we have inherited. But those prejudices can vary in the extent to which they leave us open to confront the texts that we read more or less fruitfully and our own individual relationships to our prejudices also varies." (*Ibid.*, p. 169.)

[241] Gadamer, *Philosophical Hermeneutics, op. cit.*, p. 36.

[242] *Ibid.*, p. 39.

[243] Gadamer, *Truth and Method*, trans. Joel Weinsheimer and Donald G. Marshall, *op. cit.*, p. 302.

understanding of limitation. To have limitation is also to have possibilities for expansion of one's limited perspective and to have a horizon is to be truly human, historical and open to further invitation to understand beyond one's immediate range of vision. For one not to have a horizon involves a negative implication because the person does not reach out or see far enough.

The distinctive nature of each horizon[244] means that a horizon is essentially part of the direction of our changing perspectives and it changes for one as one moves along. The horizons are similar to worldviews that expand and advance as long as we consider and accept new positions even when they are beyond our immediate reach.[245] Every worldview is a limited view/understanding of the totality of the world. Gadamer adds that we understand when the various horizons are merged together in our search for meaning. Since understanding is a continual activity, then it helps us find out that each horizon is an inadequate range of vision that needs to be enriched by integrating it with other views.[246]

The fusion leads to transformation and to communion. It could be described as the process of conversation between the various viewpoints or standpoints. According to Gadamer, it means, in such a dialogue/conversation, there is the expression of one's view point. This encounter between horizons leads to a successful transformation and communion. The notion of the fusion of horizons applies to language. Each language, according to Gadamer, is a horizon. As a horizon it expresses a worldview that we possess.

There is another perspective of the fusion of horizons.[247] They are the horizon of the text and the horizon of the reader. These horizons must be fused because hermeneutics is a theory of the real experience of thinking. Gadamer's hermeneutics focuses on the centrality of understanding. The object of hermeneutical task is the text which presents us with the subject matter for

---

[244] Charles Taylor, "Understanding the Other: A Gadamerian View on Conceptual Schemes," *Gadamer's Century: Essays in Honor of Hans-Georg Gadamer,* Jeff Malpas, Ulrich Arnswald and Jens Kertscher, eds (Cambridge, Massachusetts: The MIT Press, 2002), p. 288.

[245] Gadamer, *Hermeneutics, Religion and Ethics,* trans. Joel Weinsheimer (New Haven: Yale University Press, 1999), pp. ix-x.

[246] Gadamer, *Truth and Method,* trans. Joel Weinsheimer and Donald Marshall, *op. cit.,* p. 302.

[247] Gadamer, *Philosophical Hermeneutics, op. cit.,* p. xxxviii.

understanding. For the development of understanding there has to be the fusion of horizons of the interpreter and the text; the reader and the author etc. The subject matter during the fusion of horizons is essentially linguistic. Language is the horizon of hermeneutics. Understanding of a subject matter in hermeneutics is itself a horizon. The fusion of horizons involves the interpretation of the claim to truth communicated by each author from his/her horizon.[248]

Each horizon depicts the specific situatedness present in a worldview. A worldview as a horizon is a limited but not a closed position.[249] It is a disclosure of an experience of the world rather than a relativistic understanding of this world. Gadamer's fusion of horizons has been interpreted as the basis for cultural cum linguistic relativism. But he argues that the importance of the fusion of horizons is to hinder relativism.[250] He further explains that the views of the world are not relative in our understanding of the 'world in itself.' The views about the world are aimed at understanding the 'world-in-itself' which is also known through being-in-itself.

The idea of the fusion of horizons shows that horizons could be expanded through the integration of individual horizons. The fusion of horizons is not a mere extension of an individual fusion or perspective. The fusion of horizons describes the readiness to accommodate other limited perspectives that help shift the horizons of our knowing capacity.[251] In other words, Gadamer's fusion of horizons describes the importance of openness in the widening of horizon and understanding is the basis for the widening or broadening of horizons. This means that understanding "is always the fusion

---

[248] Jens Kertscher, "Gadamer's Ontology of Language Reconsidered," *Gadamer's Century: Essays in Honor of Hans-Georg Gadamer,* Jeff Malpas, Ulrich Arnswald and Jens Kertscher, eds (Cambridge, Massachusetts: The MIT Press, 2002), p. 147.
[249] John McDowell, "Gadamer and Davidson on Understanding and Relativism," *Gadamer's Century: Essays in Honor of Hans-Georg Gadamer,* Jeff Malpas, Ulrich Arnswald and Jens Kertscher, eds (Cambridge, Massachusetts: The MIT Press, 2002), p. 176. McDowell on the Notes section states, "This passage is concerned in particular with historical understanding, directed as our own cultural precursors, and in this context Gadamer can use the image of a single horizon that shifts with the passing of time. But the idea of horizons being fused easily transposed to any case where the occurrence of understanding involves overcoming an initial alieness." (*Ibid.*, p. 191.)
[250] *Ibid.*, p. 178.
[251] Taylor, *op. cit.*, p. 287.

of these horizons supposedly existing by themselves."[252] Our horizons change, for example, through a hermeneutical process of understanding and cultural interaction. The ability to learn new things from other cultures shows that there are no fixed horizons. This encounter offers us new ways of understanding reality.[253] Gadamer notes that for one to maintain an interdependent horizon, it demands that we have a fusion of horizons. Without the fusion of horizon it is difficult to dialogue and understand a text which speaks to us through interpretation. Gadamer explains that it is "precisely because every interpretation is concerned with the text itself.[254]

The idea of the fusion of horizons as a hermeneutical task brings out the relation that exists between the individual horizons. The fusion of horizons involves languages, temporality (in terms of past, present and future dimensions of time), traditions that are constantly mediated etc. The fusion of horizons is a process of dialogue that advances understanding to another level of clarity. It has been associated with the platonic method of dialogue. It is a

---

[252] Gadamer, *Truth and Method*, trans. Joel Weinsheimer and Donald Marshall, *op. cit.*, p. 305; Gadamer, *Wahrheit und Methode* (Tübingen: J. C. B. Mohr [Paul Siebeck] 1986), p. 311.

[253] Georgia Warnke, *Gadamer: Hermeneutics, Tradition and Reason* (Oxford: Polity Press, 1987), p. 170. Warnke addresses the influence of Hegel's *sublation* (*Aufhebung*) to Gadamer's fusion of horizons. She observes, "in my view more tenable account of consensus, Gadamer suggests that in themselves dialogue and discussion promote the progress of reason. Like Hegel, Gadamer conceives of the reciprocal integration of initially opposed opinions as a process of *sublation* (*Aufhebung*) or cancellation and preservation. At the conclusion of a conversation, the initial positions of all participants can be seen to be inadequate positions on their own and are integrated within a richer, more comprehensive view. For hermeneutic understanding it follows that we are not limited to the premises of our tradition but rather continually revise them in the encounters with and discussions we have of them. In confronting other cultures, other prejudices and, indeed, the implication that other draw from our own tradition we learn to reflect on both our assumptions and the idea of reason and to amend them in the direction for a *better* account. For Gadamer hermeneutics is a form of justification involving the dialogic adjudication of both beliefs and standards of rationality. The difference between Hegel and Gadamer in this regard is not that Gadamer no longer identifies the dialectical or dialogic process with the possibility of an advance on the part of reason; it is rather that Gadamer refuses to foreclose this advance by projecting a point of absolute knowledge at which no further dialogic encounters can develop that rationality. Gadamer therefore calls himself an advocate of the 'bad infinite' and maintains that as long as history continues, the absolutely rational position is always one the can be further enriched." (*Ibid.*, p. 170.)

[254] Gadamer, *Truth and Method*, trans. Joel Weinsheimer and Donald Marshall, *op. cit.*, p. 398; Gadamer, *Truth and Method* (New York: The Seabury Press, 1975), p. 358.

method that leads to the integration of various views with one's interlocutors.[255]

For Gadamer the fusion of horizons or perspectives takes place through a constructive process of understanding. The result of this fusion is the emergence of the higher horizon which is described as "a comprehensive horizon in which the limited horizons of text and interpreter are fused into a common view of the subject matter—the meaning."[256] The comprehensive horizon or the higher horizon could be described as a higher universality which obviously is not the result of one horizon. The higher universality goes beyond any individual horizon or perspective. It is a wider horizon with a superior vision by the one who understands.[257]

---

[255] Warnke, *op. cit.*, p. 101. Warnke relates this fusion of horizons to Socrates method of dialogue that leads to better understanding. Warnke argues, "Gadamer's reference to a unity on the subject-matter here is important. The unity with which he is concerned is not the result either of one partner's imposing his or her views on another or of our partner's simple acquiescence to the views of another. Rather, if individuals or groups come sincerely to a shared understanding of a subject-matter, the understanding they share is not the original property of one or the other but represents a new understanding of the subject-matter at issue. Gadamer's model here is that of Socratic dialogue in which the position to which Socrates and his interlocutors come at the end represents a significant advance over the position each maintained at the beginning. Each begins with certain views and assumptions but in confronting opposing views and assumptions has to reconsider and develop his or her own. The process, then, is one of integration and appropriation." (*Ibid.*, p. 101.) Warnke further explains the similar influence Hegel has in Gadamer's hermeneutics which is a form of consensus or synthesis. Warnke underscores, "In short, Gadamer's point is a Hegelian one: coming to understand a "text" involves appropriating it, integrating it within one's own understanding of the subject-matter in an awareness of both its insights and its mistakes with regard to *die Sache*. In the consensus or synthesis that results the truth of one's own position and that of the object are both preserved in a new stage of the tradition and cancelled as adequate positions on their own." (*Ibid.*, p. 103.)

[256] Gadamer, *Philosophical Hermeneutics, op. cit.*, p. xix.

[257] Warnke, *op. cit.*, p. 103. Warnke notes, "the consensus that results from hermeneutic understanding with the 'fusion of horizons.'…what Gadamer means by this 'fusion of horizons' is the integration of our historically determined concerns with the object of understanding in such a way that this integration determines the content of the object for us. In equating successful hermeneutic understanding with dialogic consensus, then, Gadamer means merely to depict the kind of mediation between past and present or between the alien and familiar that is part of any sincere attempt to understand. On this regard, hermeneutic *Verständigung* can include disagreement: we simply agree to disagree. Although we cannot break out of the tradition to which we belong, we can break with it on any given issue by emphasizing other elements of the tradition, showing the way in which the older opinion has to be modified in light of the way the evidence now looks to us and so on." (*Ibid.*, p. 103.) Gadamer, *Truth and Method* (New York: The Seabury Press, 1975), p. 240ff.

The notion of horizon relates to the idea of the hermeneutical circle discussed earlier. It is not a vicious circle that guarantees no new knowledge and understanding, but a hermeneutical circle sees each horizon as "a contextually fulfilled circle, which joins the interpreter into a unity within a processual whole."[258] As indicated earlier, the horizons express the relevance of dialogue through shared context and shared influence. The horizon of the interpreter fuses with the horizon of the text, thereby allowing us to be guided by the text. The encounter with the text (as the past horizon) provides the opportunity for new inquiries and what Gadamer calls the 'reconstituted question.'[259] The consequence of the new inquiries through the reconstituted question could be related to the notion of higher universality. However, Gadamer's idea of the fusion of horizons does not support a higher universality that is not surpassable. For him the horizon being finite in nature continues to change and gain better grounds. It moves and expands because of this interaction with other range of visions. The fusion of horizons is a form of a dialectical process that transforms the range of vision of the interpreter in the task of hermeneutics.[260] Gadamer affirms that we are aware of the historical contingency of human thinking in relation to the world. The passing nature of human knowledge or human thought is fundamental to this horizon. The fusion of horizons helps us see our past in its own being and within its own *first* horizon. Instead of forming one horizon from the two, the horizon of the reader and of the text must be fused.[261] The fusion of horizons may not necessarily be a tension free fusion. It may even become critically constructive and "the

---

[258] Gadamer "The Problem of Historical Consciousness," *op. cit.,* p. 108.
[259] http://mindflowers.net/2009/05/10/the-hermeneutics-of-ricoeur-and-gadamer-in-scriptural-and-religious-contexts/ (Accessed March 24, 2011.)
[260] Gadamer, *Philosophical Hermeneutics, op. cit.,* pp. xxxix-xl. The introduction states, "this 'higher universality' remains finite and surpassable and is not to be equated with Hegel's absolute knowledge in concepts. Gadamer draws mainly on the empirical or phenomenological side of Hegel's thought. It is not absolute knowledge, but the moving, dialectical life of reason that finds expression in Gadamer's description of what takes place in the 'fusion of horizons.' As Hegel demonstrated in the Phenomenology, every experience passes over into another experience. Understanding has this same dialectical character. We can now recognize that in its life as dialogue language is the medium in which understanding occurs. Language makes possible agreements that broaden and transform the horizons of those who use it. But every dialogue relates to the 'infinity of the unsaid,' which presents understanding with its ongoing task." (*Ibid.,* pp. xxxix-xl.)
[261] Gadamer, *Truth and Method*, trans. Joel Weinsheimer and Donald G. Marshall, *op. cit.,* p. 305.

hermeneutic task consists not in covering up this tension by attempting a naïve assimilation of the two but in consciously bringing it out."[262]

In summary, hermeneutic is an ongoing process of understanding. No single worldview as a horizon is a comprehensive experience of the world-in-itself. Each worldview has the capacity to expand in the presence of new and different worldviews. This is the openness of the fusion of horizons. Each horizon is receptive to possible corrections, especially in the face of a different worldview with better understanding. The receptivity comes through the appreciation of "insights of other worldviews in the course of coming to understand them."[263] Through the fusion of horizons we overcome the challenge of understanding the other.[264] As in human sciences, our way of understanding is open to the criticisms of other different ways of understanding. This fusion of horizons provides us with the resources to help understand the limitations of our own horizons.[265] The fusion of horizons is the integration of the understanding of traditions.[266] Gadamer's main objective is that through the task of hermeneutics we gain clear understanding of the worldviews that are part of the ultimate horizon.[267] In this way, "[E]ach

---

[262] *Ibid.*

[263] McDowell, *op. cit.*, p. 176.

[264] Taylor, *op. cit.*, p. 279. Taylor observes, "The great challenge of this century, both for politics and for social science, is that of understanding the other. The days are long gone when Europeans and other Westerners could consider their experience and culture as the norm toward with the whole of humanity was headed, so that the other could be understood as an earlier stage on the same road that they had trodden. Now we sense the full presumption involved in the idea that we already possess the key to understanding other cultures and times. But the recovery of the necessary modesty here seems always to threaten to veer into relativism, or a questioning of the very ideal of truth in human affairs. The very ideas of objectivity that underpinned Western social science seemed hard to combine with that of fundamental differences between cultures; so that real cultural openness appeared to threaten the very norms of validity on which social science rested." (*Ibid.*, p. 279.)

[265] MacIntyre, "Relativism, Power and Philosophy," *Proceedings and Addresses of the American Philosophical Association* (APA, Newark, Daleware, 1985), p. 19.

[266] Warnke, *op. cit.*, pp. 173-174. Warnke explains, "individuals and cultures integrate this understanding of others and of the differences between them within their own self-understanding, to the extent, in other words, that they learn from others and take a wider, more differentiated view, they can acquire sensitivity, subtlety....In becoming cultured we do not simply acquire better norms, values etc. We also acquire the ability to acquire them. In other words we learn tact, taste and judgement." (*Ibid.*, pp. 173-174.)

[267] McDowell explains, "When we come to understand the other subject that can involve a change in how we view the world. When the horizons fuse, the horizon within which we view the world is no longer in the same position. But what is in view, now that the horizon is in its new position, is still the world, everything that is the case, not some supposed item constituted by this particular new positioning of the horizon—everything that seems to be

cultural tradition expresses its way of thinking in the language that carries this tradition."[268] Tradition as a form of horizon of a linguistic community is a necessary condition of hermeneutics.[269] Gadamer's hermeneutical view accommodates a more extensive approach to understanding and interpretation.

2.1.5 The Significance of the Hermeneutical Situation and Effective Historical Consciousness

Hermeneutics involves dynamic hermeneutical or interpretative situations. Gadamer recognizes the importance of hermeneutical situation. The consciousness of the historico-hermeneutical situation he calls effective-historical consciousness or the consciousness of being affected by history.[270] He notes:

Consciousness of being affected by history (*wirkungsgeschichtliches bewusstsein*) is primarily consciousness of the hermeneutical *situation*. To acquire an awareness of a situation is, however, always a task of particular difficulty. The very idea of a situation means that we are not standing outside it and hence are unable to have any objective knowledge of it. We always find ourselves within a situation, and throwing light on it is a task that is never entirely completed. This is also true of the hermeneutic situation, i.e the situation in which we find ourselves with regard to the tradition that we are trying to understand. The illumination of this situation—reflection on effective history—can never be completely achieved....To be historically means that knowledge of oneself can never be complete....This almost defines the aim of philosophical hermeneutics.[271]

---

the case from within a horizon so positioned. There is no devaluing of reality's independence from thinking here." McDowell, *op. cit.*, p. 180; Gadamer, *Truth and Method* (New York: The Seabury Press, 1975), p. 273.

[268] Lawrence Kennedy Schmidt "Language in a Hermeneutic Ontology," *Language and Linguisticality in Gadamer's Hermeneutics*, Lawrence K. Schmidt, ed (Maryland: The Lexington Books, 2000), p. 3.

[269] Horizon is one's historical and cultural situation as context-bound character of interpretation.

[270] Gadamer, *Truth and Method*, trans. Joel Weinsheimer and Donald G. Marshall, *op. cit.*, p. 301; Gadamer, *Truth and Method* (New York: The Seabury Press, 1975), p. 269.

[271] *Ibid.*

How important is the 'horizon' and historical consciousness in hermeneutics? In interpretation we are always located within a situation. Also the nature of our historical situation means that we cannot completely know or understand ourselves. Our situation is always part of who we are and we never stand outside of our situation. The situation is where we discover ourselves while considering a tradition. Effective historical consciousness is focused on the awareness of our hermeneutical situation. As historical being it is impossible to have a complete knowledge of oneself. The historical situation of any interpreter presents a form of dynamism or dialectics of an incomplete self-knowledge.

The consciousness or awareness that history is ever at work is described as *wirkungsgeschichtliches Bewusstsein* (consciousness of effective history.) Consciousness of history helps "shed light on the idea of language in some phases of its history."[272] Consciousness of effective history is the same as the effect of history that cannot be completely achieved. Historically effected consciousness is present in the particular history and culture that shape this consciousness. Understanding is described as the 'effect' of history. Understanding involves the description of what we always do when we interpret things even when it occurs unconsciously. Historical consciousness is itself that mode of being that is conscious of its own historical 'being effected.' [273] It is about what happens to us over and above our wanting and doing. The historical situation of an interpreter has an effect or influence on the hermeneutical activity.[274] The past and the present historico-hermeneutical knowledge have effect on the hermeneutical process. The features of the past effect our definition or description in the present. Some events in the Middle Ages influenced the Modern period. Our process of understanding is affected by the effects of history. Gadamer explains:

> the historical consciousness has the task of understanding all the
> witnesses of a past time out of the spirit of that time, of

---

[272] Gadamer, *Philosophical Hermeneutics, op. cit.*, pp. 19-20.

[273] *Ibid.*,p. 13.

[274] http://mindflowers.net/2009/05/10/the-hermeneutics-of-ricoeur-and-gadamer-in-scriptural-and-religious-contexts/ (Accessed March 24, 2011.) According to Richard Mcgivern, "From the starting point of the interpreter's prejudice[*Vorurteile*], the location that one is situated in by the fact of language, tradition, and handed down concepts, one begins a dialogue with the past through the text....The situatedness of the individual in any context is first colored by the past's effects and impacts upon the very situation the hermeneutical search begins from." (*Ibid.*)

extricating them from the preoccupations of our own present life, and of knowing, without moral smugness, the past as a human phenomenon.[275]

Gadamer puts together the analyses of historical consciousness, historical situation and the horizon. The acquisition of a horizon is different from the acquisition of a historical situation. Our historical situation is our context of experience of tradition and a horizon relates to the individual. Each cultural worldview is a horizon with a historical situation (because it is a context of the experience of tradition.) The awareness of this historical situation is what hermeneutists refer as historical consciousness.[276] Gadamer describes historical consciousness as that awareness or illumination which comes from knowing our historical range of vision. It involves our own horizon and the external horizons related to each other. These form the one new great horizon that is an extension of what we originally had. In this way also historical consciousness is concerned with our past and the past horizons of others with regard to our tradition.[277]

The fusion of horizons is the task of the effective historical consciousness. This consciousness of our historical situation is something we cannot ontologically overcome. Our historical consciousness is self-evident to us because we are historically attuned.[278] The consciousness of the effect of history is the consciousness of our finite nature as historical beings. We are part of the situations that are affected by our historicity. Our knowledge of the world or our self-reflection on the world is mediated such that we have only but a perspective of the world. Our worldviews are our interpretations of the tradition that is also part of us.[279] Gadamer admits that with effective historical consciousness "we are self-consciously aware of both our own great historical tradition as a whole and, in their otherness, even the traditions and forms of quite different cultural worlds."[280]

---

[275] Gadamer, *Philosophical Hermeneutics, op. cit.,* p. 5.
[276] Gadamer, *Truth and Method*, trans. Joel Weinsheimer and Donald G. Marshall, *op. cit.,* p. 301; Gadamer, *Truth and Method* (New York: The Seabury Press, 1975), pp. 271-272.
[277] *Ibid.*
[278] Gadamer, *The Relevance of the Beautiful and Other Essays*, trans. Nicholas Walker, ed., with an Introduction by Robert Bernasconi (New York: Cambridge University Press, 1986), p. 11.
[279] Gadamer, *Philosophical Hermeneutics, op. cit.,* pp. xxvi-xxvii.
[280] Gadamer, *The Relevance of the Beautiful and Other Essays, op. cit.,* p. 11.

The effect of history on our consciousness comes through that which is linguistic. This is because language constitutes our human experience of our world. Gadamer writes:

The linguistic nature of this bringing into language is the same as that of the human experience of the world in general. This is what has finally led our analysis of the hermeneutical phenomenon to the discussion of the relationship between language and world.[281]

Effective historical consciousness or effective history is not only linguistic but it makes possible "the conversation between each new interpreter and the text or event he seeks to understand."[282] Gadamer's effective history demands further conversations and developing understanding. This demand for developing understanding aligns with the fusion of horizons which is the main task of effective historical consciousness. The effect of history means that we are able to fuse our different perspectives in an intercultural world. Our history is not monolithic and our temporal position is constantly changing. This situation also describes the temporality of understanding since "our understanding is oriented by the effective history or history of influences of that which we are trying to understand."[283] The consciousness of effective history is more about *being* than about consciousness since being is not fully manifest and is never fully understood. He likes effective history because of the effects of the interpreter's history on the interpreter.

Having taken a look at the main aspects of Gadamer's hermeneutical theory, I shall now focus on his treatment of the problem of understanding: language and hermeneutics. The discourse above enables us to see the important issues in Gadamer's hermeneutics and how they will apply to his analysis of language. Language is the home of being and is essential to understanding in hermeneutics.

---

[281] Gadamer, *Truth and Method*, trans. Joel Weinsheimer and Donald G. Marshall, *op. cit.*, p. 452; Gadamer, *Truth and Method* (New York: The Seabury Press, 1975), pp. 413-414.
[282] Gadamer, *Philosophical Hermeneutics, op. cit.,* p. xvii; Gadamer, *Wahrheit und Methode, op. cit.,* p. 261.
[283] Warnke, "Hermeneutics, Ethics, and Politics," The *Cambridge Companion to Gadamer*, Robert J. Dostal, ed (New York: Cambridge University Press, 2002), p. 81.

2.2 Gadamer and the Concept of 'Bildung' or Culture

Gadamer uses the concept of *"Bildung"* (culture) to illustrate on the need of formation or education in the development of human culture and understanding of self. *"Bildung"* points to a continual process or movement. It comes from a German mystique meaning as the cultivation of God's image (*Bild*) in humanity. This image needs to be cultivated by man himself. The understanding has since moved from theological to a humanistic usage. It requires a movement beyond the particular to a cultivation of the capacities for the universal or universality.[284] According to some scholars, *"Bildung"* is a process of fusion of horizons that leads to universal human transformation. This is briefly treated in Part I of *Truth and Method*.[285]

Human experiences are sources of *"Bildung"* or education. Human experiences as cultural experiences lead to the acceptance of the universal but finite nature of human existence. Culture opens us to new experiences and understandings. Culture and traditions are part of the formative principles in human life. Without culture and tradition it is difficult to understanding the meanings or the worldviews of a people. Culture determines how we conceive reality and educates us on our understanding of it.

"Bildung" is similar to Greek *"paideia"* (education, learning, and upbringing.) Hegel uses it to mean human edification. This relates to the educative and formative function of cultural studies as he would argue about experience. For Werner Jaeger, *"paideia"* means education or formation that does lead an individual to a universal understanding of human nature. However, Gadamer rejects any teleological perspective of *"paideia"* or *"Bildung"*.

Gadamer uses *"Bildung"* to imply cultivated character (*gebildet.*) For one to be cultivated, it means one is experienced (*erfahren.*) To be an experienced person means being able to accept or integrate other cultures as new cultural horizons. It means to interact and integrate other cultural views. Gadamer suggests the need to transform history and culture in order to arrive at the objective position. This position offers one the opportunity to critique

---

[284] Gadamer, *Truth and Method,* trans. Joel Weinsheimer and Donald G. Marshall, *op. cit.,* pp. 10-11.
[285] *Ibid.,* pp. 8-16.

the situation of a society. Each person is a product of a society, culture, tradition and history. We are confronted by a new culture or cultures, new experiences etc. One's experience with culture is because one is a historical being. New experiences and encounters with new cultures are possible through maintaining an attitude of openness. Openness is valuable in the encounter between cultures. When we accept a different perspective, it does not mean given up completely on our former beliefs (not the totality of our culture is given up.) "*Bilding*" or culture indicates an interactive social process in which we give and take or receive from and add to humanity's cultural development. It is "*Bilding*" (German) as in "building" (English) through a process of cultural interaction. It demands the development of universal understanding of humanity through culture, self-discipline, self-transcendence, and the integration of intercultural horizons.

This brief discussion, in my understanding, introduces us to the idea of understanding of meaning in Gadamer's hermeneutics. Culture (*Bildung*) is important in understanding language and hermeneutics, especially in considering cultural horizons and their meanings in the light of universal hermeneutics. The universality of hermeneutics is constituted by language for the purpose of understanding. The universality of hermeneutics is grounded in its linguisticality and the inner word that gives meaning and understanding. There is the universality of hermeneutics, the universality of language and the universality of thought or reason for understanding to take place. One has to remember that *logos* is considered as reason, thought, word or language.

2.3 Understanding: Gadamer's Theory of Language and the Problem of Language

In all aspects of hermeneutics previously discussed, language was always central. Gadamer, following Heidegger's enlightening consideration of language (briefly discussed in chapter one), thinks that the issue of language needs to be addressed further. For Gadamer language is at "the center of philosophical concern. Language is the fundamental mode of operation of our being-in-the-world and the all-embracing form of the constitution of the world."[286] Language as an essential structural element of understanding is present in all acts of understanding. Understanding is the central issue in

---

[286] Gadamer, *Philosophical Hermeneutics, op. cit.,* p. 3.

hermeneutics that is carried out through the medium of language. The problem of language is central to understanding the problem of hermeneutics and as a consequence at the center of philosophy. Gadamer adds that language is central because it has an interpretative use with the concepts as the inner structural element of understanding.

Understanding is linguistic and is present in every human endeavor. We exist within a linguistic world and language retains its purity in the experience of the world without enclosing us within relativity. Gadamer puts it thus:

> Understanding is language-bound... It is indeed true that we live within a language... While we live wholly within a language, the fact that we do so does not constitute linguistic relativism because there is absolutely no captivity within a language.[287]

In hermeneutics language plays a fundamental role. Language goes beyond the statements we utter through it, but this does not affect the fundamental importance of language. It is often the case that language is at times unable to exactly communicate what our thoughts are. Gadamer explains, "the task of expressing in words what they say to us seems like an infinite and hopeless undertaking....But this does not alter the fundamental priority of language."[288]

Language has intellectual quality and every language has the capacity to express reality. For Gadamer each language does it by itself in its own way. Language connects us to the world and is part of our being in the world. In hermeneutics, we develop the linguistic world since we all are "always already at home in language."[289] Through language we express, acquire universal concepts and we articulate our philosophical views about the world and reality. Language and philosophy go to together.

Gadamer in his own way criticizes the neglect of language. For him, our being-in-the-world is primordially linguistic and we live in a linguistic community. In language the reality that is beyond every individual consciousness becomes visible and it plays a role that moves beyond a

---

[287] *Ibid.,* pp. 15-16.
[288] Gadamer, *Truth and Method,* trans. Joel Weinsheimer and Donald G. Marshall, *op. cit.,* p. 402; Gadamer, *Truth and Method* (New York: The Seabury Press, 1975), p. 362.
[289] Gadamer, *Philosophical Hermeneutics, op. cit.,* p. 63.

phenomenological experience to a hermeneutical consciousness of the worldviews of cultures.[290] Through language we transmit meaning and understanding. It is in this same way that the art of understanding unfolds through language following the interaction between the past and the present experiences.

For us to understand the past and the present experiences in hermeneutics there ought to be a constitutive relation between language and reality. This constitutive relation through language is a basic condition of understanding. The possession of language "is the ontological condition for our understanding of the texts that address us."[291] Understanding presupposes our immersion in tradition of "total language dependence."[292] Language mediates between us and reality. As a medium of understanding language is not reduced to the status of mere tool of understanding. It is always constitutive of the world we understand. Gadamer observes:

> it must be emphasized that language has its true being only in dialogue, in coming to an understanding. This is not to be understood as if that were the purpose of language. Coming to an understanding is not a mere action, a purposeful activity, a setting-up of signs through which I transmit my will to others. Coming to an understanding as such, rather, does not need any tools…It is a life process in which a community of life is lived out.[293]

Since language is constitutive, then it is not merely instrumental to understanding. It is always present in the act of understanding and does not at any point become irrelevant to the quest for meaning. That means that in the knowledge of the world or of ourselves we are always involved in the use of our own language.[294] This is also what Gadamer implies when he writes that "language speaks *us*….although, of course, no one disputes the fact that it is

---

[290] Kertscher, *op. cit.*, p. 137. Gadamer, *Gesammelte Werk*, 3, (Tübingen: J. C. B. Mohr [Paul Siebeck], 1987), pp. 141-142; Gadamer on Husserl in *Gesammelte Werke*, 2, (Tübingen: J. C. B. Mohr [Paul Siebeck], 1986), p. 361.
[291] Gadamer, *Philosophical Hermeneutics, op. cit.*, p. xxix.
[292] *Ibid.*
[293] Gadamer, *Truth and Method*, trans. Joel Weinsheimer and Donald G. Marshall, *op. cit.*, p. 443; Gadamer, *Truth and Method* (New York: The Seabury Press, 1975), p. 404.
[294] Maurice Merleau-Ponty, *Signs* (Evanston, Illinois: Northwestern University Press, 1964), p. 59; Gadamer, *Philosophical Hermeneutics, op. cit.*, p. xxix.

we who speak it."[295] As linguistic beings we are spoken to through our languages.

It is through language that man *engages in* the world and whoever has language "has a world."[296] Although language is the universal medium of understanding through which we perceive the world, it does not focus on itself. This is the transparent nature of language since it makes it possible for the subject matter to be understood among people. Language reveals reality, and reality in turn does influence the use of language. Every language reveals reality from a horizon and reality takes place within language. It is in this way that language presses beyond established conventions or the societal assumptions about language. Gadamer adds, "[L]anguage is the medium in which substantive understanding and agreement takes place between two people."[297] The knowledge of language involves being open to an active participation in a transformation dialogue with others which consequently broadens one's initial horizon. In speaking we dialogue through language and we share our thoughts with some other person. This is the dialogic and disclosive nature of language which does not emphasize the individual, but presents and reveals the object of communication "before the eyes of the other person to whom I speak."[298]

As Gadamer often repeated the being that is understood is language. There is no other autonomous being outside language and this being is said through language itself. Language is always present in the disclosure of being, yet there is the "forgetfulness of language that its real being consists in what is said in it."[299] It discloses the real being of existence through what is said to us and it also reflects the self-transcending nature of language. Every language is a medium of understanding.[300] Every language reveals of being and all attempt

---

[295] *Ibid.,* p. 236.

[296] Gadamer, *Truth and Method*, trans. Joel Weinsheimer and Donald G. Marshall, *op. cit.,* p. 440.

[297] *Ibid.,* p. 386; Gadamer, *Truth and Method* (New York: The Seabury Press, 1975), pp. 345-346.

[298] Gadamer, *Philosophical Hermeneutics, op. cit.,* p. 65.

[299] *Ibid.,* p. xxx.

[300] Kertscher, *op. cit.,* p. 143. According to Kertscher, "Language is therefore the paradigm of a fundamental horizon while simultaneously being an indispensable medium of understanding. The famous and often quoted principle of Gadamer's ontology of language ("Being that can be understood is language") can be interpreted in just that sense." (*Ibid.,* p. 143.)

at language is for the disclosure of truth, the world and to express man himself. Historical situations express the world in language. Gadamer explains that language describes "a realm as indispensable to human life as the air we breathe. As Aristotle said, man is truly the being who has language. For we should let everything human be spoken to us."[301]

Language is the basis for the different cultural worlds to understand each other. Within language we merge into a common understanding of the world. There is no place for a mutual exclusive existence within language. This fusion is the ground for the encountering of the other world that stands over against us. As Gadamer notes, "the other world [that] we encounter is not only foreign but is also related to us. It has not only its own truth in itself, but also its own truth for us."[302] This view is important in understanding the later part of this thesis, especially in chapter four, using Gadamer's theory of language to understand other linguistic worlds. Every language is a view of the world which "is said or handed down in this language."[303] The use of language is not a privilege for human beings and so we possess language because we have a world of existence that is a linguistic world. The existence of a world is unique to human beings. Gadamer elaborates:

> Language is not just one of man's possessions in the world; rather, on it depends the fact that man has a *world* at all. The world as a world exists for man as for no other creature that is in the world. But this world is verbal in nature... languages are worldviews... language maintains a kind of independent life vis-à-vis the individual member of a linguistic community; and as he grows into it, it introduces him to a particular orientation and relationship to the world as well. But the ground of this statement is more important, namely that language has no independent life apart from the world that comes to language within it.[304]

He notes also that our knowledge of the world and all knowledge of us are always intrinsically influenced by the language we speak. We cannot

---

[301] Gadamer, *Philosophical Hermeneutics, op. cit.,* p. 68.
[302] Gadamer, *Truth and Method,* trans. Joel Weinsheimer and Donald G. Marshall, *op. cit.,* p. 439; Gadamer, *Truth and Method* (New York: The Seabury Press, 1975), pp. 399-400.
[303] *Ibid.*
[304] *Ibid.,* p. 440; Gadamer, *Truth and Method* (New York: The Seabury Press, 1975), pp. 401-402.

understand and give meaning to relations in the world without language. Gadamer's hermeneutics emphasizes the all-encompassing nature and the universality of language. It is universal since it involves every person and every circumstance of humanity. As universal, language is constitutive of every culture and each culture expresses itself through language. It is also infinitely used through ongoing dialogue or conversation such that even a break in conversation through language remains an ongoing process of dialogue.

Let us now discuss Gadamer in light of written language and oral tradition. I shall elaborate more on Gadamer's understanding of the problem of language in chapter four because it is the main chapter for the application of Gadamer's hermeneutics views to an African narrative text in order to underscore the universality of hermeneutics in our discourse. Also, Gadamer's theory of language, discussed above, will be used to justify my critique of Achebe's African English narrative written without fully using an African language to communicate African worldviews.

2.3.1 Written and Oral Language

Written texts present us with the real hermeneutical task, which is "the highest task of understanding."[305] A true hermeneutical task involves genuine dialogue between the written texts and the interpreter. The task of interpretation is centered on a common subject matter which written tradition consistently guarantees. Oral tradition easily loses sight of the subject matter, but focuses on the 'creative personality' or the worldviews of the individual author. In other words, oral tradition's emphasis on interpretation is more on the emotional, psychological and historical situations of the narrative more than on "a common subject matter." [306] The subject matter in hermeneutics guarantees consistency in what a text utters to generations of interpreters since "[A]ll literary documents possess a certain 'ideality of meaning' insofar as what they say to the present is in written form and is thus detached from the psychological and historical peculiarities of their origin."[307] For us to

---

[305] *Ibid.*, p. 392; Gadamer, *Truth and Method* (New York: The Seabury Press, 1975), p. 352.
[306] Gadamer, *Philosophical Hermeneutics, op. cit.,* p. xx.
[307] *Ibid.*

understand the subject matter of our discourse the emphasis of interpretation must be on language itself—a written language.

Gadamer terms his hermeneutics as an event of the act of understanding. He avoids simple "techniques and methods of interpretation, all of which assume understanding to be a deliberate product of self-conscious reflection."[308] Hermeneutics is not purely technique and method of interpretation but more of a linguistic activity. In a written language, the intellectual quality is preserved to allow for interpretation and understanding. Gadamer expounds:

> In writing, language gains its true ideality, for in encountering a written tradition understanding consciousness acquires its full sovereignty. Its being does not depend on anything. Thus reading consciousness is in potential possession of its history…Writing is not mere accident or mere supplement that qualitatively changes nothing in the course of oral tradition. Certainly, there can be a will to make things continue, a will to permanence, without writing. But only a written tradition can detach itself from the mere continuance of the vestiges of past life, remnants from which one human being can by inference piece out another existence.[309]

For Gadamer, linguistic tradition essentially involves 'something handed down.' It could be orally given through repetition of stories, legendary tales, myths or as a written text that is clear to read and easy to investigate. Unlike the oral tradition that depends on repetition, in a written tradition the full interpretation is realized because the subject matter is clearly seen and does not depend on being repeated. The past and the present are available because all necessary information about a people or culture is written down and the intellectual quality is preserved.

The quality of information received through oral tradition is easily lost. Oral tradition has lost many of its genuine history because of poor documentation. The failure of oral tradition to preserve intellectual quality of

---

[308] *Ibid.*, p. xxviii.
[309] Gadamer, *Truth and Method*, trans. Joel Weinsheimer and Donald G. Marshall, *op. cit.*, pp. 392-393; Gadamer, *Truth and Method* (New York: The Seabury Press, 1975), pp. 352-353.

information or the ideality of the word causes the loss of the continuity of memory. Memory is an important factor in the interpretation of worldviews. Gadamer explains:

> A written tradition is not a fragment of a past world, but has already raised itself beyond this into the sphere of the meaning that it expresses. The ideality of the word is what everything linguistic beyond the finitude and transience that characterize other remnants of past existence. It is not this document, as a piece of the past, that is the bearer of tradition but the continuity of memory. Through it tradition becomes part of our own world, and thus what it communicates can be stated immediately. Where we have a written tradition, we are not just told a particular thing, but a past humanity itself becomes present to us in its general relation to the world.[310]

Now with literature and documents, we have access to information. Gadamer recalls Plato's support for oral tradition in philosophical studies. Plato writes that written tradition has the problem of falling into misunderstanding, especially with the passage of time. The spoken words could be better interpreted following emotional elements, the manner of speaking, the tempo and the influencing conditions "in which it is spoken."[311] A written tradition easily overlooks the tempo and tone of voice used in the oral communication of facts. Gadamer observes:

> The task of understanding is presented with particular clarity when we recognize this weakness of all writing. We need only recall what Plato said, namely that the specific weakness of writing was that no one could come to the aid of the written word if it falls victim to misunderstanding, intentional or unintentional.[312]

But a written text has equally a good advantage in the communication of meaning. An important advantage of written tradition is that it provides us with the "abstract ideality of language. Hence the meaning of something written is fundamentally identifiable and repeatable."[313] However, speech/utterance shares also in the ideality of the meaning in communication. Gadamer affirms

---

[310] *Ibid.*, p. 392; Gadamer, *Truth and Method* (New York: The Seabury Press, 1975), p. 352.
[311] *Ibid.*, p. 395; Gadamer, *Truth and Method* (New York: The Seabury Press, 1975), p. 355.
[312]*Ibid.*, p. 394. Gadamer thinks that Plato's rejection of the written tradition is based on his (Plato) effort to cover up problems in his writing and art. See Plato, *Seventh Letter* 341c, 344c, and *Phaedrus*, 275.
[313] *Ibid.*

that writing possesses the advantage of presenting the hermeneutical problem with purity. He focuses more on the advantages of written tradition to hermeneutics. There is the clarity in information without the interference of contingent factors that hinder access to truth. He states:

> In fact, the particular weakness of writing, its greater helplessness as compared to speech, has another side to it, in that it demonstrates with redoubled clarity the dialectical task of understanding. As in conversation, understanding here too must try to strengthen the meaning of what is said. What is stated in the text must be detached from all contingent factors and grasped in its full ideality, in which alone it has validity. Thus, precisely because it entirely detaches the sense of what is said from the person saying it, the written word makes the understanding reader the arbiter of its claim to truth. The reader experiences what is addressed to him and what he understands in its validity. What he understands is always more than an unfamiliar opinion: it is always possible truth. This is what emerges from the detaching what is spoken from the speaker and from the permanence that writing bestows.[314]

Written language sustains the existence of the linguistic tradition. In Gadamer's perspective, the hermeneutical depth of the subject matter in a text is better understood in a tradition that cherishes the preservation of facts through writing and documentation. He observes that there is an advantages to written tradition since people often see whatever is written as self-authenticating. In a written tradition what is preserved is not merely a fragment of a past world but an appropriation of genuine history that is part of humanity itself which is made present to us.

Every society has its own language that presents or addresses it. In Gadamer's hermeneutics, language helps express the fact that we have a world. He makes reference to the use of an African language. An African language has its originality and addresses its world, like any living language it equally has a conceptual universality and pragmatic meaning. This pragmatic meaning is important for universality of hermeneutics. The use of a concept in different particular contexts presents different connotations in interpretation. Gadamer observes:

---

[314] *Ibid.*, pp. 395-396.

There is an African language that has two hundred different words for camel, according to the camel's particular circumstances and relationships to the desert-dwellers. The specific meaning that "camel" has in all these different denominations makes it seem an entirely different creature.[315] In such cases we can say that there is an extreme tension between the genus and the linguistic designation. But we can also say that the tendency towards conceptual universality and that towards pragmatic meaning are never completely harmonized in any living language.[316]

Following the above, the language of each people communicates their worldviews and each person lives in language. The language we speak as part of the world is capable of describing our world. Using a foreign language may not provide one with the appropriateness that a homeland language could provide. Gadamer's comment about the multiple words one African language uses to describe 'camel' because of the slightest change of circumstances in relation to part of the camel applies to this discourse on translation (into another language.) In this way he explains the capability of any language to describe its reality in the most appropriate way more than that another language could translate it in original sense. Gadamer opines:

> When a person lives in a language, he is filled with the sense of the unsurpassable appropriateness of the words he uses for the subject matter he is talking about. It seems impossible that other words in other languages could name the things equally well. The suitable word always seems to be one's own and unique, just as the thing referred to is always unique. The agony of translation consists ultimately in the fact that the original words seems to be inseparable from the things they refer to, so that in order to make a text intelligible one often has to give an interpretative paraphrase of it rather than translate it.[317]

Written traditions provide us with the primary object of hermeneutics. Language is at the center of hermeneutics. Every language is capable of being

---

[315] Ernst Cassirer, *Philosophy of Symbolic Forms* (Yale 1953 [7th ed. 1968]), p. 290.
[316] Gadamer, *Truth and Method*, trans. Joel Weinsheimer and Donald G. Marshall, *op. cit.*, p. 434; Gadamer, *Truth and Method* (New York: The Seabury Press, 1975), pp. 394-395.
[317] *Ibid.*, p. 403.

used for understanding and useful to hermeneutics because that language is written down. Gadamer's views above will later be used in chapter four in commending an African narrative by Achebe and the effort he made in putting such narrative in a written language (English.) My criticism will only focus on why Achebe failed to put Igbo language (an African language) into full written form, which should bring out the intellectual quality of the language and the philosophical depth of its meaning, especially in a post-colonial world and in an emerging world of dialogical civilization. Let us now discuss the second aspect of the problem of understanding which is the problem of hermeneutics.

2.4 Understanding: The Problem of Hermeneutics

According to Gadamer:

> [T]he classical discipline concerned with the art of understanding texts is hermeneutics…Understanding must be conceived as a part of the event in which the meaning of all statements-those of art and all other kind of tradition-is formed and made complete.[318]

Hermeneutics concerns itself with the phenomenon of understanding and the process of acquiring meaning from texts or objects. Without the problem of understanding there would be no need for hermeneutics. Gadamer points out also that "there would be no hermeneutical task if there were no mutual understanding that has been disturbed and that those involved in a conversation must search for and find again together."[319] In hermeneutics, when something is not intelligible to us, we are worried about understanding it. Hermeneutics as an art of understanding involves understanding everything that could be understood. German romantic hermeneutics, especially Schleiermacher, described hermeneutics as the task of "avoiding misunderstanding,"[320] and the expression of meaning through language.

Hermeneutics is the expression of meaning through language. Hermeneutics and language are inseparable in the understanding of the world.

---

[318] *Ibid.*, p. 157.
[319] Gadamer, *Philosophical Hermeneutics, op. cit.*, pp. 25-26.
[320] *Ibid.*, p. 98.

There is an essential relation between thinking and speaking-thought and language. We understand and interpret people's thoughts through the medium of language. Every person's understanding of the world is determined by the linguistic world. To understand a person or a text is to understand the language of the person's linguistic world or the dominant language of one's milieu for being that is understood is language itself. Our understanding is purely linguistic. Gadamer further adds that understanding means "assimilating what is said to the point that it becomes one's own."[321]

Briefly we recall above, section *2.1.1* (*hermeneutical circle*) of the present thesis, that Gadamer's hermeneutic theory emphasizes the quintessential relationship between the whole and its parts. The parts or the details are necessary in the comprehension of the whole. The whole is essential in the understanding of the various parts and there has to be a form of textual unity. For this unity to be achieved, a full circle of moving from whole to the parts and from the parts to the whole is required. Gadamer is not the first to make use of this approach in hermeneutics. It has been an ancient practice to understand rhetoric, but now he uses it in hermeneutical theory.[322] This theory urges that we understand the text's linguistic parts and structure by understanding in the context of the whole and then through the part, which is in coherence with the whole.

Gadamer also urges that we can understand the views of writers since there could be other deeper meanings with time. Hermeneutics does not pursue only one original meaning or the author's original intention. It goes beyond this common level to solving the problem of meaning which is the problem of hermeneutics. Gadamer writes:

> The customary way of defining the meaning of a text has been to identify it with the subjective act of intending of its author. The task of understanding is then construed as the recapturing or repetition of this original intention. Such a theory of meaning has obvious advantage, not the least of which is that it seems to make

---

[321] Gadamer, *Truth and Method*, trans. Joel Weinsheimer and Donald G. Marshall, *op. cit.*, p. 400; Gadamer, *Truth and Method* (New York: The Seabury Press, 1975), p. 360.
[322] Wachterhauser, *op. cit.*, pp. 77-78, n. 4. See Tilottama Rajan, "Hermeneutics," *The Johns Hopkins Guide to Literary Theory and Criticism,* ed. Michael Groden and Martin Kreiswirth), [cited 26 November, 2004.]
Online:http://www.press.jhu.edu/books/hopkins_guideto_literary_theory/hermeneutics_1.html.) (Accessed March 24, 2011.)

possible a definitive, canonical interpretation. Because the author intended something specific, the interpretation that recovers and represents that original intention is the correct one that banishes all competing interpretations as incorrect. Just as scientific experiments can be repeated exactly any number of times under the same conditions and mathematical problems have but one answer, so the author's intention constitutes a kind of fact, a "meaning-in-itself," which is repeated by the correct interpretation.[323]

Writing involves many influencing factors and some of these factors are unconscious environmental factors like culture, values, traditions, languages, proverbs, myths and others. These are reflected in the structure of the texts and determine how we understand them. The process of understanding involves a putting together of the various parts into a whole for meaningfulness, it also involves the consciousness of the effect or the influence of history in having a clear interpretation of a text. This helps the interpreter to be more conscious of things than the author. Some may refer to it as a form of 'reconstruction' that leads to clear understanding.

Gadamer's perception of hermeneutics is more than a mere reconstruction of events for clear understanding or for acquiring meaning. Does understanding mean a reproduction or a reconstruction of original production? Reconstruction does not offer us new understanding/meaning. It however returns us to the recovery of old meaning. Hermeneutics, for Gadamer, in this case, will become a pointless endeavor when we look at man and his changing/situational experiences in the same way and with only one obsolete meaning or overused meaning. There is always a new meaning received in reading the same text at different times. We always understand differently, especially with the change of interest in a text read by a different generation of interpreters. Gadamer critically argues that the "reconstruction"

---

[323]Gadamer, *Philosophical Hermeneutics, op. cit.,* pp. xxiii-xxiv. The editor's introduction holds that "Just as scientific experiments can be repeated exactly any number of times under the same conditions and mathematical problems have but one answer, so the author's intention constitutes a kind of fact, a 'meaning-in-itself,' which is repeated by the correct interpretation. While there may be varying explications of the significance of the text for us, it has only one meaning, and that is what the creator meant by his word or by his work of art." (*Ibid*, pp. xxiii-xxiv.)

[324] of the conditions that influenced the writing of a text and its original intention could still be done, but it does not bring us closer to the full meaning of a work of art or text. Understanding as the goal of hermeneutics is a productive endeavor rather than a mere reproduction of meaning. We should not be obsessed with the original production of what was done in the past.

Gadamer further critiques this Schleiermacher's reconstructive view of hermeneutics by asking if the question of the original world is the primary concern of hermeneutic. He thinks it is contrary to the idea of classic understanding of the work of art. The meaning of the work of art is continual to the generation or the age that newly questions it with different interests. What is important to Schleiermacher's hermeneutics, in Gadamer's view, is to understand the point of contact or the recovery of this point of contact and the writer's original words in order to avoid "misunderstanding."[325] Gadamer prefers that we go beyond this definitive-meaning-based form of hermeneutics and embrace the one that reveals new meaning. One of Gadamer's principal contributions to hermeneutics is that he shifts the focus of hermeneutics from 'reproduction' or 'reconstructive' form of interpretation and understanding. Understanding is not merely a product of self-conscious reflection. It is rather a linguistic process that involves—"language and the understanding of transmitted meaning—[these] are not two processes, but are affirmed by Gadamer as one and the same."[326]

Gadamer's philosophical hermeneutics demands "a kind of openness to the text."[327] This means that the individual horizons are open to the interaction with other different horizons such that the result of the merging of different perspectives will help us identify how what may be strange or not familiar to us may not be considered as meaningless, but could be related to what we have in our world. This process of understanding that culminates in the fusion of horizons "has more in common with a dialogue between persons"[328] and the dialogue between people. We shall consider this as Gadamer's effort in

---

[324] Gadamer, *Truth and Method*, trans. Joel Weinsheimer and Donald G. Marshall, *op. cit.*, p. 191.
[325] *Ibid.*, p. 185. Schleiermacher's position is the re-establishing or reproducing the writer's original word. This view will be relevant to Achebe's work because he is reconstructing or reproducing the worldviews of African people.
[326] Gadamer, *Philosophical Hermeneutics, op. cit.*, p. xxviii.
[327] Taylor, *op. cit.*, p. 288.
[328] Gadamer, *Philosophical Hermeneutics, op. cit.*, p. xix.

drawing attention to the interpersonal and intercultural aspect of his hermeneutics. This is important in Gadamer's project and to my work with Gadamer in this thesis. There is the language we speak and the language that emerges in an attempt to understand other traditions and people. His hermeneutics allows the fusion of alternative horizons and richer ontology of language that emerges through understanding.[329] The problem of hermeneutics essentially lies "in showing that a language-view is a worldview…it is the basis of a far-reaching anthropological insight."[330]

We recall that the essential ingredients used in the practice of hermeneutics are the relevant resources of getting at deeper or inner meaning.[331] Every aspect of the human experience of the world is an object of meaning and understanding.[332] Our encounter with the world requires deriving meaningfulness from each encounter. These encounters include our political, economic, and social relationships that are part of our life-world. Gadamer expounds that the principle of hermeneutics requires that everything that needs to be understood is among the primary object of hermeneutics. It is within hermeneutics that every being is known in its world or community. Hermeneutics takes place in every human community and it is a form of game of interpretation that is constitutive of our *quotidian* or everyday life. We also involve in the game of interpretation to be understood and to understand other people. This game, which Gadamer understands as a form of play or the genuine involvement in a true act of mutual self-giving, in order to arrive at understanding, is a "process of interpretation [that] takes place whenever we 'understand'."[333]

Gadamer adds that the process of understanding involves universality in the communication of meaning. This process of understanding is more than the

---

[329] Taylor, *op. cit.*, p. 292.
[330] Gadamer, *Truth and Method*, trans. Joel Weinsheimer and Donald G. Marshall, *op. cit.*, p. 440; Gadamer, *Truth and Method* (New York: The Seabury Press, 1975), pp. 400-401.
[331] MacIntyre, *op. cit.*, p. 170. See Gadamer, *Hegel's Dialectic: Five Hermeneutical Studies*, trans. Christopher Smith (New Haven: Yale University Press, 1976), p. 93. MacIntyre explains, "The resources of hermeneutics are the resources of language and it is to language and only to language that Gadamer ascribes a condition that is beyond critique and beyond prescription. 'Word themselves prescribe the only way in which we can put them to use. One refers to that as proper 'usage'—something which does not depend on us, but rather we on it." (*Ibid.*, p. 93.)
[332] Gadamer, *Philosophical Hermeneutics*, pp. 31-32.
[333] *Ibid.*, p. 32.

givens of our transmitted culture to include other givens of the world around and beyond us. He sees the universality of hermeneutics as an all involving process or an unrestricted scope of understanding. Understanding as the medium of hermeneutics involves always a new meaning and a pointer to a deeper meaning or understanding. Gadamer further explains:

> [T]he universality of the hermeneutical perspective is all-encompassing… It means that everything points to another thing. This 'everything' is not an assertion as to how it encounters man's understanding. There is nothing that cannot mean something to it. But the statement implies something else as well: nothing comes forth in the one meaning that is simply offered to us.[334]

This is why it is important in hermeneutics to get access to the many meanings related to a hermeneutical object. Gadamer considers the object of hermeneutics as the whole of the experience of the world, including all traditions. All traditions, as something handed down to us or to generations, are the corpus of our experience of the world. Tradition, he notes "encompasses institutions and life-forms as well as texts…within the process of integration that is involved in all human life that stands within traditions."[335]

The discussion so far relates the problem of language and hermeneutics. All forms of interpretation are truly linguistic and reality is understood linguistically. It is not contrary to understanding to talk of language when discussing hermeneutics. We cannot overlook the role of language when attempting to understand hermeneutics. As Gadamer affirms that in all forms of interpretation whatever that is intelligible is communicable through language. Language is constitutive of our experiences and our understanding of our experience. However, whatever that may not be linguistic still has the capacity to be interpreted linguistically. Our tradition, in a general sense, may not be linguistic but everything is explainable or could be explained through language.[336]

If hermeneutics is the discourse of understanding, language makes understanding possible. Hermeneutics as understanding does not mean that

---

[334] *Ibid.*, p. 103.
[335] *Ibid.*, p. 96.
[336] *Ibid.*, p. 99.

language is a meaningful windowless isolation such that a translation from one language to another is impossible. The point is the following:

> Understanding is essentially linguistic, but in such fashion that it transcends the limits of any particular language, thus mediating between the familiar and the alien. The particular language with which we live is not closed off monadically against what is foreign to it. Instead it is porous and open to expansion and absorption to ever new mediated content.[337]

The hermeneutical process of questions and answers is an essential part of interpretation. We have to inquire for more information from utterances, explanation etc in order to understand an author or a text. We could use other ways of formulation or expressions to better understand an intended meaning. Gadamer recognizes that in narratives and dialogue with an interpreter the author or speaker involves the fusion of perspectives. Even any momentary stop of a conversation does not mean that dialogue is over. A break in conversation is part and parcel of the entire dialogue to understand each other. He adds that with an interpreter the author holds together "what is said and addressed to the other person... It is this infinity of the unsaid--this relation to the whole of being that is disclosed in what is said-into which the one who understands is drawn."[338]

Gadamer considers the role of hermeneutics in literary texts and the communication of truth to be classified within the human sciences rather than the natural sciences. The truth of hermeneutics is not like the fixed knowledge common in the natural sciences. The interpretation of texts offers one the opportunity of accessing different standpoints in which new perspectives are heard. He observes the unique nature of human sciences as distinct from natural sciences. As part of the human sciences, modern historical research is about the transmission of meaning /tradition. The object of historical research is man in his changing circumstances or conditions, not determined purely by the law of science and scientific verifications. Human sciences are guided by what is given and what the interests in tradition by the generations of interpreters are. Every new voice has something new to tell us and every new experience of history is a new voice that ought to be listened to. Gadamer concludes on the difference between the natural sciences and human sciences:

---

[337] *Ibid.*
[338] Gadamer, *Philosophical Hermeneutics, op. cit.,* p. xxxii.

this is precisely what distinguishes the human sciences from the natural sciences. Whereas the object of the natural sciences can be described idealiter as what would be known in the perfect knowledge of nature, it is senseless to speak of a perfect knowledge of history, and for this reason it is not possible to speak of an "object in itself" toward which its research is directed.[339]

Hermeneutics concerns itself with the human sciences that are open to the uncertain dynamics of human historical experience. The human sciences lack the predictabilities of the natural sciences. Unlike the natural sciences that are more objective and limited, human sciences are more suitable for unlimited hermeneutical initiatives in order to get at meanings.

With the above discourse, we addressed the universality of hermeneutics and how we understand when we encounter texts and other people. Gadamer's view of hermeneutics does situate and help us understand the intercultural problem of language and hermeneutics to be considered in chapter three (Achebe's narrative of tragedy and contemporary African thought on the notion of person.) Later in chapter four I will have a clear application of Gadamer's intercultural approach to the problem.

2.4.1 Written Tradition and Literature

In literature the worldviews of a people are disclosed through language. The use of language in the literature of a people provides one with a new standpoint and it reflects the truth of the people specific to them. Gadamer argues that language expresses a view of the world during our conversations with others or during our study of text or literature. For him literature

has acquired its own contemporaneity with every present. To understand it does not mean primarily to reason one's way back into the past, but to have a present involvement in what is said. It is not really about a relationship between persons, between the reader and the author (who is perhaps quite unknown), but about sharing in what the text shares with us. The meaning of what is

---

[339] Gadamer, *Truth and Method*, trans. Joel Weinsheimer and Donald G. Marshall, *op. cit.*, p. 285.

said is, when we understand it, quite independent of whether the traditionary text gives us a picture of the author and of whether or not we want to interpret it as a historical source. Let us here recall that the task of hermeneutics was originally and chiefly the understanding of texts.[340]

Writing a literary work or narrative is like creating a work of art. Narrative is an important object of hermeneutics and written texts, as Gadamer notes, are the real object of the hermeneutical task. The ancient dialogues of philosophers and historical narrative of writers have been used for understanding and further interpretation of the period. For instance, Plato's dialogues and Aristotle's works are 'literature' for hermeneutical understanding among medieval, modern and contemporary philosophers. Most of the highlights of the influence of Plato on Gadamer's hermeneutics were discussed in chapter one above. Plato's dialogues are important to Gadamer especially in the communication of meaning; the representation of what is said by interlocutors; the explanation of the message that are beyond human understanding; the intelligibility of what is in a text; the inner unity of what is said and that the meaning of a word lies in the depth of the soul (inner word); the presence of motivation, intention, and situation in what is communicated to us; the avoidance of misrepresentation in written words; the role of language for conventional or natural use; and how to arrive at meaning without necessarily focusing solely on the logics. One's attention is also drawn to the idea of focusing on the subject matter of the text and on the role of the dialectical fusion of perspectives that leads to a better understanding in a dialogue.

In Plato's time, poetic and philosophical traditions have become 'literature' for understanding. For Gadamer, Plato's dialogues are useful for the 'interpretation' of texts used by the sophists in order to teach or instruct.
Plato's dialogues are models of the hermeneutical process in this dialectical sense, and the unique power of his philosophy owes much to the sense we have in reading him that we participate in the very life of understanding as a movement that bears all participants beyond their initial horizons.[341]

---

[340] *Ibid.*, p. 393.
[341] Gadamer, *Philosophical Hermeneutics, op. cit.*, p. xxii.

Gadamer's approach to literature shows the historical dimension of the hermeneutical task of understanding and meaning. The historical situation of a philosopher is an important place to proceed with the task of hermeneutics. Universal hermeneutics demands that we have a situation as the locus of interpretation:

> it is not only ancient texts that betray to the interpreter when and where they were most likely written. Mommsen's History of Rome-a veritable masterpiece of critical-historical methodology-gives us just as unequivocal indications of the 'hermeneutical situation' in which it was written and proves to be the child of its age rather than the simple result of the application of a method by an anonymous 'knowing subject.'[342]

The historical situation and experience of war-time Europe partly influenced Gadamer's hermeneutical task on conversation, communication and dialogue. Dialogue is the new culture in a world devastated by imperialism, hegemony, human violence and lack of peaceful collaboration. We require dialogue or communication to find solutions to the threats of human co-existence. Gadamer describes it as an "open and nonmanipulative communication"[343] for peaceful co-existence in Europe. We accomplish it through a hermeneutics of true mutual dialogue, linguistic analysis of the views of others, and a new understanding. The demands of living in a new world of dialogical civilization are, among other things, that we see the need for a new philosophical approach to hermeneutics in which we reconsider our own views after having listened to other perspectives. Gadamer refers to it as "a philosophy which teaches us to see the justification for the other's point of view and which thus makes us doubt our own."[344] He addresses the possibility of a common human civilization through hermeneutics, written texts and literature.

There are other aspects in written tradition and literature. The use of language in narrative literature is one aspect, while the other aspect is that there has to be a familiar world of exchange between the texts and the

---

[342] *Ibid.*, p. xviii.
[343] Dieter Misgeld and Graeme Nicholson, eds. *Hans-Georg Gadamer on Education, Poetry, and History: Applied Hermeneutics*, trans. by Lawrence Schmidt and Monica Reuss, (New York: State University of New York Press, 1992), p. xvii.
[344] *Ibid.*, p. xviii.

interpreters. These factors are important in the communication of one's world and worldviews in a different language. Focusing on language is one issue, but it is difficult to speak to an unfamiliar world. As Gadamer notes, the being that is understood is language and language is constitutive of the world. An unfamiliar world could be presented to others through language. However, this language has to be understood and interpreted to be able to appreciate its meaning or what it presents.[345]

Let us take a look at Gadamer's discourse on the hermeneutical relevance of Aristotle's notion of tragedy as an important aspect of a written tradition and literature (*Poetics.*) The purpose of this section is to relate Gadamer's use of Aristotle's notion of tragedy to African narrative of tragedy (in chapter three) as a way of communicating meaning and understanding of the worldviews that may be foreign but not totally different from Western philosophical worldview. As my thesis project vision /view, Gadamer's hermeneutics serves the meeting point/ or provides the framework for intercultural hermeneutical transitions/interactions between these different philosophico-cultural worlds. He also provides the hermeneutical justifications for understanding Achebe's African thought in its own right (although foreign) since "it has not only its own truth in itself but also its own truth for us,"[346] especially when we have a claim of universality and the possibility of universal understanding.

2.5 Gadamer on the Hermeneutical Relevance of Aristotle's Notion of Tragedy

I shall now discuss Gadamer's use of Aristotle's notion of tragedy to show the aesthetics of a work of art and the relevance of the experience of truth in works of art. Aristotle's notion of tragedy includes: plot, character, diction, spectacle etc in order to communicate the inner meaning and truth. I shall later relate Gadamer's notion of tragedy and Achebe's notion of tragedy where they share some meeting points. It is important that we mention some relevant issues in relations to both notions of tragedy but drawing comparisons or establishing differences is not the concern of this research. My primary

---

[345] Gadamer, *Truth and Method,* trans. Joel Weinsheimer and Donald G. Marshall, *op. cit.*, pp. 439- 440; Gadamer, *Truth and Method* (New York: The Seabury Press, 1975), pp. 400- 401.
[346] *Ibid.*, p. 439.

concern is to establish the communal notion of tragedy in Achebe's African tragedy. How Achebe's narrative tragedy resonates with communal tragedy rather than with a personal tragedy as in Aristotle's is to be justified in this text, especially in chapters three and four. One has to recall that Gadamer's use of Aristotle's notion of tragedy is not intrinsically and completely related to Achebe's use of African notion of tragedy. These are two different perspectives with different purposes/goals. One thing is clear, Achebe's text as a whole appears to be about an African heroic-tragedy while Gadamer's notion of Aristotle's tragedy is to experience and understand truth or meaning. Both are related as representation or communication of meaning and as literature/texts. I think one could still relate Gadamer's hermeneutical principles to Achebe's notion of African tragedy without a detailed discourse of Aristotle's notion of tragedy in the *Poetics*.

In Aristotle's *Poetics* the use of the notion of tragedy has seen some modifications, although it has retained a sort of common essence: a series of tragic events that affect an individual or a group. According to Aristotle, tragedy is:

> a representation of an action that is heroic and complete and of a certain magnitude--by means of language enriched with all kinds of ornament, each used separately in the different parts of the play: it represents men in action and does not use narrative, and through pity and fear it effects relief to these and similar emotions. (1449bff)[347]

It is a representation or "a mimesis... of fearful and pitiful events, and this effect comes about when things happen unexpectedly... (52a 2-4.)"[348] The important aspect of this representation is the heroic action (1449bff) and not a representation of people. In tragedy we express true sympathy for the sufferings and the unfortunate circumstances of the hero character. In writing

---

[347] Aristotle, *Poetics*, trans. William Hamilton Fyfe (London: William Heinemann Ltd., 1932.)

[348] Stephen Halliwell, *Aristotle's Poetics* (North Carolina: The University of North Carolina Press, 1986), p. 171; See Ross, *op. cit.*, (2003.) Ross considers mimesis as art of recognition and representation.

tragedy the narrative focuses on the "character-study" (1450aff.)[349] Stephen Halliwell, a scholar in Aristotle, comments:

> The heroes of tragedy (to use 'hero' once more in its Greek not in its Romantic sense) are, according to Aristotle, to be humanized so as to allow true sympathy with their misfortune and suffering, but without their being reduced thereby to the level of perfectly ordinary humanity. They are to be close enough in nature to the audience to elicit full pity and fear, yet they must remain sufficiently heroic to excite a special and heightened degree of these emotions.[350]

Aristotle avoids dissociating fear and pity in treating his theory of the experience of tragic drama. He observes that tragedy evokes emotions: fear and pity. The experience of these emotions affects the spectators who are essential characters in the description of tragedy. The hero (agent) suffers misfortune or loss of external fortune, his loss of possessions and properties discloses the presence of pain and destruction. In Aristotle's narrative:

> theory places the weight of the experience of tragedy onto the transformation in the external fortunes of the agents rather than on the ethical nature of the characters and their actions. …It is, then, the possession of exceptional human status or prosperity (but not ethical excellence) which opens up the possibility of the 'pain and destruction' and the most moving kinds of instability, of the type around which the ideal tragedy of the *Poetics* is built.[351]

Gadamer holds that Aristotle's theory of tragedy provides a good instance of the narrative of the structure of being, which manifests in dramas 'in theaters' or in works of art. Tragic narrative or tragedy belongs to the sphere of aesthetics. In aesthetic, there are plays and representations of reality. He explains:

> Aristotle's theory of tragedy may serve to exemplify the structure of aesthetic being as a whole. To be sure, It is situated in the context of a poetics and seems to apply only for dramatic poetry.

---

[349] Aristotle, *Poetics, op. cit.*
[350] Halliwell, *op. cit.*, p. 179.
[351] *Ibid.*, pp. 179-180.

However, the tragic is a fundamental phenomenon, a structure of meaning that does not exist only in tragedy, the tragic work of art in the narrower sense, but also in other artistic genres, especially epic... Indeed, it is not even a specifically artistic phenomenon, for it is also found in life. For this reason, modern scholars (Richard Hamann, Max Scheler[352]) see the tragic as something extra-aesthetic, an ethical and metaphysical phenomenon that enters into the sphere of aesthetic problem only from outside.[353]

As Gadamer notes, the theory of the tragic play shows the essence of the tragic through poetics.[354] There may not be only one particular reason to reflect on the notion of tragedy. It could be for aesthetic, dramatic, poetic or epic reasons. There are different ways that tragedy has been presented in the history of thought. For instance, it is different from Attic to Euripides, from Aeschylus to Shakespeare's tragedies as noted by Gadamer. We also have the classical, modern (Kierkegaard's) and contemporary tragedies with one unifying essence that Aristotle emphasized as the emotional effects on the audience connecting them with the situation of the hero character. Gadamer briefly traces the history and concludes that "[W]hat we find reflected in thought about the tragic, from Aristotle down to the present, is certainly no unchangeable essence." [355]

In a concise approach, Gadamer brings all the necessary issues about tragedy together when he describes it as:

the unity of a tragic course of events that is experienced as such. But what is experienced as a tragic course of events—even if it is not a play that is shown on the stage but a tragedy in 'life'—is a closed circle of meaning that of itself resists all penetration and interference. What is understood as tragic must simply be accepted. Hence it is, in fact, a phenomenon basic on the 'aesthetic'. We learn from Aristotle that the representation of the

---

[352] Hamann and Scheler hold that the tragic may not have any aesthetic relevance. Gadamer's accepts the aesthetic aspect in tragedy.
[353] Gadamer, *Truth and Method*, trans. Joel Weinsheimer and Donald G. Marshall, *op. cit.*, p. 125; Gadamer, *Truth and Method* (New York: The Seabury Press, 1975), p. 114.
[354] *Ibid.* See Ross, *op. cit.* Poetry as work of art.
[355] *Ibid.*, p. 125; Gadamer, *Truth and Method* (New York: The Seabury Press, 1975), pp. 114-115.

tragic action has a specific effect on the spectator. The representation works through *eleos* and *phobos*.[356]

One could ask why was tragedy discussed at all by Gadamer? The reason is: because the significance of the theory of tragedy is within the structure of aesthetics. The modifications present in Aristotle are understandable in regard to the structure and narrative of aesthetics. Gadamer argues that in the definition of tragedy Aristotle discusses about a unity of tragic successive events, especially in real life situation. Also, even in a dramatic representation, it is a tragedy of an imaginative 'life'. The aesthetic value of this representation is there because of the emotional effects on the audience. Gadamer is right when he describes tragedy from an 'aesthetic' and representational perspective which causes a known specific effect on the spectators of that tragic drama.[357]

Gadamer's aim in the discussion on tragedy is to bring in the role of art in the form of imitation or representation of life situation in the communication of meaning. For him tragedy is described through art which is one of the ways to the disclosure and understanding of truth. The disclosure of truth does depend on the relation of art to human historical awareness of meaning made present through art or aesthetics. Our concepts are bound to be different on how they are used in describing our worldviews. Gadamer appeals to such understanding of "imitation, play, symbol, and festival with the aim of showing their relevance to modern… art… [He] strives to bring his reflections on art into conformity with his account of historical consciousness."[358] He also highlights the relevance of narratives in the presentation of truth within the approach of the human sciences. The importance of language or word in the interpretation of thought about the narrative of tragedy is part of Gadamer's reason of using Aristotle's work. The language used in the discourse puts across the *logos apophantikos* as propositions that evoke emotions. There is also the place of different kinds of narratives about tragedy but with some common basic identities. There are examples of what the narrative of tragedy could be in other artistic genres as mentioned above. We recall that other aspects of the importance of Aristotle's narrative to Gadamer were discussed in details in chapter one on Aristotle's influence in hermeneutics. The above

---

[356] *Ibid.*, p. 126.
[357] *Ibid.*
[358] Gadamer, *The Relevance of the Beautiful and Other Essays, op. cit.*, p. xviii.

are some of the important points of Gadamer's analysis of the hermeneutical relevance of Aristotle's theory of tragedy and its narrative (as literature.)

In summary, Gadamer's hermeneutics sees meaning and understanding as content-oriented, not author-oriented activity. The main problem of understanding is the problem of hermeneutics and language. Written language and literature provide us with real hermeneutical tasks because of their hermeneutical quality of preserving information as texts or narratives. This applies to Gadamer's example on the relevance of Aristotle's theory of tragedy as a written hermeneutical narrative.

2.6 Conclusion

Gadamer's hermeneutical framework is appropriate in the general art of understanding of texts. What is essential in his philosophical hermeneutics is not what is based on rules or methods but rather to lived experience. He rejects every form of logical and mechanical or natural science method-based application of hermeneutics. Despite various historical situations there are conclusions that philosophers and writers can reach: that means historical situations are not definitive determinant factors in interpretation. We obviously do reach certain conclusions but they need to be justified.[359] This is the role of hermeneutics and historical conditions. But does ongoing interpretation mean there is no conclusive position or understanding? Well, in a situation where understanding is difficult, then the demands for the task of hermeneutics become paramount.

---

[359] MacIntyre, *op. cit.,* pp. 161-162. MacIntyre raises some critical questions. He argues that "The concept of conclusive argument is ineliminable from interpretations of philosophical texts. About the contents advanced by the author of any philosophical text we cannot avoid asking three questions: are the arguments presented for this or that conclusion presented as conclusive. If so, was the author, given the premises of and the presuppositions underlying those arguments, right to treat them as conclusive? And should we now, given our presuppositions and beliefs about the truth or falsity of those premises, treat them as conclusive? If so, then there are questions, concepts, and standards that are to some significant degree shared by philosophers at work in very different historical contexts with very different beliefs and presuppositions, namely those questions, concepts and standards that are involved in asking and answering questions about whether this or that argument is or is not conclusive." (*Ibid.,* pp. 161-162.)

Hermeneutics requires openness to meaning and understanding. Gadamer's hermeneutic principles of hermeneutical circle, the role of prejudice, temporal distance, the fusion of horizons and effective historical consciousness are important in our search for clear understanding and the role of the universality of hermeneutics. We understand better when hermeneutics is done with narrative literature or written texts that present us with reliable and intelligible contents. Written language plays a significant role in understanding aesthetics. In using the example of Aristotle's notion of tragedy Gadamer considers how aesthetics helps in the communication of inner meaning and understanding. He expresses the need to extend our quest for truth by starting from what is most common to us. That is: from art, to history and then to philosophy (in terms of language.) The quest for truth and the understanding of meaning are part of this universality of hermeneutics. The understanding of meaning involves everything that can lead us to truth. The subtle and demanding difficulty in understanding the universality of hermeneutics is in dealing with the problem of hermeneutics and the problem of language as the two sides of understanding (in philosophical hermeneutics) because, as Gadamer notes, our exercise of the capacity for understanding is impossible if we do not involve our own "worldview and language-view."[360]

---

[360] Gadamer, *Truth and Method,* trans. Joel Weinsheimer and Donald G. Marshall, *op. cit.,* p. 440; Gadamer, *Truth and Method* (New York: The Seabury Press, 1975), pp. 400-401.

CHAPTER 3

Achebe's Narrative and Contemporary African Philosophical Thought

3.1 Achebe's Narrative: Language and Narrative of Tragedy in Chinua Achebe's Things Fall Apart and Contemporary African Philosophical Thought on the Notion of Person

In this section, I first briefly present the common definition/view of culture used by Achebe and other African scholars in this chapter that are related to Gadamer's hermeneutic concept of *Bildung* (applied as culture.) This is important in understanding the intercultural aspect of this discourse. It is also necessary because language is an essential aspect of culture and hermeneutics which form the core aspect of this book. I will later carefully address the philosophical content of this work through hermeneutics and language. The purpose of this chapter is to present the narratives of Achebe's *Things Fall Apart* and contemporary African philosophical thought on the notion of person in order to justify a communal interpretation of African tragedy. This African philosophical notion of person as a cultural or traditional understanding of person will be integrated in chapter four through the hermeneutical principle of prejudice (tradition as prejudice, as pre-judgment or fore-knowledge/fore-meaning) and the fusion of cultural perspectives with part of our hermeneutical theme: *Okonkwo: obsession with heroic cultural personage leading to tragedy* in order for us to gain new understanding from the text.

3.2 African Thought on Culture

Culture comes from the Latin word "*cultura*" which refers to the art of "putting into use", or "to make use of" [361] something. It relates to the English word "cultivate." [362] In this sense "*cultura*" is same as the German word

---

[361] Anozie Onyema, *The Igbo Culture and the Formation of Conscience* (Owerri: Assumpta Press, 1999), pp. 92-93.
[362] *Ibid.*

"*Bildung*" taken above by Gadamer to mean "cultivation"[363] or the process of cultivation or formation. Culture or '*Bildung*' connotes the formation or development of an object or a person (animate object.) It involves everything about the development of an individual or a people, which includes intellectual, physical, social, hermeneutical etc. Through culture we develop ourselves and our understanding of the world/reality around us. According to an African scholar Anozie Onyema, Professor of Theology at the Catholic Institute of West African, Port-Harcourt, Nigeria, "[C]ulture is more than one can simply define. It is all things seen and unseen, heard and unheard, experienced and not experienced. Culture develops with the people!"[364] Onyema makes reference to Raymond Williams' article "*Culture and Civilization*" were he (Williams) explains that:

> the concept of culture was developed in four ways, all of which still affects its meaning. First, culture came to mean 'a general state or habit of the mind,' with close relations to the idea of human perfection. Second, it came to mean, 'a general state of intellectual and moral development in a society as a whole.' Thirdly, it came to mean 'the general body of arts and intellectual work.' Fourth, it came to mean, 'the whole way of life, material, intellectual, and spiritual, of a given society'.[365]

For Ernst Cassirer, culture is "the process of man's progressive self-liberation…. In all of them man discovers and proves a new power - the power to build up a world of his own, an 'ideal' world."[366] That means- culture is the way of life of a people or the ensemble of a people's way of life in attempt to understand their world. It includes language, art, religion and, science. Edward Burnett Tylor goes further to add that culture "is that complex whole which includes knowledge, belief, art, morals, law, customs, and any other capabilities and habits acquired by man as a member of society."[367] It is with

---

[363] Gadamer, *Truth and Method,* trans. Joel Weinsheimer and Donald G. Marshall, *op. cit.,* pp. 70-76.
[364] Onyema, *The Igbo Culture and the Formation of Conscience, op. cit.,* p. 92.
[365] Raymond Williams, "Culture and Civilization," *The Encyclopedia of Philosophy, Paul Edward,* ed (New York: Macmillian Publishing Co, Inc & The Free Press: 1967, vol. 11), p. 273; See Onyema, *op. cit.,* p. 93.
[366] Ernst Cassirer, *An Essay on Man* (New Haven and London: Yale University Press, 1967 (1st Ed., 1944)), pp. 70-71.
[367] Edward Burnett Tylor, *Primitive Culture* (London: John Murray, 1871), p. 5.

this common understanding that African scholars mentioned in this chapter three make their contributions to African philosophical thought and Achebe's African notion of tragedy narrative.

For another African scholar Elochukwu E. Uzukwu, Associate Professor, Pierre Schouver Chair, Department of Theology at Duquesne University, Pittsburgh:

> Oftentimes when one talks about African culture, minds are filled with dress, dance, colour, quaint art work-modes of the past. But culture is dynamic and living (reality) and not only the past-oriented. It embraces socio-economic and political organizations of a people within a given environment, it has a depth-level (generally called structural history) where people struggle to express and reflect on the mystery of its contact with the universe. At this depth-level the question of life and death, of God and the spirits undergirding the universe are posed.[368]

Culture is the dynamic generality of a people's worldviews. It involves every aspect of their life as a group. This is mainly how most African scholars define or describe culture[369]. It is also in this light that I apply it in my discourse on Gadamer. My task is not to identify the difference between Africans and Gadamer's understanding of culture, but to initiate a dialogic hermeneutics in which Gadamer's universality of hermeneutics and his other hermeneutical principles become a paradigm for addressing the intercultural problem of language and hermeneutics (which is a problem of understanding and meaning) that arise from the encounter between cultures or cultural perspectives during the colonial period and after. The hermeneutical application will be done in chapter four with Gadamer's hermeneutics directly bearing on Achebe's text.

Now let me focus on the overview of Achebe narrative text and its historical background. This is important for scholars/readers who are not familiar with Achebe's background. However, according to Gadamer, this is

---

[368] Elochukwu. E. Uzukwu, *Church and Inculturation* (Nigeria: Pacific College Press Ltd., 1985), p. 25; See Uzukwu, "Inculturation of Eucharistic Celebration in Africa," *African Christian Studies*, (1983) vol. 1, p. 14.
[369] Tylor, *Primitive Culture, op. cit.*, p. 5.

not necessary in philosophical hermeneutics. It is not important to know the author's background. What is required is the author's text. Nevertheless, I think it will do no one any harm to provide as much information as possible in a new discipline like *African* philosophy and its use of hermeneutics-as part of the universality of hermeneutics.

3.3 Achebe's Background

Achebe received Western education and was familiar with ethnographic literature about the Igbo. Ode Ogede, Professor of Language and Literature at the Department of English and Mass Communication, North Carolina Central University, Durham, explains that Achebe aimed at narrating the originality of an African society.[370] His narrative is about the life-world and events of his people. Ogede argues:

> he(Achebe) has also given readers a novel with an unequalled display of talent which ranks among the best works of world fiction, utilizing the pressure of recorded human events as the organizing principle of narrative structure. *Things Fall Apart* can justifiably be considered the earliest novel to successfully bring together in a conglomerate many of the themes and narratives techniques that now define the genre of realistic historical fiction in modern African literature. It is unparalleled in its elegance, lucidity, and felicity of expression; today anyone with an idea of life in Africa either acquired it through *Things Fall Apart* or soon becomes acquainted with it, because it stands out as a novel that has unquestionably opened exceptional possibilities for the genre of realistic historical fiction to unlock a window on a fast-disappearing world.[371]

---

[370] Joseph McLaren, "Things Fall Apart: Cultural and Historical Contexts," *Critical Insights: Things Fall Apart*, Keith Booker, ed (Pasadena, California: Salem Press, 2011), p. 19; See Alan R. Friesen, "Okonkwo's Suicide as an Affirmative Act: Do Things Really Fall Apart?," *Critical Insights, op. cit.*
[371] Ode Ogede, *Achebe's Things Fall Apart: A Reader's Guide* (London: Continuum International Publishing Group, 2007), pp. ix-x.

Before Achebe wrote this novel, there were a few well-written works about Africa. Some writings had a distorted view of the genuineness of the African thought and life-world, for instance, some writings of G.W. F. Hegel[372] and Conrad's *Heart of Darkness* mentioned above. Achebe uses the effectiveness of narrative to draw attention to African worldviews.[373] Despite the difficulties of misinterpretation caused by using English language, Achebe accepts his approach as the best way to unravel the true cultural and philosophical heritage of his people. Ogede further explains:

> Though such large questions about the goals of narrative are never easy to tackle, Achebe would not be intimidated. So, he reminded his then newly emerging audience of readers to be aware of the significance with the art of storytelling was acquiring for his new nation, as deriving its special effect from leading the people to a larger understanding of their cultural heritage. He also made known that he personally sees his novelistic ambition as being to 'help my society regain belief in itself... He goes on to add that it is the duty of the African writer to lead 'the task of re-education and regeneration that must be done'[374]

Things Fall Apart's influential position among African novels is undoubtedly convincing. It has been a major source of information about African culture, history and philosophy of existence. Its style of communication excites readers in their attempts to understand and interpret African worldviews following Achebe's "inventive use of language, plot,

---

[372] McLaren, *op. cit.,* p. 23. McLaren admits, "Selden Rodman correctly identified Achebe's purpose-to give an insider's view of an African society. However, the language of his praise also contains what has become, for contemporary critics, a problematic labeling of traditional African society. The word "primitive," so widely used before and after the 1950s, was often accompanied by similar terms, such as "native" and "tribe," all of which tend to relegate African ethnicities to positions of backwardness and savagery. These ideas were inheritances of the eighteenth century, passed down by such thinkers as the German philosopher Georg Wilhelm Hegel, who viewed African societies as outside of history, in a "completely wild and untamed state," and... lacking ... developing any culture." See Selden Rodman, "The White Man's Faith," Review of *Things Fall Apart, by Chinua Achebe*, New York Times *Book Review* 22 February, 1959, p. 28; p. 93; p. 98; See McLaren, *op. cit.,* pp. 23-24.
[373] Ogede, *op. cit.,* p. x.
[374] *Ibid.,* pp. xi-xii; See Chinua Achebe, *Morning Yet On Creation Day: Essays* (London: Heinemann, 1975), p. 71.

setting, imagery, narrative devices, and characterization."[375] *Things Fall Apart* accomplishes a significant goal: To produce a written publication of African reality. Simon Gikandi, Professor of English at Princeton University and scholar in modern African novel, admits that Achebe was one of the "writers to recognize the function of the novel not solely as a mode of representing reality, but one which had limitless possibilities of inventing a new national community"[376] Achebe's representation of African worldviews comes as one that "forces us to see anew the fluidity of self-understanding as well as class alignments in a living African culture."[377] His narrative characters humanize African culture, philosophy and thought.[378]

The main hermeneutical purpose of Achebe is putting Africa at the center of critical thinking and focusing his novel on Igbo worldviews. He presents the narrative as he experienced it among his people. He equally reconstructs the "Igbo world that had existed before his birth… by presenting the effects of colonialism on individual Igbo people… and on the villages of Umuofia and Mbanta, which are replicas of actual Igbo villages."[379] Toyin Falola, a Nigerian historian and professor of African Studies (the Frances Higginbotham Nalle Centennial Professor in History), University of Texas at Austin, admits that this is the real historical and cultural situation of the Igbo at the close of the nineteenth century.[380] However, it is real as much as it reflects Igbo world, but its unique situation is that "[T]he village of Umuofia… 'is somewhat derived from Ogidi, Achebe's 'hometown.'"[381] Achebe's story tallies with the historical fact of the Igbo. As Christian Anieke, Professor of English and American Literature and Comparative Linguistics, notes:

> The first contact of Igbo land with Christian missionaries (often
> referred to by Achebe in his novels) was in the second half of the

---

[375] *Ibid.*, p. xii.
[376] Simon Gikandi, *Reading Chinua Achebe: Language and Ideology in Fiction* (London: James Currey, 1991), p. 3.
[377] George Olakunle, *Relocating Agency: Modernity and African Letters* (Albany: State University of New York Press, 2003), p. 176.
[378] McLaren, *op. cit.*, p. 23.
[379] *Ibid.*, p. 24.
[380] Toyin Falola, *The History of Nigeria* (Westport, CT: Greenwood, 1999), p. 67. See the religious aspect of this colonial influence in Emmanuel Ayankanmi Ayandele, *The Missionary Impact on Modern Nigeria, 1842-1914: A Political and Social Analysis* (New York: Humanities Press, 1967), p. 5; See John E. Eberegbulam Njoku, *The Igbos of Nigeria: Ancient Rites, Changes, and Survival* (Lewiston, New York: Mellen, 1990), p. 61.
[381] McLaren, *op. cit.*, p. 26.

19th century. On 27th July 1857 a group of Church Missionary Society (CMS) led by Ajai Crowther arrived in Igbo land and established the first mission station in Onitsha.[382] Many of the conflicts with the evangelical missionaries mentioned by Achebe in the *Things Fall Apart* have a historical basis in similar conflicts with the evangelicals in the 1930s.[383] The arrival of the missionaries in the second half of the 19th century was the beginning of major changes that would take place in Igbo land… Some of the wars mentioned by Achebe in *Things Fall Apart*… are actually his recollections of the stories he heard about these conflicts.[384]

Following the above, one understands that Achebe's fiction has real historical background with real Igbo people. In order to authentically tell African story, Achebe avoids being a one-dimensional writer. His approach is honest, and he presents the Igbo people as "purposeful creators of their own world and unique history."[385] This is specifically clear in his tragedy narrative.

The 19th Century period of the Igbos is part of the time of colonial infiltration and exploration for economic control in Africa. Many African communities were still intact with their own cultural values, customs and religious practices. Achebe's time witnessed the coming of many Europeans as colonizers and as Christian evangelizers. As I noted above, it was a time of influence through Western education. Many young graduates from Great Britain/Europe came to teach at Nigerian university colleges. The young teachers used foreign books and narratives to teach African students. Some of the narratives were not appealing to the worldviews of students like Achebe and Wole Soyinka (was awarded the 1986 Nobel Prize in Literature, first African at the time) and others. In the excitement for independence, some students began to write in defense of their African thought, culture and

---

[382] Ezenwa Ohaeto, *Chinua Achebe: A Biography* (Oxford: James Currey Ltd, 1997), p. 12.
[383] *Ibid.*
[384] Christian Anieke, *Problems of Intercultural Communication and Understanding in Achebe's Representation of the Igbo and their Culture* (Enugu: Mbaeze Printing Press, 2008), p. 19. He is also the Pro-chancellor of GO-University, Enugu, Nigeria and a member of International Association of Post-Colonial Literature Professors.
[385] Micere Githae-Mugo, *Visions of Africa: The Fiction of Chinua Achebe, Margaret Laurence, Elspeth Huxley, and Ngugi wa Thiong'o* (Nairobi: Kenya Literature Bureau, 1978), p. 29.

worldviews. This situation has continued and later influenced present young African scholars to develop interest in African thought or philosophy. This has been recognized at some universities and institutions of higher learning as African Studies, African Philosophy or *African Hermeneutic Philosophy*, Ethno-philosophy etc. This is the historico-hermeneutical situation of the post-colonial or post-independence scholarship and the horizon of this present research. This book follows this tradition as a new horizon of getting at new meanings through reading a classic African text in light of Gadamer's universality of hermeneutics as a framework. It is a new horizon that seeks genuine intercultural understanding through language and hermeneutics, especially in applying the hermeneutics to Achebe's tragedy narrative.

Did Achebe's tragedy narrative solely come from African worldviews or was he influenced by Greek tragedy in Aristotle? How did Achebe communicate tragedy that corresponds to Aristotle's description? Some scholars argue that Achebe borrowed from Western philosophy. In Ogede's words:

> The infrastructural frame is evidently Western, modeled as *Things Fall Apart*'s plot is on the Aristotelian convention of tragedy, but the dominant rhetorical ploy used by Achebe are derived from oral tradition, one of the favourite indigenous arts of his people.[386]

Achebe had rejected earlier in an interview the argument that he borrowed from Greek tragedy in Aristotle. In an interview conducted by Charles H. Rowell, founder of Callaloo: a Journal of African Diaspora Arts and Letters (Southern University in Baton Rouge, Louisiana), about the comments of critics in this regard, Achebe replies:

No, I don't think I was responding to that particular format. This is not, of course, to say that there is no relationship between these [Greek and African Tragedies]. If we are to believe what we are hearing these days, the Greeks did not drop from the sky. They evolved in a certain place which was very close to Africa. Very close to Egypt, which in itself was also very close to the Sudan

---

[386] Ogede, *op. cit.,* p. 17.

and Nubia, which was very close to West Africa. So it may well turn out, believe it or not, that some of the things Aristotle was saying about tragedy were not really unheard of in other cultures. It's just that we are not yet ready to make these quantum leaps! For instance, it has been shown that one-third of the entire vocabulary of ancient Greek came from Egypt and the Middle East. And so obviously there were links with us which the Greeks themselves apparently had no problem acknowledging....In any event, I think a lot of what Aristotle says makes sense. Putting it in a neat, schematic way may be peculiar to the Greek way of thinking about the hero. But the idea is not necessarily foreign to other people: the man who's larger than life, who exemplifies virtues that are admired by the community, but also a man who for all that is still human. He can have flaws, you see. All that seems to me to be very elegantly underlined in Aristotle's work. I think they are there in human nature itself and would be found in other traditions even if they were not spelled out in the same exactly way."[387]

My task is not to further discuss the comments of critics but to inquire about a possible uniqueness in African notion of tragedy following my interpretation of *Things Fall Apart* and Igbo worldviews. Achebe's African notion of tragedy does not suggest of any significant difference from any other philosophical notions of tragedy.[388] He accepts there could be a historical relation between Aristotle's and Africans. Moreover, he observes that tragedy is common to cultures and peoples. Following this explanation, one could say that there are some similarities between Aristotle and Achebe's. For them tragedy affects the life of a known hero, who possesses some supernatural status, and is admired by the community. The tragic situation of the known hero evokes fear in the community and rouses sympathy in the spectators. One specific issue that Achebe admits is Aristotle's schematic and technical approach to his discourse on tragedy. The misfortune that befalls the hero is not of his making. In

---

[387] Charles H. Rowell, "An Interview with Chinua Achebe," *Chinua Achebe's Things Fall Apart: a casebook*, Isidore Okpewho, ed (Oxford: Oxford University Press, 2003), pp. 265-266.
[388] See Anieke, *op. cit.,* pp. 42-45; See David I. Ker, *The African Novel and the Modernist Tradition* (New York: Peter Lang, 1997), p. 27.

Achebe's work, Okonkwo's tragedy is associated with his *Chi* or his Fate.[389] This is an important remark which will be later philosophically and hermeneutically discussed in chapter four.

At this point, I shall now focus on another important area of my thesis with regard to tragedy narrative. Here we take a look at the hermeneutics of language used by Achebe in his narrative. What is the function of language (English language) in his narrative and could any other language have been better in understanding his narrative?

3.4 An Overview of Achebe's Narrative Chapters

Things Fall Apart is a fiction book by Achebe. It was published when most works of fiction about Africa were written primarily by Europeans. Achebe's book is a narrative set to reflect the Igbo African world of the late 1800s to early 1900s in a village of Umuofia. As a novel published during the agitation for independence among Africa countries from the European colonial administrations, it is part of the quest for critical philosophical reflection of African beingness/existence, belongingness, African philosophical identity, recognition, self-determination and nationhood.[390]

Many African countries shortly began to determine the course of their nationhood. For instance, Ghana had her independence in 1958 and Nigeria got hers in 1960. Also with Joseph Conrad's *Heart of Darkness* which was a popular colonial narrative at this time, that misrepresented African ideas and cultures, many young African scholars began to get involved in critical thinking and the publication of their thoughts. With this exciting experience of self-determination and belongingness, Achebe sets for himself the goal to provide narratives of African philosophical life-world (in literary context) from an African perspective.[391] This period of the late 1950s is classified as a

---

[389] Fate is an essential part of Okonkwo's tragedy in Achebe. Stephen Halliwell acknowledges the possibility of difference in considering the Greek's use of tragedy. He notes, "Tragedy's access to deep feelings of pity and fear in its audience presupposes a delicate tension whereby an affinity ('likeness') with the tragic characters can be experienced, but without the erasure of altruistic by self-regarding emotion which *too close* an identification would produce." See Stephen Halliwell, *Aristotle's Poetics, op. cit.*, pp. 178-179.

[390] McLaren, *op. cit.*, p. 19; See Alan R. Friesen, "Okonkwo's Suicide as an Affirmative Act: Do Things Really Fall Apart?," *Critical Insights, op. cit.*

[391] *Ibid.*

historical and cultural epoch that puts in written language the worldviews of the Igbo of Nigeria. Michael J. Echeruo,[392] William Safire Professor of Modern Letters in the English Department of Syracuse University, New York, USA, acknowledges that most cultural narratives and fictions about Africa were then written by Europeans "for the education and entertainment of the [European] author's native readers" and not truly "about Africa in any important sense."[393]

My purpose here is to present the chapters of Achebe's text that set the tone for a hermeneutical narrative of tragedy. I shall focus on the significant situations leading to what is considered as tragedy in Achebe. The actual interpretation of this narrative in the light of Gadamer's claim of the universality of hermeneutics and the hermeneutics principles will take place in chapter four below. Part of what we have here in chapter three could be referred to as the Igbo African hermeneutics or understanding of meanings of some African concepts. Let us now look at the chapters of Achebe's *Things Fall Apart* text.[394]

Chapters one to three: Okonkwo was the son of a lazy and unsuccessful man called Unoka. Although Unoka was poor and lazy, he was known for his love of music as a skilled flute player, for his use of language and proverbs. Okonkwo was sad about his father's unsuccessful life. But he became a wealthy farmer through hard work and was a respected man in his community (Umuofia.) As a young man, he brought honor to his village by defeating the great Amalinze the Cat in a wrestling match. Okonkwo was a great hero-personality and well-known in the community. It was not long after that he started to display an exaggerated perception of himself.

After the murder of a young woman of Okonkwo's village by someone from Mbaino, Okonkwo was sent to deliver a message to Mbaino people that they make reparation for the death of the young woman by handing over to Umuofia a virgin maid and a young man, or get ready for war. Mbaino people agreed by handing to Okonkwo a virgin and young man named Ikemefuna.

---

[392] He is a literary critic. He is a notable critic of western writers on Africa. He is a member of the Modern Language Association of America (MLA.)

[393] Michael Joseph Echeruo, *Joyce Cary and the Novel of Africa* (London: Longman, 1973), pp. 1-26; See McLaren, "Things Fall Apart: Cultural and Historical Contexts," *op. cit.*, p. 19.

[394] http://www.sparknotes.com/lit/things/section1.rhtml (Accessed September 24, 2013.) I have developed my own relevant analyses of the chapters of Achebe's at the influence of the works from Sparknotes and others.

When he returned to Umuofia, the virgin maid was given to Ogbuefi Udo, as a wife, while Ikemefuna was asked to live with Okonkwo. Ikemefuna was with Okonkwo's family for three years. He was well-loved in Okonkwo's household and became a good influence to Okonkwo's first son Nwoye, who Okonkwo considered to be lazy as his own father (Unoka.) Nwoye was twelve years old, while Ikemefuna was fifteen years old. In order to maintain his hero-status, fame and wealth, Okonkwo was very demanding of his family members, especially the boys.

Okonkwo became a successful farmer[395] by borrowing some yam seeds from Nwakibie (a famous farmer) in his village who admired Okonkwo for his hard work and great wrestling qualities. He gave Okonkwo more yam seeds than he requested (800 yam seeds). Okonkwo also received help from other people of good will in the community. When that year's harvest went through difficulties, because of drought, Okonkwo was not lucky because he had planted most of his yam seeds at the time. His family went through a rough time, but he persevered (*Analysis:* The peaceful co-existence and mutual love of Umuofia is seen in the friendship and support people give to one another. Nwakibe is willing to help Okonkwo, even beyond Okonkwo's expectations, by offering him more yam seeds for his planting. He loves Okonkwo for his hard work and fame. In the village, people sharing drinks and kola nuts show the peacefulness or the desire for peaceful existence in the community. When Unoka had a guest whom he owes, he welcomes the guest with a gift of kola nut. However, this does not prevent the guest from explaining the real purpose of his visit, even when it is such a sensitive matter as paying an old debt. Unoka uses suitable proverbs to communicate in beautiful ways that he is unable to pay his debt. It appears Achebe's text wants to present African in a unique perspective of being capable of using deep meaning and complex language to communicate her traditions and complex life-world. Earlier reports from colonialists considered Africans as having no clear culture/as savages but Achebe's text presents Africans as people who love language, communicate with proverbs and speech patterns, with literary and non-literary meanings. Although Unoka was good with words and proverbs, Okonkwo avoids being like his father (Unoka), Okonkwo becomes so obsessed and abusive in his own fatherly role. He hates the lazy trait of his father.)

---

[395] Tedros Kiros, *Moral Philosophy and Development: The Condition in Africa* (Ohio University Center for International Studies-Monographs in International Studies Africa Series Number 61, Athens, Ohio 1992), p. 169.

Chapter four: After a difficult farming season, Okonkwo worked on his crops and eventually succeeded in having a good harvest. The situation set the stage for the wrongheaded aspect of Okonkwo's life. People began to complain of his pride and arrogance while dealing with less fortunate members of the community. During the Week of Peace Okonkwo beat one of his wives (Ojiugo.) He was asked to make a sacrifice—*nso ani*—to appease the god of the land whom he had offended by breaking the peace of the Sacred Week. Okonkwo repented of his transgression, paid the fine and brought the materials for the sacrifice. After the Week of Peace, it was not long before the planting season started.

Chapter five: Shortly before the harvest season, a time to celebrate the New Yam festival, there were less work to be done and this was not a happy time for Okonkwo who liked to keep himself busy. One day, while he was about to go hunting, his second wife Ekwefi made a remark about his hunting gun that was as good as a dead gun or what she referred as "guns that were never shot,"[396] Okonkwo in anger fired the gun at her, but missed. One recalls that Ekwefi, Okonkwo's second wife, married him because of his wrestling strength and manliness. It is after the New Yam festival that the community had its wrestling match season.

Chapters six and seven: The wrestling matches were good for the young people of different age grades. Maduka, the son of Obierika, Okonkwo's friend won one of the wrestling matches which were the occasion to show manliness, bring fame and accolades to one's community.

Now, it was almost three years since Ikemefuna joined Okonkwo's family. One of the elders of the community, Ogbuefi Ezeudu, visited Okonkwo and advised him not to get involved in the killing of Ikemefuna since the young boy has so much adapted to being almost a family member of Okonkwo. He regarded Okonkwo as 'father.' Ikemefuna was a good friend of Nwoye (Okonkwo's son) and has told Nwoye folklores/stories from his own Mbaino community. Some of these folklores were never heard before in Umuofia. On the day of Ikemefuna's sacrifice, Okonkwo killed Ikemefuna himself in the bush. Nwoye had a bad feeling that his friend had been killed. He could tell because his father's mood changed after 'traveling with Ikemefuna.' (**Analysis for chapters four to seven:** Ikemefuna brings something

---

[396] Achebe, *Things Fall Apart* (Canada: Anchor Canada edition 2009), p. 39.

unique and different from his own community and background to Okonkwo (by extension Umuofia.) He adds some excitements to Nwoye's boring experience with his overbearing father. The intercultural situation with the colonial masters starts in a difficult way. There is the stereotype to lump all communities under one form of culture. Among the Igbo people alone, there is the *subculture* that shows a little instance of the difference among the unity of the Igbo and by extension Africans.

Although one regularly read of internecine wars in Achebe's text, one also notes that it was not a simple issue to declare war against another village. The village that has been wronged has to consult with the Oracles of their land to help determine what lies in the future, whether the war is just, whether it is going to be successful or not. It is a culture that emphasizes peaceful co-existence and any war fought ought to be a just war. Okonkwo delivers Umuofia's message to the people of Mbaino to allow them time to choose between peace and war. The entire community weighs the situation and prefers to make some reparations for the death of a young woman from Umuofia. In a similar way, when Okonkwo violated the Week of Peace by beating one of his wives, he was asked by the chief priest to make some reparations for putting the peace of the community in danger. Okonkwo was able to make the required sacrifices for peace to rain in Umuofia. So there is a culture of interpersonal understanding and inter-communal peaceful existence. Reparations and sacrifices were ways of leading every person and community on the path of peace. It is also means nothing is totally destroyed or one's fortune totally taken away. When reparations are made, then there is forgiveness, hope and a new beginning again. The belief in *Chi* among the people also helps allow peace to reign. The notion of *Chi* shall be discussed later in chapter four. *Chi* helps hinder extremes of pride and sadness of failure. Everyone's *Chi* is there to support one to succeed or to manage his/her shame without taking all the blames. Okonkwo apparently bears the blames for his abusive relationship with his family members because of his phobia of the weakness of his father (Unoka) and the cultural pressure (obsession with heroic cultural personage) of his society that sees the manliness character as a determinant of a successful person or a person of great status.)

Chapter eight: After the death of Ikemefuna, Okonkwo became depressed and would not eat very well. However, he tried to brighten himself up in order not to be seen as weak and unmanly. He visited his friend Obierika

140

to congratulate his son Maduka on his victory during the wrestling match. Maduka's manliness and bravery show his is set for a successful life. During his visit to his friend Obierika, a discussion arose about why Obierika did not participate in the killing of Ikemefuna. Obierika felt it was not up to him (Okonkwo) to kill Ikemefuna. For Okonkwo, if the killing of Ikemefuna had happened during the busier time of the year, it would have been easier for him to forget the incident by focusing on his huge farming responsibilities. It was not long while Okonkwo and Obierika were discussing the marriage visit of Obierika's in-laws-to-be that they received the news of the death of Ogbuefi Ezeudu, the oldest man in the village. It was also while visiting Obierika's family that news about the arrival of the white men in nearby village came to Okonkwo's notice. (*Analysis:* Okonkwo did not follow the prudent advice of an elder of his community. He determines to see the commands of the Oracle get accomplished and he wants to show he is man enough in doing the difficult task for the people. As a community warrior, he is never ready to give away his bravery. Okonkwo has a strong personality and willingness to protect the traditions of his ancestors, especially in killing Ikemefuna. Obierika thinks that it is a more appropriate thing to avoid participating in the killing of Ikemefuna. He seems to question some of the practices of his community in contrast to Okonkwo's excessive attachment to the traditions of his people. Although the manliness of Obierika is not in question, but his loyalty to his ancestral traditions is apparent. Okonkwo prefers to follow the practices of his people without questioning it at all. Nwoye, his son, is more like Obierika in questioning some of the practices of the community.)

Chapter nine: Okonkwo had a tough family incident. One night one of his wives (Ekwefi) woke him up to report that Ezinma his daughter was dying. Ekwefi has got only Ezinma after losing about nine children at infancy. She had given her children different Igbo names that are symbolic and with deeper traditional meanings. One, she named *Onwubiko*—meaning "Death, I implore you," and, the other, *Ozoemena*—meaning "May it not happen again." For the Igbo there is always a meaning to a name. *Ezinma* means "Good path or the future looks good" (*Ezi*—'path', *nma*—'good.') Ezinma's situation made Okonkwo seek for the herbs to cure his daughter and even went further to make inquiries from a medicine man who told him that Ezinma was an *Ogbanje*—"a 'wicked' child that torments parents." An *Ogbanje* is a 'problem' child that re-enters its mother womb only to be born and to die too soon to cause parents grief. (*Analysis:* A *needy* child is a *special* child to the mother and father. Ezinma's health situation and her mother's history of losing babies cause her to be loved as a special child. Ekwefi and Ezinma are not a typical mother and daughter. Ezinma is a good companion to her mother who has gone through pains of losing her children. The cooperation between the three wives of Okonkwo is exemplary. They are very supportive of Ekwefi and she is not jealous of any of them because of their children. She worries because of her not-so-lucky motherhood situation. Okonkwo is protective and supportive of Ekwefi and Ezinma. The names given to the dead children reveal an important aspect of Igbo practice. Their stories are part of their names. These names show the philosophical and hermeneutical meanings of Igbo names and how they explain or throw light on the situation or the narratives surrounding a person's birth or history. One could gain deeper meaning by thinking through the names in the narratives. We shall further discuss the hermeneutics of Igbo names in the narrative under this chapter three, *3.5.1*, and the intercultural problem of language in chapter four, *4. 1*.

Chapters ten to thirteen: There was a ceremonial gathering in the village to administer justice in the community. It was administered through *Egwugwu* considered to be the clan's ancestral spirit but some people believed that *Egwugwu* is really the masked men who acted like spirits. This group resolved disputes between husbands and wives (family problems), and other small problems in the community. Okonkwo, it is believed, is a member of this group.

In Okonkwo's family, Ekwefi told a story to her daughter and this story has a message or meaning to teach her about greed. In the folklore, the tortoise and the birds were all invited to a party in heaven. The tortoise deceived the birds by claiming his name is "All of you." When food and drinks were provided at the occasion, the host said they belonged to "All of you" and the tortoise claimed they were his since he goes by the name "All of you." He took away all the food and drinks. But when it was time to return to earth, the birds retaliated and punished the tortoise by not providing him with some of their feathers to fly back to earth. Even when one of the birds offered to help the tortoise deliver his message to his wife to prepare a safe landing place for him, the bird gave false information that tortoise has asked for stones and sharp objects in his compound set for his arrival. The tortoise actually asked for some safety foams or air bags for safe landing from heaven. Sadly, the tortoise fell on the hard earth and crashed. This story explained how the tortoise got a patched-up like shell. While Ekwefi was telling the story, Chielo, the priestess of the Oracle of the Hills and Caves arrived to carry Ezinma to the cave of the Oracle because the Oracle demanded to see Ezinma. Chielo warned Okonkwo and Ekwefi not to defy the message or demands of the gods. Ekwefi followed the priestess to the place, and Okonkwo later came to see the health situation of his family members. (*Analysis:* The depth of African meanings could be communicated through allegories and so a named object cannot be taken literally in a narrative. Tortoise is known for his wisdom or witty life. Birds are known for generosity and friendship. It is like in Philo's allegorical interpretation (in chapter one) where objects represent something different and deeper meaning. The visit of the priestess is to transmit a message to the family of Okonkwo about the demands of the Oracle. This is similar to the Greek notion of hermeneutics that is considered as a message coming from the gods and needs to be explained to the people.)

(*Chapter thirteen*): Shortly after the death of Ogbuefi Ezeudu, there were preparations for his burial. Ezeudu was a respected man in the community and had many titles (he had taken three of all four titles of the land.) He was the elderly man that visited Okonkwo to advise him against participating in killing Ikemefuna. In a bid to give the elder citizen a befitting funeral by using his gun to honor Ogbuefi Ezendu, Okonkwo accidentally killed the sixteen-year old son of Ogbuefi Ezeudu (the deceased.) For such incidents, it is evil to spill the blood of a clansman, although it was all an accident. It was an abomination to the Earth goddess. In the apparent absence of other options to appease the goddess of the land, Okonkwo is left with one option: to immediately flee with his family from his community. (*Analysis:* Okonkwo pays the price for the purification of the land by leaving Umuofia to his maternal land (Mbanta) for a seven-year exile and his compound is reduced to rubbles. Okonkwo's exile was a way of giving the family of Ezeudu and the community the time to heal and forget the incident. Okonkwo has already paid the price of that unfortunate incident by losing his home. Obierika, Okonkwo's friend, participates in the destruction of his house. One may wonder why Obierika participated in destroying Okonkwo's house (even when Okonkwo is still regarded a village hero and warrior) but yet Obierika would not participate in fulfilling the demands of the Oracle that Ikemefuna must die. He is actually reluctant to participate in such demand by the Earth goddess for an accidental killing of a sixteen-year old boy (Ezeudu's son.))

Chapters fourteen to sixteen: At his maternal land, Okonkwo was received by his uncle Uchendu and his people. They helped him build his new house, offered him a piece of land to farm, and seeds for planting. Okonkwo hoped to rise in prominence and success, but thing did not work out at first. Unfortunately, the first planting did not go very well and Okonkwo became depressed. Uchendu had to make Okonkwo regain his confidence by letting him know of his (Uchendu's) own pains and loses in life. He wanted to let him know that he had earlier lost wives and children, but life has to go on. There is hope in the future. Life is most important.

(*Chapter fifteen*): It was not long Okonkwo was visited by his friend Obierika with some local currencies from selling some of Okonkwo's yams. He also reported to Okonkwo the recent intercultural problems going on in their community since the arrival of the white man and his Christian group. Already an ugly incident had taken place between the people of Abame and the colonial masters. The Abame people consulted with their Oracle which 'prophesied' that Abame will be invaded by the colonizers and that will lead to the destruction of the land of Abame. The people of Abame tried to prevent it by first attacking the one single white man they saw in their community. The colonial masters knowing that one of them has been killed attacked in return and destroyed Abame. Uchendu wanted to know from Obierika what the white man said to Abame people that warranted their killing him. For Obierika, the white man said something that the people of Abame did not "understand"-this is the main issue of hermeneutics to understand what the other has to say. Okonkwo wished that the Abame people had obeyed their Oracle by getting better prepared for war with the colonial masters.

(*Chapter sixteen*): Obierika visited Okonkwo for the second time. He reported to Okonkwo about seeing his son, Nwoye, who has joined the Christian group–part of the colonial group that invaded Umuofia. One of the interpreters of the white men, Mr. Kiaga, was known to speak a different dialect that has a funny sound when expressing Igbo word for "myself" (*Ikem*) that comes off as "my buttock" (*ikem*). This caused people to make fun of Mr. Kiaga. The Christian group preached about one God that has a son and is also a *Trinity*. This is contrary to the worldviews of Umuofia people. They could not fathom a God having a son and that also means having a wife. The Christian group considered Umuofia gods as false gods. This did not go well with the people because their culture/religion was considered inferior to the

Christian missionaries. This situation presented the depth of misunderstanding and misrepresentation in the narrative (***Analysis:*** The role of the maternal land cannot be overemphasized. The name- *Nneka* (Mother is supreme/great) - is justified in Okonkwo seeking refuge in his mother's hometown (feminine world.) The situation contrasts with Okonkwo's exaggeration of the masculine aspect of his personality. His helpless exile shows the weakness in his life— the feminine personality. He finds it difficult to accept being exiled from his community where he is famous and respected. Uchendu, his maternal uncle, rebukes Okonkwo and reminds him that he is not alone in his difficulties. He reminds him the true meaning of "Nneka" in his current situation.

Okonkwo's friend Obierika visits him for the first time with money from the sale of Okonkwo's farm produce. Okonkwo is happy for his friends visit but then the coming of the Christian missionaries to Umuofia worries him because the traditions of his ancestors are under attack. The intercultural relationship starts on a negative perspective between the colonizers and the local people. One group condemns the activities of the other. The conversion of the people of Umuofia and other communities must be carried out as a force of change by the European Christian group, while the Christian group is a force that must be attacked in return by the local people. The tragic intercultural consequences of this misunderstanding have not been clearly foreseen by both cultures: Africans and Europeans.)

Chapters seventeen to nineteen: The missionaries or the Christian group received a piece of land to build their church. The elders and the community gave them the 'Evil' forest, hoping that they will be afraid to build their church there or even that the bad spirits of the evil forest will attack them before twenty-eight days. But after twenty-eight days nothing happened to them. The missionaries were happy for the land and since nothing happened to them many of the local people began to convert to this new 'fearless' religion. Many other people converted to the new religion were referred as the *efulefu* (people without title or unworthy of recognition in the community.) Okonkwo considered Nwoye's conversion (abandoning his ancestral religion) a non-manly approach to life. Nwoye has started already to progress in his education with the Christian group. Some of the Christian members started to attack the traditions of Umuofia people. In Mbanta, the elders agreed to ostracize those who joined the missionaries, but they did not send them out of Mbanta as Okonkwo had hoped. It was not long, one of the new converts who boasted of killing a Sacred python (a sacred animal in the community) died and the elders concluded that the ancestors have defended or re-affirmed themselves.

Okonkwo's seven years in exile was nearing completion. He was excited to return to Umuofia as a successful man, even in a foreign land. He organized a generous feast for his maternal Uncle's families, thanked them for their welcome and support all these seven years. However, deep within him, Okonkwo always wished that his accomplishments had happened in Umuofia rather than elsewhere. At the feast, Okonkwo was reminded again about the Christian missionaries and the changes they have brought in Umuofia and how the young people have been led to believe that the new religion was better and offered them education. The conflict between the traditional religion and the Christian religion continued. (**Analysis:** The arrival of the missionaries causes some opposition among the people with regard to respect of their traditional practices. The new group destroys the socio-political structure and values of the people with regard to leadership (Elders were respected before.) There was disunity among the local people. The Christian missionaries welcomed people who were never regarded in the community and so gave them a sense of belonging. Although the community seems to be a welcoming place for people, it still set people at the margins of life. The Christian group offers hope and opportunities to those who were dissatisfied with some of the traditional religious practices. The outcasts or *osu* found a new voice and a new family in the Christian group. Not everyone is as unwelcoming to the Christian group as Okonkwo. His maternal uncle Uchendu is very thoughtful and ready to accept a genuine intercultural relationship between the people and the new religionists.)

Chapters twenty to twenty-one: Okonkwo had his new home built in Umuofia. He had advised his daughters not to marry in Mbanta but to wait until they returned to Umuofia. It appeared this decision was made to show Okonkwo's control of his family and his determination for them to be well-known in their community. Okonkwo had to wait until his return to encourage his two sons to take titles so as to keep them focused on the traditions of their ancestors. During a discussion, Okonkwo and his friend Obierika talked about the harm done to their community by the Christian missionaries/new culture. Okonkwo was surprised that Umuofia had not done anything to stop this conversion. He was also aware of a young man in Aneto who was hanged by the colonial administration/government.

On a positive side, the Christian missionaries have really transformed the communities, with schools, hospitals, education and skill-acquisition centers. Mr. Brown was known to have adopted a better policy of intercultural practice, mutual understanding and respect among the two religions adherents. He encouraged Umuofians to make use of the opportunities so that more young interpreters from outside Umuofia will not take the jobs and determine the 'destiny' of Umuofia people. Mr. Brown did not stay that long before he took ill. He had to return back to his homeland, but he was quite good in respecting the differences of the people. He was replaced by Reverend Smith. Following Okonkwo's return, his disappointment about Umuofia was that things were no longer the same. He could not offer his boys the opportunities to get initiated into *ozo* ceremonial title because it was done every three year and had to wait until it was time again to take the titles.(**Analysis:** Achebe's text is not a one-sided evaluation of the activities of the Christian missionaries in his community. He presents a balanced evaluation of the colonial intercultural practices. There are some socio-economic benefits arising from the cross-cultural interactions of these two religions/cultures. In the end, Obierika thinks that Igbo language is difficult to understand and any encounter without language is almost impossible. Language is important in understanding any culture. Achebe's text also shows how culture and language are bound together.)

Chapter twenty-two: Reverend Smith was not as compassionate as Mr. Brown. He demanded total acceptance of the bible from his church men and women. He changed Mr. Brown's accommodating and tolerant intercultural approach. Following the change of leadership among the Christian missionaries, the new converts were very orthodox and more zealous to confront the traditional religionists. One of the new converts, Enoch, threatened to unmask the *Egwugwu* during the festival that honors the Earth deity. To unmask the *Egwugwu* is considered a *deicide* (equals to killing of an ancestral spirit.) For doing this, the *Egwugwu* group destroyed Enoch's home and threatened to destroy the church as well in order to cleanse the land of Enoch's evil action. During the confrontation between *Egwugwu* and the Christian group, Reverend Smith's interpreter tried to avoid an ugly situation by translating in a less direct and harsh manner what Reverend Smith said, which the interpreter thought would cause more problems if the people had understood it. Despite the interpreter saying that Reverend Smith has promised to the take care of the situation himself, the *Egwugwu* group went ahead and destroyed the church.

Chapter twenty-three: The new development excited Okonkwo. At least the *Egwugwu* group had stood up against the Christian missionaries. He was not completely happy that the Christian group was not killed or sent out from Umuofia. When the District Commissioner returned from his travels, he invited the elders of Umuofia for a meeting, where he promised that a peaceful resolution will be accomplished. Unfortunately, he spoke to Umuofia elders in a condescending manner and said he wanted the Umuofia people to resolve the issues as friends. Because the District Commissioner suggested resolving the issues as friends, it made the elders who had gone to that meeting with their machetes (should there be need for self-defense) put them down on the floor. The elders were deceived by the District Commissioner and were arrested by a group of soldiers, and imprisoned for several days. They suffered physical and emotional abuses while in jail. Although the Court had asked that each elder will be released on bail after paying two hundred cowries (local currency), the court messengers/ interpreters asked for two hundred and fifty cowries so that the make some profits out of the people. They court messengers demanded that the fine must be paid or the elders will be hanged. The town crier announced to the community about the situation and they began to plan to raise the money to bail their elders. (*Analysis:* Reverend Smith's intercultural policies change was a very strict relationship of "black and white." He had no plans to accommodate the Igbo traditional beliefs and practices. The confrontations between the groups become violent, especially now that communication has failed. The language gap between the colonial masters and the people was so wide. Even when the interpreters try to play a little role to resolve issues, it was difficult to arrive at something mutually accommodating. Somehow Mr. Brown's argument is vindicated that the people of Umuofia should educate themselves so that other people will not determine their future progress. It seems Mr. Brown name is symbolic here because his name suggests another possibility of color—meaning everything about life is not only 'white or black.' There is also the 'grey or brown' (Mr. Brown) aspect that we have to tread carefully with and thoughtfully understand. Enoch appears to contrast with Okonkwo. Unlike Okonkwo's father, Enoch's father is known to be the son of the snake-priest (the royal python) and this makes his killing the sacred python a very serious offense. His temperament reminds us of Okonkwo and his interest to get rid of the Christian group in order to preserve the cultural traditions of his ancestors. For Enoch it was to get rid of the ancestral traditions of his people.)

Chapter twenty-four: The elders were released from jail where they were emotional and physically abused and humiliated. The village was in utmost silence and gloomy. The next day the elders gathered to discuss the events that have taken place. Okonkwo had decided to stand up for himself no matter what the village people have chosen to do, especially if it is contrary to preserving the traditions of their ancestor or going to war. While the meeting was going on, five court messengers approached the elders and demanded that the meeting be stopped because the District Commissioner had said so. Okonkwo was not happy and so used his machete to kill one of them and the rest of the court messengers ran away. When he expected his people of Umuofia to defend their land and fight to the last man, his people disappointed him. He was disappointed that they could not act as one people and finish off the rest of the court messengers. With the recent happenings, "Umuofia has already been transmogrified into a clay-footed giant. Okonkwo's disappointment is unimaginable. He goes away and commits suicide. Things have indeed fallen apart in the Igbo society Umuofia!"[397] It was the end of a life of series of tragic events.

Chapter twenty-five: The District Commissioner arrived at Okonkwo's compound to arrest him for killing one of the court messengers. He met with a number of elders who were discussing the recent events and the tragedy that has befallen them. The District Commissioner asked of Okonkwo but no one would tell him were he was. With a threat to imprison all the elders, one of them Obierika accepted to take the District Commissioner to were Okonkwo was. It was then the District Commissioner saw Okonkwo's body dangling from a tree. He had committed suicide. As the custom was, when one commits suicide, the person's body is regarded as evil and only strangers could touch the body. Obierika expressed his frustration against the colonial masters represented by the District Commissioner and Reverend Smith for being responsible for Okonkwo's death. They have pushed him to the wall. Obierika requests from the District Commissioner that his messenger (being strangers) should help bury Okonkwo's body. The District Commissioner was initially hesitant but later agreed to allow only his messengers to help with burying the body.

---

[397] Anieke, *op. cit.*, p. 39.

The District Commissioner left with excitement on having learned a few new things about the Igbo African traditions and culture—suicide is considered as evil and strangers bury those who committed suicide. He hopes that the information he gathered from Okonkwo's incident will form a paragraph or a chapter of his book entitled: *The Pacification of the Primitive Tribes of the Lower Niger*. (This may be another book like the *Heart of Darkness* where writers tell stories about things they do not clearly understand within the African community.) (*Analysis:* Okonkwo chooses to address the confrontation by the colonial masters in his own way in order to protect his ancestral traditions. He terribly feels the humiliation that threatens his ancestral traditions and the imprisonment that makes him look like a pauper in a community he is regarded a hero/ a warrior. The District Commissioner frustrates the opportunity to understand the people more because he was misrepresenting the culture of Umuofia people. He thinks that the local people are good at using superfluous words, instead of listening to understand that Igbos love to speak in a particular manner. The local people like their proverbs and wise sayings. Unfortunately, Okonkwo's tragic death is considered as a good highlight in the District Commissioner's forthcoming book on Africa. He fails to see the tragedy and pain in the community.

From the events in the book, there is a complex situation in understanding if Okonkwo's death is a personal tragedy or determined by his *Chi*—which will suggest a communal tragedy. It depends on the reader or the interpreter to justify his/her position through his/her arguments about whose tragedy it is. One thing is certain, that Achebe did not present a perfect picture of African culture. He also wants to present a balanced view of the colonial masters and their operations in Umuofia. The intercultural situation re-echoes the demand for further effort in intercultural understanding in our current philosophical and hermeneutical world. So far the colonialists have provided an account of the local people to serve the interest of the colonial masters and Achebe tells his own story or his own interpretation of his philosophical world as an African.)

From the above, there are two sides of one intercultural problem that I will like to focus on: **a**) *Problem of Language*, and **b**) *Problem of Hermeneutics/interpretation* are the two sides of the one problem of understanding.

3.5 Achebe and Language

There is no doubt that Achebe's Western education was instrumental to his use of English language. Western colonial education was part of the influencing factors that motivated his fiction novel in response to what he read from some English European writers about his African people. Francis Abiola Irele, an African literary scholar and Visiting Professor of African and African American Studies and of Romance Languages and Literatures at Harvard University, argues that Achebe is a man of two worlds: a) a pre-colonial African, and b) Western world of experience. These influenced his creative awareness and the sensibilities of his education affected his ability in the reconstruction of his narrative. It is on the sad experiences of the colonial days that Achebe's narrative is based. His education gave him his status "as a Westernized African, the product of Christian education."[398] This view about his new status as a Westernized African does imply that using English language was a privilege, a sign of acceptance and a form of compliance in narrative about African reality from a perspective that does not communicate the totality of the truth and meaning of his world, although he had the good intention to do so.

With the influence of his Western colonial education, Achebe insists that using English language was the best available option at the time of writing his novel. English language was the main educational language[399] of the then Igbo communities during the colonial era. In 1964, Achebe said: "Is it right that a man should abandon his mother tongue for someone else's? It looks like a dreadful betrayal and produces a guilty feeling. But for me there is no other choice. I have been given the language and I intend to us it."[400] Ogede explains:

> Achebe addressed the debate regarding the appropriate language
> of African literature in an essay entitled 'The African Writer and

---

[398] http://web.africa.ufl.edu/asq/v4/v4i3a1.htm (Accessed March 18, 2011.) Francis Abiola Irele, "The Tragic Conflict in the Novels of Chinua Achebe," *Critical Perspectives on Chinua Achebe*, Lyn Innes and Bernth Lindfors, eds (Washington DC: Three Continents Press, 1978.)

[399] Pandurang, *op. cit.*, p. 345.

[400] Ngugi wa Thiong'o, *Decolonising the Mind: The Politics of Language in African Literature* (London: Heinemann, 1986), p. 7; Kalu Ogbaa, *Understanding Things Fall Apart: A Student Casebook to Issues, Sources, and Historical Documents* (Westport, Connecticut: The Greenwood Press, 1999), p. 195.

the English Language', in which he envisions 'a new voice coming out of Africa, speaking of African experience in a world-wide language'. This domesticated English language, he writes, must be one 'prepared to pay... submission to many different kinds of use'; a language able to' bring out' the African writer's 'message best' without being altered 'to the extent that its value as a medium of international language will be lost'.[401]

Achebe formulated a language-style in which to tell his African story. He was concerned with how to tell his story and the language to articulate it. Isidore Okpewho, Doctor of Comparative Literature from the University of Denver, USA, commends Achebe's original English novel. Okpewho points out that there was a form of conflict between indigenous language and the language of empowerment. The language of empowerment for the Anglophone, which is English, serves those who use it for economic purposes and status. Okpewho is of the opinion that Achebe was systemic in bringing in the indigenous language with English.[402]

According to Abdul Janmohamed, Professor of English University of California, Berkeley, for an African writer the decision to use English as the language of communication is beclouded by paradoxes and contradictions. It is difficult for an African writer not to write in English "because he was born in a British colony and can receive formal education only in English... he recreated himself ... by adopting the appropriate European language as well as literary forms."[403] But in order to accommodate the realities of the two worlds and cultures that confronted Achebe, he decided to bring in Igbo words in his English narrative. He truly had the interest to develop his language (Igbo) so he domesticated an Igbo-based English narrative. *Things Fall Apart* is a return to cultural hermeneutics and the renewal of a culture. Achebe's narrative is an attempt to save African culture and worldviews from the ontological and hermeneutical problem of misrepresentation. This argument for a true ontological representation of one's reality strengthens my argument that an

---

[401] Ogede, *op. cit.*, p. 97.

[402] Isidore Okpewho, "On the Concept: "Commonwealth Literature," *Meditations on African Literature*, Dubem Okafor, ed (CT: Greenwood Press, 2001), pp. 35-38.

[403] Abdul Janmohamed, "Sophisticated Primitivism: The Syncretism of Oral and Literate Modes in Achebe's *Things Fall Apart*," *Chinua Achebe Things Fall Apart (Authoritative Text, Contexts and Criticism)*, Francis Abiola Irele, ed (New York: W. W. Norton & Company, 2009), p. 572.

indigenous African life-world and its meaning ought to be communicated fu.
in an African language. This agrees with Achebe's own confirmed opinion that
before writing his narrative "that his earliest sensibilities were enshrined in the
Igbo language and storytelling tradition while growing up 'fond of stories and
intrigued by language-first Igbo, spoken with such eloquence by the old men
of the village, and later English which I began to learn at the age of eight'."[404]
This addresses the almost inevitable situation that Achebe found himself with
regard to English usage. He had a limited option to use the language of his
education and Igbo language of his culture. In order to bring in a sort of
adaptability, he puts in the Igbo words as would be the case in a normal oral
tradition.

3.5.1 Achebe: English and Igbo Languages

Okonkwo's world is an Igbo world. Igbo language is the language of
conversation of the people of Umuofia. Language and human finitude go
together. Language and thinking go together as words and concepts go
together. In dialogues or conversations we make use of language. Conversation
is always going on and in it is an infinite task for mutual understanding to take
place. The basic structure of language is mutual understanding
(*Übereinkommen*) in a conversation. Does Achebe's use of English language
constitute any difficulties to understanding Africans by the Europeans?
Although this question does not follow from the teaching of philosophical
hermeneutics, as some scholars hold, it follows from the concern of
understanding true meaning itself and how our thought and language match
with reality. We are always after understanding something and we question
whatever hinders accessing a people's truth. Meanwhile, Achebe's main
purpose is clear: telling African truths by Africans themselves.[405]

Achebe adopts the use of Igbo concepts mixed in an English language
narrative[406] for the purpose of receptivity of his work. As I indicated earlier,
there is a cultural proximity in Achebe's use of Igbo concepts and English

---

[404] Ogede, *op. cit.,* pp. 10-11.
[405] This issue will be further addressed in chapter four (Application of Gadamer's hermeneutics.)
[406] Some have described it as "Engli-Igbo"-a combination of English and Igbo languages or Igbo flavored English language. Christian Anieke affirms that Achebe's novels are full of Engli-Igbo or bilingualism. See Anieke, *op. cit.*, p. 63. See McLaren, *op. cit.*, p. 27-28.

Achebe uses the Igbo names of the individuals and their
ties. These names are meant to reflect the reality of the people. It is
hermeneutics of the Igbo worldview which does assist African and
foreign readers of Achebe's literature. Without this knowledge, it is difficult to
understand the deep thoughts in Achebe's Igbo narrative. Igbo language has a
complex cultural subtext, like any other language, a transliteration may not
represent the reality of the people as it was intended or the truth of their world
as it ought to be understood. For instance, if Achebe had written the
'Masquerade', the concept of "Egwugwu" will be lost or almost meaningless
in the narrative. *Egwugwu* means in Igbo hermeneutics—"one who
impersonates one of the ancestral spirits of the village." Its duty is to uphold
justice and solve family problems. To attack *Egwugwu* is not to attack a fellow
mortal. It is to attack a spirit. Igbo names are very helpful in carrying out a
genuine hermeneutical task in Igbo world. In the text, Ekwefi calls one of her
dead children "*Onwuma*"---meaning "Death may please himself."[407] The story
of her family is understood in the names given to the children. We shall
discuss this further in chapter four. When an English person says: "Mr.
Smith"—it is just "Mr. Smith" or with a little add story about "Mr. Smith." For
the Igbos it is quite different. Another good example is: my full name is
written- '*Stanley Uche Anozie*.' In deep Igbo hermeneutics, "***Stanley***" provides
no meaning to an Igbo person other than it is an English Christian name,
whereas "*Uche*" and "*Anozie*" are more thought-filled names and deeply
meaningful for the Igbo African person. "*Uche*" is a short for "*Uche-chukwu*"
or "*Uche-chi*" (*Chi* for God) meaning "God's will or the will of God";
"Anozie" meanings "I have settled down." It could also be used to explain
"one who has overcome a difficult challenge."

Another good example is Achebe (the author of our narrative text). His
full name reads "*Albert Chinualumogu Achebe*." The name "***Albert***" has no
hermeneutical meaning for the Igbo people of Achebe's narrative, except that
it is an English Christian baptismal name. The meaningful part of Achebe's
names are "*Chinua*" which is a short for "*Chinua-lumogu*" meaning "May my
God (*Chi*) fight for me or may my God (*Chi*) fight my battle for me or standup
in my defense." The author's last name "*Achebe*" is a short form of a long

---

[407] Achebe, *Things Fall Apart* (Canada: Anchor Canada edition, 2009), p. 77.

meaning. "*Chebe*" means "to protect or to guard."[408] The closely related root meaning is from another Igbo name: "*Anichebem*" meaning "May the Land (or the Land deity) protect me." "*Ani*" means "Land" or "Earth" and "*ichebem*" meaning "a personal request to be protected by the god of the Land or the Earth goddess." One recalls that the Earth goddess in *Things Fall Apart* narrative received many sacrifices of reparations or purification from people who violated her commands to avoid calamity befalling the entire people.[409] "*Chi-chebem*" and "*Nna-chebem*" (*Chi* or *Nna* means God) are other ways of saying the same the Igbo name "*Achebe*" meaning also "May God or god protect me." This answers the question: does the use of English language constitute any difficulties in understanding Africans? Again, this shall be further discussed in chapter four. According to McLaren, "the Igbo of that period would have expressed themselves in Igbo.... unlike Conrad in *Heart of Darkness*...[Achebe] he has maintained the spirit of the oral tradition by incorporating elements of it."[410]

Igbo tradition was an oral tradition. Achebe combines the Igbo and English languages for effective communication. He makes Igbo language enjoy the relevance of a written tradition. The aesthetics of Achebe's style of making Igbo part of a written tradition is seen, for instance, in this line: Ekwefi commands her daughter Ezinna to remove her waist beads: "Remove your *jigida* first."[411] Ogede referencing Achebe's language style observes:

> English and Igbo thought patterns fuse harmoniously. As good an example as any of this linguistic harmony is Ekwefi's reprimanding comments to her daughter Ezinna while the two help in getting the food ready for the bride-pricing reception of Akueke, Obierika's daughter: 'Remove your *jigida* first,' her mother warned as she moved near the fireplace to bring the pestle resting against the wall. 'Everyday I tell you that *jigida* and fire

---

[408] I use "guard me" because the Igbos are known to travel on business trips or for economic reasons and so will ordinarily ask the gods of their land to guard or protect them on the journey.

[409] Achebe, *Things Fall Apart, op. cit.,* pp. 30-31. The priest of the Earth goddess, Ani, calls Okonkwo and warns him "The evil you have done can ruin the whole clan. The earth goddess whom you have insulted may refuse to give us her increase, and we shall all perish." This similar situation happens when Okonkwo accidentally kills Ogbuefi Ezeudu's son (*Ibid.*, pp. 124-125.) I prefer to use capital letter to begin Land or Earth as a mark of religious respect of these concepts.

[410] McLaren, *op. cit.,* pp. 27-28.

[411] Achebe, *Things Fall Apart, op. cit.,* p. 71.

are not friends. But you will never hear. You grew ears for decoration, not for hearing. One of these days your *jigida* will catch fire on your waist, and then you will know'. This passage summons to life not only the rhythm, rhetoric and verbal echo, but also the light, gentle tenor of Igbo speech, which, rendered into English, gives the remarks they carry a new vigour.[412]

Achebe had many ways to narrate his story which could be different from an English person's approach to narrative. He has a peculiar control and usage of English language with Igbo concepts which gives him the advantage of a genuine novelist and a historical authenticity. The basis for this historical authenticity is because of Achebe's use of English language. This argument we have already criticized above because it is a status of colonial privilege to identify with its 'language of privilege.' Achebe by his use of English positively develops many prose styles in line with communicating the subject matter of his narrative. So he is more of a Europeanized African rather than "an illiterate village elder."[413] In other words, it is an issue of privilege, a new status issue to communicate the truth of African world first in a foreign language rather than a hermeneutic matter. As a valid hermeneutic concern for Achebe himself, he tries to address this problem which means he (Achebe) acknowledges that there is a language (interpretation) problem.[414]

According to Obiwu Iwuanyawu, Director of Writing Center at Central State University in Wilberforce, Ohio, Achebe acknowledges the demand for literature in African language. However, he felt his target of creating a language for African narrative has been accomplished. He has tried to accommodate this language change in his other writings. Presently, there are about five known translations of *Things Fall Apart* into Igbo-going on simultaneously and also translations into five other African languages, like Kikuyu, Yoruba etc. *Things Fall Apart* has been translated into fifty languages and sold about ten million copies which explain how successful it has been.

---

[412] Ogede, *op. cit.*, pp. 21-22; Achebe, *Things Fall Apart* (Canada: Anchor Canada edition, 2009), p. 71.
[413] Lindfors, *op. cit.*, p. 556; See Lindfors, "African Vernacular Styles in Nigerian Fiction," *CLA Journal*, 9 (1966), pp. 265-273; Gerald Moore, "English Words, African Lives," *Presence Africaine*, No. 54 (1965), pp. 90-101; Ezekiel Mphahlele, "The Language of African Literature," *Harvard Educational Review*, 34 (Spring 1964), pp. 298-305; Jones, *op. cit.*, pp. 39-43.
[414] *Ibid.*

Part of the success of this work is based on the style: the use of English and Igbo languages. According to Janmohamed's analysis:

> In fact, the congruence between the style, elements of the narrative structure, and characterization, on the one hand, and the nature of the culture represented, on the other, account for the success of the novel: because Achebe is able to capture the flavour of an oral society in his style and narrative organization, *Things Fall Apart* is able to represent successfully the specificity of a culture alien to most Western readers.[415]

There is a successful reception of Achebe's work in English and its support for Igbo language concepts. This sets the situation for a fusion of linguistic perspectives or horizons. Achebe introduces a new aspect in African-English-language narrative. Although he communicates with some agreements or considerations with the local Igbo language and its resonance, he fails short of his initial project in transmitting the totality of the truth and meaning of the people. This is where philosophy and hermeneutics are important in finding out ways of improving on what has been contributed by critiquing Achebe's views and failures. Each language possesses certain qualities for the communication of the truth of its world and it is at the level of application and translation from one language to the other that the fusion of horizons is easily understood. There are some fusions of perspectives when Achebe adapted some Igbo thought pattern and wise sayings to be able to put them in English expressions or transliterations.[416] Through the publication of *Things Fall Apart*, Achebe gives Igbo language and worldview the publicity that it deserves. It does reveal *some* African true identity through an African voice. Ogede explains:

> the 'remarkable assimilation of African and European features' that 'not only brought into fiction in English an integrated African world, but also achieved the feat of presenting that world in its entirety in an unrelated language. Achebe's debt to the oral tradition is expressly in his creation of a new English style that follows and derives from his own Igbo African vernacular, idiom, rhythm, and tenor of speech. Above all, he exhibits a remarkable grasp of the proverb, which constitutes for the Igbo the "palm-oil with which words are eaten"' (1975: 251). And

---

[415] Janmohamed, *op. cit.*, p. 579.
[416] Ogede, *op. cit.*, p. 36.

recent evaluation by eminent folklorist Isidore Okpewho extends this affirmation, describing the text as 'an unusual novel not only for the "strange" world it portrays but equally for the familiar touch Achebe brings to the English medium of his writing' (2003: 39). The achievement of this novel, Okpewho restates, lies in initiating 'a vogue in postcolonial African literature whereby writers, while representing their societies in a European language, endeavored to create a space for their indigenous sensibilities in both sound (African words inserted here and there) and sense (peculiar ways of meaning)'.[417]

One recalls Ogede's analysis of Okpewho about Achebe's use of English. Achebe brings an effective fusion from English language and the sensibilities of the African people. That is the procedure of a classic postcolonial African literature and its demands. The questions are: Does a current analysis of this situation require a different approach that emphasizes the capability of each language alone to deliver clearly its understanding of reality? Do we need a "method" like Achebe's or a principle to determine what the art of narration and the preferred language should be? Some other African scholars agree that Achebe's contributions through a written tradition have put oral Igbo tradition in a good light. Gikandi appreciates Achebe's contributions to pedagogy and interpretation of African worldviews.[418] No doubt Achebe's narrative is an important work in African thought and philosophical studies. Like any subject matter that needs to be continually articulated, the good in Achebe's works needs to be evaluated in a contemporary light of the role of language. As one of the great narratives of our time, it requires that we look at the text from a new perspective in order to develop "a deeper understanding of Africa at a significant period of its history and a formative time in European imperial expansion in Africa than exists in any other novel."[419] Understanding the reality of Achebe's people is important. It is not merely about language of narrative. Achebe develops a form of integrating Igbo word use into English language to be able to communicate African worldviews and narrative. Ogede also observes that the English language provides an overwhelming advantage to Achebe:

---

[417] *Ibid*., p. 95.
[418] Achebe, "Novelist as Teacher," 1965, p. 72.
[419] Ogede, *op. cit.*, p. ix.

Nevertheless, by giving his writing international currency, English has turned out to be more an enabling than an inhibiting factor to him... This is an English language that has been adjusted to serve as a vehicle for conveying the potency of Igbo idioms, turns of phrase, concepts, ideas and words. Many tacitly assume that, to meet the demand to express Igbo concepts and ideas accurately, Achebe had to reconfigure in a second-language situation the tenor of his native idiom.[420]

In recent discussions on the hermeneutical problems of Achebe's English literature, Achebe reiterates that English language has not hindered the understanding of Igbo worldview but has disclosed it to the international community more than any other. But Janmohamed's concern is that:

[U]nlike English, most African languages were non-literate and that the noetic structures of these oral cultures are significantly different from those of chirographic ones. The African writer who uses English, then, is faced at some level with the paradox of representing the experience of oral cultures through literate language and forms. Chinua Achebe...is... aware of this problem and has depicted in his fiction not only the material, political, and social destruction of indigenous societies caused by colonization but also the subtle annihilation of the conservative, homeostatic oral culture.[421]

However, one understands that scholars are aware of the positive fusion of perspectives that emanates from this synthesis of cultures, oral and written languages: Igbo oral tradition and Western written tradition etc. African scholars now make use of these positive qualities in written language and tradition to effectively present African worldviews and genuine philosophical mode of existence.

3.6 Achebe: Mode of Existence and the Unfolding of History in *Things Fall Apart*

Achebe's work is a clarion call to a new understanding and a new mode of existence in relation to humanity and to reality in general. It is a mode of existence which demands an ontological change in the vision of life of a

---

[420] *Ibid.*, p. 23.
[421] Janmohamed, *op. cit.*, p. 573.

people. *Things Fall Apart* is also an invitation to a cultural consciousness and continuity with some modifications. Achebe's hero-character's suicide is not a closure. It is rather a new beginning of the uncertain future that has to come for the people of Umuofia, for Africa and for the world. What unfolds is the consciousness of history and consciousness of our historical situation. It unfolds not as a totally new project but as a cultural discontinuity as well as an ontological continuity in a new mode of being for authentic intercultural relations within a global world determined by socio-cultural, socio-economic and philosophical factors. In the spirit of Achebe's narrative, the new mode is a pointer to the 'tragedy' of the past intercultural events and encounter that had to happen for a new horizon to arrive.[422]

In Achebe's word, *Things Fall Apart* establishes the demand for a new mode of being and understanding. The world of the Umuofian has to comply with the changing world around them. Could the demand for a new mode of being be a pointer to the tragedy of the community rather than of an individual (like Okonkwo)? Achebe describes the uniqueness of this new mode of existence that takes place in Umuofia. It appears as an eventful night - "a terrible night" [423] and a scene that could only mean-the change of the *old order* of things, where death (of the old order) implies the need for a new beginning in the life of the community. Achebe describes it thus:

> That night the Mother of the Spirits walked the length and breadth of the clan, weeping for her murdered son. It was a terrible night. Not even the oldest man in Umuofia had ever heard such a strange and fearful sound, and it was never to be heard again. It seemed as if the very soul of the tribe wept for a great evil that was coming - its own death.[424]

This "terrible night" welcomes a new beginning in the community as a night that equally affects the life of the gods of the land. The new beginning is the transition that occurs when what 'has never happened before' (symbolized in the terrible night and the gods weeping) began to happen. When what has earlier been considered as an issue of imagination and regarded as almost impossibility happened, then the new phase of expectation has dawn. The new must now begin. When the gods weep, it means a tragic history of the people

---

[422] http://web.africa.ufl.edu/asq/v4/v4i3a1.htm (Accessed March 18, 2011.)
[423] Achebe, *Things Fall Apart, op. cit.,* pp. 186-187.
[424] *Ibid.*

or something of immense significance has happened that demands a profound community response. In the text, it says: "All our gods are weeping. *Idemili* is weeping. *Ogwugwu* is weeping. *Agbala* is weeping, and all the others…"[425] In Irele's explanation:

> The epochal significance of the passage is intensified, assumes cosmic resonance, in the lament that pours out of one of the characters… Okika's lament directs us to the heart of Achebe's novel: it is as an elegy that incorporates a tragic vision of history that *Things Fall Apart* elicits the strongest and deepest response.[426]

Although Achebe's work is fictional, it captures the stylistic impression of a developing history or an unfolding history in a particular Igbo community. The final aspect of this terrible night or tragic events has taken place. While the elders of the community gathered to find a lasting solution to their confrontations with the colonial masters (District Commissioner and Reverend Smith), Okonkwo then kills one of the court messengers for attempting to stop their emergency community meeting and he goes to commit suicide. Once Okonkwo killed himself, a new dawn in Umuofia begins. It is the new dawn of genuine and hopeful intercultural understanding because a price has been paid by Okonkwo with his life. The future of this intercultural relationship is now the today of the African world/ experience and other (Western etc) cultural experiences. The need for genuine intercultural understanding still lingers. Certainly it is a form of intercultural exchange following the new mode of experiencing reality. This new mode of experience is the measure of the aesthetic of reality and as such most current. It is a genuine combination of African and Western worldviews. Irele adumbrates these intercultural and unfolding historical implications:

> The transition of Achebe's style from an epic mode to one associated with the novel provides an indication of the changing modes of this relation. This stylistic evolution of the novel may be interpreted as the scriptural sign of a corresponding

---

[425] *Ibid.*, p. 203. This situation could also be used to justify the communal tragedy in Achebe. The gods could not weep if only an individual crisis is involved. It is a communal "we" tragedy that is why the gods weep.

[426] http://web.africa.ufl.edu/asq/v4/v4i3a1.htm (Accessed March 18, 2011.) Achebe, *Things Fall Apart* (Canada: Anchor Canada edition, 2009), p. 203.

adjustment of the writer's vision, reflecting his sense, as the narrative develops, of the pressure of history as it begins to exert itself upon the community that is the subject of the novel. This seems to accord with a Hegelian conception of history as the unfolding saga of modernity, with the modern novel as its imaginative equivalent. The received opinion stemming from these sources has tended to understand modernity as a historical phenomenon arising primarily from the Western experience and as the paradigm that commands the writing of scientific history, and, as a consequence, the emergence of the novel, the literary genre that is thought to be most closely associated with modern culture. In this view, the novel as a specific modern genre affords a new medium for the construction in aesthetic and moral terms of a vision of a totality no longer immediately available to consciousness in the fragmented, reified world of modern civilization.[427]

In *Things Fall Apart*, Achebe accomplishes the sole goal of projecting Igbo worldviews as a *part* of the *whole* historical reality. Igbo world of reality is no different from the other worlds of reality. In fact, it is part of the totality of the human experience seen from the perspective of Africans and within the historicity of a common humanity (our collective being-ness.) Neil Ten Kortenaar, Professor and Director Center for Comparative Literature, University of Toronto, argues that Achebe's vision was to historicize the Igbo people and, by extension, to posit the historicity of the African people. Achebe's hero character Okonkwo is a character whose life ignites "the Igbos' entry into history."[428] Achebe's narrative places his socio-cultural ideas in line with the conception of history. These cultural ideas become part of a general historical reality which is about a human world realized in each culture. His

[427] *Ibid.* See Georg Wilhelm Friedrich Hegel, *Reason in History*, trans. Robert S. Hartman (Englewoods Cliffs, New Jersey: Prentice Hall, 1953); See also Lindfors, "The Palm Oil with which Words are Eaten," *African Literature Today*, (1968), pp. 3-18; See Georg Lukacs, *The Theory of the Novel* (Cambridge, Mass: Harvard University Press, 1977); Steven Lukes, *Essays in Social Theory* (New York: Columbia University Press, 1977.)
[428] Neil Ten Kortenaar, "How the Centre is Made to Hold in Things Fall Apart," *Postcolonial Literatures: Achebe, Ngugi, Desai, Walcott*, Michael Parker and Roger Starkey, eds (Houndmills, Basingstoke: Macmillan, 1995), p. 45.

narrative presents a creative reconstruction of the historicity of African experience and African dimension of our collective Dasein (being.)[429]

In Achebe's work one perceives the becoming of history and becoming of being. Achebe's fictional novel resonates with a reflection on the becoming of African being. Thus his "work enacts a double movement of consciousness... A travelling... towards a cosmopolitan modern identity at the same time as a journeying back to regain a threatened past and selfhood."[430] These dual aspects come directly into view in *Things Fall Apart*, "in which Achebe begins to elaborate a historical vision that encompasses both a revaluation of the African past and its critical appraisal."[431]

Achebe's work is part of the historical material of a culture. But some other philosophers would regard this historical material of a culture as peculiar to pre-history, mythic and transient tradition.[432] Kortenaar admits that Achebe regrets the possibility of his work being considered in such a manner, "however, is not the precolonial world... but the pre-colonial world's potential, all that it might have become."[433] It is clear that Achebe is building the case of African becoming without dwelling on the past of pre-colonial Africa. His narrative is the narrative of the life-world of his people that goes on in the future. The future of his people is in continuity and not totally realized. This is the nature of our contemporary life-world to relate to our unrealized future and its understanding.[434] For us, it has to be hermeneutically and philosophically continued and realized. The way to its realization is through a profound sense of hermeneutics (understanding meanings.)

The philosophical dimension of Achebe's work addressing the notion of becoming is also about the transformation of a people. Most of Achebe's works are following the direction of this African historical and philosophical

---

[429] http://web.africa.ufl.edu/asq/v4/v4i3a1.htm (Accessed March 18, 2011.)
[430] Achebe, "What Has Literature Got to Do with It?," Chinua Achebe, *Hopes and Impediments, Selected Essays* (New York: Anchor Books, 1989), p. 110.
[431] Irele, "Introduction," *Chinua Achebe Things Fall Apart, op. cit.*, p. xxi.
[432] http://web.africa.ufl.edu/asq/v4/v4i3a1.htm (Accessed March 18, 2011.) Irele analyzes what he sees as the movement of history as depicted in Hegel's *Philosophy of History* where he identifies issues that he regarded as pre-historical and transient rather than the essential part of original history.
[433] Neil Ten Kortenaar, "The Question of Modern African Tragedy," *Chinua Achebe Things Fall Apart (Authoritative Text, Contexts and Criticism)*, Francis Abiola Irele, ed (New York: W. W. Norton & Company, 2009), pp. 342-343.
[434] *Ibid.*, p. 343.

becoming or African transformation. As noted, Achebe is not interested in the total restoration of the 'glorious' past of African society, but he is pursuing the necessary transition and transformation that must follow this intercultural encounter. This intercultural encounter does not leave any of the parties as they were before the encounter. Everyone or every culture has something to learn and something to offer in that encounter. It is about the innate philosophical evolution of African society which ought to come through moments of crisis (catharsis or purification or self-evaluation) and reach fulfillment through a gradual process of "African Becoming."[435] Achebe calls it a philosophy of great depth of the Africans which is what he tries to capture in *Things Fall Apart*. He says, "African peoples...frequently had a philosophy of great depth and value and beauty"[436] in narratives.

3.7 Achebe: Narratives

African philosophical mode of existence and their history of becoming are portrayed in hermeneutical narratives or discourses. Achebe uses the effectiveness of Igbo proverbs to communicate his sense of African becoming. The relevant proverbs aspect shall be discussed in chapter four below. Achebe's hermeneutical narrative is acknowledged because of its humanization of the Igbo, especially in a world where colonialism did not offer much positive reports about the culture of the 'colonized' people or the philosophical "Other". Achebe's narrative brings to light the ontological universality as well as the particular dimensions of Igbo Africans. Achebe's hermeneutical narrative is "a story in which Africa would be 'seen in all its grandeur and all its weakness.'"[437]

Achebe's *Things Fall Apart* is a book of a unique nature. Through fictional characters and communities it involves African experience that reflects the life of a true historical people following their encounter with Western culture. Irele describes Achebe's narrative:

---

[435] Irele, "The Tragic Conflict in the Novels of Chinua Achebe," *Critical Perspectives on Chinua Achebe, op. cit.,* p. 21.

[436] Chinua Achebe, "The Role of the Writer in a New Nation," *Nigeria Magazine*, No. 81 (June 1964), p. 157; See also Lindfors, "The Palm-oil with which Achebe's Words are Eaten," *Chinua Achebe Things Fall Apart, op. cit.,* p. 555.

[437] McLaren, "Things Fall Apart: Cultural and Historical Contexts," *op. cit.,* p. 28; See Kate Turkington, *Chinua Achebe*: "Things Fall Apart" (London: Edward Arnold, 1977), p. 110.

In its specific reference to the African experience, *Things Fall Apart* has assumed a historical significance, for although it is not a historical novel in the usual sense of the term—that is, of a fictional re-enactment of real facts—it is a work that is governed by an acute sense of the determining power of events. This observation applies to all of Achebe's fiction, in which the African experience assumes its full human and narrative scope in the modern novel....Achebe has sought not merely to explore the African experience as shaped by the colonial encounter, but also to re-create in imaginative terms the complex dimensions of the African world, and thus to restore to the continent its character as a theater of human endeavour and cultural accomplishment.[438]

As fictional and non-historical novel, *Things Fall Apart* reenacts the cultural world of the Igbo Africans. The historicity of this book is not in the ordinary sense of history since it does not deal with "real events of the past, featuring real historical personalities as characters".[439] We see various forms of histories that are fictional but yet respond or relate to the hermeneutical and philosophical truth of the people. Achebe's narrative unfolds as a result of his creative faculty. He is able to reconstruct the events of his historical world (as a child, a teenager and an educated adult.) It may not be considered in a strict sense a historical book but it has the depth of truth of the people communicated in an imaginative way. The point to observe here is that narratives or the power to narratives is what is common to all human societies. It is about the "significance of narrative as a universal phenomenon."[440] Achebe's narrative has succeeded in bringing fiction and history together in an inclusive manner, while involving truth, life, experience, imitation and representation.

In my view there is a harmony between fiction and reality in Achebe. His fiction is not totally outside the real. The names of characters in *Things Fall Apart* may be imaginary but their actions express a truth in the world of concrete actions of true Igbo people. There is a connection between fiction and history in the text. The real world of experience serves as referent to our narrative while the events in the fiction are symbolic representation of lived experiences. This narrative expresses truth and "transforms these events into

---

[438] Irele, "Introduction," *Chinua Achebe Things Fall Apart, op. cit.*, p. xxi.
[439] http://web.africa.ufl.edu/asq/v4/v4i3a1.htm (Accessed March 18, 2011.)
[440] *Ibid.*

intimations of patterns of meaning that any literal representation of them as facts could never produce'."[441]

In another way, Achebe's work could be interpreted as an effort to use imaginative creativity to shape African experience in true history. It is a history that is drawn out for generations of Igbo scholars to read, philosophically consider, and to keep record. As was earlier mentioned, Achebe uses fiction to draw attention to the historical identity of Africans, especially the Igbo. It is a form of cultural consciousness, preservation and recollection.[442] Irele explains:

> This seems to me the direction of meaning in Achebe's fiction, which, in its immediate reference, represents an imaginative remapping of the African experience within the space of history, the literary mode deployed as a means of shaping consciousness for the confrontation of the new realities on the horizon of African being. The ironies and the ambivalence that underscore the drama of cultural memory in his first novel emerge in a new light from this perspective, attesting to a sombre consciousness but one resolutely oriented towards a future envisioned as pregnant with new possibilities.[443]

Achebe's hermeneutical narrative is like other philosophical narratives that focus on general human condition: our being-there-in-existence with the exigencies of life; human fragility and facticity; and being-in-the-world; our-togetherness-with-others; our anxiety and our totality of experience etc., and in its specific significance as African experience. African experience is all part of human existential situations. It has the common characteristics of great tragedies in literature (Western, Christian etc.) For the African, whose story it is about, it must have a central and distinctive role. Our human finitude and changing circumstances, our worries, our concerns, cares, worries, are part of

---

[441] *Ibid.* See Hayden White, *The Content of the Form: Narrative Discourse and Historical Representation* (Baltimore: Johns Hopkins University Press, 1987), pp. 44-45. A similar work has been done with another fiction: *The Lord of the Rings* by *J. R. R. Tolkien*, which is a fictional work but one derives ethical implications from the plot and characters in the novel. See Stanley Uche Anozie, "Fate and Morality in J. R. R. Tolkien's *The Lord of the Rings* and Plato's *Ring of Gyges*," (Unpublished Seminar Paper, Saint Paul University, Ottawa, June 2010.)

[442] http://web.africa.ufl.edu/asq/v4/v4i3a1.htm (Accessed March 18, 2011.)

[443] *Ibid.*

Dasein's experience. It involves finding out our potencies which includes our positive potencies and our negative potencies. As positive potencies, tragedy leaves us with the desire of what to do to overcome our negative circumstances and improve our lives. The negative potencies leave us with concerns about what could happen to us following what we have witnessed in the life of another. Tragedy leaves us with some effects of emotional nature. We are worried and concerned about experiences of the main character, while we are afraid that his/her situation could become our fate. Thus:

> it contains of the general human condition....The description applies equally to all the great tragedies of world literature,...As a necessary component of its exploration of the African experience, *Things Fall Apart* embodies this fundamental truth of the imaginative vision.[444]

African writers and philosophers dwell on issues that focus on the reality of African life-world and authentic African experience. It means focusing on "the dignity of self and society by representing them, in the best instances, in a manner that he considers unidealized but more authentic."[445] Authenticity is a concept similar to Gadamer's truth. I will apply only Gadamer's views in relation to Achebe in the next chapter.

The shifting perspective from African narrative to a Western mode of understanding is in the long run for a cultural recollection or cultural memory, the communication of the details of Igbo African life-world. *Things Fall Apart* is a project geared at facilitating cultural memory, recollection and revival. Irele concludes:

> The novel's imaginative scope thus extends beyond mere documentation to convey, through the careful reproduction of its marking details, the distinctive character of Igbo tribal life as experienced by its subjects, the felt texture from which it derives its universal significance. It is this that gives *Things Fall Apart*

---

[444]*Ibid.* See Roland Barthes, *Le Degre zero de l'ecriture* (Paris: Editions de Seuil, 1953.) The English translation by Ann Lavers and Colin Smith, *Writing Degree Zero* (New York: Hill and Wang, 1968; Barthes, Sur Racine, Paris: Editions du Seuil, 1963 (Collection Pierres vives); Barthes S/Z. Paris: Editions du Seuil 1970 (Collection Points) English Translation Richard Miller, New York: Hill and Wang, 1986.
[445] Janmohamed, *op. cit.*, p. 571.

its power of conviction and validates the project of cultural memory attested by the novel. [446]

Let me now elaborate on Achebe's fictional narrative with regard to his use of the notion of person. Although Achebe did not discuss the notion of person directly, we see in his narrative a hermeneutical theme for personhood in African narrative. I shall present the contemporary African philosophical notion of the person in order to help us justify the argument about the communal notion of tragedy. In chapter four I shall be relating or integrating our hermeneutical themes from Achebe's narratives and the notion of person (as ontologically a relational being) as part of the traditions or prejudices of tradition, fusion of perspectives etc., for understanding our text.

3.8 Achebe and Contemporary African Philosophical Notion of the Person and Community

Achebe did not discuss the notion of person, but he made use of the heroic cultural personage which we will use as a hermeneutical theme in chapter four. We are only introducing the notion of person here to enrich our discussion as part of African philosophical thought in general. This discourse will be used in chapter four to argue in support of my interpretation of Achebe's tragedy as a communal tragedy rather than a personal tragedy.

It is important to consider contemporary African philosophical notion of the person and community in order to see what contributions it may provide to understanding Achebe's Okonkwo (tragic hero character.) The African concept of the person, in my analysis,[447] has two views that complement each other: (i) Person as the beauty of life, and (ii) Person as relational--"I am because we are."

---

[446] http://web.africa.ufl.edu/asq/v4/v4i3a1.htm (Accessed March 18, 2011.)

[447] I have carried some research in this area. See Stanley Uche Anozie, "Authentic Integration Process in Canada and the Contemporary African Concept of the Human Person: Martin Buber's I-Thou Socio- philosophy," (Unpublished Philosophy Master's Thesis, Dominican University College, Ottawa, August, 2009.) See also Stanley Uche Anozie, "Human Rights and Nigeria Niger-Delta Oil Crisis: Alan Gewirth—The Community of Rights," (Unpublished Public Ethics Master's Research Paper, Saint Paul University, Ottawa, August, 2010.)

3.8.1 Person as the Beauty of Life

Like most African communities and nations, the Igbo, a major ethnic group in Southeastern Nigeria, uses the terms "human being" and "person" interchangeably. Being called a human being is the same as being called a person, and *vice versa*.[448] The Igbo language considers *person* as *Mmadu (Mma-du)*, which is the combination of *Mma* (Beauty) and *Ndu* (Life.) The concept of person is the concept of the beauty of life; indeed the concept of the beauty of all created things in their totality. Human beings make the world beautiful and meaningful.[449] The Igbo notion of the person as "beauty of life" reminds some philosophers of the traditional doctrine of the "transcendentals", the essential properties of being, to which the beautiful is counted (next to the one, the true, and the good). Commenting on the African philosophical notion of person as "the beauty of life", Francis C. O. Njoku, Dean of Philosophy, Claretian Institute of Philosophy, Maryland, Owerri, Nigeria, sees in beauty:

> a manifestation of their metaphysical essence: humans are the beauty of earthly life, and as a home beauty,[450] they represent the totality of all as an expression of this beauty. They are persons by virtue of being endowed with beauty at creation. Their personhood is not socially acquired or to be decided by a court of law but they are naturally persons.[451]

Philosophically speaking, there is an intrinsic connection between person and beauty. The beautiful is understood as what reveals itself. In the description of the person as the beauty of life we recognize something of the Heideggerian[452] notions of being (*Sein*) and of the human being (*Da-sein*)[453]:

---

[448] Obi J. Oguejiofor, ed., *Philosophy, Democracy and Responsible Governance in Africa* (Munster: Lit Verlag, 2003), p. 82.

[449] William Shakespeare is acknowledged as having described man as "the beauty of the world" (Hamlet Act 2, Scene 2.)

[450] 'Home beauty' is an expression of beauty in its totality and in its nearness to creation/humanity.

[451] Francis O. C. Njoku, *Development and African Philosophy: A Theoretical Reconstruction of African Socio-Political Economy* (New York: iUniverse, Inc., 2004), p. 163 (Footnote); Oguejiofor, ed., *op. cit.,* pp. 81-82.

[452] Charles B. Guignon, "Martin Heidegger," *The Cambridge Dictionary of Philosophy,* Robert Audi, ed (Cambridge: Cambridge University Press, second edition, 1999), pp. 370-373.

being reveals, manifests, and discloses itself through, in, and to others. It is through human being (*Dasein*) that being (*Sein*) discloses itself. A person is a being "whose essential structures are centered in disclosedness."[454] Something similar is expressed in the word "*Existenz*"-'to stand out'; the idea of person means standing out and disclosure of (the human) being through its beauty. The notion of person as the beauty of existence is common among Africans. Richard C. Onwuanibe, former Associate Professor, Cleveland State University, Ohio elaborates that for the Igbo:

> [T]rue personhood, as pure subject, is not something that can be analyzed into anything... Personhood is a manifestation or presence even through a body, but never identifiable with it. Since 'person' is primitive, the inability to analyze person (*qua* subject or soul) is not an argument for its non-existence but for its 'transcendence' or 'no-thingness'. In Ibo greetings... Nobody greets a body but 'what' is manifest through the body. [455]

The quotation of Onwuanibe underscores the metaphysical, transcendent dimension of the person, which is an essential topic among African philosophers. Person has a physical (material or bodily) and a spiritual (transcendent) aspect. African philosophical thought conceives of person as a totality of spirit (soul) and body. The Bantus of Eastern and Central Africa and the Igbo have a common understanding of personhood in this regard. For Pierre Marie Emonet, "[T]he person is a whole, integrating soul and body."[456] Onwuanibe explains, "[T]he Ibo [Igbo] notions of soul (*mkpuru obi*) and spirit (*mmuo*), as essential aspects of man, bear out the transcendence of the human person from the metaphysical point of view."[457] There is something similar in

---

[453] Barry Hallen, "Phenomenology and the Exposition of African Traditional Thought," *African Philosophy,* Claude Sumner, ed (Addis Ababa: Addis Ababa University Press, second edition, 1998), pp. 51-52.

[454] Martin Heidegger, *Being and Time*, trans. Joan Stambaugh (New York: State University of New York Press, 1996), p. 20 (18); p. 231 (213.)

[455] Richard C. Onwuanibe, "The Human Person and Immortality in Ibo (African) Metaphysics," *African Philosophy: An Introduction*, Richard A. Wright, ed (New York: University Press of America, 1984), p. 186.

[456] Pierre-Marie Emonet, *The Greatest Marvel of Nature: An Introduction to The Philosophy of the Human Person*, trans. Robert R. Barr (New York: The Crossroad Publishing Company, 2000), p. 128; See J. F. Donceel, *Philosophical Anthropology* (New York: Sheed and Ward, 1967), p. 463. He writes about person that, "he is a spirit, albeit in matter, because the core of his being is self-consciousness."

[457] Onwuanibe, *op. cit.*, p. 185. Jacques Maritain clearly addresses the metaphysical aspects in the concept of individual and the concept of person. He clarifies, "There is not in me one

Senegal (West Africa), for instance, in Wolof, the main language of Senegal, spirit is translated as *"xel, sago,* or *degal,"* while matter or body is *"lef"* (thing) or *"yaram"* (body.)[458]

In an African context, the rational discourse on dignity of the person will have to take into account the African perspective on the transcendent aspect of person. Every person is unique, special, and transcendentally connected to the divine *Chi-neke* (Igbo—southeastern Nigeria), *Oluwa* (Yoruba, Nigeria), *Borbore* (Akan, Ghana), *Unkulunkulu* (Zulu, South Africa.)[459] Onwuanibe explains the metaphysical, divine aspect the African attributes to the person as follows:

> The realm of the immaterial... includes the divine, and metaphysics is not complete without the treatment of God, the highest Being and His relationship to lesser beings such as humans... In the Ibo conception of man, man is oriented to the divine. [460]

These ideas show that in African thought, a person has to be thought of as a subject, rather than a mere object–if we accept Onwuanibe's distinction. Onwuanibe states, "Object-oriented thinking aims at controlling and exploiting the other, while subject-oriented thinking feels the demand of the freedom of the other."[461] Being a subject rather than an object, the person is not to be used,

---

reality, called my individual, and another reality, called my person. One and the same being is an individual, in one sense, and a person, in another sense. Our whole being is an individual by reason of that in us which derives from matter, and a person by reason of that in us which derives from spirit.... No doubt, each of my acts is simultaneously the act of myself as an individual and the act of myself as a person." See Jacques Maritain, *The Social and Political Philosophy of Jacques Maritain,* Joseph W. Evans and Leo R. Ward, eds. (New York: Image Books, 1965), pp. 22-23. Maritain says that individuality and personality (person) "are the two metaphysical aspects of the human being." (22.)

[458] Léopold Sédar Senghor, "Negritude: A Humanism of the Twentieth Century (1966)," *I am Because We Are: Readings in Black Philosophy*, Fred Lee Hord (Mzee Lasana Okpara) and Jonathan Scott Lee, eds (Amherst: University of Massachusetts Press, 1995), p. 48.

[459] John Samuel Mbiti, *African Religions and Philosophy* (London: Heinemann Educational Books Ltd, 1969), pp. 29-38.

[460] Onwuanibe, *op. cit.*, p. 192.

[461] *Ibid.*, p. 186.

abused, and exploited.[462] As person, the individual is an end in itself with dignity.

This discourse helps us to connect the notion of person as the beauty of life and as relational (I am because we are) to the idea of a tragic hero whose failure is hermeneutically a communal tragedy, rather than a personal tragedy.

3.8.2 Person as Relational—"I am because we are"

African thinkers try to develop a notion of person in which traditional African elements as well as the idea of an individual with human rights are respected. In this notion, concepts like: person, mutuality, and interpersonal community need balancing. African philosophy of the person centers on "I am because we are, and since we are therefore I am."[463] The African philosophical paradigm for thinking about the person is the paradigm of *"I-We"*; i.e., it strives for a dialectical balance between "I" and "we". The person is an individual in a community of persons. African society puts more emphasis on the community than on the individuals. It is based "more on solidarity than on the activity and needs of the individual, more on the community of persons than on their autonomy. Ours is a community society."[464] Scholars and philosophers like William Sweet,[465] Panteleon Iroegbu[466]etc, who have done research on the African philosophical notion of person and socio-philosophical thought, would commonly call the African notion of person 'communitarian.'

The African communitarian notion of person does affirm independent rational beings and also insists on the intrinsic relational nature of the person, who is related to other persons in the community. It is a notion of person as an

---

[462] Even the consideration of people as simple consumers in a welfare system could be seen as objectification. See Leslie Armour, *The Idea of Canada and The Crisis of Community* (Ottawa: Steel Rail Publishing, 1981), p. 56.

[463] Mbiti, *op. cit.,* p. 113.

[464] Léopold Sédar Senghor, *On African Socialism*, trans. Mercer Cook (New York: Praeger, 1964), pp. 93-94.

[465] He is a Canadian philosopher. Sweet is Professor of Philosophy and Director of the Center for Philosophy, Theology, and Cultural Traditions at St. Francis Xavier University.

[466] Panteleon Iroegbu, *Appropriate Ecclesiology (Through Narrative Theology to an African Church)* (Owerri: International Universities Press, 1996), p. 92. Iroegbu describes this community based understanding of person as "Umunna" or in terms of "being-with-the-others."

individual within a community. One could ask how this conception of the independent rational being in a community different from Aristotle or Boethius?[467]

Aristotle considers person as an independent rational soul or with the power to think. A person has body and soul but the principle of the human body is the soul which is substance or form of the body. The soul is a necessary condition for the body to be called a human person. The soul is the efficient cause of the human person. The human person has rationality-the power of thinking as its distinct characteristic. The soul is important in Aristotle's discussion on the human person. Our actions must reflect the logical result of thought which is shared with other persons in a community. A person's individual interest is not more than the community's interest. The person ought to be at the service of the common good of the community. He/she is incomplete without the community. Similar to this is the classical definition of person according to Boethius (480-525.) Person is "an individual substance of a rational nature (est naturae rationabilis individua substantia.)"[468] The Latin word for person–*persona*--relates to the mask worn by an actor, the role or the character of an actor, or to an individual. Gradually, it has come to mean, "something which is self-existent, that is, not a property or a part of another thing but a thing in its own right."[469] It further describes "an individual, intransmissible (incommunicable), rational essence which is self-existent."[470] Personhood is now perceived in the sense of relation, being-with others. Personhood implies being in human community. The community determines some of what happens in its relation to a single person. For most Africans:

> the reality of the communal world takes precedence over the reality of individual life histories, whatever these may be. And this primacy is meant to apply not only ontologically, but also in regard to epistemic accessibility. It is in rootedness in an ongoing

---

[467] Some scholars are concerned about this issue with regard to Africans and Aristotle's or any other views of person and community.

[468] Boethius, *Tractates Consolation*, trans. H. F. Stewart and E. K. Rand (London: Harvard University Press, 1953), pp. 84-85. Boethius's definition of person has been criticized by existentialists (Existentialist Thomists) as disregarding the existential aspect of person and making person merely essence (essentialism.)

[469] Warren Bourgeois, *Persons: What Philosophers Say About You* (Waterloo: Wilfrid Laurier University Press, 2003), p. 400.

[470] *Ibid.*, p. 103.

human community that the individual comes to see himself as man, and it is by first knowing this community as a stubborn perduring fact of the psychophysical world that the individual also comes to know himself as a durable, more or less permanent, fact of this world. [471]

This concept of the *"I-We"* is based on dependence and reciprocity. Ethnologists and other writers recognize the unity, the balance, and the harmony that ideally exists between the community and the person. The community has "priority over the individual without crushing him, but allowing him to blossom as a person."[472] But the question that needs to be addressed is: if the interest of one collides with the other what happens? Can the person lose his status as an 'end in itself', a subject? Following my earlier comment about African philosophy of person, it considers person as a subject rather than an object, it is the community that determines what and whose interest ought to be protected when there is a collision of interests. The community arbitrates between the two individuals. The interest of an elder is much more important than that of a younger person. The interest of an elderly person who is closer to the ancestors and gods is considered more than that of an ordinary member of the community. The particular interest of a pregnant woman (because of her situation) is more than that of a man or a young person because the baby (life in her) could be a respected ancestor reincarnating or coming back to life (still closer to the ancestral world.) The interest to be served could be determined by what is best for the supernatural world rather than the physical world. The interests of the chief priests of the gods of the land are considered more than any other in the community. We recall that the community has the final say and any individual's interest is relatively secondary to the primary vision/interest of the community. However, whatever interest that is protected, the individual is indirectly served through that of the community. The individual is an end-with-the-community or Others. He is not

---

[471] Ifeanyi A. Menkiti, "Person and Community in African Traditional Thought," *African Philosophy: An Introduction,* Richard A. Wright, ed (New York: University Press of America (Third Edition) 1984), pp. 171-172.

[472] Senghor, "Negritude: A Humanism of the Twentieth Century (1966)," *op. cit.,* p. 50; See Kwame Gyekye, "Person and Community in African Thought," *Person and Community,* Kwasi Wiredu and Kwame Gyekye, eds (Washington, D. C.: The Council for Research in Values and Philosophy, Vol. 1, 1992), p. 101. He explains, "[T]he type of social structure or arrangement evolved by a particular society seems to reflect –and be influenced by –the public conceptions of personhood held in the society."

an end in itself without the community. The relevance of the concept of *"I-We"* is in seeking a balance between person and community.

The dominant emphasis on the community in the African notion of person has been criticized by people like Kwame Gyekye, a Ghanaian philosopher and a Visiting Professor of African-American Studies at Temple University, Philadelphia, Pennsylvania; and Njoku. They are concerned that the individual dimensions of the person's well-being are neglected. The overbearing precedence of community over the individual person calls for some individualist alternatives. The concern is that this communitarian notion of person may limit or undermine the inviolable rights/dignity of the person as an individual, especially when it focuses on the rights of the community or associates the rights of the individual as subordinate to that of the community (as in I am because We are.) The concern is to ensure against the community interfering with an individual's responsibility and hence prevent his freedom and well-being from being sacrificed to a presumed higher common goal. Among other African philosophers, Gyekye criticizes the African notion of person because of its implications for human well-being. He states:

> it is possible for people to assume offhandedly that with its emphasis on communal values, collective good and shared ends, communitarianism invariably conceives the person as wholly constituted by social relationships; that it tends to whittle down the moral autonomy of the person; that it makes the being and life of the individual person totally dependent on the activities, values, projects, practices and ends of the community; and consequently, that it diminishes his freedom and capability to choose or question or re-evaluate the shared values of the community. [473]

---

[473] Gyekye, *op. cit.*, p. 102; See John Coates, *The Crisis of The Human Person: Some Personalist Interpretations* (London: Longmans, Green and Co, 1949), p. 12. Coates notes, "Maritain's distinction between the person and the individual…. It is based, first of all, on a recognition that because man has a need of his fellows to perfect his specific activity, he is on that account an individual part of a city or community, so that a submission of his own to the larger good, where the two conflict, is called for by reason." Chinua Achebe, *The Trouble with Nigeria* (Enugu: Fourth Dimension Publishing Co. Ltd, 1983), p. 58, p. 60, p. 62. Achebe's use of individualistic ethics for the Igbo seems to me a later development considering the long years of communalism and it could also spring from the years of socio-economic neglect and abuse of the fundamental rights of the people.

In the later part of the above quote, Gyekye emphasizes the individual's freedom and ability to be critical of the shared values of one's community, one understands that that there is an obvious obstacle to individual's freedom and well-being but the desire to question the values of the community is part of the ongoing discourse between individuals and their communities for a better society. Peaceful existence, freedom and human rights are subject matters that will always be part of any developing and developed society. The difference for these societies is that in a developing society the agitations and the dialogue for change go on. In the developed society, it is more of maintaining and securing the democratic principles to sustain freedom, rule of law and citizen mind.[474] This is why critical or reflective thinking is part of every human organization even when it is denied or the opportunity is frustrated.

African philosophers have expressed concerns about the repercussions of the African notion of person on the individual. Many Africans share the conviction that the idea "I am because we are" (I-We) is apt to express and justify their notion of community; but that this idea may have negative implications for individual members of the community. The community sanctions the protection of individual well-being and encourages this political notion of person. A political notion of person recognizes person as the product of a social agreement- a member of a community. The person is totally dependent on the community to have rights and freedoms. This applies to African communities that only recognize the social rights of the person as long as they are in accord with the good of the community. Njoku adds, "[E]vidently, the community in the African sense presents itself as the greatest infallible judge and distributor of resources for social living. Rights are then community-sanctioned."[475] It is easy to notice the devaluation of the person as an ontological and irreplaceable being in this situation. The ontological notion of person emphasizes that the person is incommunicable entity with rational soul. The person is an 'end in itself.' A person is a being with free essence and dignity through creation.

Considering the above, it is difficult to hold on to the *"I-We"* person view as conceived by contemporary African philosophical thought. If one

---

[474] See Bernard Bosanquet, *The Philosophical Theory of the State* (Kitchener, Ontario: Batoche Books, 2001, originally published in 1899), p. 186. Bernard Bosanquet--a British philosopher and social reformer.
[475] Njoku, *op. cit.,* pp. 154-155.

looks at the ontological and the political notions of person separately, then the "I-We" person will be different, but to separate the ontological and the political does not mean much in African worldview. In fact, the ontological and the political are inseparable because the real world of being (spiritual) and physical world are somehow connected. There is always continuity from one level to the other, and vice versa. However, Benezet Bujo, an African and Professor of Theology at University of Fribourg, Switzerland, in defense of *"I-We"* person and community philosophical thought, explains that:

> Because there is interdependence between the community and the individual, the community must not subordinate what is particular, but should promote and support it, because without the individuality of the single members it would totally disintegrate. Interaction, within the African context, makes it clear that the individual is an incomplete being who is basically dependent on the community. [476]

The view of Léopold Sédar Senghor[477] remains relevant here when he describes this *"I-We"* as "essentially relations with others, an opening out to the world, contact and participation with others."[478] This concept of the *"I-We"* as Senghor further clarifies is based on dialogue and reciprocity. This point addresses the argument by Njoku as not so comprehensive and grounded. Senghor again explains that ethnologists have often praised the "unity, the balance, and the harmony… founded on dialogue and reciprocity, the group had priority over the individual without crushing him."[479] The main criticism against the African concept of person and community is that it sometimes devalues the individual's well-being and is unable to guarantee a protecting-community.

---

[476] Benezet Bujo, *The Ethical Dimension of Community: The African Model and The Dialogue Between North and South* (Nairobi: Paulines Publication Africa, 1998), p. 148.

[477] He was a Senegalese poet, politician and cultural theorist.

[478] Senghor, "Negritude: A Humanism of the Twentieth Century (1966)," *op. cit.,* p. 46. This point is the popular "Negritude" philosophy on who the African is or emphasis on the African personality. It is a kind of ethno-philosophy.

[479] Senghor, *op. cit.,* p. 50. See Gyekye, *op. cit.,* p. 101. He explains, "The existence of any social structure is an outstanding, in fact, a necessary feature of every human society. A social structure is evolved not only to give effect to certain conceptions of human nature, but also to provide a framework for both the realization of the potentials, goals and hopes of the individual members of the society and the continuous existence and survival of the society. The type of social structure or arrangement evolved by a particular society seems to reflect –and be influenced by –the public conceptions of personhood held in the society."

The African notion of person is important in light of Achebe's presentation of Okonkwo's crisis that leads to tragedy in the novel, especially because of "Okonkwo's exaggerated sense of self."[480] It helps in establishing the argument that Okonkwo's tragedy is in fact a communal tragedy rather than merely an individual or personal tragedy. The African philosophical notion of person will be considered in chapter four as part of the prejudices, fusion of horizons etc as principle of hermeneutics in understanding.

In summary, Achebe accomplishes his main objective of telling African story from an African voice and correctly presents the truth of his world. He also made use of effective Igbo proverbs (which we moved to chapter four) in communicating the worldviews of his people. His mastery of the language of his education is shown in his translation of Igbo proverbs and ideas in clearly chosen words. His use of metaphor and figures of speech are close to the realities of African thought. With these literary skills and linguistic acuity, he is able to convince his readers "that African peoples did, not hear of culture for the first time from Europeans; that their societies were not mindless but frequently had a philosophy of great depth and value and beauty, that they had poetry."[481]

Achebe understands that the intercultural situation between his people's culture and the European culture brought new perspectives. The situation has also shown the demand for a new mode of existence that is part of the common unfolding of history. His attention is drawn to narrating the story of this cultural encounter, especially in a positive and productive light. Achebe tries his best to describe this cross-cultural interaction from the perspective of an Igbo African person. It is this genuine goal that makes Achebe's narrative a cross-cultural interaction which is "an opportunity for unity instead of the alienation."[482] The cross-cultural interaction is a form of comparative study, the relation of the peoples and cultures. It also does not overlook the complexes, the "crossroads of cultures"[483] that are natural to such fusion of perspectives or cultures.

---

[480] http://web.africa.ufl.edu/asq/v4/v4i3a1.htm (Accessed March 18, 2011.)

[481] Lindfors, *op. cit.*, p. 571; See also Chinua Achebe, 'The Role of the Writer in a New Nation," *Nigeria Magazine*, No. 81 (June 1964), p. 157.

[482] Ogede, *op. cit.*, p. 7.

[483] Chinua Achebe, *Hopes and Impediments*: Selected Essays (NY: Anchor Books, 1989), p. 34; See also Begam, *op. cit.*, p. 221.

I have also looked at the contemporary African philosophical notion of person and community in order to help us understand Achebe's perspective of Okonkwo's hero person image that may have led to his tragic end. Somehow one is able to situate the personal and the communal aspects of the notion of tragedy among Africans. If a person has an essential ontological and relational nature as "I-We", then the implication for communal tragedy is obvious. African notion of person is as ontological as Aristotle's and Boethius' but it is more communitarian than individual.

Achebe's goal is "a profound understanding of the modes of life and expression among the Igbo, and thus establishes a more complete perspective on African life than was available before its publication."[484] Achebe does not argue that the situation of the Igbo before the encounter with Western cultures was completely in perfect condition. He has not argued that he is providing a unilateral narrative of an African culture and society. His primary purpose is to present in the most authentic manner the historical reality of his people and making it possible to get a genuine critique or appraisal by scholars and readers. In general his narrative reflects "the self-questioning and the internal debates related to the culture." [485] The focus for Achebe is on his contributions to African worldviews, interpretation or African hermeneutics. Achebe's traditional background had a preference for oral tradition of communication. The encounter with the West has provided the opportunity to communicate the historical reality of the Igbo world in a written language.

Achebe assumes this responsibility to narrate the story of the African in its true hermeneutical and historical context. He displays a great knowledge of the use of English language and the ability to reach his non-African audience. But the choice of English, although it did make *Things Fall Apart* get access to millions of readers outside the Igbo culture, it as well raises some hermeneutical questions and which we attempted to address.[486]

3.9 Conclusion

Achebe's goal is to "help my [his] society regain belief in itself and put away the complexes of the years of denigration and self-abasement. And it is

---

[484] Irele, "Introduction," *Chinua Achebe Things Fall Apart, op. cit.*, p. xvii.
[485] *Ibid.*, p. xvi.
[486] Ode Ogede, *Chinua Achebe and the Politics of Representation* (Trenton: NJ: Africa World Press, 2001), pp. 17-18.

essentially a question of education."[487] To accomplish this singular task he presents his narrative in the synthesis of cultures and languages thereby initiating what Gareth Griffiths calls "a world language."[488] Achebe's narrative in Igbo language would have better communicated tragedy in light of African language, thought and philosophy. We already saw the hermeneutics of Igbo names/objects and the rich meaning they communicate to us. Language is an essential aspect of culture and hermeneutics. I think that there is at least one serious criticism against Achebe. That is: he is constrained to seek the approval of 'colonial English language': a language suitable for all cultures and places. It seems there is an excessive dependence on the language (English) beyond its capacity in communicating Igbo worldviews and the truth of their experiences and history.[489] The discourse about cultural and linguistic interactions ought to be pursued further through questioning the emerging intercultural problem of language and hermeneutics present in Achebe's first novel. This is important if we are to truly understand *Things Fall Apart* and African philosophical worldviews, with specific reference to communal tragedy. Every good narrative discloses the truth of our world and the unfolding of history of our common beingness. Achebe's narrative presents us with the opportunity for Igbo African hermeneutics as part of general hermeneutics and philosophy.

As long as African philosophical thinking is concerned, one has to bear in mind that not every part of the discourse above is *abstract philosophy*. For the most part, African or *'Africana philosophy'* portrays a reflection on the realities of life, philosophy of life or thought about existence important to people of African descent. It is more on the practical rather than on the theoretical side of philosophy. In Prof. Tsenay Serequeberhan words, "[T]he discourse of African philosophy…is a reflective and critical effort to rethink the African situation beyond the confines of Eurocentric concepts and categories."[490] Hermeneutics is an essential aspect of this discourse of African

---

[487] Chinua Achebe, *Morning Yet On Creation Day: Essays* (London: Heinemann, 1975), p. 71.

[488] Gareth Grifiths, "Language and Action in the Novels of Achebe," *Critical Perspectives on Chinua Achebe*, Lyn Innes and Bernth Lindfors, eds (Washingston D.C.: Three Continents Press, 1978), p. 70.

[489] Janmohamed, *op. cit.*, pp. 585-586.

[490] Serequeberhan, ed., *African Philosophy: The Essential Readings*, *op. cit.*, pp. 22-23; See also Serequeberhan, *The Hermeneutics of African Philosophy: Horizon and Discourse* (New York: Routledge, 1994.)

philosophy. As we know, philosophy includes metaphysics, epistemology, ethics, anthropology, culture, religion, values etc. There is Thomistic philosophy and there is Jewish philosophy, Oriental philosophy etc. There is Analytic philosophy and there is Continental philosophy etc. Philosophy is not only one thing alone and it is not about one area of the world or reality.

From my reading of Achebe's text and the summary of the chapters of his text above, there are two sides of one intercultural problem that are raised through the narrative. They are: **a**) *Problem of Language*, and **b**) *Problem of Hermeneutics/interpretation*. These are the two sides of the one problem of understanding in general. In chapter four, I shall use Gadamer's claim of the universality of hermeneutics and his principles of philosophical hermeneutics to bear on language and hermeneutics. I will argue that addressing the intercultural problem of language and the problem of hermeneutics in the text, especially about interpreting African communal tragedy, is possible through using Gadamer's framework. Okonkwo's series of tragic events are essentially and hermeneutically the communal tragedy of Umuofia. Gadamer provides us with the platform and a meeting point to understand deeper truths and meanings in an African text.

CHAPTER 4

Gadamer and Achebe: The Intercultural Problem of Language and Hermeneutics

4.1 The Intercultural Problem of Language

In this chapter I will bring Gadamerian hermeneutics to bear on my reading of Achebe's *Things Fall Apart*. This is especially so because of the claim of the universality of hermeneutics with regard to understanding, language and hermeneutics. I engage or dialogue with Achebe's text. However, I make references to views of experts or authorities in African philosophical thought or Achebean scholars. As we recognize in hermeneutics, dialogue involves listening to or accommodating other views, especially if they are foundational views in the development of a particular thought or understanding. Gadamer considers these as good prejudices and/or horizons that we work with.

This chapter is simply set to relate Gadamer's aspects of hermeneutics with Achebe's narrative text. The intercultural problem of language (*4.1*) strictly focuses on the written tradition (literature) and the *linguistic* implications of Achebe's use of English language, and why Igbo (African) language could have been better used, although each language is able to communicate meaning through dialogue rather than in the use of exact words or similar words in translations for understanding others/texts. There is understanding in the act of dialogue itself. The intercultural problem of hermeneutics (*4.2*) focuses on understanding the hermeneutical meanings in Achebe's notion of tragedy narrative (without focusing solely on *language* (linguistic re-presentation) but also on *meaningfulness*, *hermeneutical re-presentation* and the *communication* of *communitarian* understanding of African tragedy as part of African hermeneutics of existence--or--African intercultural experience with Western culture/colonial agency in Achebe.) The *4.2.2* subsection is situated under interpretation/hermeneutic (the intercultural problem of hermeneutics) because I use relevant Gadamer's hermeneutical principles to develop some hermeneutical themes from Achebe's text to better understand communal *personhood* of the tragic Hero-Character (Okonkwo),

African notion of communal tragedy, the understanding of *Chi proverbs* in *Things Fall Apart* and the African notion of *Chi*. For one to clearly understand some of the *Chi proverbs*, one needs to understand the usage of *Chi* with its ontological and religious interpretive implications. The interpretive connections between Gadamer and Achebe in this chapter are only on relevant universal hermeneutical themes and principles (*4.2.2 e*; *4.2.4* and *4.2.5*) in order to develop and advance a 'unique' understanding of our universality of hermeneutics project in Achebe's text: the *communal aspect* of tragedy. In other words, the *communal* aspect of tragedy is the deeper/inner meaning that is not immediately discerned from Achebe's text without the careful use of Gadamer's principles for the conditions of understanding and the universal hermeneutic principles. Let me now provide a description of what intercultural problem of language and hermeneutics means in understanding deeper meanings, especially with regard to African philosophical thought and intercultural experience in Achebe's text.

The intercultural problem of language is the problem or the concern about the problem of language and how it is used in the communication of meaning among people who speak from different cultural backgrounds and of different languages. Interculturality is a common feature of most multicultural societies and is of a peculiar philosophical interest in a post-colonial world. In such a world, one is confronted by a situation that requires that conversation or dialogue must take place between people of different cultural worlds, perspectives and linguistic usage. For instance, in Canada, whenever there is need for a dialogue to take place between a French Canadian (that speaks and understands only French very well) and an English Canadian (that speaks and understands only English very well) in which each only speaks and understands very well one of Canada's two official languages as a *native language*, then there one experiences an intercultural problem of language. That is the situation of the intercultural problem of language because both of the parties need to make sense of what the other person is communicating or the meaning in his/her communication. It is not merely an issue of having a translator or an interpreter, but making sense of the 'inner meaning' or the reality or truth that has been communicated through another language and worldview. In a similar way, when the traditional Africans were encountered by the Europeans in their communities, it was an intercultural situation of how would they understand the language of each other or the inner meanings of their languages.

Gadamer describes this situation as how one understands "what the other person wanted to say and said in that he left much unsaid."[491] It is not about the translator or interpreter providing a *copy* of what is said or reproduced in exact terms. It is about making what is said intelligible (in its meaning) to the other person despite the language or worldview differences. Language (not particular language) in this case is the "realm of human being-together, the realm of common understanding."[492] This kind of situation for conversation/dialogue must have taken place between traditional Africans in Nigeria and the European missionaries and colonizers (who could not speak or understand the inner meanings of the local African languages) in Achebe's text. In the present, for Africans to be understood by Europeans, and vice versa, there ought to be an intercultural approach because of the problem of language as means to address the general problem of understanding or comprehension of meaning. Some consider this problem in the context of hermeneutics as the intercultural dialogue between people of different cultures and languages. This common intercultural problem of understanding has continued to be an important part of hermeneutics in general that needs to be addressed through what has been referred to as dialogic hermeneutics in a world of cultural identity, recognition, mutual respect and mutual understanding. For this thesis, Gadamer provides the framework to address this problem or difficulty. The difficulties for these different socio-cultural groups of people are: what happens with their different languages if they must understand each other? How does genuine comprehension of inner meaning and understanding take place without further misunderstanding and misrepresentation of any of these groups of people?

Within the context of African people, one has to bear in mind the intercultural concerns or difficulties caused by a book like Conrad's *The Heart of Darkness* mentioned above in the general introduction, or the colonial intercultural situation at the background of Achebe's narrative. Another aspect to this intercultural problem of language, as part of the problem of the understanding, is the criticism by some African scholars against Achebe's *English* literature (non-African language literature.) Foremost in this language criticism against Achebe are Ngugi wa Thiong'o (an African scholar), Abdul Janmohamed, and many others. The concerns of this section of the thesis are: **a)** to acknowledge and articulate the condition for the possibility as well as the legitimacy of the intercultural problem of language, especially following the

---

[491] Gadamer, *Philosophical Hermeneutics, op. cit.*, p. 68.
[492] *Ibid.*

colonial experience and continued experience in most African countries, and **b)** how Gadamer provides a valid philosophical and hermeneutical answer to this intercultural problem of language raised by Achebe's English narrative and the consequent criticisms of Achebe by fellow African scholars. The language problem is obviously there, as the opponents of Achebe argue, but is it really an ontological and hermeneutical problem of understanding? Let us take a look at Gadamer's philosophical hermeneutics and the claim of universality of hermeneutics as the framework in addressing this intercultural problem of language.

Gadamer's main task is to focus on the philosophic aspect of the language of hermeneutics. The goal is to understand the act and language of communication in which the truth of being is genuinely understood. As his central assertion suggests, "Being that can be understood is language,"[493] which means his hermeneutics does not intend an absolute or complete comprehension of being. It is rather about our hermeneutical experience and how we understood our hermeneutical experience of being through language. It means we are focusing on the ontological constitution of understanding by language and its relation to beings. The universality of language in the understanding of reality is fundamental and central in hermeneutics.

The question of the problem of language has taken a central position in recent philosophical discussions. Our experience of the world is an experience expressed through language or in a verbal form. Although earlier philosophers such as Schleiermacher, Heidegger, and others have directed their attentions to the role of scientific methods and the natural sciences in conceiving the world as part of a disposal *world* of technology, Gadamer pushes the focus by bringing language at the core of philosophical understanding that links us to the non-manipulable aspects of our existence and the experience of truth without domination through scientific method. Natural science and scientific method see the objective world as a world of technology, a world to be used rather than a world to be truly experienced through interpretive language and understood with respect. The aspect of hermeneutics that involves language

---

[493] Gadamer, *Truth and Method,* trans. Joel Weinsheimer and Donald G. Marshall, *op. cit.*, p. 470; Jeff Malpas, Ulrich Arnswald and Jens Kertscher, eds. *Gadamer's Century: Essays in Honor of Hans-Georg Gadamer* (Cambridge, Massachusetts: The MIT Press, 2002), p. 154.

emphasizes and helps us to reconnect with the essential issues of our existence, our being and the constitution of our world or reality in general.[494]

Following the linguistic constitution of our world and reality, it is appropriate to say that the problem of language is an essential part of the universality of hermeneutics. In Gadamer's theory language is present in every human endeavor, even in the world of science. It is all-encompassing. Language retains its purity in the world of literary art. As Gadamer says, it does not enclose us within a world of relativity.[495] He adds, "not even within our native language. We all experience this when we learn a foreign language, especially on journeys insofar as we master the foreign language to some extent."[496]

Achebe as we have discussed in chapter three learned the use of English language (mastered it as some say) as a foreign language through Western colonial education. He, through his narrative, recognizes the fact that English language is a language of colonial empowerment within his cultural world and that he had no choice but to use it as such. A new foreign language, as Gadamer notes, does not put us in a relativity of any world. It rather opens us to understanding the reality of the world of the new language. The person is able to accept the new language and its relation to reality without enclosing oneself in the relativity of one's native world. One rather gains new understanding through the new language and one's native/original language. This applies to Achebe who had Igbo language as his original language but was compelled through colonial policies to acquire a new language (English) and used it communicate the understanding of his African world.

In line with Gadamer's rejection of captivity within a language or relativity of our linguistic world, Achebe at some points introduces some Igbo words in his English narrative in order to develop understanding between the two languages and cultures as if in a regular consultation with his native/original language and world in order to avoid any misrepresentation in his narrative. But Gadamer argues that learning a foreign language or communicating through a foreign language does not require "constantly

---

[494] Gadamer, *Philosophical Hermeneutics, op. cit.*, pp. 3-4.
[495] *Ibid.*, pp. 15-16; p. 67.
[496] *Ibid.*

consulting inwardly our own world and its vocabulary."[497] However, it does not mean that one cannot endeavor to communicate in another language. Gadamer's point is that an author's original or native language or language of the homeland should never be seen as a hindrance to the narrative of non-African or African worldviews, especially because we "live within a language"[498] and that language-every language for that matter-has the capacity for the universal hermeneutical task of understanding. But there are some healthy intelligible concerns.

The first concern or difficulty for Achebe to write in Igbo language would be the problem of understanding but hermeneutics provides that further aspect of interpretation and "the saying-further (*Weitersagen*) of a message."[499] Each language has a claim to the universality that is appropriate to understanding, as Gadamer notes. This is because what should be understood should be understood through language which is a basic principle of hermeneutics. Gadamer further expounds that language involves the interaction of the inner and the external aspects in understanding. This means that words carry inner or deeper meaning in a discourse.[500]

Let us recall that the central place of language as the medium through which hermeneutics is carried out has been discussed at length in chapter two above. Following this role of language in understanding, it is equally a central problem of hermeneutics. Language guides one and determines the hermeneutic act of understanding through interpretation. Through interpretation one presents in clearer or more explicit terms the structure of understanding thereby help resolve the problem of hermeneutics. In general the problem of language and the problem of hermeneutics are all part of one central problem of understanding (applied as interpretation.) Gadamer explains:

> the hermeneutic problem acquired systematic importance because
> the romantics recognized the inner unity of intelligere and
> explicare. Interpretation is not an occasional, post facto
> supplement to understanding; rather, understanding is always

---

[497] *Ibid.*
[498] *Ibid.*, pp. 15-16.
[499] *Ibid.*, p. 17. Achebe's concern will be: is Igbo language understandable to many educated people in the world? How could he reach out to enough people through his narrative in Igbo?
[500] *Ibid.*

interpretation, and hence interpretation is the explicit form of understanding. In accordance with this insight, interpretative language and concepts are also an inner structural element of understanding.[501]

Gadamer's theory of language, in addressing this one problem of understanding, introduces a form of language revolution into philosophy. The use of language goes beyond a phenomenological method of experience to a conscious hermeneutical reflection on everyday existence and the worldviews of cultures.[502] For him, our understanding requires us to integrate the temporal aspects of human experience, whether as past, present or the future in ways that provide meaning and reveal the reality of language, because as Gadamer says, it "unfolds a phenomenology of language"[503] in the world of human experience.

Human experience of the world brings to light these inseparable but limited relations in understanding. Meanwhile, although our perspectives are given pre-reflectively, our understanding is limited because of the limits of our language. That implies that "there is no 'world in itself' beyond its presence as the subject matter of a particular language community."[504] In Gadamer's view reality has to be expressed as the subject matter of a dialogue through language. The relation between reality and language is such that does not create, control and objectify materials. It means, "[O]ur possession of language, or better, our possession by language, is the ontological condition for our understanding of the texts that address us."[505] The possession of language as a condition for understanding is not about the ontology for "self-founding," but presupposes that our immersion in tradition is linguistic rather than emphasize on methodology and objective control. We are immersed in our ontology of "total language dependence."[506] Language discovers the unknown but it is not *a means* of representing a truth already known. In this way

---

[501] Gadamer, *Truth and Method,* trans. Joel Weinsheimer and Donald G. Marshall , *op. cit.,* p. 306; Gadamer, *Truth and Method* (New York: The Seabury Press, 1975), p. 274.
[502] Kertscher, *op. cit.,* p. 137; See Gadamer, *Gesammelte Werk,* 3 (Tübingen: J. C. B. Mohr [Paul Siebeck], 1987), pp. 141-142; See also Gadamer on Husserl in *Gesammelte Werke,* 2 (Tübingen: J. C. B. Mohr [Paul Siebeck], 1986), p. 361.
[503] Gadamer, *Philosophical Hermeneutics, op. cit.,* p. xxviii.
[504] *Ibid.,* pp. xxviii-xxix.
[505] *Ibid.,* p. xxix.
[506] *Ibid.*

language is not reduced to the status of mere tool of understanding. There is no extra-linguistic relation with the world that puts this "world into the instrumentation of language. To begin by assuming such a schema is to reduce language to the status of a tool, which fails to grasp its all-encompassing, world-constituting significance."[507]

Gadamer further explains that language is not an object or something that we use and reject after it has done its service. Also we do not find ourselves as consciousness over against the world, i.e., as a tool of understanding in a wordless condition. Our knowledge of ourselves is linguistic and it is essential to our being human. It ought not to be seen as an object for it is in essence *what we are*, i.e., *our* language and it *speaks us*. When Gadamer says that *language speaks us,* it implies that our language of existence (any language) is capable of expressing our worldviews. As human beings who have languages, we are spoken to through our respective languages. Gadamer accepts that language and understanding are inseparable structural aspects of our being-in-the-world.[508] Language is not an optional condition of understanding.[509] Through the language we use, the objects of our concern appear to us depending on the world already disclosed to us. We are always directed or oriented to a particular world by means of language. As Gadamer recommends we focus on the actual *life* of language as speaking, which is a process of communication that is dialogical rather than focus only on the "form or structure of language."[510]

Following Gadamer's claim of universality of hermeneutics on our discourse on language above, I think, it is possible and pertinent for Achebe to express African reality in African language since language, any language, is inseparable from reality. Achebe does not use African language *per se* in pursuing his *African* narrative task. His view and use of language generate some hermeneutical difficulties in the translation and contemporary reading of his narrative literature. Each language is appropriate for hermeneutics because each language uses its exact words to communicate understanding in its very way. A language can have a suitable or appropriate word that uniquely describes an object within its cultural world. However, other cultures do not

---

[507] Gadamer, *Philosophical Hermeneutics, op. cit.,* p. xxix.
[508] Heidegger's influence on Gadamer is well known at this point.
[509] Gadamer, *Philosophical Hermeneutics, op. cit.,* p. xxix.
[510] *Ibid.,* p. xxx. Editor's Introduction.

necessarily have words to describe the same word, but through dialogue interlocutors can make up for the lack of word. The cultural world of a society is the same as the world one confronts in hermeneutics. As Gadamer states:

> When person lives in a language, he is filled with the sense of the unsurpassable appropriateness of the words he uses for the subject matter he is talking about. It seems impossible that other words in other languages could name the objects equally well. The suitable word always seems to be one's own and unique, just as the thing referred to is always unique. The agony of translation consists ultimately in the fact that the original words seems to be inseparable from the things they refer to, so that to make a text intelligible one often has to give an interpretative paraphrase of it rather than translate it. The more sensitively our historical consciousness reacts, the more it seems to be aware of the untranslatability of the unfamiliar.[511]

Our language is an essential part of our existence which is transmitted as traditions to future generations. The use of an African language or a continental African language in writing African literature could be interpreted as part of what Gadamer describes as the "power of 'tradition.' "[512] Language provides us with the resources to present, preserve and guard our traditions that connect us to the world.[513] Certainly Gadamer is right that every language is able to say whatever it wants to say. But according to African scholars and linguists, language only better says whatever it says within its cultural milieu of understanding. A language may say whatever it wants to say, but it does not communicate meaning to other person who is not able to understand that particular language (a linguist argument.) How will one know that a language has effectively communicated a particular meaning when one does not understand or use that language to express understanding? Gadamer's response is that it is only in dialogue, although it seems to us that our language does a better job at representing our reality. This is why in some of the examples of Igbo proverbs in Achebe one still has to provide some explanations or transliterations of their meanings for a non-Igbo reader. This explanation or transliteration is a confirmation of the universality of hermeneutics. Achebe's

---

[511] Gadamer, *Truth and Method,* trans. Joel Weinsheimer and Donald G. Marshall, *op. cit.,* p. 403; Gadamer, *Truth and Method* (New York: The Seabury Press, 1975), p. 363.
[512] Gadamer, *Philosophical Hermeneutics, op. cit.,* p. 29.
[513] *Ibid.*

use of English language (other than an African language), some African scholars argue, denies African narrative literature the nuances it may have in disclosing Africans' perception of their world and in the continual transmission/preservation of their African worldviews. This obviously is contrary to hermeneutics as Gadamer perceives it.

The disclosive function of language is of importance to hermeneutics. Language reveals the world around us and does not focus on itself but through language reality or our subject matter is understood. With this disclosive nature of language one knows how to "make oneself understood by others regarding the subject matter."[514] Language discloses reality and reality does influence language. Language strives to press beyond the limits of established conventions while it discloses reality. The question that is often raised by African scholars and linguists (and may not be so important to non-African readers or important to hermeneutists) is: was Achebe justified in using English language since he is only using it to make his culture (his subject matter)-African worldviews understood? One recalls that English language at this time was an important language within Achebe's world. He describes his approach as "speaking of African experience in a world–wide language."[515] This domesticated language is "able to' bring out' the African writer's 'message best' without being altered 'to the extent that its value as a medium of international language will be lost'."[516] Achebe uses a new approach to language that presents African world "through mediated lenses."[517] Again, does the situation justify Achebe's choice of English language? According to Gadamer, there is no problem with using another language. However, one has to recall that Gadamer, for this book, does not only provide a hermeneutical *framework* but he also provides an *optimistic platform* and *a meeting point* to advance the interpretation/understanding of the other (i.e. an African other.) In light of the universality of hermeneutics as constituted by language, there is an ontological and hermeneutical justification for Achebe's use of English language, but the reason against its justification by some African scholars is rather ideological, philosophical as well as political.

---

[514] *Ibid.*, p. xxx.
[515] Okpewho, "Introduction," *Chinua Achebe's Things Fall Apart: A Casebook, op. cit.*, pp. 28-29.
[516] Ogede, *op. cit.*, p. 97.
[517] Francoise Lionet affirms that the encounter of two languages (African and European) offers the local people to be creative in incorporating useful "Western" tools, techniques, or strategies into their own cosmology or Weltanschauung." –See Ogede, *op. cit.*, p. 97.

On Achebe's second concern or difficulty, one has to recall that in chapter three it was clearly noted that the colonial English language was a privilege matter or a socio-political matter. Those of Achebe's age bracket and above who could not express themselves in English or in Europeanized African way were considered illiterate people. Using English language was a tool to foster acceptability and belongingness to a colonial world with colonial 'philosophy' and perspective. (The English colonizers used the policy of 'Association'—that means that the colonized maintain some of their cultural practices and identities while the colonizers occupy the positions of administration in their Euro-African economic relations. The French used the policy of 'Assimilation'—that means that the colonized are meant to become part of one French cultural identity by adopting French language and culture. It is the 19th and 20th Centuries' policy of expanding French culture in their colonies. One could relate or compare the situation with Gadamer's objections to Heidegger's involvement with National Socialism (Nazi Germany) and cultural imperialism of his time.) Gadamer recommends that the effort to foster 'a great community' includes living without fear of exploitation, non use of means of oppression and hegemony, and recognition of cultural identity (as horizon.) I think Achebe directly and indirectly acknowledges this constraint in using English language to express the truth of Igbo world because he saw it as a problem for his African characters to express themselves in a language they do not speak or understand. This is his second concern or difficulty and his first concern was that Igbo language has no wide recognition and readership. Thus Achebe tries to "resolve this problem"[518] by adopting an African vernacular style in order to inject a new vigor into English language mode of expression which does not truly capture African meanings as they are intended. Meanwhile, the attempt by Achebe confirms the ability for any language to apprehend any cultural reality.

For Gadamer, there is no *special method* to get at the truth. Every language describes reality from a horizon. Although Gadamer's claim of universality of hermeneutics accepts that language is always more than a tool, Achebe's use of English language as a tool in his narratives does suggest that one could go further in seeing language as the very medium by which we apprehend and understand our world. This we know corresponds to the ontological and universal nature of language, as Gadamer states. But I argue

---

[518] Lindfors, *op. cit.*, p. 556.

that Achebe's use of English language to present African worldviews (in an effort to avoid misrepresentation) does create an intercultural problem of language since a particular language (English) is *used* as a means. It also expresses that when a language is used (it always is in a sense), and in this case to disseminate African thought or African experience, especially following a history of colonial misrepresentation, misunderstanding and hegemony. But yet language goes beyond our use of it. Meanwhile, the strength of the argument against Achebe's approach is strongly on the colonial utilitarian application of language which failed to adequately present the inner meaning and totality of the African world without some serious difficulties of understanding that arose from the encounter between these two cultures and different languages.

Language is the mirror through which we look at the worldviews of a people. If language is analogically a mirror through which worldviews are expressed, I think, from a linguistic and politico-philosophical perspective, that Achebe's usage of English language somehow denies Igbo language and African people the opportunity to genuinely present African thought, epistemologies, ontology of person as communal and worldviews to other cultures. In a simple term, I will say that Achebe's approach takes away the opportunity for African language to develop its possibilities and suitably transmit its nuance of reality, especially in a colonial and post-colonial world because it was not fully applied in the narrative. Every hermeneutical theory is not merely a linguistic theory but also an ontological theory for understanding 'being' and 'truth' for African people, African experience and the development of African languages.

Now let us take a look at the fusion of both languages in Achebe's narrative since he adopted an African vernacular style to English language. How does that apply to Gadamer's philosophical hermeneutics and its claim of universality of hermeneutics? Gadamer's philosophical hermeneutics does use the understanding of horizons-the fusion of horizons-which helps us to comprehend reality in general to encourage a further application of language. In this way he offers us a framework to address the intercultural problem of language and hermeneutics because no one person or culture understands all about reality.

In providing a framework, Gadamer does not argue against the justification for choosing English language since reality could be accessed by *any* language, but he justifies the universal capacity of language-any language for that matter-to be used in the task of hermeneutics. This point goes to support the understanding that the language of a people reflects the reality of the people in question. It is not that English language cannot reflect reality; rather it promotes English culture/people than the people of other linguistic culture. In a way this is not a hermeneutical issue, as some scholars will argue. Every language certainly has the capacity to communicate reality but a specific language is most suitable for the specific people it belongs to as part of their life-world. It means that to avoid using an African language creates some nuance challenges (that can be overcome through dialogue) in reflecting African worldviews in some specific contexts. For instance, to translate *Umuofia* as "people of the forest"[519] (Joseph McLaren's translation) or "people of the bush" does not truly capture the inner meaning of that name and it could be derogatory for the native speakers of Igbo language. Igbo names in the narrative like "Ikemefuna" (meaning--May my strength not be lost), "Okonkwo," (meaning--A male child born on *Nkwo* market day)[520] "Nneka" (meaning--Mother is superior or precious) etc have deeper hermeneutical implications or bear hermeneutical weight in understanding the context and the specific message in the text. No good English transliteration will suitably capture the philosophical meaning without drowning the precision and clear points these names make in the narrative or text. Another good example is Achebe's proverb: "Whenever you see a toad jumping in the broad daylight, then know that something is after its life."[521] The Igbo language rendering of this proverb is: *Awo anaghi agba ọsọ ehihie n'efu.* The English translation of it in the text does not bring out the deeper meaning and the philosophical depth of this proverb or help a non-Igbo person/reader to appreciate its hermeneutical purpose in that part of the narrative.

The 'toad' in that proverb context stands for man in his ontological and existential situation. The toad has to move/run/jump because there is an urgent

---

[519] McLaren, *op. cit.*, pp. 27-28.

[520] The Igbo people have four days in a week. There are four market days: Eke, Orie, Afor and Nkwo. Children are named according to the market day they were born or because something very significant happened around that time of their birth or because wishes are fulfilled. When one is not aware of these situations, it is possible to misunderstand the inner meaning of the names.

[521] Achebe, *Things Fall Apart* (Canada: Anchor Canada edition 2009), p. 203.

situation (life and death, important issue.) Madu translates it in as: "The nocturnal toad does not run during the day in vain."[522] One could consider Madu's translation as closer to the inner meaning of that Igbo proverb than Achebe's. But none of these captures, in my view, the coded meaning of the proverb in the situation under consideration. This is why in my later analysis of this proverb it has a precise hermeneutic meaning as "urgency or importance" based on the contexts and the subject matter of the discussion in Achebe's part of the text (Gadamer's principles of hermeneutic circle, going back and forth, whole and part, and vice versa etc were applied in this case.) The argument is that the promotion of indigenous African language in Achebe would have enabled the indigenous language, through writing, gain its "true ideality"[523] and its true intellectual quality. The capacity of every language to have intellectual quality means that each language is able to philosophically express its world in its own way, independent of how other cultures perceive reality.

As noted, in every language there is a unity of thought and reality. When that truth which is being communicated to us is not well uttered then more harm is done than good. It means that African people and their languages lose more because of lack of development of their philosophical linguistic heritage. In the way that Achebe had it, English language gains more because he incorporates the Igbo expressions within English, thereby showing how philosophically dynamic and vibrant English is in the fusion of languages. Now, if the issue is on the 'truth for us', then it ought to be what 'the truth we wish to communicate to others is all about', i.e., Igbo African experience of truth given to the rest of the world. It is about what we mean to communicate and not what the languages of the 'reader', 'hearer' or 'listener' will like us communicate to him/her. What determines the content of communication is the subject matter or reality of the speaker or writer and not the reader or listener. 'Listening' involves overcoming your own negative prejudices and socio-historical conditions in order to understand the truth of what has been presented to you as it was intended, and more. Let us take a look at the second aspect of this intercultural problem of language which is ontologically and

---

[522] Madu, *African Symbols, Proverbs and Myths: The Hermeneutics of Destiny, op. cit.*, p. 217.
[523] Gadamer, *Truth and Method* , trans. Joel Weinsheimer and Donald G. Marshall, *op. cit.*, p. 392; p. 394; Gadamer, *Truth and Method* (New York: The Seabury Press, 1975), pp. 352-353.

hermeneutically based, not from the linguistic and political perspective of African scholars and linguists.

This is where Gadamer's framework helps the intercultural problem of language. So far we have discussed the linguistic perspective that articulates and supports African language development or a continental African language for the communication of African truth and meanings in text or narrative. According to Gadamer:

> this question is simply how every language, despite its difference from other languages, can say everything it wants. Linguistics teaches us that every language does this in its own way. But we then ask, how, amid the variety of these forms of utterance, there is still the intimate unity of thought and speech, so that everything that has been transmitted in writing can be understood. Thus we are interested in the opposite of what linguistics tried to investigate. The intimate unity of language and thought is the premise from which linguistics too starts. It is this alone that has made it a science.[524]

Gadamer's position is different from the view of the linguistic above who insist that their particular language best communicates reality in its own way. His view is that our being-in-the-world is shaped by language.[525] He maintains that in language reality becomes visible to us. This aspect of the argument is the hermeneutical justification of Gadamer on the use of any foreign language to communicate a worldview.

In Gadamer's hermeneutical and ontological view, people like Achebe are able to communicate the reality of their world in any foreign language of their choice as long as they master and understand the foreign language in question for their narrative. The cherished purpose of the classic work of Achebe is because it shows or expresses an African truth and intelligible worldviews. The heart of Gadamer's hermeneutical project is that there is the language we speak and the language that emerges in an attempt to understand other traditions/people's worldviews. This makes Gadamer's approach appropriate in addressing Achebe's difficulties, especially for the African scholars who critique his narrative from a linguistic and political perspective.

---

[524] *Ibid.*, p. 403.
[525] McDowell, *op. cit.*, p. 183.

What Gadamer is after is not a discussion on linguistics but on the inner constitution of understanding by language as such.

As an inner constitution of understanding, language view is a view of the world or and a view of the world is a view of reality. Gadamer further solidifies this argument when he states that reality takes place within language. This is part of the essential meaning of the universality of hermeneutics that is grounded in within language. He says:

> Reality does not happen "behind the back" of language; it happens rather behind the backs of those who live in the subjective opinion that they have understood "the world" (or can no longer understand it); that is, reality happens precisely *within* language.[526]

The reality in question is the reality that is found *within* or within the *inner* language. As he noted earlier, there are the outer word and the inner word (logos or language.) It is in the inner word or language that the universality of hermeneutics is understood. It is in the inner universality that all these particular languages and different people (different cultures) are able to communicate meanings that are also truly understood. This view recalls the history of the development of philosophical hermeneutics and the claim of the universality of hermeneutics in which Plato, Aristotle, Augustine, Husserl etc were of great importance to Gadamer. The λόγος προφορικός (*logos prophorikos*) and λόγος ἐνδιάθετος (*logos endiathetos*) are essential parts of the understanding. The *logos endiathetos* (inner word) describes this inner constitution that makes it possible for our thought to be united in the description of the same reality despite our different languages. Whatever is said in a language could as well be communicated in another language, for instance, in the metaphysics of beauty. The Greek word for the beautiful is 'kalon' could be expressed in German as 'schön' (adjective for beautiful), or in African Igbo language as 'mma' (*mara mma*—beautiful.)[527] For these different languages, the essence (the inner meaning) of the beautiful is expressible or communicable by the respective languages in its own way and also through dialogue. That means there is again an inner or spiritual dimension to language. This is the area that Gadamer is interested in as long as hermeneutics

---

[526] Gadamer, *Philosophical Hermeneutics, op. cit.*, p. 35.
[527] See my reflection above on African notion of the person as the beauty of life (mma, mma ndu, madu.)

and ontology is concerned. It shows the hermeneutical richness of language and Gadamer's hermeneutics guarantees the development to a richer language[528] through intercultural encounter.

The richness of language is truly seen in its being the universal means of understanding[529] and to know a language is to be open to "participation [participate] in a dialogue with others that transforms and broadens the horizons from which we start."[530] The being in language is that which is said through language itself. Using a language would mean being less aware of the language itself. This is the meaning of the "forgetfulness of language that its real being consists in what is said in it. What is said in it constitutes the common world in which we live."[531] Gadamer observes that what is said in language is part of the common world of our experience. The common world of our experience is communicated to us through literature or texts. Language gives us the real being of existence through what is said to us. To speak a language means to communicate, to share one's thoughts and so speak to someone. It is the dialogic aspect of language that emphasizes less of the individual (I-lessness) and thus places the object of communication "before the eyes of the other person to whom I speak."[532] There is no individual language. Every language has the role to communicate and in communicating we go beyond ourselves.

The role of language is the communication of the truth in every linguistic world. Language makes it possible for the different cultural worlds to understand each other. In language there is no mutual exclusive existence because it is within language that we encounter common understanding. This encounter is the basis for an intercultural world in which each foreign world offers something to the other. Gadamer says, "[T]he other world that stands over against us is not only a foreign, but a relatively other world. It does not have its own truth simply *for itself* but also its truth *for us*." [533] It is in this light that Achebe's use of English language has thoughtfully and philosophically communicated the truth of the subject matter for itself and also its truth for us

---

[528] Taylor, *op. cit.*, p. 292.
[529] Gadamer, *Philosophical Hermeneutics, op. cit.*, p. xxx.
[530] *Ibid.*
[531] *Ibid.*, p. 65.
[532] *Ibid.*
[533] *Ibid.*, p. xxxix.

(others.) Achebe's narrative has some truths to share with the rest of the world and it does communicate these truths in Gadamer's view.

Language reveals truth and man uses language to reveal or express himself, according to Gadamer. Every human being lives within an environment that has language. This is part of our historical fate put thus: "Every historical situation elicits new attempts to render the world into language. Each makes its contribution to the tradition....As Heidegger has said, we are therefore always 'on the way to language'." [534] Gadamer explains that we do not choose our language, but we could develop our language while we communicate the truth of our world. Since we do not choose our language, then this choice/ situation is part of our historical fate. Our hermeneutical task provides the opportunities for the development of the infinite possibilities of our language as the medium of understanding our being. This relates to Gadamer's comment about Aristotle that "man is truly the being who has language"[535] and language reflects our being/world.

For Gadamer, "every language is a view of the world, it is not primarily because it is a particular type of language...but because of what is said or handed down in this language." [536] The possession of language is not a privilege for some human beings. To possess a language is to possess a world. Since we possess language in a linguistic world, then we have a world of existence to describe. Igbo language (as an African language) necessarily describes a world of its own—an Igbo African world, a world of its experience. Gadamer elaborates, "[L]anguage is not just one of man's possessions in the world; rather, on it depends the fact that man has a world at all"[537] that is communicable through language. At this level, each of us is able to communicate with the other because our understanding is ontologically dependent on the inner or inner unity of language and not necessarily on the particular type or original language of our conversation. It is also dependent on the universality of reason.

---

[534] *Ibid.*,pp. lv-lvi.
[535] *Ibid.*, p. 68.
[536] Gadamer, *Truth and Method* , trans. Joel Weinsheimer and Donald G. Marshall, *op. cit.*, pp. 438-439.
[537] *Ibid.*, p. 440.

In summary, every language communicates its own view of reality and worldviews. Gadamer's theory of language affirms that through language one comprehends the world-views of different cultures, peoples and their experience of reality. He notes that every language is essentially communicable of all human knowledge of the world.[538] He further argues that the wholeness of human existence in the world is understood through language. There are two situations and answers in the question of the intercultural problem of language in this section.

From the first perspective, some African scholars and linguists argue, on a philosophical and political basis, that Achebe uses English language in his narrative for a colonial utilitarian purpose, and more so as a privilege tool for Western acceptance and recognition. By doing that, he is accused of ideologically, politically and philosophically (but not hermeneutically for Gadamer) hindering the development of Igbo African language which is also African view of reality in a colonial and post-colonial world. But some scholars may argue that this political or ideological concern is counter to hermeneutics. However, one could add that hermeneutics is involved in everything, political, ideological or not. In this regard some examples of misconstrued proverb and names were provided from Achebe's text.

From the second perspective, based on Gadamer's universality of hermeneutics view, the main argument in defense of an author like Achebe is that we are not discussing linguists' view of language. We are rather discussing the hermeneutical and ontological view of language that does not suggest that only one's particular language can accurately communicate the truth of one's world. There is a unity of thought and language. It is not impossible that other languages could translate well our words. Each language can do it in its own way. So the essential interpersonal and intercultural problem of language is best addressed through the universality of hermeneutics and the place of 'inner' language in the communication of meaning and truth. The inner meaning is where communication is universal. This makes the intercultural problem of language a *surmountable problem* by dialogue for Gadamer because we can understand other languages within the inner unity of language. It is in the spirit of the inner language that we are united in

---

[538] Gadamer, *Philosophical Hermeneutics, op. cit.,* p. 61.

understanding as *I* and *Thou* (interpersonal as well as intercultural) in dialogue/conversation.[539]

Some of the important features of language, according to Gadamer, are: a) its "I-lessness," disclosive and dialogic. To speak means to speak to someone, b) there is the universality of language. Every people/culture makes use of language to express itself and be understood by others.

Let me now discuss Gadamer and Achebe in the context of a written language tradition (literature). One has to remember that we are only relating Gadamer's relevant arguments to where they connect to Achebe's narrative/literature and purpose of written tradition in light of the claim of the universality of hermeneutics and to further address the intercultural problem of language.

4.1.1 Gadamer and Achebe: Written Tradition (Literature)

Schleiermacher is credited to be the first to recognize the place of hermeneutics in oral tradition. However, Gadamer thinks that Plato had earlier expressed concerns that written tradition has more problems in interpretation because it causes more misunderstanding and misrepresentation than oral tradition.[540] Hermeneutics deals with the problem of understanding the utterances of people and not only written texts. Gadamer affirms:

> the task of hermeneutics was first and foremost the understanding of texts. Schleiermacher was the first to downplay the importance of writing for the hermeneutical problem because he saw that the problem of understanding was raised--and perhaps in its fullest form—by oral utterance too....In actual fact, writing is central to the hermeneutical phenomenon insofar as its detachment both from the writer or author and from a specifically addressed recipient or reader gives it a life of its own. What is fixed in writing has raised itself into public sphere of meaning in which everyone who can read has an equal share.[541]

---

[539] *Ibid.*, pp. 65-66.
[540] See Plato, *Seventh Letter* 341c, 344c, and *Phaedrus* 275.
[541] Gadamer, *Truth and Method*, trans. Joel Weinsheimer and Donald G. Marshall, *op. cit.*, p. 393.

An important advantage of written tradition is that we understand a written text based on what it says to the reader or interpreter. It allows for comprehension of new meaning without emphasizing the psychological aspect of the writer. This makes the meaning of whatever is written down to be "fundamentally identifiable and repeatable."[542] Written tradition provides us with texts for clear thoughts. Gadamer explains the hermeneutical benefits of a written tradition:

> our understanding remains curiously unsure and fragmentary when we have no written tradition of a culture but only dumb monuments, and we do not call this information about the past 'history'. Texts, on the other hand, always express a whole…in every detail when they can be interpreted as writing…Thus written texts present the real hermeneutical task. Writing involves self-alienation. Overcoming it, reading the text, is thus the highest task of understanding. Even the pure signs of an inscription can be seen properly and articulated correctly only if the text can be transformed back into language.[543]

Most African traditional societies depend on oral tradition in communicating their worldviews. This situation hampers the understanding of African thoughts. Achebe could be said to be among those that started the revolution from oral to written tradition in African thought/literature. This is a major problem to African communities and the communication of the truth of their historical experience. This is one of the gains of Achebe's contributions through his tragedy narrative. In Achebe's literature one sees the relevance of Gadamer's view that written texts provide the material for real hermeneutical task[544] and the effective communication of a people's world of experience. As Gadamer affirms, an oral tradition is deficient in carrying out the real hermeneutical task. But written tradition provides the wholeness necessary in interpretation. Achebe's written narrative accomplishes an important task of expressing and correcting some of the misrepresentations of African philosophical worldviews. Written tradition is consistent, reliable, durable, and expresses the wholeness in history which is part of the universality of

---

[542] *Ibid.*, p. 394.
[543] *Ibid.*, p. 392.
[544] *Ibid.*

hermeneutics. In my view, Janmohamed, an Achebean commentator, describes the advantage of written tradition in a way similar to Gadamer:

> When an utterance 'is put in writing it can be inspected in much greater detail, in its parts as well as in its whole, backwards as well as forwards, out of context as well as in its setting; in other words, it can be subjected to a quite different type of scrutiny and critique than is possible with purely verbal communication. Speech is no longer tied to an 'occasion'; it becomes timeless. Nor is it attached to a person; no paper, it becomes more abstract, more depersonalized.'[545]

In this way the task of interpretation is centered on a common subject matter which written tradition consistently guarantees. Oral tradition could easily lose sight of the subject matter. For Gadamer, focusing on the subject matter is central to hermeneutics. A true hermeneutical task involves genuine dialogue between the written texts and the reader/interpreter. The conversational partners focus on "a common subject matter." [546] The subject matter in hermeneutics guarantees consistency in what a text utters to generations of hermeneutists and moreover "[A]ll literary documents possess a certain 'ideality of meaning' insofar as what they say to the present is in written form and is thus detached from the psychological and historical peculiarities of their origin."[547] For us to understand the subject matter of our discourse the emphasis of interpretation must be on language itself—a written language. In this light there is a firm connection between Gadamer's idea of the universality of hermeneutics and what Achebe accomplished in putting African narrative in a written tradition.

Gadamer equally focuses his hermeneutics on the act of understanding as an event. The act of understanding involves the interpreter and the text as essential to his hermeneutical principle. In this way he avoids simple "techniques and methods of interpretation, all of which assume understanding to be a deliberate product of self-conscious reflection."[548] Hermeneutics is not

---

[545] Abdul Janmohamed, "Sophisticated Primitivism: The Syncretism of Oral and Literate Modes in Achebe's *Things Fall Apart*," *Chinua Achebe Things Fall Apart (Authoritative Text, Contexts and Criticism)*, Francis Abiola Irele, ed (New York: W. W. Norton & Company, 2009), p. 574.
[546] Gadamer, *Philosophical Hermeneutics, op. cit.*, p. xx.
[547] *Ibid.*
[548] *Ibid.*, p. xxviii.

mainly technique and method of interpretation but more of a linguistic activity in which the now and past interrelate in language.[549] Gadamer adds that through writing language develops true conceptual quality and so gains its full value.

What is handed down as tradition could be orally given through repetition of stories, myths or texts that are clear and easy to investigate. There is constant availability and intellectual quality in what has been handed in writing. While oral tradition is repetitive, written tradition realizes full interpretation because of the subject matter. The past and the present are available because all necessary information about a people's worldview is written down and not through repetition. African tradition is a victim of this huge chasm between the past and the present because of the hermeneutical disconnect between them (the African past and the present.) In oral tradition one loses some of the qualities of communication preserved in human history and the loss of the continuity that one gets from the effective use of memory. In Gadamer's understanding this is one of the contributions of Hegel when he quotes him as saying that transmission of history is to "make memory last."[550] In a typical oral tradition as well as in a written tradition society the power of memory is undeniably crucial in the re-presentation and interpretation of worldviews, and transmission of tradition (oral and written.)

Gadamer makes reference to Plato's concern about written tradition and argues that written tradition does have its own weaknesses, especially when its contents are misunderstood.[551] He adds that the context in which something is spoken to us could affect the meaning and interpretation of what is said to us. It is not only the context or circumstances of the spoken word, but it could have a different meaning because of "the manner of speaking, the tone of voice, the tempo."[552] But, writing equally means having 'an equal share' of material for the task of understanding. One basic advantage of written tradition is that what is written is presented in its ideality and identity. However, we do

---

[549] *Ibid.*
[550] Gadamer, *Truth and Method*, trans. Joel Weinsheimer and Donald G. Marshall, *op. cit.*, p. 393.
[551] Gadamer thinks that Plato's position that written tradition has more problem of misunderstanding is based on Plato's effort to cover up problems in his writing and art. See Plato, *Seventh Letter* 341c, 344c, and *Phaedrus,* 275.
[552] Gadamer, *Truth and Method*, trans. Joel Weinsheimer and Donald G. Marshall, *op. cit.*, p. 395.

recognize that speech also carries with it the ideality of the meaning and understanding. Although Gadamer rejects the attempt to make hermeneutics a science in the light of the method of the natural sciences, he does not reject being methodological in hermeneutics. He affirms that writing presents us with the pure quality of information and understanding rather than in an oral tradition.

In African tradition, it is important to observe the advantage or role of oral tradition. The spoken words could be better interpreted following emotional elements, tone, and circumstance. It also focuses on the 'creative personality' of the individual. Gadamer's critical view is appropriate to Igbo African oral tradition because of the place of the psychological, emotional and situational elements in oral tradition. Oral tradition lacks the safety for understanding. He recommends moving the focus of hermeneutics from an oral to a written one. Written tradition encourages the grasping of full meaning and validity in the communication of truth and meaning. Gadamer explains that written tradition presents us with high level opportunities for arriving at objectivity in the claim to truth and has self-authenticity. Human experiences and understanding are best made present through a written tradition.[553]

Hermeneutics deals with understanding texts and literature is like any written transmitted or handed text that needs to be understood. For Gadamer literature as text provides hermeneutics its object for application of interpretation. The most important part is in the effect of communication emerging from a given text.[554] Narrative literature is an important object of hermeneutics. Similarly, Plato's dialogues as literature serve for the hermeneutical understanding among contemporary philosophers. Gadamer describes these dialogues (narratives) as having useful dialectical and hermeneutical values.[555] His approach to literature shows the historical dimension of the hermeneutical task of understanding and meaning. The historical situation of a philosopher is an important place to proceed with the task of hermeneutics. Universal hermeneutics requires that one identifies the

---

[553] Gadamer observes that there is an advantage in written tradition since people often see whatever is written as self-authenticating.
[554] Gadamer, *Truth and Method*, trans. Joel Weinsheimer and Donald G. Marshall, *op. cit.*, p. 393.
[555] Gadamer, *Philosophical Hermeneutics, op. cit.*, p. xxii.

hermeneutical situation of interpretation. Gadamer includes literary narratives like *Mommsen's History of Rome* as one of such written narratives with a clear historico-hermeneutical situation.[556] It is this historio-hermeneutical relevance that connects Gadamer's hermeneutics to Achebe's fictional narrative with a true historico-hermeneutical situation in which it was written.

Following the above, Achebe's *Things Fall Apart*, as a literature, relates with the historico-hermeneutical situation in which it is written in order to disclose understanding and meaning. For Gadamer it is the function of a philosopher to be aware of the hermeneutical tension between the goal and the nature of the reality he/she wishes to uncover. For one to be aware of the tension it requires being conscious of the hermeneutical situation and text/literature at the center of interpretation. Hermeneutics must start from the situation that a person seeking to understanding has a bond with and whatever that is transmitted in text. It has to be connected with the tradition from which the text or literature speaks.

The literature of a people gives one a new perspective of understanding them. Gadamer holds that in the learning analysis of literature one has access to what is handed through language. This point underscores my concern that Achebe has problems with using English rather than Igbo language for expressing Igbo worldviews in literature. The content and nuances of literature are primarily transmitted through the language of the people, i.e. the language of their daily lives. Some of his English narrative lines do not adequately represent exact Igbo worldviews, for instance in the transliteration of some Igbo proverbs, the presentation of the notion of *Chi* as merely individual fate in understanding tragedy etc. This book articulates these issues later in this chapter under the intercultural problem of hermeneutics.

Whenever Achebe uses English language, he ought to be open to accept the interpretive implications it brings within the standpoint of the African narrative. There is quite a complex linguistic relation here between the text and the interpreter. The authentic communication of one's worldviews or the meanings in a work of literature involves language and a familiar world. There has to be a meeting point or point of contact for genuine communication to

---

[556] *Ibid.*, p. xviii. The historical book "Mommsen's History of Rome" is a product of its time and the influence of the period.

take place. This point of contact is one of the conditions of understanding in which the worldviews and languages are both put into consideration.

In Achebe's narrative literature one sees a piece of literary art or the experience of art, as Gadamer describes it. Understanding Achebe's narrative literature requires coming close to the being of meaning of what has been transmitted. That is the being of meaning of African thought transmitted in texts. Gadamer observes, "[B]ut it is true of everything that has come down to us by being written down that here a will to permanence has created the unique forms of continuance that we call literature."[557] In light of Gadamer's view on the universality of hermeneutics, Achebe's narrative literature communicates meaning and thus serves as art of understanding African worldviews in its truthfulness. Achebe has put literature to mimetic use, but his language of narrative has obstructed in some ways the actualization of true understanding of African worldview, philosophy and thought especially in the specific experience of tragedy. Understanding a text like his may involve some hermeneutical difficulties.

Despite these difficulties, Achebe accepts that literature is one of the best ways to unravel the true cultural and philosophical thoughts of his people and of educating people through narratives. He affirms that literature provides a way to assist our societies and communities assume the leadership role in the education of young African scholars and the true transmission of African worldviews by Africans themselves.[558] In Gadamer's supportive view, such written texts or literature are necessary in the development of reading consciousness which leads to a historical consciousness and the preservation of historical tradition. Now one could critically apply this understanding to what advantages a written Igbo or any African language literature would have been to the development of a reading consciousness and historical consciousness among African scholars and students. Had this been the case with Achebe's text (in Igbo language), then our hermeneutical task will be purely and directly on it as the "highest task of understanding."[559] In another

---

[557] Gadamer, *Truth and Method*, trans. Joel Weinsheimer and Donald G. Marshall, *op. cit.*, p. 393.
[558] Achebe, *Morning Yet On Creation Day, op. cit.*, p. 71; See Ogede, *Achebe's Things Fall Apart: A Reader's Guide, op. cit.*, pp. xi-xii.
[559] Gadamer, *Truth and Method*, trans. Joel Weinsheimer and Donald G. Marshall, *op. cit.*, p. 392. The access to the written text is when the task of hermeneutics really begins could be related to the beginning of not just *full sovereignty* (that is not dependent on anything else to understand the text) but also leads to a socio-cultural sovereignty were people's true

way, it is not only the continuity of memory and developing reading historical consciousness but also what Gadamer refers at the acquisition of *full sovereignty* (understanding is not dependent on emotions, on unsure repetitions, but on pure text.)

The most effective way to see the depth of the hermeneutical task in Achebe's literature and the art of understanding of literary text of a people's worldviews is in recalling the general history of hermeneutics. Hermeneutics starts as an "ancillary to theology and philology,"[560] which develops to become a system at the basis of all human sciences. The historical development of this science is summarized by Gadamer:

> It is not only the written tradition that is estranged and in need of new and more vital assimilation; everything that is no longer immediately situated in a world—that is, all tradition, whether art or the other spiritual creations of the past: law, religion, philosophy, and so forth—is estranged from its original meaning and depends on the unlocking and mediating…. It is to the *rise of historical consciousness* that hermeneutics owes its centrality within the human sciences.[561]

In light of Gadamer's comments above, it shows another advantage/gain in the contributions of Achebe. Achebe's narrative is a literary text of African people's thought and tradition. His task is to develop a means for better understanding and appropriate assimilation[562] of African worldviews, especially its traditional, social, religious, linguistic, ontological and philosophical truth. There is an apparent agreement between Gadamer and Achebe on the role of hermeneutics in the interpretation of texts by providing access to different viewpoints. Gadamer re-emphasizes the distinction between the task of hermeneutics as human science in seeking knowledge guided by current interest in tradition and the desire for perfect knowledge by the natural sciences. Hermeneutics as a branch of the human sciences is like the historical science. Hermeneutics provides us with the ongoing inquiry to understanding

---

meanings are understood. This view is sympathetic to African scholars and linguistic critique of Achebe's English literature.

[560] Gadamer, *Truth and Method*, trans. Joel Weinsheimer and Donald G. Marshall, *op. cit.*, p. 157; Gadamer, *Truth and Method* (New York: The Seabury Press, 1975), p. 146.
[561] *Ibid.*, pp. 157-158.
[562] *Ibid.*

and disclosure of meaning. In a similar manner, and in the light of the advantages/gains of Achebe's work, his purpose of narrative is to disclose the original world of his historical people and to avoid further misrepresentation of his people's worldviews. My hermeneutical task in this section is to see how Achebe accomplishes his purpose and, if not, how he could have developed a productive universal hermeneutics following Gadamer's philosophical hermeneutical contributions.

Achebe's work, in the light of its gains or accomplishments, is an attempt at the communication and preservation of the original history of a people within its original context. But the problems of temporal distance relating this original history, the original hermeneutical context, the meaning of the narrative and the language we use in communicating these original worldviews are issues that concern philosophers, hermeneutists and literary theorists. The cultural and historical background/context of any literature is important in understanding its meaning. However, this does not require the reconstruction of the past. Achebe himself is of the view that his narrative is a hermeneutical reconstruction of the history about his people and what he remembers of it. He reconstructs the world of his people and he equally reconstructs the villages of Umuofia and Mbanta to reflect actual Igbo village communities. Somehow, to a great extent, these village communities resonate to the nineteenth century[563] historical and cultural life situations of our people. One could describe Achebe's narrative of these historical and cultural situations as an act of fictional reconstruction or re-enactment and the communication of meaning/understanding. The African experience of this historical time has been influence by the effect of the colonial intercultural encounter. For Achebe, in *Things Fall Apart*, re-enacting or reconstructing is one of the best ways to restore the distorted representation of African world, its human and cultural achievements.[564]

Now from the perspective of what is lost through Achebe's narrative, his reconstructive view of hermeneutics is not in harmony with how Gadamer perceives hermeneutics. Hermeneutics is not a reconstruction of events for understanding. Gadamer argues that the reconstruction of the original situations or restoration of it will only lead to a pointless endeavor which

---

[563] Falola, *op. cit.*, p. 67; See Ayandele, *op. cit.*, p. 5; See Njoku, *op. cit.*, p. 61.
[564] Irele, "Introduction," *Chinua Achebe Things Fall Apart, op. cit.*, p. xxi.

provides us with a dead meaning.[565] If Achebe's narrative project in English is solely reconstructive and an attempt to restore African worldviews following European writers' misrepresentations as he said, then it is obvious why the project is inadequate because it focuses only on the past with no new meaning. But Achebe's position agrees with Schleiermacher's hermeneutics discussed earlier (in chapter one) which supports the restoration and reconstruction[566] of original situations in history rather than with Gadamer's.

Gadamer criticizes the view of hermeneutics as reconstruction by insisting in its inadequacy. He explains that this is "in fact, Schleiermacher's conception and the tacit premise of his entire hermeneutics....historical knowledge opens the possibility of replacing what is lost and reconstructing tradition, inasmuch as it restores the original occasion and circumstances."[567] In my analysis, Achebe's narrative approach is for Gadamer not a productive form of universal hermeneutics. For what is reconstructed is never the original world. It seems a futile reconstruction in order to connect with the history of our existence or the history of our being. Connecting with the history of our past is not all that is required in universal hermeneutics, but we are also required to gain access to new meaning which involves using new interests, new circumstances and new generational perspectives to look at the same reality or text.

The important aspect connecting Achebe and Gadamer is that Gadamer insists that we try to understand the texts of writers because they could have deeper meanings with time. Hermeneutics does not describe the activities of the natural sciences which has one single meaning (original meaning.) Gadamer wishes to go beyond this kind of customary form of hermeneutics that is solely based on the author's intention. Interpretation would mean only a repetition of the obvious subjective intention of the author. Hermeneutics goes beyond this level to solve the problem of meaning which is the same as the problem of hermeneutics.

---

[565] Gadamer, *Truth and Method*, trans. Joel Weinsheimer and Donald G. Marshall, *op. cit.*, p. 160.
[566] *Ibid.*, p. 159.
[567] *Ibid.* Schleiermacher's view is about re-establishing or reproducing the writer's original word. However, this view is relevant to Achebe's work because he was reconstructing or reproducing the worldviews of his African people.

Gadamer's hermeneutic proposal does not emphasize an *ultimate* or a *definitive* interpretation, but allows for competing interpretations knowing that meanings abound with time and varied situations of present interpreter or reader.[568] It is in this way that the positive aspect of Achebe's written narrative is truly appreciated. *Things Fall Apart* as a written text-becomes a subject matter-for continued critical and hermeneutical reflections as it is for this book. Like Gadamer says, there is no definitive interpretation since new meaning come with time and with the change of interest of generations as it is in our case (a new generation's interpretation of Achebe's text.)

In the above subsection, I have discussed the intercultural problem of language in the context of written tradition/literature with a view to understand Achebe's narrative and point out what were gained and also lost in the narrative in terms of language. African philosophical thought gained among other things through **a**) the introduction of a written tradition and literature, and **b**) a new way to preserve and support oral narratives. But it lost through **a**) negligence of the rich capabilities of Igbo language use in written narratives, the alteration of the linguistic uniqueness and style of communication of Igbo worldviews, **b**) the opportunity to enhance the formation of reading and historical consciousness leading to full (hermeneutical) sovereignty in understanding Igbo or African texts and philosophical thinking. Gadamer's hermeneutical contributions provide us with the standard for these critical evaluations that bring us new complex meanings rather than the reconstructive meaning (original meaning or second creation of old meaning.)

I shall now turn to the intercultural problem of hermeneutics to see how Gadamer addresses it. We have to remember that most aspects of the problem of language also apply to the problem of hermeneutics. Despite this unique and subtle connection between language and hermeneutics, I shall try as much as possible to explain distinctly these closely related aspects of the universality of hermeneutics, and avoid some unnecessary repetitions.

---

[568]Gadamer, *Philosophical Hermeneutics, op. cit.,* pp. xxiii-xxiv. A scientific problem like a mathematical problem has but one answer and it has only one meaning. Hermeneutics is different and is more dynamic with meanings. (*Ibid*, pp. xxiii-xxiv.)

4.2 Gadamer and Achebe: The Intercultural Problem of Hermeneutics

The intercultural problem of hermeneutics is not any different from the intercultural problem of language as long as the problem of understanding is concerned. The background explanations offered above on the colonial policies of assimilation and association are also part of this section. On the intercultural problem of language, we focused on the interaction between the two cultures (African and European) in understanding each, especially African worldviews from the perspective of African language usage having been the victim of colonial misrepresentation. At this point, we are focusing on the role of hermeneutics in the intercultural process of interpretation and understanding. How does one in using English language understand the depth of the meaning that a text (*Things Fall Apart*), according Gadamer, "shares with us"?[569] How could English cultural perspective effectively understand or communicate African world views? The answer again is through dialogue between both. In this case, hermeneutics is not interested in the author (Achebe) or his personal state of mind. Our focus is on understanding the text (*Things Fall Apart*) as the main hermeneutical object. We shall be using Gadamer's hermeneutical principles to unveil the meanings present in Achebe's narrative,[570] especially with regard to explaining the communal meaning of tragedy in African worldview. We must come with our good prejudice, which includes our educational background, cultural values, our "fore-meaning" or "pre-understanding" to be able to explore the dialogue in the text. In an age of globalization, people of different cultures meet and hermeneutical understanding ought to transcend to acquire new meanings. This is an attempt at getting at deeper philosophical meaning through the universality of hermeneutics. Understanding is no longer a method of inquiry about a given object but it is an ongoing process of tradition. It is the correlating of one's hermeneutical situation and the text like Achebe's for deeper meanings.

---

[569] Gadamer, *Truth and Method*, trans. Joel Weinsheimer and Donald G. Marshall, *op. cit.*, p. 393.

[570] In chapter twenty-one of Achebe's narrative, he shows a kind of approach to the intercultural problem of hermeneutics introduced by Mr. Brown (the new white missionary in Umuofia.) Achebe writes, "Mr. Brown came to be respected even by the clan, because he trod softly on its faith…Neither of them succeeded in converting the other but they learned more about their different beliefs." See Achebe, *Things Fall Apart* (Canada: Anchor Canada edition, 2009), pp. 178-179.

For Gadamer there is a new challenge because hermeneutics encounters "literature and poetry, the humanities and classical studies... to grow beyond the limits of history as it has been and slowly to become ready to enter into a set of global relations."[571] His observation justifies the significant place of Achebe's narrative literature in this research as in applied hermeneutics. Although we may have different cultures with "varieties of histories and people,"[572] there is a common hermeneutical task which is based on the universality of language and on "a worldwide conversation of cultures."[573] During Gadamer's time, his cultural *cum* historical situations shaped his hermeneutical reflections. There were records of poets and writers describing their experience of German culture during the war. It was a difficult time in European history. In light of Achebe's narrative literature for understanding African Igbo people, one could argue that Europe, as a people or culture, was going through its own *"Things Fall Apart"*, especially in Gadamer's Germany. The experiences of culture that Achebe addresses are relevant to Gadamer's view of philosophical hermeneutics.[574] Achebe's literary art as narrative literature is a mode of this universality of hermeneutics (of understanding) we articulate through language. It presents us with historical situation for understanding the events that took place in his culture.

As I earlier discussed in chapter two, historical situations influence thinking. The devastations of the World War periods evoked or resurrected the use of values of dialogue and peaceful collaboration among peoples and cultures of these periods. Through the intercultural experience there emerges a new world of collaborative civilization justified by a new form of philosophy of existence, meaning or hermeneutics. It also requires that every relevant view on life/ reality ought to be considered and could even mean putting our own worldviews into serious critical re-evaluation for peaceful human co-existence. This might be regarded as the hermeneutics of mutual understanding or mutual dialogue[575] or dialogic hermeneutics, which is what addressing the intercultural problem of language and hermeneutics accomplishes.

---

[571] Misgeld and Nicholson, *op. cit.,* pp. xiii-xiv.
[572] *Ibid.,* p. xiv.
[573] *Ibid.*
[574] *Ibid.,* p. xv. Gadamer will appreciate Achebe's narrative literature of the worldviews of his people as Gadamer appreciated Osip Mandelstam (a Russian Jewish Poet) poetry.
[575] *Ibid.,* p. xviii.

For dialogue and mutual understanding, the problem of language is part of the general problem of hermeneutics.[576] Whatever that gives experience is an object of understanding. This experience is common to all human beings; it forms the structure of our human knowledge and language. Our experience of the world is made present through the medium of language and in that way has become the object of hermeneutics through which we describe our world and our relation with one another. Gadamer repeatedly describes it as the language through which we encounter ourselves, our beingness.

Hermeneutics as the game of interpretation is constitutive of our daily life and this game "takes place whenever we 'understand'."[577] We understand because we have the universality of language present in hermeneutics. For Gadamer our understanding points out the universality of hermeneutics in which language transmits everything, including arts, culture, proverbs, worldviews etc. Language is part of the sphere of understanding in which the totality of what forms our epistemic world is disclosed as something comprehended.[578] This totality of what forms our known world is comprehended gradually through continued interpretation as an explicit project of understanding.

In *Things Fall Apart* and in light of Achebe's narrative contributions, we go beyond the simple interpretation that comes through the narrative itself. After over sixty years of its publication, it is important that African scholars and others develop new interests in the hermeneutics of Achebe's narrative literature. The meaning in his work is not yet exhausted. As Gadamer observes, every historical period understands a particular text in its specific way. Each historical people within a historical period ought to develop interest in the text of their general tradition that demands comprehension or understanding. In that case, it offers us new understanding of the text because it speaks as a text and not dependent on the psychological state of the author. We have to free ourselves of these contingencies of the author so that the true meaning of a text will emerge.

---

[576] Gadamer, *Philosophical Hermeneutics, op. cit.*, pp. 25-26.
[577] *Ibid.*, p. 32.
[578] *Ibid.*, pp. 25-26.

My hermeneutical task now is to inquire how in narratives each experience or meaning directs us to another experience or meaning,[579] especially with reference to tragedy. This process will help us highlight the advantages/gains of Achebe's interpretive contribution through the use of Gadamer's hermeneutical conditions of understanding. Achebe's narrative literature has a significant mode of representing reality and with other ways of presenting a form of new social consciousness and national identity.[580] His articulation of African worldviews creates awareness of the continued possibilities for understanding of his cultural world.[581] Through Gadamer's hermeneutics and Achebe's narrative approach we encounter new meanings in a worldview. The task of hermeneutics in this regard is that issues are debated and re-examined for better understanding. It is part of the reflective creativity in understanding of literature or a novel like Achebe's. The new accomplishment of this process of reflective creativity is that every aspect of a people's culture and value system is continually reviewed and constructively evaluated.

Hermeneutics-as an art of understanding-is involved whenever what is said is not directly comprehensible, but still needs to be understood. In other words, we have an intelligible text that needs to be understood handed over through tradition. Thus far Achebe's narrative task is to avoid misunderstanding and false information. But in some ways Achebe fails to completely avoid this misunderstanding. I shall take a look at his notion of tragedy—Igbo African tragedy. In my view, Gadamer's hermeneutical framework as an optimistic platform, the communal notion of the person and reflections on the notion of *Chi* and the *Chi proverbs* are important in the interpretation of Okonkwo's tragedy: Is African tragedy more of a communal than a personal tragedy?

The discussion so far explains the intercultural problem of hermeneutics *à la* the intercultural problem of language. It also points out what have been gained (advantages) and what may have been lost (disadvantages) in Achebe's narrative. For Gadamer, all forms of interpretation are truly linguistic and reality is understood linguistically.[582] But it does not mean that we are closed

---

[579] Gadamer, *Philosophical Hermeneutics, op. cit.,* p. 103.
[580] Gikandi, *op. cit.,* p. 3.
[581] Olakunle. *op. cit.,* p. 176.
[582] Gadamer, *Philosophical Hermeneutics, op. cit.,* p. 99.

off in the relativity of a particular language. It is the character of language that its mediation involves openness and absorption. Openness and absorption are helpful conditions in understanding Achebe's work and how it applies to other cultures, but it is not closed off to what might be different and strange. Reason goes above every other language and it makes understanding possible through language. The hermeneutical experience is conceived in language, expressed in words and "[W]ords themselves prescribe the only way in which we can put them to use."[583]

Achebe as a writer understands the role of native language in narrative literature. He seems to have moved beyond the Igbo language in order to express thoughts that concern the African mind. These questioning thoughts are better presented through literature in a written tradition. There are varieties of interpretations providing us with new comprehensions and fresh understanding.[584] Achebe's *Things Fall Apart* appears to be variedly interpreted because there is no standard interpretation which sets a single direction for understanding *it*. Now let us see if Achebe's work implies other interpretations for interpreters and readers, especially for other African readers and for us. This we shall see through the application of Gadamer's principles of hermeneutics, the claim of the universality of hermeneutics and the conditions of understanding to Achebe's text and his notion of tragedy.

4.2.1 Application of Gadamer's Hermeneutic Principles and Theory of Language to Understand African Notion of Tragedy

Gadamer uses the concepts of hermeneutics to mean interpretation, translation and application. Hermeneutics involves the act of application as a condition of understanding and for the purpose of understanding and to derive meaning. Application means integrating our understanding to a contemporary context thereby developing new meanings and self-understanding. The event of tragedy is an 'experience',[585] a hermeneutical experience. Gadamer notes, "[W]e emphasized that the experience (Erfahrung) of meaning which takes

---

[583] MacIntyre, *op. cit.*, p. 170; See Gadamer, *Hegel's Dialectic: Five Hermeneutical Studies, op. cit.*, p. 93.
[584] Gadamer, *Philosophical Hermeneutics, op. cit.*, pp. xxv-xxvi.
[585] Gadamer describes tragedy in terms of the aesthetic of work of art, with the emotions of fear and pity and relation to the reactions of spectators. My approach to tragedy is interpretive--strictly a series of tragic experiences of life.

place in understanding always includes application."[586] Application as hermeneutics is an essential part of the phenomenon of understanding. We move from a general situation to involve ourselves with a present situation or particular context of understanding. In this case, how do we apply philosophical hermeneutics to Achebe's notion of tragedy and so understand African worldviews? Gadamer argues that interpretation involves using the traditional text by applying it to a particular situation and to oneself. The traditional text is not only given to the interpreter. For one to understand what constitutes the meaning and the importance of the text, i.e., universal has to be applied to a situation and to an interpreter.

Tragedy is a result of a series of grave experiences in life and it is the "unity of a tragic course of events that is experienced as such."[587] Gadamer briefly considers tragedy from Aristotle's *Poetics* and uses it to exemplify the whole structure of aesthetic being (as part of the experience of truth through art.) For Aristotle, the experience of tragedy is not based on the moral or ethical life of the characters in a narrative. Tragedy portrays the exceptional human conditions of the hero-character which contrast with the emergence of pain, displeasure and destruction. The contrast is revealed because of the opposites between the prosperity/splendor and lose/destruction that underline tragedy and tragic event. This is for Aristotle the ideal picture of tragedy in his discussions in the *Poetics*.[588] I have purposely chosen to avoid some aspects of Aristotle's tragedy in the *Poetics* by not focusing on diction, melody, and spectacle. These are not required in our discussion of African tragedy. I am also not trying to present any differences between Achebe's and Aristotle's theory of tragedy. It is proper to allow African notion of tragedy to independently showcase itself without necessarily emphasizing some comparisons with Western notion of tragedy. I think any other approach will leave us with a faulty result with the intercultural problem of understanding similar to the colonial days when every cultural meaning has to be solely verified /certified by a colonial standard on what qualifies as genuine thought/philosophy or what does not. Intercultural understanding or interculturality requires seeing/understanding others as they are and not necessarily if they are like us. It is with this purposefulness of making

---

[586] Gadamer, *Truth and Method*, trans. Joel Weinsheimer and Donald G. Marshall, *op. cit.*, p. 385; Gadamer, *Truth and Method* (New York: The Seabury Press, 1975), pp. 345-346.
[587] *Ibid.*, p. 126.
[588] Halliwell, *op. cit.*, pp. 179-180.

intelligible a given text, in its own merits, that Gadamer's hermeneutical approach serves as a paradigm or provides a framework for addressing the intercultural problem of hermeneutics (understanding)[589] with a specific reference to tragedy.

Gadamer discusses the hermeneutical relevance of Aristotle's theory of tragedy within the structure of aesthetics. Tragedy is a form of aesthetic representation that reveals the difficult or suffering situations of the hero-character. Gadamer argues that all the conditions involved by Aristotle are important in the definition of tragedy, but he also notes that the effect on the spectator or audience must be considered.[590] Tragedy has the effects of fear and pity on the spectators of a tragic play, especially because of what happens to the hero-character. The effect of tragedy on the spectators is essential to aesthetics. It is also part of a work of art that has hermeneutical significance. The effect of tragedy is that we become aware of human finite nature through suffering. It includes the experience of the unlimited and uncertain nature of the future. The experience of tragedy is what happens to us and yet we cannot prevent it from happening. Gadamer points out that:

> What a man has to learn through suffering is not this or that particular thing, but insight into the limitations of humanity, into the absoluteness of the barrier that separates man from the divine. It is ultimately a religious insight—that kind of insight which gave birth to Greek tragedy.[591]

This is similar to the experience of suffering and limitation of humanity in Achebe's hero character Okonkwo. While avoiding a repetition of the whole Okonkwo tragedy which has been earlier presented in chapter three, permit me to bring in the highlights to refresh our minds on the features in Achebe's hero-character, especially in this chapter on hermeneutical application. Okonkwo was a man of humble beginning with some difficulties in establishing himself. His father Unoka is known only for his love of music and his seeming laziness. Okonkwo confronted this sad experience by often recalling his father's inability to address his own life needs. In order to overcome this experience, he

---

[589] Charles Taylor sees this form of hermeneutics as the hermeneutics of recognition which is not necessarily an acceptance. It means seeing others as they are.
[590] Gadamer, *Truth and Method*, trans. Joel Weinsheimer and Donald G. Marshall, *op. cit.*, p.126; Gadamer, *Truth and Method* (New York: The Seabury Press, 1975), pp. 114-115.
[591] *Ibid.*, p. 351.

longed for power and greatness, doing his best to rise in status as a known farmer and a warrior. According to Achebe, through personal effort and commitment Okonkwo became the hero of Umuofia, but his world turned around when he accidentally killed a young member of his village. As custom demands, the youth and some other individuals had to destroy Okonkwo's compound in accordance with the directive of the goddesses of the land. The destruction of Okonkwo's compound was carried out with their minds set at cleansing their community of the evil brought on it by Okonkwo's action.

This is the first aspect of the series of tragedies to affect Okonkwo. According to some commentators, Achebe's notion of tragedy comes from the influence of Western culture. His notion of tragedy could be said to have been influenced by the Aristotelian notion and modification of tragedy as aesthetic because of English language usage (Western.) But in Gadamer's view the experience of tragedy is common in all human society. The life-world of other peoples and cultures are not completely foreign or in contradistinction to our own. In other words, Achebe's narrative of the experience of tragedy is an imitation of "life" of a hero in an African world. It is the mimesis or representation of the *Weltanschauung* of a people as work of art. Gadamer notes that to the present time "the mimesis theory still retains something of its old validity...There remains a continuity of meaning which links the work of art with the existing world and from which even the alienated consciousness of a cultured society never quite detaches itself."[592]

Gadamer observes that the notion of tragedy has retained some classic sense of the role of destiny, but we now have other different notions like, the modern notion of tragedy, the Christian notion of tragedy. Achebe like Gadamer argues that there could be various notions[593] of tragedy without necessarily being the same as that of Greek tragedy. There is no reason to justify a single format for understanding tragedy. Achebe explains further that Aristotle's Greek tragedy narrative is peculiar to the Greek *Weltanschauung* but it is not completely new to other human traditions, like the African, in general, or the Igbos, in particular. Achebe, Gadamer and Aristotle include the necessary conditions to identify tragedy, especially the hero-status enjoyed by the main character and the feeling of pain and pity by the community for what

---

[592] *Ibid.*, p. 129; Gadamer, *Truth and Method* (New York: The Seabury Press, 1975), p. 118.
[593] *Ibid.*, pp. 126-127. Gadamer mentions Christian tragedy and modern tragedy. One could also say African tragedy, European tragedy etc.

has befallen a known and admired individual/hero-character. This notion of tragedy is embedded in human nature.[594] Although Achebe's highlights the human flaws and the capacity to express virtues that endeared the hero-character to the community, the notion of tragedy can easily be described as applicable to most societies.

Achebe's view of African tragedy has a hermeneutical challenge which demands openness and understanding. Achebe and Gadamer's perspectives reject categorizing *different* worldviews as *lesser, erroneous* and *undeveloped*. This is what Gadamer calls 'openness.' [595] "He rejects closing oneself: 'reflecting [myself] out of [my] relation to the other and so becoming unreachable by him."[596] Through this way we see that understanding is always a process of the fusing of perspectives that could independently exist.[597] As Achebe explains, tragedy is present in human nature *per se* and in other traditions, "even if they were not spelled out in the same exactly way."[598]

Let us now use some of the hermeneutical principles to address Achebe's narrative in order to buttress my position that Okonkwo's tragedy is a communal tragedy. I shall use the hermeneutical circle, prejudices, the fusion of horizons etc., and their implications very prominently in this section.

Achebe's narrative has to be analyzed as a whole (language) and in parts (as in words and texts.) The language style, the various proverbs, and wise sayings need to lead us to an understanding of the whole text. The traditional, cultural and philosophical prejudices as long as they are good prejudices are necessary in getting at the true meaning of the African tragedy narrative. His whole text (*Things Fall Apart*) needs to be critically and hermeneutically interpreted to arrive even at a complex but true meaning. The going back and forth through the chapters and the paragraphs need to lead us to a whole meaning and understanding. As Gadamer explains, "the circular movement of understanding runs backward and forward along the text and ceases when the text is perfectly understood."[599] In this way the true African notion of tragedy

---

[594] Rowell, *op. cit.,* pp. 265-266.

[595] Taylor, *op. cit.,* p. 296.

[596] *Ibid.*

[597] See Gadamer, *Philosophical Hermeneutics, op. cit.,* p. xix.

[598] Rowell, *op. cit.,* pp. 265-266.

[599] Gadamer, *Truth and Method,* trans. Joel Weinsheimer and Donald G. Marshall, op. cit., p. 293; Gadamer, *Truth and Method* (New York: The Seabury Press, 1975), p. 261.

is properly understood. It is only within that context that the intercultural problem of language (misrepresentation through English language) and hermeneutics (personal interpretation of African tragedy) is resolved. Also what the author has provided in the text is what attracts our attention. We have to focus on recapturing the perspective within which he formulated his views.[600] Gadamer stresses that the interpreter focuses on that which is universal in other to understand the content of the text and what constitutes its meaning. His philosophical hermeneutics accommodates an extensive and exhaustive aspect of understanding and interpretation.

Let us look at the various themes that have been worked out to justify communal tragedy (following my interpretation of Achebe) using Gadamer's hermeneutical circle which requires going back and forth through the words, sentences, proverbs, paragraphs and chapters of Achebe's narrative, the fusions of the various perspectives/horizons of the text, the influence of temporal distance and effects of history in understanding Achebe's text/discourse etc. One has to bear in mind that some of these principles, like hermeneutical circle, have been used by other (past) hermeneutists to gain meaning. In our case, Gadamer is a contemporary *avant garde* of these principles through his philosophical hermeneutics. These hermeneutical principles are almost part of our unconscious everyday life. But for a conscious reflective approach, the discourse below has been inspired by Gadamer's emphasis on these intrinsically-related hermeneutical principles. I will describe as '*hermeneutical themes*' some of the main topics/themes in Achebe and African philosophical thought to justify this book's interpretations on the communal tragedy in Achebe's text.

---

[600] Segrave, *op. cit.* See Gadamer, *Truth and Method* (New York: The Seabury Press, 1975), p. 259.

4.2.2 Gadamer's Hermeneutical Circle and Achebe's Notion of Tragedy:

Some Hermeneutical Themes for Understanding African 'Communal' Tragedy

a. Okonkwo's Fame and the Tragic Killing of Ikemefuna

I have used various hermeneutical principles of Gadamer, especially the hermeneutical circle—while dialoguing with the chapters and paragraphs of Achebe's text—to develop my own hermeneutical themes to confirm communal tragedy. While using the hermeneutical circle, other principles were applied through a necessary implication and extension. The meaning derived from the narrative text is that: As a hero of Umuofia, Okonkwo was asked by the elders of the community to keep Ikemefuna, a boy taken as reparation for the killing of a lady from Umuofia. Ikemefuna lives for three years in the household of Okonkwo, such that he almost becomes a member of Okonkwo's family. He calls Okonkwo 'father,' having adapted to his new family and community. Ikemefuna and Nwoye (Okonkwo's son) are best friends. After three years the community oracle demands that Ikemefuna be sacrificed. As it turns out, on the appointed day of sacrifice, it was Okonkwo (his adopted father) who kills Ikemefuna when he ran to him for protection.

Ritual killing is part of the then Igbo cultural life. It could be religiously sanctioned by the Oracles, but often there are alternative sacrifices as recommended by the Oracle's chief priest or priestess. In Achebe's *Things Fall Apart* Ikemefuna is killed as a ritual sacrifice. Irele notes, "the young boy's ritual killing, an act against nature in which his father participates. The fate of Ikemefuna, its stark revelation of the grim underside of the tribal ethos."[601] Prior to the killing of Ikemefuna, Achebe narrates that Ogbuefi Ezeudu (a community elder) warns Okonkwo:

> That boy calls you father. Do not bear a hand in his death... Yes,
> Umuofia has decided to kill him. The Oracle of the Hills and the
> Caves has pronounced it. They will take him outside Umuofia as

---

[601] http://web.africa.ufl.edu/asq/v4/v4i3a1.htm (Accessed March 18, 2011.)

is the custom, and kill him there. But I want you to have nothing to do with it. He calls you father.[602]

With the application of Gadamer's hermeneutical principles, the conditions of understanding and theory of language we shall better see and understand a distinction in Achebe's notion of tragedy. Achebe's Okonkwo and Ikemefuna are doomed in accordance with the demands of the Oracle. Ikemefuna's fate shows the cultural value of the people and its difficult side.[603] In chapter seven of the text, Achebe narrates that although the Umuofia people have decided to kill Ikemefuna, his death must take place outside the community.[604] For some hermeneutists Okonkwo violated the demands of the Oracle when he killed Ikemefuna. But Okonkwo himself argues that for killing Ikemefuna it will be unacceptable for the Earth [goddess] to reproach him for keeping her orders. [605]

In line with this meaning, Okonkwo was never clearly ordered not to get involved or to stay out of it, "and so cannot be faulted for disobeying an elder by landing the fatal blow"[606] that kills Ikemefuna.[607] That means, for him to do anything otherwise would have been clearly against the will of the Oracle.[608] But one may disagree and argue that Okonkwo violated the law of the gods by killing Ikemefuna.[609] The precise law of the gods here, I should explain, is the law or the demand of the Earth goddess (Ala.)

In chapter two of this thesis, Gadamer's philosophical hermeneutical theory and the conditions of understanding, we recall, recognize the essential

---

[602] Achebe, *Things Fall Apart* (Canada: Anchor Canada edition, 2009), p. 57; See also Ndiawar Sarr, "The Center Holds: The Resilience of Ibo Culture in *Things Fall Apart*," *Global Perspectives on Teaching Literature*, Sandra Ward Lott, Maureen S. G. Hawkins, et al, eds (Illinois: National Council of Teachers of English, 1993), p. 349.

[603] http://web.africa.ufl.edu/asq/v4/v4i3a1.htm (Accessed March 18, 2011.)

[604] Achebe, *Things Fall Apart* (Canada: Anchor Canada edition, 2009), p. 57; Achebe, *Things Fall Apart* (NY: Fawcett Crest, 1959), p. 57; See also Sarr, *op. cit.,* p. 349.

[605] Achebe, *Things Fall Apart, op. cit.,* p. 67.

[606] Alan R. Friesen, Okonkwo's Suicide as an Affirmative Act: Do Things Really Fall Apart?," *Critical Insights: Things Fall Apart*, Keith Booker, ed (Pasadena, California: Salem Press, 2011), p. 286.

[607] David Hoegberg, "Principle and Practice: The Logic of Cultural Violence in Achebe's Things Fall Apart," *Critical Insights: Things Fall Apart*, Keith Booker, ed (Pasadena, California: Salem Press, 2011), p. 145. Hoegberg explores the issue of violence and the consequent tragedy in Igbo cultural world.

[608] Friesen, *op. cit.,* p. 286. Friesen thinks that Ikemefuna was saved from other more cruel fate.

[609] Jude Chudi Okpala, "Igbo Metaphysics in Chinua Achebe's *Things Fall Apart*," *Callaloo* 25, (2002), p. 562.

relationship between these conditions or principles in hermeneutics. These conditions of understanding or principles demand that one understands the various parts of the text and the fusion of horizons/aspects to gain better understanding or comprehension.[610] Nowhere in the text does it indicate that Okonkwo plans to disobey the commands of the goddess of the land. Using the universality in hermeneutics principles, in chapter seven of the text, Okonkwo was never 'ordered' (only an advice was offered to him) to avoid involving himself with the killing of Ikemefuna, and so cannot be blamed for fulfilling a sacred duty.[611]

There seems to be a philosophical puzzle[612] here in understanding what the Oracle demands for failure to execute Ikemefuna. Ogbuefi Ezeudu was interested in discouraging Okonkwo from actively participating in the execution.[613] Anything contrary to fulfilling this duty will be tantamount to disobeying the Oracle. Why did the Oracle not clearly suggest that another person fulfills its demands knowing the tragic implications for Okonkwo? Why did the community not choose someone else to take care of Ikemefuna knowing that Okonkwo's pride is his worst enemy? The apparent philosophical paradox understanding what the Oracle really demands[614] is what Gadamer refers as a situation that requires more critical reflections and re-examinations. With a further reflection on the various detailed statements and contexts of the narrative, it is difficult to argue that Okonkwo is intent in disobeying the Oracle. However, one acquiesces that Okonkwo is overzealous in carrying out these instructions from the gods or goddesses. He is quite aware of the consequent traditional implications of overlooking the demands of the Oracle. This argument is a fortiori to the fact that Okonkwo's aim at the end of the

---

[610] Wachterhauser, *op. cit.*, pp. 77-78, n. 4; See Rajan, "Hermeneutics," *op. cit.*

[611] Friesen, *op. cit.*, p. 286.

[612] Patrick C. Nnoromele, "The Plight of a Hero in Achebe's Things Fall Apart," *Critical Insights: Things Fall Apart*, Keith Booker, ed (Pasadena, California: Salem Press, 2011), p. 274. Here we try to explain Nnoromele understanding of the puzzle or paradox. In Nnoromele's view, "[T]he cultural practice was that when the gods or goddesses demanded anyone for sacrifice, the family must be excluded because the Umuofia people believed that the emotional attachment the family might have for the individual would interfere with the process or the obligation to execute the demands of the Oracle. Hence, Ogbuefi Ezeudu sought for at least a passive compromise from Okonkwo." (pp. 276-277.) Achebe, *Things Fall Apart* (Portsmouth: Heinemann, 1996), p. 22.

[613] Achebe, *Things Fall Apart* (Canada: Anchor Canada edition, 2009), p. 57.

[614] Okpala, *op. cit.,* p. 562; Achebe, *Things Fall Apart* (Canada: Anchor Canada edition, 2009), p. 57; pp. 66-67; Achebe, *Things Fall Apart* (Portsmouth: Heinemann, 1996), p. 22; Nnoromele, *op. cit.*, p. 274.

narrative is to insist on the culture of Umuofia rather than on the culture[615] of the missionaries.

After the death of Ikemefuna, Okonkwo questioned his friend Obierika for not getting involved in killing Ikemefuna. Obierika philosophically answers, "[B]ut the Oracle did not ask me to carry out its decision."[616] Again, following Gadamerian hermeneutical circle (and by extension the fusion of horizons) approach--there is nothing in any other parts of Achebe's text to indicate that Okonkwo violated the demands of the Oracle. Obierika only felt that the Oracle did not ask him to do the act, while sees it differently (an order that must be obeyed by whoever.)

Okonkwo's desire for fame and hero status influenced his decision to kill Ikemefuna himself. In the end, it means that Ikemefuna was doomed to die, but it was not up to Okonkwo to do it himself. Moreover, to be able to analyze and interpret the message of the gods or goddesses is important in African worldviews and value system. The messages of the gods/goddesses are not always clear and so required that the elders (African gerontocracy) sit together to further discuss, reflect and analyze the message from the Oracle. This is in accord with Western original religious use of hermeneutics. The messenger of *Hermes* is said to help the people understand the message communicated to them. Irele explains:

> the dialogue that elders [such as Ezeudu, Ezenwa, and Obierika] engage in with their own culture throughout the novel points to the process by which the principles governing the world concept and value system of the tribe are constantly debated, re-examined, and in this way, retrospectively rationalized. Thus, as represented by Chinua Achebe, and contrary to the discourse of colonial anthropology, Umuofia, the primordial Igbo village, emerges as a locus of reflective civility.[617]

Now let us take a look at another hermeneutical theme: Okonkwo: the cultural martial ethos, in line with discerning the communal tragedy situation from the text.

---

[615] Culture could be interpreted as 'civilization.'
[616] Achebe, *Things Fall Apart, op. cit.*, p. 66.
[617] http://web.africa.ufl.edu/asq/v4/v4i3a1.htm (Accessed March 18, 2011.)

b. Okonkwo: Cultural Martial Ethos

In this subsection, using the hermeneutical principles, including the hermeneutical situation and fusion of horizons/perspectives etc., in the texts one is able to discern deeper meanings. In Achebe's text there is a culture that admires a martial ethos, a form of bravery. It, however, involves a disposition, of the kind seen in a soldier in line of duty. The soldier knows that he is in war and should be ready to deliver in the business of the day. This is the kind of situation that is often experienced in a traditional Igbo society (our hermeneutical situation, influenced by the effects of history.) People are business minded and ready to show bravery. This situation often gives way to tragic consequences, especially by the brave people in the community. The brave, the mighty and the powerful dominate almost every aspect of the life of the community. Okonkwo seems to be set for a tragic end because of his obsession with Igbo cultural martial ethos.

A martial ethos comes also with the dialectics of a cultural society that readily distinguishes between the brave[618] and the coward, the advantaged and the disadvantaged, the able and the challenged. The brave, robust and powerful are categorized, excessively praised and their qualities promoted, while the *not-so-powerful* are treated as cowards, weaklings and sometimes outright treated as being lazy. Irele observes that Okonkwo is the antithesis of his own father. He takes up an opposite character of being a fearful person.[619] Achebe writes:

> He [Okonkwo] was a man of action, a man of war. Unlike his father he could stand the look of blood. In Umuofia's latest war he was the first to bring home a human head. That was his fifth head, and he was not an old man yet. On great occasions, such as the funeral of a village celebrity he drank his palm-wine from his first human head.[620]

---

[618] D. N. Mkhize, "The Portrayal of Igbo Culture in Zulu," *Chinua Achebe's Things Fall Apart*, Harold Bloom, ed (NY: Infobase Publishers, 2010), p. 34. Mkhize makes references to the role of Oracles and going to war in Igboland. This I interpret as part of the religio-cultural worldview of the Igbo.

[619] http://web.africa.ufl.edu/asq/v4/v4i3a1.htm (Accessed March 18, 2011.)

[620] Achebe, *Things Fall Apart* (Canada: Anchor Canada edition, 2009), p. 10; See Achebe, *Things Fall Apart*, (London: Heinemann, 1958), p. 8; Mkhize, "The Portrayal of Igbo Culture in Zulu, *op. cit.*, p. 34.

The young members of the community are meant to learn to identify with individuals known to possess these 'virtues' or ethos. This affirms the role of the community in this regard. Okonkwo's community worldview treasures and esteems the martial ethos he identifies with and the community respects "those men who win distinction on the battlefield ('in Umuofia.)"[621] These Igbo worldviews and cultural values are there to influence the young. We are all products of our society and we make our societies. One gathers from the narrative that it is within such an influencing society that Okonkwo developed his character (the hermeneutical circle could indirectly involve temporal distance and effective history.) Achebe casts Okonkwo "in a heroic mold, as befits his warrior status. The portrait we have of him is that of 'a man of action,'[622] in deliberate contrast to the reflective character of his friend Obierika."[623] It is a well-known cultural trait of the Igbo society to show heroism. Igbo culture demands the "exhibition of acts of heroism," and a "personal achievement [is]… revered."[624] Most African writers and scholars admit that martial ethos is part of the core values of the Igbo and it is part of the essential formation of every Igbo person. One could only conclude that Okonkwo did act and live according to his cultural beliefs. His community values were strong influences on his life. [625]

Achebe's narrative shows that Igbo cultural tradition has many instances of internecine or community wars between communities, especially over land disputes, retributive violence among communities etc. Such community wars are most often justified through religious rituals and Oracle consultations. Those who have achieved significant status in the community are classed based on public display of aggressiveness, prowess, and war trophies (display of conquered people and their heads) during war. In regard to these war trophies that encourage violence, Achebe writes, Okonkwo was "a man of

---

[621] Richard Begam, "Achebe's Sense of an Ending: History and Tragedy in *Things Fall Apart*," *Critical Insights: Things Fall Apart*, Keith Booker, ed (Pasadena, California: Salem Press, 2011), p. 209.

[622] Achebe, *Things Fall Apart* (Canada: Anchor Canada edition 2009), p. 10; Achebe, *op. cit.*, p. 8; Mkhize, *op. cit.*, p. 34.

[623] Francis Abiola Irele, "Introduction," *Things Fall Apart Chinua Achebe: A Norton Critical Edition*, Francis Abiola Irele, ed (NY: W. W. Norton and Co, Inc, 2009), p. xiii.

[624] Ifeoma Onyemelukwe, "Search for Lost Identity in Achebe's *Things Fall Apart*," *Emerging Perspectives on Chinua Achebe*, Ernest N. Emenyonu, ed (Trenton, New Jersey: Africa World Press, Inc, Volume 1, 2004), p. 40.

[625] Ode Ogede, *Achebe's Things Fall Apart: A Reader's Guide* (London: Continuum International Publishing Group, 2007), pp. 19-20.

war".[626] In the text, Achebe presents Okonkwo as a man who derived much pleasure in expressing his passion to get into war and conquer his community's enemies. However, Okonkwo's community was very good at negotiating with enemy communities to avoid going into an unnecessary war. Achebe writes:

> But the war that now threatened was a just war. Even the enemy clan knew that. And so when Okonkwo of Umuofia arrived at Mbaino as the proud and imperious emissary of war, he was treated with great honor and respect, and two days later he returned home with a lad of fifteen and a young virgin. The lad's name was Ikemefuna, whose sad story is still told in Umuofia unto this day.[627]

War-mongering attitudes are ways of urging violent aggression and involve reminiscing on the bounties of war or war-ransom. Alan R. Friesen agrees with this interpretation in what he calls "the war-ransom"[628] that could be prevalent in internecine wars between communities in Igboland. These war-mongering enabling cultural practices are present in Igbo linguistic expression and peculiar proverbs. For instance, *Chi onye adighi n'izu ma mmadu egbuna ya* (If one's *Chi* (fate or destiny) is not in agreement, nobody can kill him); *Onyem n'egbu na mmadu agam egbu kwa ya na mmuo* (A person I kill in life I will kill also him in spirit-world.) Achebe provides these other proverbs to set the stage for the final confrontation. He uses these other proverbs a) "Whenever you see a toad jumping in broad daylight, then know that something is after its life."[629] (Igbo proverb--*Awo anaghi agba ọsọ ehihe n'efu*), b) "Eneka the bird was asked why he was always on the wing and he replied: Men have learned to shoot without missing their mark and I have learned to fly without perching on a twig" (Igbo proverb--*Diochi muta igba agaghi, eneka amuta ufe akwusighi.*) These proverbs above are specifically used in this context to develop and advance the hermeneutical theme of "Okonkwo: cultural marital ethos" or thoughts about Okonkwo's warlike attitude.

---

[626] Achebe, *Things Fall Apart* (Canada: Anchor Canada edition, 2009), p. 10; See Achebe, *Things Fall Apart*, (London: Heinemann, 1958), p. 8; Mkhize, *op. cit.*, p. 34.

[627] *Ibid.*, p. 12; See Patrick C. Nnoromele, "The Plight of a Hero in Achebe's *Things Fall Apart*," *Critical Insights: Things Fall Apart*, Keith Booker, ed (Pasadena, California: Salem Press, 2011), p. 272.

[628] Friesen, *op. cit.*, p. 272.

[629] Achebe, *Things Fall Apart* (Canada: Anchor Canada edition, 2009), p. 203.

Another hermeneutical theme that attracts our attention in Achebe's narrative is Okonkwo's obsession with heroic cultural personage leading to tragedy. As we noted above, these hermeneutical themes are arrived at through the application of hermeneutical principles like hermeneutical circle etc., to get new meaning by comparing and contrasting the comments, perspective of the various chapters and pages in the texts.

c. Okonkwo: Obsession with Heroic Cultural Personage Leading to Tragedy

We shall discuss this hermeneutical theme bearing in mind African notion of person discussed in chapter three above (the hermeneutical circle is here related to the fusion of horizons and good prejudices.) This notion as part of African tradition is a kind of good prejudice that we carry with us in the interpretation of Achebe's text. It is part of 'fore-knowledge' that constitutes and influences our understanding of what the content of the text means, especially with regard to the hermeneutical theme-*Okonkwo: Obsession with Heroic Cultural Personage Leading to Communal Tragedy.*

Achebe's presentation of Okonkwo shows a character whose tragic end was influenced by many factors. One of it is that Okonkwo has an ideal Igbo cultural personage. It is a cultural personage that struggles for recognition. A cultural personage struggling for recognition is a conspicuous theme developed in Okonkwo's story.[630] Igbo culture sometimes overemphasized personage and self-image. It is a culture that is obsessed with the personality cult image. Using the hermeneutical circle of the whole and details of the text, i.e., in the various passages of the text, it affirms that Okonkwo is a man obsessed with self and personal realizations. It is as if the whole narrative is about a man and his self-dreams. Even his aspirations are sometimes contrasted to his father's failures and lack of self-determination to become in the community a success-story or hero-personality. Achebe acknowledges this issue when he explains that "Okonkwo was not a man of thought but of action. But in absence of work, talking was the next best."[631]

---

[630] http://web.africa.ufl.edu/asq/v4/v4i3a1.htm (Accessed March 18, 2011.)
[631] Achebe, *Things Fall Apart* (Canada: Anchor Canada edition, 2009), p. 69.

One is of the impression that Okonkwo is an ideal of a community's hero personality, but it is rather his distorted obsession to self. Like Achebe notes, Okonkwo was after his selfish personal ideal. Reading further in the narrative Okonkwo places much emphasis on his self-esteem and how times have changed in the qualities of great personalities the community now has. Achebe has Okonkwo say, "I think it is good that our clan hold the *ozo* title in high esteem. In those other clan you speak of, *ozo* [community title] is so low that every beggar takes it."[632] Irele captures this point when he argues that we are alerted that Okonkwo's "manly ideal is excessive and even wrongheaded."[633] It somehow indicates to us that Okonkwo impending tragedy is set to happen because of his wrong choices and desires. One has to note that in Greek tragedy, especially Aristotle's, pity for the tragic hero is based on the fact that he is not completely responsible for his downfall or misfortune. In Okonkwo's case his misfortune is attributed to his wrongheadedness and excessive quest for self-image. The anti-climax of this self-ideal was when Okonkwo returned to Umuofia but not to a hero's welcome and eventually lost everything, including his social standing, and it dawned on him that his final downfall is inevitable.[634] He was a victim of his own cultural-person-ideal-image obsession. This is interpreted and described as a cultural trait for survival (survivalist culture) because of the social situation in the community. When certain personalities in the community are idolized, praised and emulated for their warlike life, it becomes the way of life for the young for security, opportunity and identity. At some point, many people identify with these outstanding individuals as a sort of survival mechanism. In other words, this survivalist mentality is sustained by the dependence of some African communities on the physical strength and accomplishments of their illustrious individuals. The successful individuals are there for the communities' survival, provide social security and to build social solidarity. Achebe's Umuofia clearly portrays this survivalist culture and community.

---

[632] *Ibid.*, pp. 69-70.

[633] http://web.africa.ufl.edu/asq/v4/v4i3a1.htm (Accessed March 18, 2011.) Prof. D. Ipperciel argues that in Greek tragedy pity is shown to the tragic hero because he/she is not responsible for his/her downfall. This is also in line with my reading of Greek tragedy, especially in Aristotle. Meanwhile, despite this difference with African tragedy narrative, I am interested in a hermeneutic presentation of Igbo African tragedy and its subtle implications. My task is about what other cultures have to give us as their meaning and truths.

[634] *Ibid.*

Irele agrees with this point as a survival principle and culture. He notes, "[I]n the case of Okonkwo, he is a man who has grown up in a community which, because of its passionate desire for survival, places its faith above all in the individual quality of 'manliness'."[635] Following the interpretation of the various aspects of Achebe's narrative, this cultural principle and practice nurture violence and confrontational qualities in the young, especially when they have to fight their way through obstacles. To survive means or demands a form of struggle which is often violent when it meets another violent force or opposition. This is how a survivalist attitude becomes a common lifestyle in a society. We are what our society makes us, but not completely. Certainly there are some exemplary individuals who could resist some negative socio-cultural influences in their community/society. In some African societies poverty and unemployment have continued to influence a survivalist view of life. Education, economic progress and empowerment are ways of critically addressing the negative effects of a survivalist culture.[636] There is a mutual reciprocal situation between society and the individual. This as a consequence influences a community and the individual members of the community. From the text Okonkwo is a product of his society because his society has made him by proposing to him their philosophy of life, their desirable social values, conducts, collective expectations and other determinations (temporal distance applied.)

The survivalist cultural attitude is perceived in the show of 'manliness', which is associated with fierce approach to things of life. It could manifest at some point as perversions, especially when one is desperate to survive, be heroic and be recognized. There is the demand for social conformity, but is it rather more of social non-conformity in the case of Okonkwo and his obsessions. The possession of power sometimes leads to the show of power and dominance. In a society of inequalities those who possess power impose it against the will of others. This can only be perpetuated through violence, intimidation and fear.[637]

---

[635] Francis Abiola Irele, "The Tragic Conflict in the Novels of Chinua Achebe," *Critical Perspectives on Chinua Achebe*, Lyn Innes and Bernth Lindfors, eds (Washington D.C.: Three Continents Press, 1978), p. 11.

[636] I have discussed a related issue in ---Stanley Uche Anozie, "Human Rights and Terrorism: The Niger Delta Oil War," *Morality and Terrorism*, Mahmoud Masaeli, ed (California: Nortia Press, 2012), pp. 207-222.

[637] Irele, "Introduction," *Things Fall Apart Chinua Achebe: A Norton Critical Edition*, Francis Abiola Irele, ed., *op. cit.*, p. xiv.

In chapter thirteen of Achebe's narrative (hermeneutical circle, fusion of horizons etc are applied to develop the thoughts), after the accidental killing of Ogbuefi Ezeudu's son by Okonkwo, his compound was destroyed.[638] Okonkwo was forced into exile with his whole family. It was a tragedy. One sees the systematic approach employed in the destruction of Okonkwo's compound and how the 'act of destruction' was dissociated from an 'act of hatred.' There is a deep socio-philosophical implication here that the Umuofia community followed some social laws and *mores,* even when the consequences are grave. Achebe explains the justice in the destruction, "[I]t was the justice of the earth goddess, and they were merely her messengers."[639] Okonkwo's years in exile show the tragedy of a man who has been separated from his community where he was held a hero. In Achebe's narrative, Okonkwo's return from exile opens to him a new chapter of *"Things Fall Apart."* His community has since moved on without him and he may never meet up with the new social challenges of his community. Many things have changed since his exile. This change leads to a series of negative events in Okonkwo's life until he could no longer cope. Following the events that happened at Okonkwo's return from exile, the hermeneutical understanding is that his excitements at returning home (to his old hero personality ideal and his accomplishments in another land--Mbanta) gave way to frustration with coping with the new world of Umuofia. He in anger beheads a servant of the District Commissioner and this leads to the final tragic event: His takes his own life.

Okonkwo's life has been one with a series of struggle to achieve greatness and excellence.[640] In the end, he did fail and this implies a personal tragedy as some scholars read it. His failure resonates with human tragic situation in life. Okonkwo's life challenges are identified in every culture and community. In another way, the struggles of Okonkwo also portray the struggles of his community. His rise and fall reflects the rise and fall of his society. If a survivalist society depends on the success of its prominent individuals for social security (notion of person: I am because we, and because we are therefore I am), then the parallel implication is that Okonkwo's misfortune is misfortune for his community/society. Achebe concludes his

---

[638] Achebe, *Things Fall Apart* (Canada: Anchor Canada edition, 2009), p. 125; Achebe, *Things Fall Apart* (London: Heinemann, 1958), p. 88.

[639] *Ibid.*

[640] Bernth Lindfors, "The Palm-oil with which Achebe's Words are Eaten," *Chinua Achebe Things Fall Apart (Authoritative Text, Contexts and Criticism)*, Francis Abiola Irele, ed (New York: W. W. Norton & Company, 2009), p. 559.

narrative with Obierika's (Okonkwo's reflective friend) word: "That man was one of the greatest men in Umuofia. You drove him to kill himself; and now he will be buried like a dog."[641]

In summary, *Things Fall Apart* shows a man who is insistent in his actions and at times appears innocent and sincere in his purpose. It seems that he developed these habits because of his life's ambition: a community hero and a man of pride. The colonial masters represented by the District Commissioner is convinced that he is "bringing 'civilization' to Umuofia as the elders of Umuofia are convinced that he is destroying civilization."[642] Okonkwo stands out to protect this civilization of his people, but on some occasions he makes it difficult to identify him as a custodian of his culture or civilization or "a headstrong outlaw."[643]

The philosophical aspect of the hermeneutics task is that Okonkwo appears not to represent the total reality of an Igbo person as presented in Achebe's English literature. Okonkwo reflects a personhood with bad temper and obsessive fear in his conflict against Western culture. It seems other people in the community had a different approach to the crisis of civilizations going on in Umuofia. It was not as if they supported the new culture but they were set to confront it in a different way from Okonkwo's.[644] Had Achebe told his story 'first' in Igbo language, he would have communicated African thought and reality in a way that Okonkwo's person is easily identified with the African notion of person and community as presented in chapter three above. This would have helped us truly understand the communal tragedy in the narrative. The communal meaning of African notion of the person has a subtle philosophical significance (as good prejudice necessary for interpretation) in understanding African notion of tragedy. A person cannot be otherwise, i.e., he/she as an individual lives in a community of persons. This

---

[641] Achebe, *Things Fall Apart* (Canada: Anchor Canada edition, 2009), p. 208.

[642] Eldred Jones, "Language and Theme in 'Things Fall Apart'," *Review of English Literature*, v. 4 (1964), pp. 39-43.

[643] Ogede, *op. cit.,* pp. 19-20.

[644] When the Commissioner came to arrest Okonkwo and found out that he had killed himself, the one of the men in the crowd with Obierika (Okonkwo's friend) says, "It is against our custom... His body is evil, and only strangers may touch it. That is why we ask your people to bring him down, because you are strangers." There is still this intercultural problem of hermeneutics between the two cultures: the Umuofian and the Strangers.

makes sense with the heroic cultural personage who is respected for his contributions to his/her community.

d. Gadamer and Achebe: Hermeneutics of African (Igbo) Chi Proverbs in the Narrative

The Igbo are known to express themselves with craft by using wise sayings. Their speech patterns give them the ability to use many short phrases and more words to address sensitive issues among them. Proverbs could be used to make discussions short or to prolong discursive negotiations. It could also be used to make understanding difficult for the uninitiated or keep discussions among the elders' forum. Proverbs could be used to present literal thoughts and non-literal/complicated thoughts that are best said in not very clear manner (with hidden meanings.) This makes proverbs to be described as having 'coded message' or deeper meaning beyond the surface words. This is what makes the Igbo a "proverb-loving people."[645]

In the text, Achebe notes, "Among the Ibo [Igbo] the art of conversation is regarded very highly, and proverbs are the palm-oil with which words are eaten."[646] That means narratives in Igbo culture go with a style of speaking and through wise sayings. This is an essential cultural heritage of the Igbo. In the narrative, the proverbs capture the cultural and linguistic heritage of the Igbo in words that must be explained through careful interpretive approach. Sometimes the proverbs are seen as general principles of life and community living that ought to be interpreted within a situation through application. For instance, Okonkwo's success as a wrestler and a wealthy farmer is carefully and thoughtfully presented in the text in this way: "Age was respected among his people, but achievement was revered. As the elders said, if a child washed his hands he could eat with kings. Okonkwo has clearly washed his hands and so he ate with kings and elders."[647] This text highlights that Okonkwo's accomplishment speaks for itself. He has merited the status of being classed among kings or respected as belonging to the elite of his community. This

---

[645] Anieke, *op. cit.*, p. 107.

[646] Achebe, *Things Fall Apart* (Canada: Anchor Canada edition, 2009), p. 7; Lindfors, "The Palm-oil with which Achebe's Words are Eaten," *Chinua Achebe Things Fall Apart, op. cit.*, p. 555; See also Lindfors, "The Palm-oil with which Achebe's Words are Eaten," *Critical Perspectives on Chinua Achebe, op. cit.*, pp. 47-66.

[647] *Ibid.*, p. 8; Achebe, *Things Fall Apart* (New York: Anchor, 1959), p. 8.

shows the beauty and reason for applying proverbs in Igbo narratives and communication. One is intrigued in the way words are used to capture the meaning of the subject matter in the narrative and the proverb "is groomed and dressed for general consumption... [and] fosters the perception of understanding."[648]

Gadamer's hermeneutics principles (especially good prejudices, hermeneutical circle, fusion of horizons/perspective of the *Chi* proverbs etc) are spontaneously or naturally applied by us in Achebe's text chapters. These principles are used to engage Achebe's text in a dialogue and critical discussion. I shall follow a specific structure of this book in order to discuss the notion of *Chi* at a later and suitable part of this work. This will not affect the true meaning of the whole text.

In the text, one of the elders of the community who was imprisoned by the District Commissioner addresses the people. He uses a proverb: "My father used to say to me: Whenever you see a toad jumping in broad daylight, then know that something is after its life."[649] In other words, "[A] toad does not run in the daytime for nothing." This proverb addresses the importance of an event: the urgent meeting taking place after the imprisonment of the elders during the colonial time. For the people of Umuofia it is a situation of grave concern and the reason of such gathering is as such urgent and important. Anieke observes that the English language equivalent is "[T]here is no smoke without fire."[650] I am cautious in using this equivalent since "no smoke without fire" describes more of a philosophical problem of causality rather than "reason for an event" or the importance or *urgency* of a matter. As briefly mentioned above on *4.2* (*the intercultural problem of language*), following the interpretive process of Gadamer, in which the whole text and the particular aspects of the text are applied for true meaning and also the fusion of the various perspectives or contexts of the text, my simple equivalent to that proverb is that there is always a reason for a thing to happen (not as a material cause, but urgency.) This meaning could only be arrived at by looking at the situations before and after the proverb. Umuofia community has been

---

[648] Oliver Lovesey, "Making Use of the Past in *Things Fall Apart*," *Chinua Achebe's Things Fall Apart*, ed. Harold Bloom (NY: Infobase Publishers, 2010), p. 128; See Achebe, *Things Fall Apart* (New York: Anchor, 1959), p. 20.
[649] Achebe, *Things Fall Apart* (Canada: Anchor Canada edition, 2009), p. 203.
[650] Anieke, *op. cit.*, p. 110.

confronted by a strange system (culture) that does not accord respect to her cultural values/respect for elders, so there is a situation of urgency and importance to address this anomaly. Focusing on causality, in my reading of it, does not totally and truly capture the coded content of that proverb. The use of proverbs is the Igbo way of reflecting the wisdom of its community, the traditions that must be handed down or transmitted through direct application in narratives. Proverbs provide the clearness that the narrative seeks to be comprehended by Igbo and foreigners alike.

In chapter fourteen of the text another proverb is used. It says, "[I]f a man said yea his *chi* also affirmed."[651] This proverb illustrates the double aspects of human existence. The double aspects are the divine and the human aspects of existence. For a person to accomplish anything in Igbo worldviews he/she must live in accord with his/her destiny or fate. It involves an unpredictable aspect which implies that a person has to first accept that he/she is capable of accomplishing a task before one's *Chi* (personal god or guardian) concurs with the same task.

A further discussion of the role of *Chi* in Igbo African worldviews is necessary because of *Chi*'s place in the proverbs and in the events that happen in people's life. A subtle but important distinction here is that *Chi* is started with a capital letter to associate it with Igbo religion (as respect to the divine or a higher being.)[652] However, I will retain the use of *chi* (starting with small letter) as in the text. They both mean the same thing. For the Igbo, according to Anieke, *Chi* is an important concept in traditional society. "*Chi* can be defined as personal destiny, or personalized providence, of the individual which shapes their history and destiny. Some see *Chi* as a divine emanation from God which is responsible for the individual's fate or destiny."[653] The complexity of meanings about the specific role of the *Chi* is still present in the above statement. But *Chi* involves element of both fate and faith (personal duty blessed by one's *Chi*),[654] in terms of the support one receives from the gods in order to succeed in one's individual task. It is in this sense (application of the

---

[651] Achebe, *Things Fall Apart* (Canada: Anchor Canada edition, 2009), p. 131; Achebe, *Things Fall Apart* (London: Heinemann, 1958), p. 165.

[652] I choose to capitalize '*Chi*' considering its religious connotation in African thought. The role of *Chi* or fate is essential in Okonkwo's tragedy.

[653] Anieke, *op. cit.*, p. 34; See Pauline Aligwekwe, *Continuity of Traditional Values, The Igbo of Nigeria* (Owerri: 1991), p. 173; See Elizabeth Isichei, *A History of the Igbo People* (London: The Macmillan Press, 1976), p. 75.

[654] Madu, *op. cit.*, p. 183.

fusion of horizons/perspectives) that *Chi's* role could also imply the task of a mediator. One's relationship to the Supreme Being (God) is determined by one's relations to his/her *Chi*. Since *Chi* is only an individual relationship, rather than universal, there could be a lucky person (with a good luck *Chi* (*Chioma*)) or even a bad luck person (with bad luck *Chi* (*Chiojoo*).) This reminds us about the place of predestination and freewill in Igbo traditional world. In relation to the above, there are other proverbs among the Igbo that affirm predestination. For example: *Onye kwe ma chi ya ekweghi, o ga-egbu onwe ya?* (If one says yes and his/her *Chi* disagrees, should one commit suicide?) While presenting the Igbo proverbs in Igbo above, one recalls the argument in the earlier part of this thesis that English language translation or transliteration of Igbo proverbs and narratives hindered the communication of their true inner meaning. Achebe ought to have the narrative *first* communicated in Igbo language to protect its true meanings and philosophical understanding.

When some of the people of the community referred to Okonkwo as one who is pushing his luck and desperate with the gods, Achebe describes the scene in a proverbial manner, "people said he (Okonkwo) had no respect for the gods of his clan. His enemies said his good fortune had gone to his head. They called him the little bird *nza* (Igbo name for a small bird) who so far forgot himself after a heavy meal that he challenged his *chi*."[655] The essence of the *Chi* proverbs in the narrative is to sharpen the image of the hero (Okonkwo) and clearly presents the depth of his struggles [with fate.] This same situation is reinforced through other *Chi* proverbs (in chapter fourteen) when Okonkwo returned to his community after his exile of seven years. Achebe's text presents it thus:

> Clearly his personal god or *chi* was not made for great things. A man could not rise beyond the destiny of his *chi*. The saying of the elders was not true-that if a man said yea his *chi* also affirmed. Here was a man whose *chi* said nay despite his own affirmation.[656]

---

[655] Achebe, *Things Fall Apart* (Canada: Anchor Canada edition, 2009), p. 31; Achebe, *Things Fall Apart* (London: Heinemann, 1958), p. 26.
[656] *Ibid.*,p. 131; See also Lindfors, "The Palm-oil with which Achebe's Words are Eaten," *Chinua Achebe Things Fall Apart, op. cit.,* p. 560.

Okonkwo's character clearly surfaces at the stages of his life and within his quest for heroic status. Achebe paints a picture of a man who easily forgets and who hopes that the best has been set for him by destiny. While in exile Okonkwo's accomplishments grew and after his return to Umuofia things seem to improve for him. People felt "that his *chi* [fate or god] might now be making amends for the past disaster"[657] (in chapter twenty.) It appears that the gods could change their mind and make things better. In normal parlance, only finite human being could "be making amends."[658] In the quote above, it states, "[C]learly his personal god or *chi* was not made for great things."[659] The text seems to imply that Okonkwo's *Chi* or destiny was unchangeable unless through the mistakes of the gods. I think Okonkwo could not change his own fate by himself alone without the higher approval of his *Chi*. If this is the case, it is in agreement with the line "that his *chi* might now be making amends for the past disaster"[660] (in chapter twenty—we are dialoguing with these chapters as horizons and parts of the whole text.) Nevertheless, the line of argument may have to be read as only *a wish* of Okonkwo "that now... (my addition expressing only the wish of Okonkwo) his *chi* might be making amends."[661] But some African philosophers and hermeneutists argue that Okonkwo's accomplishments were not the designs of the gods but only his personal efforts. I think that means the contributions of his *Chi* are not considered or simply insignificant. My conclusion is that Okonkwo's destiny was unchanged and his successes were from his destiny (although he worked hard.) This conclusion leads us closer to the fact that African tragedy in the text is about communal tragedy of the Umuofia people. Okonkwo's fate is his community's fate.

I shall now proceed in this section of chapter four to present the African notion of *Chi* as pure African philosophical and hermeneutical theme since we have talked about some '*Chi* proverbs' in Achebe's text above.

---

[657] *Ibid.*, p. 172; Achebe, *Things Fall Apart* (London: Heinemann, 1958), p. 154.
[658] *Ibid.*
[659] *Ibid.*, p. 117.
[660] *Ibid.*, p. 172.
[661] This is my reading of that line to express only a wish or a possibility for Okonkwo. Lindfors affirms the complex nature proverbs. There are proverbs that express different views on the same issue. Lindfors, "The Palm-oil with which Achebe's Words are Eaten," *Chinua Achebe Things Fall Apart, op. cit.,* p. 561.

e. Gadamer and Achebe: The Hermeneutical Principle of Prejudice and the Hermeneutical Theme of the African Notion of Chi

Earlier we discussed the *chi* under "*Chi* proverbs" or as used in proverbs. In this section I will be discussing it as a hermeneutical theme or as an African philosophical notion in order to justify my argument about 'communal' tragedy. In other words, my task here is to inquire about African communal notion of tragedy using the notion of *Chi* (as good prejudice or fore-meaning from African tradition or horizons of possibilities) to justify my interpretation of *Things Fall Apart* in light of Gadamer's claims of the universality of hermeneutics and the conditions of understanding. If Achebe's African notion of tragedy is slightly unique from the Greek's,[662] how does Gadamer's hermeneutics help us to unravel this subtle uniqueness?

The text on Achebe's notion of tragedy relates with Okonkwo's *Chi* or fate.[663] The term *Chi* provides a subtle distinction between African and Greek notions of tragedy. Gadamer's hermeneutical style requires that "understanding...be put in question."[664] This involves applying the hermeneutical process of dialogue or conversation with the different parts of the text to understand new meanings coming from the narrative. We are also using the principle of legitimate and good prejudices which allows our prior knowledge and prejudgments to positively bear on our present inquiry or practice of hermeneutics. As we recall prejudices are ontological to us and constitute our knowledge acquisition or our act of interpretation. It is an essential part of our historical reality and so we cannot overcome all our prejudices, but we could direct them to useful means in order to engage with the text as Gadamer suggests. The knowledge and philosophical thought about African notion of *Chi* are aspects of the good prejudices which help to inform us on the true meaning of our text.

As earlier narrated, between chapters twenty and twenty-five, Okonkwo is confronted by a new culture and religion after his return to his village. His path to tragedy started as soon as he killed a court messenger of the District Commissioner (in chapter twenty-four leading to chapter twenty-five.) His disappointment, which is another form of tragedy, is that his people could not

---

[662] See Anieke, *op. cit.,* pp. 42-45; See Ker, *op. cit.*, p. 27.
[663] For the role of fate in tragedy: See Halliwell, *op. cit.,* pp. 178-179.
[664] Taylor, *op. cit.*, p. 280.

rise up in his defense or his people have been compromised. Okonkwo's disappointment gives way to despair and consequent suicide.[665] In the text, Obierika, Okonkwo's friend, remonstrates that the new culture/civilization and religion has sent Okonkwo to an early grave. This argument suggests that Okonkwo through the narrative did not see any reason to act contrary to the wish of the gods and goddesses of his land. It is rather Okonkwo's fate or destiny or *Chi* that saw him end his life in tragedy. Achebe uses such proverbs as these to get this point across. We have to remember that these proverbs ought to be written as they are translated in the text (English.) The proverbs are: (a) "as a man danced so the drums were beaten for him" [666]-meaning that success is determined outside an individual. Achebe also adds (b) "when a man says yes his *chi* says yes also"-meaning that "Okonkwo said yes very strongly; so his *chi* agreed. And not only his *chi* but his clan too, because it judged a man by the work of his hands."[667] It is a positive meaning of *Chi* notion in chapter four of Achebe's text. These are the primary proverbs that suggest success and fortune in life and their relation to fate.

Success or failure in life is measured in Igbo worldviews according to how one lived with one's destiny or fate or *Chi*. *Chi* defines an individual's personal destiny and the role of providence.[668] This shows that it includes the presence of fate and personal decisions approved by one's *Chi*.[669] The hermeneutical meaning of the narrative in this regard is that one needs to receive the approval of his god in other to accomplish set goals. *Chi's* role does involve some complex meanings because it is related to many aspects of an individual's life. This is in line with Gadamer's view of possible complexity of meanings or new comprehensions[670] about specific hermeneutical objects or

---

[665] Anieke, *op. cit.*, p. 39.

[666] Achebe, *Things Fall Apart* (London: Heinemann, 1958), p. 165.

[667] Achebe, *Things Fall Apart* (Canada: Anchor Canada edition, 2009), p. 27.

[668] Anieke, *op. cit.*, p. 34; See Aligwekwe, *op. cit.*, p. 173; See Isichei, *op. cit.*, p. 75.

[669] Madu, *op. cit.*, p. 183.

[670] Gadamer, *Philosophical Hermeneutics, op. cit.*, pp. xxv-xxvi. There is the possibility of immediate changes in interpretation. Even an individual's interpretation could be altered in a couple of minutes. According to MacIntyre, "[I]n this way philosophical issues that had previously seemed to be closed and settled may always be reopened. What had appeared to be conclusive arguments against some position turn out not to be conclusive after all, perhaps because the position against which they were directed had been reinterpreted, perhaps because the arguments have been reevaluated. About the possibility of reinterpretation, Gadamer has written that it always confronts the reader of a text; "The line of meaning that the text manifests to him as he reads it always and necessarily breaks off in an open indeterminacy. He can, indeed he must, accept the fact that future generations will

texts. In comparing chapter four and chapter fourteen of the narrative-- the positive meaning of *Chi* turns to a negative use in the later chapter. The text states about Okonkwo, "[C]learly his personal god or *chi* was not made for great things. A man could not rise beyond the destiny of his *chi*. The saying of the elders was not true—that if a man said yea his *chi* also affirmed. Here was a man whose *chi* said nay despite his own affirmation."[671]

I will like to keep Igbo proverbs as they are to avoid distortion and misrepresentation: Igbo proverbs used in justifying the interpretation of the role of fate or destiny in African tragedy are many. However, I will focus on the ones provided in Achebe above: *Onye kwe ma chi ya ekweghi, o ga-egbu onwe ya?* (If one says yes and his/her *Chi* disagrees, should one commit suicide?) Achebe also describes a similar proverb which notes that Okonkwo was disrespectful to the gods of the land. Other people in the community who are critical of Okonkwo's behavior often called him the arrogant man who has let his good fortune take over his reason. In their frustration with Okonkwo they used the image of a very little bird *nza* (Igbo name for a small bird) to describe him. The little bird *nza* is contrasted to the *heavy* meal and the *heavy* hands of the powerful *Chi*/god. This proverbial argument against fate is rather a single argument by those in the community who hated Okonkwo's demeanor, but not necessarily the truth about Okonkwo. His character clearly shows the nature of his struggles with fate. Achebe highlights the role of destiny in tragedy when he recalls that Okonkwo's personal *Chi*/god may not have set him up for heroic things or on famous path. It is beyond the power of a mere mortal to succeed/ rise over the determinations of his powerful *Chi*.[672]

Now let us look at another part of the series of tragic events in the text in which *Chi* was referred. Achebe clearly affirms that despite the odds of being forced to live in a foreign land with limited opportunities, Okonkwo's success grew even while he was in exile. What is the meaning of this return to a community that sent him away after destroying all he had worked for? It could

---

understand differently what he has read in the text." But the possibility of such a change in understanding is not only a matter of the perspective of some future generation. A single reader's perspective changes over time; what was at one time at or near the horizon may always become part of the foreground. And so it is always possible that my future reading of some passage within a text or some text or some body of texts will not be the same as my present reading." See MacIntyre, *op. cit.*, p. 160.

[671] Achebe, *Things Fall Apart* (Canada: Anchor Canada edition, 2009), p. 131.

[672] *Ibid.* See also Lindfors, *op. cit.*, p. 560.

be seen from the hermeneutical circle perspective as the return to a new beginning in which tragedy is truly understood as having a strong communal implication. Okonkwo returning with success to his original community hermeneutically seems to indicate that his success is a private accomplishment (because he became successful every place he went.) Also, Okonkwo, without returning to his community, would suggest an individual tragedy because his initial tragic situation leads him to that individual (with his family) exile. But further in the text, Achebe recalls that Umuofia people believe Okonkwo's fortune must be coming to him because of the new blessings of his *Chi* [god] after the past destructions he experienced.[673] Achebe's text equally suggests that Okonkwo's *Chi* or destiny is unchangeable. His fate befalls on him with the approval of his *Chi*.[674] The consideration of any change in destiny is only a confirmation of the ability of the personal god to make necessary changes which is perceived as an act of amendment by a higher being. Philosophically this is difficult since a higher (divine) being does not need to change his/her mind. Doing so will raise some epistemological concerns of a higher being not possessing *ab initio* and in totality a fuller knowledge of the reality around him, especially in relation to mere mortals. Despite this seeming difficulty, the interpretation of this amendment/change of mind by a divine being--*Chi* could be read as an act permissible *only* by one's *Chi* for a person who is consistent with the demands of his personal *Chi*. It is an adjustment made by the divine for people loyal to his/her commands. It is simply *gratis* (out of kindness or favor or compliment.) This point again confirms my interpretation and conclusion that Achebe's Okonkwo was faithful to the commands of the Oracle and obedient to the cause of his religion.[675] As Gadamer recommends, hermeneutics has the task of going beyond the comments of the author through the continued dialogues of understanding, the questions and responses that express better the thoughts of the author, the consideration of temporal

---

[673] Achebe, *Things Fall Apart* (Canada: Anchor Canada edition, 2009), p. 172.

[674] I am of the view that we are establishing dialogues with Achebe since, according to Gadamer, in dialogue we understand what we have said, especially after being questioned by others about our utterances. Kertscher explains, "According to Gadamer, as speakers, we are in the same situation as when we are hearers, since we only come to understand what we have said through our interpretative engagement with others in which the meanings of our own utterances as well as theirs are questioned, responded to, and worked out. What we mean is articulated and exhibited through our utterance and responses, that is, through linguistic and practical activities in which utterances are embedded. On this basis Gadamer is not only attempting to avoid objectivistic views of meaning and understanding but also to establish the productive dimension of understanding." See Kertscher, *op. cit.*, p. 145.

[675] Kertscher, *op. cit.*, p. 145.

distance the analysis of particulars and details. That means one could articulate better what Achebe intended through his narrative. [676]

Gadamer's claim of the universality of hermeneutics supports the use of the argument on hermeneutical circle (as a condition of understanding.) Meanwhile, an incomplete application of this principle does lead to the *conclusion* by some African philosophers and hermeneutists that Okonkwo's accomplishments were not the designs of the gods but only his individual efforts. For instance, Lindfors' position (conclusion) is that Okonkwo's successes were not based on fate or destiny. However, Okonkwo faces a series of tragic events and finally takes his own life because he was wrong in allowing his ego to take over his reason by seeking to achieve greatness in a desperate manner. This, for Lindfors, is what makes Okonkwo a tragic hero. He agrees with this interpretation that Okonkwo's accomplishments are not the designs of the gods, rather "Okonkwo erred by daring to attempt something he did not have the power to achieve."[677] I think that this conclusion could only be arrived at by *not* critically following Gadamer's principles of the universality of hermeneutics, like analyzing the particulars and the details of the texts, and vice versa, and other hermeneutical conditions of understanding in the narrative. In other words, there are no other parts of Achebe's narrative that suggested or convincingly suggested Lindfors' conclusion. The cultural traditions and the background narratives do not affirm holding Okonkwo responsible for misunderstanding the Oracle of the land. Okonkwo is only left with a subtle suggestion by the elder in the community which may not be the true understanding of the demands of the Oracle (but about the use of prudence.) Gadamer clearly notes that "the arbitrariness of a corrupt text can

---

[676] *Ibid.,* pp. 144-145. Kertscher observes, "we are inclined to accept the speaker's own explanation of what he has said as adequate to provide an account of the meaning of the sentence in question. We thus concede that speaker has what is known as "first-person authority" on the assumption that the author of an utterance will best know what he has said. According to Gadamer, however, we have to give up this view: the sense of a sentence is not something that is simply present and needs only to be discovered. That this is so is evident when one asks how the intention of the speaker is present in cases of misunderstanding. The answer is that the intentions is only accessible on the basis of information acquired from the speaker—we can ask him what he has meant by using certain words or how he uses certain expressions. Having done so, we can suggest another formulation for his utterances, add comments, explanations, or interpretations. In doing so, we determine the sense of what is said on the basis of a dialogue that encompasses both ourselves and our interlocutor and in which the interlocutor's own initial understanding is not only drawn upon, but may also end up being progressively altered."
[677] Lindfors, *op. cit.,* p. 563.

be corrected if the context as a whole is understood."[678] Achebe's narrative has to involve the contexts or situations describing the tragic events surrounding Okonkwo.

My two hermeneutical conclusions after using the hermeneutical circle, the good prejudices, and by extension some other principles of Gadamer, are that: first, Okonkwo was faithful to his *Chi* and to the Oracle, and secondly, Okonkwo's success was from his *Chi* (and so fate) and not necessarily from his hard work. These show that Okonkwo has no question to answer about his fate. His seeming 'personal' tragedy is a tragedy that has befallen Umuofia as a community going through the actual intercultural problem or crisis. It is thus how things are for the people of Umuofia. It is their communal tragedy or fate.

Following the discourse above, *Chi* proverbs or predestination proverbs co-exist with anti-predestination proverbs shows the complex nature of the Igbo culture.[679] Thus there are elements of both vividness and complexity in understanding the true meaning attached to a proverb. It is generally used to transmit traditional wisdom in a linguistic way and the concise worldviews of the people.[680] The proverb is deep with "coded message... The appropriateness of the proverb lies in the way it is quoted to capture a state of mind."[681]

Achebe's African oral tradition is peculiar with the use of proverbs as an essential part of its conversation style, the richness of its linguistic abilities and its aesthetics of communication. The depth of communication delivered through proverbs requires a thorough hermeneutical task to unravel the totality of meaning of the proverbs because they have deeper meaning than the words present. If one has no adequate education about Igbo (African) usage of proverbs in the discourse, then it is difficult to understand the true message intended in the discourse. In a narrative, names, objects, properties, words, figures of speech, metaphors etc. could carry much hermeneutical weight in a particular culture, in this case, the African Igbo people.

---

[678] Gadamer, *Truth and Method*, trans. Joel Weinsheimer and Donald G. Marshall, *op. cit.*, p. 392; Gadamer, *Truth and Method* (New York: The Seabury Press, 1975), p. 352.
[679] Anieke, *op. cit.*, p. 110.
[680] Arthur Ravenscroft, *Chinua Achebe* (London: Longmans, Green and co Ltd, 1969), p. 16.
[681] Ogede, *op. cit.*, p. 30.

Achebe equally used other figures of speech and styles, not only proverbs, but similes, metaphors etc, like "a bush-fire in the harmattan"[682]; "like pouring grains of corn into a bag full of holes,"[683] "as busy as an anti-hill"[684] etc. I argue that Achebe does not only employ African vernacular style to his dialogue but he narrates the story with "proverbs and similes which help to evoke the cultural milieu in which the action takes place."[685] With a careful interplay of proverbs, Igbo metaphors and terms in his text, Achebe refuses to accept that African narratives need to be written in African languages.[686]

Proverbs make communication easy and more effective. They have their own depth that they introduce in African discourse. Achebe's use of proverb gives his writing the color of its African-ness and the uniqueness of Africanity. The proverbs give a linguistic value to the narrative. This makes the novel easy to understand and interpret because the proverbs are pointers to the message of the narrative. I have to conclude with Lindfors' words that proverbs "provide a 'grammar of values' by which the deeds of a hero can be measured and evaluated. By studying Achebe's proverbs we are better able to interpret his novels."[687]

Let us now look at some other proverbs present in Achebe's work. Although not all the proverbs are relevant to our research and advancement of the understanding of the communal aspect of tragedy, the common ones present in the narrative need to be clearly understand to improve understanding of African existence and worldviews.

4.2.3 Some Other Proverbs and their Meanings in Achebe's *Things Fall Apart*

These proverbs in this subsection were not considered among the '*Chi*' proverbs that we thoughtfully explained above. These proverbs are not afterthoughts but are generally essential in African hermeneutical thought. In

---

[682] Achebe, *Things Fall Apart* (Canada: Anchor Canada edition, 2009), p.1; Achebe, *Things Fall Apart* (London: Heinemann, 1958), p. 1.
[683] *Ibid.*, p. 22.
[684] Achebe, *Things Fall Apart* (London: Heinemann, 1958), p. 100.
[685] Lindfors, *op. cit.*, p. 557.
[686] McLaren, "Things Fall Apart: Cultural and Historical Contexts," *op. cit.*, pp. 27-28.
[687] Lindfors, *op. cit.*, pp. 558-559; Lindfors acknowledges the source of this view "grammar of values" from Melville Jean Herskovits, *Dahomean Narrative* (Evanston, 1958), p. 56; See Austin J. Shelton, "The 'Palm-Oil' of Language: Proverbs in Chinua Achebe's Novels," *Modern Language Quarterly*, 30, No. 1 (1969), pp. 86-111.

other words, we will make references to these 'other' proverbs present in the text and, for lack of space, briefly highlight their core meanings as coded words. One has to recall that the whole text of *Things Fall Apart* is the main object of hermeneutics. We do not intend to make a long and extensive hermeneutic project with these non-*Chi* proverbs but to recognize their being part of Achebe's narrative and for the communication of inner meaning.

Here are some of them used by Achebe in the text:

- "[T]he sun will shine on those who stand before it shines on those who kneel under them."[688] This proverb suggests the levels of considerations that the gods grant to people and their status. Achebe also presents other examples of a cultural tradition that had attachment to accomplishments and societal status.
- "if a child washed his hands he could eat with kings." [689]A child shapes his own destiny. It means a well-groomed person succeeds or grows to enjoy with kings or the company of successful people or people of honor.
- In chapter one the proverb states, "He who brings *kola* brings life."[690] Kola nut is a caffeine-containing African nut (of evergreen trees of genus *Cola* –it is native to tropical rainforest of African) eaten before or during discussion. It has a bitter taste and is regarded as a stimulant to reduce the effects of hunger and fatigue. The presence of kola affirms the formal beginning of a gathering or meeting of the community. It is an essential edible in Igbo ceremonies. It is also used as a sign of welcome to guests in homes. Kola is interpreted as life-giving fruit. It is believed that from the seed springs out life–a living tree. In Anieke's view, "kola is 'a force that unites the living, the dead, and the supernatural forces in one place'. Therefore, to bring kola is to express a wish for unity with supernatural forces[691] and with fellow human beings; in other words, to bring life."[692]

---

[688] Achebe, *Things Fall Apart* (London: Heinemann, 1958), p. 5.

[689] *Ibid.,* p. 6.

[690] Achebe, *Things Fall Apart* (Canada: Anchor Canada edition, 2009), p. 6; Achebe, *Things Fall Apart* (London: Heinemann, 1958), p. 5; Anieke, *op. cit.*, p. 108.

[691] Anayochukwu Okoli, *A Sojourner in Her Own Tribe* (Enugu: Mekanand Publications, 1998), p. 50. Kola is used during prayers to invoke the assistance of the ancestors and initiate mutual communion. Anieke, *op. cit.*, p. 33.

[692] Anieke, *op. cit.*, p. 108.

- In chapter three the text states, "an old woman is always uneasy when dry bones are mentioned in a proverb."[693] The incident surrounding this proverb helps recall to Okonkwo the story of his father's laziness. Okonkwo is sensitive to certain symbols, objects and images used in community discussions. It also means when something worry us, anything said relating to it keeps us on the edge or get nervous and concerned. We become very sensitive because of our worrying or not so proud situations.

- In chapter three the proverb says, "[T]he lizard that jumped from the high iroko tree to the ground said he would praise himself if no one else did."[694] It means sometimes self-praise is acceptable. We live for ourselves. The iroko tree (Chorophoria excelsa) is commonly seen in west coast of tropical Africa. It is a hardwood, tough and dense of mostly brown color. It is also called *African Teak.*

- In chapter eight the proverb says, "A child's fingers are not scalded by a piece of hot yam which its mother puts into its palm."[695] Okonkwo uses this to justify his killing of Ikemefuna and why the Earth goddess ought not to punish him. If a higher being demands a tough task from a person, then the task does not hurt the person.

- "If I fall down for you and you fall down for me, it is play."[696] This is the proverbs the people introduce in negotiations as to demand compromise and mutual understanding or mutual considerations. In Anieke's analysis, "This proverb expresses a desire for compromise in dealing with people and issues. A deal is likely to go through if each party is ready for some compromise (German— *Entgegenkommen*)."[697]

- In chapter seventeen, the text uses a wise saying or proverb, "Living fire begets cold, impotent ash."[698] Okonkwo recalls the personality differences between him and his son (Nwoye.) Okonkwo considers himself as "a flaming fire"[699] while his son is a weakling ("begotten a woman for a son".) It is about the puzzling effects of some causes. Fire

---

[693] Achebe, *Things Fall Apart* (Canada: Anchor Canada edition, 2009), p. 21.
[694] *Ibid.*
[695] *Ibid.*, p. 67.
[696] Achebe, *Things Fall Apart* (London: Heinemann, 1958), p. 51; See Anieke, *op. cit.*, p. 109.
[697] Anieke, *op. cit.*, p. 109.
[698] Achebe, *Things Fall Apart* (Canada: Anchor Canada edition, 2009), p. 153.
[699] *Ibid.*

leaves you with cold ash. Fire is the cause of cold ash. But fire is strong and exciting, but when it goes off it leaves cold ash.

- Another proverb says: "as a man danced so the drums were beaten for him"[700]-meaning that what dictates success is from a world outside an individual or beyond and only the beyond that determines the nature of success of an individual.

Igbo proverbs could have multiple applications and interpretations at a time: "Sometimes in Achebe's novels one finds proverbs expressing different views on the same subject."[701] There is no one proverb that provides the 'total picture' of a situation. Each proverb speaks or answers from a perspective. That means that one has to carefully understand and interpret the contents of the proverbs to take the true meanings out of them. Okonkwo as a character is aware of the complex interpretive quality of his people's proverbs. He could interpretively relate "When mother cow is chewing grass its young ones watch its mouth"[702] with "A chick that will grow into a cock can be spotted the very day it hatches.[703]" When Okonkwo noticed the irony, or even the dialectics, of the situation in his own family: his father was lazy, he himself was heroic and famous, while his son Nwoye had nothing to hold as his trade and reputation, Okonkwo is said to have sighed heavily, "[A]nd immediately Okonkwo's [his] eyes were opened and he saw the whole matter clearly."[704]

There is a number of issues not disclosed but they can only be accessed through the hermeneutical process of questions and answers as an essential part of interpretation.[705] We have to inquire for more information from utterances, explanations, and other precisions in order to understand an author or a text.[706] In writing many factors are involved,[707] e.g., languages, contexts, proverbs and various tropes. Narratives and dialogue offer us many information that demand interpretation and comprehension of meanings. There is still more to be understood from a simple narrative, including some hidden

---

[700] Achebe, *Things Fall Apart* (London: Heinemann, 1958), p. 165.
[701] Lindfors, *op. cit.,* p. 561.
[702] Achebe, *Things Fall Apart* (Canada: Anchor Canada edition, 2009), pp. 70-71; Achebe, *Things Fall Apart* (London: Heinemann, 1958), p. 62.
[703] *Ibid.,* p. 66; Achebe, *Things Fall Apart* (London: Heinemann, 1958), p. 58.
[704] *Ibid.,* p. 153; Achebe, *Things Fall Apart* (London: Heinemann, 1958), p. 138.
[705] Kertscher, *op. cit.,* pp. 144-145.
[706] *Ibid.,* p. 192.
[707] *Ibid.,* p. 190.

meanings.[708] The ongoing dialogue with Achebe's narrative is part of the process of hermeneutics that emphasizes clarity of meaning. Achebe's narrative has not said the final word and, as contemporary interpreters and researchers, we are expected to see Achebe's literary art from new perspectives and in contemporary light.

Our hermeneutical task so far is to understand Achebe within our present historical contexts and it is not merely to reproduce Achebe's intention. Gadamer's condition of understanding demands that interpretation does not have to be solely dependent on the situation/ context of the author. New meanings are received following ongoing interpretation, the central interest of the generation of interpreters and the time in understanding.[709]

I shall now take a look at the unfolding of history and the fusion of horizons in relation to contemporary African thought. Achebe's hero-tragic book is about the unfolding of history and the new change in understanding. Our project so far is the application of Gadamer's hermeneutical framework to justify the universality of hermeneutics and its conditions of understanding of any text.

---

[708] Gadamer, *Philosophical Hermeneutics, op. cit.,* p. xxxii.

[709] Gadamer describes contemporaneity to involve, "[l]isteners of the day before yesterday as well as of the day after tomorrow are always among those to whom one speaks as a contemporary. Where are we to draw the line that excludes a reader from being addressed? What are contemporaries and what is a text's claim to truth in the face of this multifarious mixture of past and future? The idea of the original reader is full of unexamined idealization. Furthermore, our conception of the nature of literary tradition contains a fundamental objection to the hermeneutical legitimacy of the idea of the original reader. We saw that literature is defined by the will to hand on. But a person who copies and passes on is doing it for his own contemporaries. Thus the reference to the original reader, like that to the meaning of the author, seems to offer only a very crude historico-hermeneutical criterion which cannot really limit the horizon of a text's meaning. What is fixed in writing has detached itself from the contingency of its origin and its author and made itself free for new relationships. Normative concepts such as the author's meaning or the original reader's understanding represent in fact only an empty space that is filled from time to time in understanding." Gadamer, Truth and Method, trans. Joel Weinsheimer and Donald G. Marshall, op. cit., pp. 396-397; See also Gadamer, *Truth and Method* (New York: The Seabury Press, 1975), pp. 356-357.

4.2.4 Interculturality: The Unfolding of History, the Fusion of Horizons and Contemporary African Thought

Gadamer's use of the hermeneutical principle of fusion of horizons has been considered by some scholars as reminding us of Hegel's concept of the universal history. Hegel holds that progress in history is not material, but part of humanity's spiritual development. Our experiences are the essential part of development of the universal history of Being. This progress is through the historical dialectics of thesis, antithesis and synthesis in Hegel's view. Gadamer's view of hermeneutics somehow advances Hegel's universal history. For Gadamer, the experience of Europe of his time and the need for European integration is part of history. It is in this similar manner that the experiences of the process of emancipation and end of colonial rule in former colonial countries under Europe are part of history (especially for African scholars and students.) Every historical experience is part of our global experience and history. Every development of worldviews and understanding are because of the historical situations of the time and are all part of the universal history of our peaceful existence. The intercultural efforts to reconcile African rooted cultures/values of their life-world with Western style economic progress or foreign colonial cultures are part of the universal history of human experience. In Gadamer's view every worldview or every perspective of reality is required in the effort to arrive at understanding and disclosure of meaning. Every worldview is part of the whole view of the world. This is similar to Hegel's use of the dialectics in history through the process of *Aufhebung* (means in German 'to cancel', 'to preserve,' 'to raise up' or 'to sublate') that does not require the elimination of whatever is important in the process of knowledge and history. The universal history expressed through *Aufhebung* (cancellation and preservation or resolution) is central in understanding the notion of the fusion of horizons. Gadamer's hermeneutics shows a real support for the use of "the concept of fusion of horizons, where the ultimate horizon…implied…the direction of every individual event of fusion."[710] One also recalls that Gadamer is critical of identifying his work with Hegel's form of dialectics. It is not our goal in this section to identify Gadamer with Hegel's whole views.

---

[710] Gadamer, *Philosophical Hermeneutics, op. cit.,* p. 36.

Following my analysis of Achebe's *Things Fall Apart*, it is my views that it be interpreted as an unfolding narrative history of a particular people-the Igbo people, being part of the unfolding of universal history. It is relates to what Gadamer describes as the part of the "objective course of history."[711] Achebe's work is itself a hermeneutic understanding of the worldviews of his people, thought and culture. It is the communication of meaning and understanding from his people's socio-cultural perspective. Achebe's narrative addresses some aspects of the intercultural problem of understanding and language by relating the two different cultural ranges of vision. In this way he aligns with Gadamer's "fusion of horizons"[712] thereby suggesting that we are not limited or bound to the premise of our traditions. It helps us recognize intercultural differences and to tolerate plurality.

Every cultural perspective is a horizon. We need the fusion of horizons for greater understanding and for genuine conversations to take place among people of different cultural worlds. In so doing social alienation is overcome and a true intercultural world is developed. In the fusion or merging of horizons we have a central direction for our diverse and limited understanding, due to the finite and particular nature of human knowledge. Gadamer explains that the horizon is a limited range of vision and it requires the emergence of new horizons. A new horizon that emerges implies the continuity for reaching out to new frontiers with new meanings. That means one is not constrained to what is nearest to him/her. Our encounter with tradition involves the acknowledgement of our relative knowledge to what is present to us, the need to inquire further or to expand our horizon. Our horizon is also part of our hermeneutical situation. We are in this hermeneutical situation because we have a horizon.

Gadamer articulates the importance of the fusion of the horizons in regard to language. Understanding and interpretation of meanings come through language. Gadamer states:

The guiding idea... *is that the fusion of horizons that takes place in understanding is actually the achievement of language.* Admittedly, what language is belongs among the most

[711] Gadamer, *Truth and Method*, trans. Joel Weinsheimer and Donald G. Marshall, *op. cit.*, p. 296.
[712] Gadamer, *Philosophical Hermeneutics, op. cit.*, p. 39; Warnke, *Gadamer: Hermeneutics, Tradition and Reason* (Oxford: Polity Press, 1987), p. 170.

mysterious questions that man ponders. Language is so uncannily near to our thinking, and when it functions it is so little an object, that it seems to conceal its own being from us.[713]

Language helps us get acquainted with the perspective of our world and the subject matter that interests us.[714] This fusion of horizons is caused by the shift one makes for the new objects that were not part of one's first range of vision. It is not a mere extension of a fusion. The fusion of horizons best describes the intercultural activities that allow us to be aware of the different ways of looking at things, accept the different opinions of other cultures and integrate them to our worldviews. Charles Taylor,[715] a Gadamerian commentator, states with regard to the intercultural aspect of the fusion of horizons:

> The 'horizons' here are at first distinct, they are the way that each has of understanding the human condition in their nonidentity. The "fusion" comes about when one (or both) undergo[es] a shift; the horizon is extended so as to make room for the object that before did not fit within it. For instance, we become aware that there are different ways of believing things, one of which is holding them as a "personal opinion." This was all that we allowed for before, but now we have space for other ways and can therefore accommodate the beliefs of a quite different culture. Our horizon is extended to take in this possibility, which was beyond its limit before. But this is better seen as a fusion rather than just as an extension of horizons, because at the same time we are introducing a language to talk about their beliefs that represent an extension in relation to their language… So the new language used here, which places 'opinions' alongside other modes of believing as possible alternative ways of holding things true, opens a broader horizon, extending beyond both the original ones and in a sense combining them.[716]

---

[713] Gadamer, *Truth and Method* , trans. Joel Weinsheimer and Donald G. Marshall, *op. cit.*, p. 370.

[714] Gadamer, *Philosophical Hermeneutics, op. cit.*, p. xxxviii.

[715] I choose to introduce Charles Taylor because of his unique application of Gadamer's views to intercultural understanding and dialogue, especially in Western conception of selfhood. This is really a contemporary application of Gadamer's view in a multicultural world.

[716] Taylor, *op. cit.*, p. 287.

Gadamer's fusion of horizons is about the openness for a broader horizon. It is the extension of understanding, especially since individual horizons could be independently understood. He presents understanding as something that takes place when independent horizons encounter each other. The encounter of the various cultures of the world creates the need for the fusion of perspectives and offers new ways of understanding reality. There is always room for some intercultural dialogue and deeper hermeneutical understanding. This room for intercultural dialogue relates to the integration of cultural worlds while retaining useful values or visions of life which are far from perfect. That means, although there are distinct horizons, they are not fixed horizons or 'perfect' horizons.[717]

Meanwhile, one has to address some questions often raised by objecting views since not everyone is familiar with Gadamer's view on the fusion of horizons: is there a distinction of horizons or is there a continuity of horizon? Have we only one horizon that extends? I think these are valid questions, however, some may disagree that Gadamer did not intend to see these as problems. Gadamer addresses these questions by arguing that the idea of the fusion of horizons shows that part of the hermeneutical task involves the encounter between traditions as limited range of vision of our world existence. Like any encounter, there is bound to be tension between each of the horizons with an attempt at developing a perfect single horizon. That means to consider a fusion of horizons as giving rise to one perfectly understood "world" is controversial and indefensible. In another way, Gadamer describes this fusion as the transmission of the past and the future that are constitutively mediated. Let me provide a brief analysis of how this fusion of horizons applies to Achebe's text.

Like Gadamer's fusion of horizons, Achebe argues that the horizon of the Igbo people before the encounter with Western cultures was a limited horizon. Achebe's understanding of the fusion of horizons or perspectives acknowledges limitations of horizons within intercultural situations. But a better intercultural understanding could provide us with more peaceful understanding of the different cultures.[718] Achebe's text agrees with Gadamer's

---

[717] *Ibid.*, p. 290.
[718] Lloyd W. Brown, "Cultural Norms and Modes of Perception in Achebe's Fiction," *Critical Perspectives on Chinua Achebe*, Lyn Innes and Bernth Lindfors, eds (Washington D.C.: Three Continents Press, 1978), p. 35.

view that intercultural encounter brings new perspectives and ways of understanding Africa. He weighs the weakness of traditional African society in the light of Western standard in the modern period. The confrontational nature of the initial cultural interactions gave rise to a form of agitating quest for self-identity and nationhood, which in turn left everyone with deep emphasis on cultural differences, especially in the mode of understanding others.

A good intercultural understanding of each other's cultural perspective has always been a possibility, but the era of colonial conflict between the two cultures exposes the limitations of each cultural perspective rather than for an honest intercultural understanding to take place. Achebe's work presents the new horizons for intercultural relationships thereby bringing in a form of internal harmony or acceptance. He brings in a critical and constructive way the cultural encounter could take place by focusing on the positive elements for the progress of our universal existence.[719] It is not just for the Africans to see but for the European to reappraise their philosophical and anthropological comprehensions of African world and its past. Although Achebe's cross-cultural interactions narrative lays many emphases on the perspective of an Igbo African person, it also lays a general foundation for further hermeneutical inquiry in philosophical thinking and cultural dialogue, and to develop an intercultural opportunity that focuses on the positive elements for progress with others rather than on alienation of others.[720] These are part of the gains of the narrative. Yet one cannot overlook the intrigues and complicated demands in accomplishing this much progress or fusion with our various cultural perspectives.[721] The fusion of horizons is the same as the synthesis of cultures in Achebe. In Ogede's words, Achebe uses this view

> to convey his fascination with the idea of Igbo and European cultures co-existing on an equal footing, a concept of cross-cultural interaction which he himself characterizes as a 'crossroads of cultures'. But his essayistic representations of the stances of the Igbo encounter with Europe as a graceful fusion of cultures.[722]

---

[719] Ogede, *Achebe's Things Fall Apart: A Reader's Guide, op. cit.,* p. 7.
[720] Some have referred this intercultural solution of the problems as part of internal harmonization or acceptance of other philosophico-cultural views.
[721] Achebe, *Hopes and Impediments, op. cit.,* p. 34; See Begam, *op. cit.,* p. 221.
[722] Ogede, *op. cit.,* p. 6.

The fusion of horizons of cultures or the cross-cultural interaction is not fully appreciated, especially when it is seen from the negative side—colonialism. But we have to go beyond this negative situation to allow a creative fusion of rich perspectives of the cultures involved. It means the integration of differing perspectives that lead to the profound understanding or a better understanding of the subject matter (that is also the meaning which is the focus of all involved in the dialogue.) This provides the platform for a dialogic consensus[723] because of the amalgam of different positions. It also requires a level of dialogic openness in accepting to reconsider one's standpoint based on the counter-examples or objections of others. It is the way to gain better understanding because all the parties to the dialogue or conversation have a new informed understanding influenced by all the different considerations and better articulated privileged position. This result is accomplished through constructive criticisms and rational dialogue.[724]

For Gadamer, a privileged position is constructively evaluated through rational criticism. A horizon or perspective needs to integrate with other horizons. It is the process of understanding that leads to consequent genuine hermeneutical productivity. The emerging higher horizon is also referred to as the more comprehensive horizon that overcomes the negative limitations of the texts and interpreters or readers by drawing our attention only to the subject matter and its meanings.[725] But one has to raise some ideological concerns emanating from this fusion of horizons of cultures in Achebe's text. How valuable is this fusion of horizons in an intercultural world? By using English language does Achebe really provide a substantial opportunity for African philosophical culture? Is it merely a superficial dialogic relation that plays in the end to the good of the colonial language rather than to African language development in narratives and use in philosophical thinking? [726]

Despite these ideological concerns, Achebe succeeds (as an advantage) in presenting African experience in a language that is variegated with Igbo concepts, style of thought and narrative aesthetics. Ogede argues that:

---

[723] Warnke, *Gadamer: Hermeneutics, Tradition and Reason* (Oxford: Polity Press, 1987), *pp.* 169-170.
[724] *Ibid.*
[725] Gadamer, *Philosophical Hermeneutics, op. cit.,* p. xix.
[726] Janmohamed, *op. cit.,* p. 572.

the encounter has led to artistic fusion and a generous flowering of letters. Politically, bringing Africa and Europe together created difficult companions. But the books that have come out of the marriage, like Achebe's *Things Fall Apart,* bear the marks of a variegated gallery of art with remarkable vitality which can be imagined to be the product of only one kind of experience: the unique chemistry of conditions of unresolved contradictions to which colonization gave vent. Partly because Igbo forms of vernacular rhetoric tend to blend themselves easily with English expression, they allow for full-scale fictional exploration in *Things Fall Apart,* leading to a new form of language that enables Achebe to present Africa to the world through mediated lenses. That is why it's not entirely correct to conclude that Achebe's 'newly acquired tongue' necessarily places his ideas at 'a considerable structural and expressive remove from the speech modes, habits of thought, and cultural codes of the historical community whose experience he undertakes to record in his fiction'....[727] On the contrary, as a literature of cultural hybridization, the hallmarks of *Things Fall Apart*'s accomplishments lie in conveying an amazing story with great aesthetic effect, exemplifying in so doing a supreme instance of successful pastiche.[728]

The African and Western fusion of horizons or encounter of worldviews has led to an intercultural life and understanding in the contemporary world. There is dialogue between languages, cultures, perspectives, and worldviews. That is why we can understand other people and interpret their reality. It is how an intercultural fusion of horizons leads to a higher horizon and to a higher universality. The new emerging horizon is not the exclusive accomplishment of one horizon or one people. Gadamer explains that it does not get rid of particularity, but it brings all to a higher level of application or universality (superior vision.) The going back and forth, and back again, involved in the fusion of horizons could only be negatively understood or end on the wrong side if we end discussion. The main aim of the fusion is the ongoing dialogue

---

[727] Francoise Lionet affirms that the encounter of two languages (African and European) offers the local people creativity in incorporating useful "Western" tools, techniques, or strategies into their own cosmology or Weltanschauung"–See Ogede, *op. cit.,* p. 97.
[728] Ogede, *op. cit.,* p. 21.

that is a form of self-purification. The negative and the positive are all integrated (one recalls Hegel's dialectics and the cancellations.)

The distinctive nature of each horizon[729] allows for a wider range of vision following the intercultural encounter of these worldviews. [730] Gadamer brings everything together through his view of the fusion, dialogue and openness. He, like Achebe, insists that a horizon is the perspective that we have and this perspective changes depending on our place and the daily experience or the number of passing experiences. There should be no abstraction of horizon. Our views change and our horizons of the world change as well. This is exactly the core interpretation that Gadamer guides one to gets from Achebe's narrative literature. The new horizon that emerges from these interactions of culture is a new view of the world. It is not the world-in-itself, but another extended view of the world or understanding of the world. It is another position of appreciation of "reality's independence from thinking."[731] The reality that is beyond each one of us and each of the cultures of the world is the ultimate horizon which we are and at the same time situated within.

The higher horizon is always beyond each one of us and our individual worldviews. Gadamer describes this higher horizon as that which is always beyond our reach, but we never give up in desiring to get at it in terms of better understanding or reaching out to higher meanings.[732] The point is that every worldview has the world in view as *everything that is* the case, not as *everything that it takes* to be the case. We have not yet arrived at everything or the wholeness of being/reality itself. There is always a continual merging of the different worldviews or horizons, including the old and the new; the familiar and the unfamiliar or alien; the part with the whole; and the past with the present.

Another way to articulate Gadamer's idea of the fusion of horizons in Achebe is the aspect of language: the fusion of oral and written languages in the narrative. Language provides some useful assistance in presenting Africa's worldviews to other cultures. The aesthetic nature of African culture reflects in

---

[729] Taylor, *op. cit.,* p. 288.
[730] Brown, *op. cit.,* p. 35.
[731] McDowell, *op. cit.,* p. 180. New horizon gives us new position to understand reality.
[732] Gadamer, *Hermeneutics, Religion and Ethics, op. cit.,* pp. ix-x.

the style of its self-expression. Achebe's use of written fictional style of narratives clearly portrays the historical reality of a people.[733] That is what makes Achebe's project unique because it comes up with a world text which is the result of authentic fusion of horizons of cultures and traditions (oral and written.) Irele says:

> Achebe's integration of these oral forms into this novel lends complexity to its mode of signification, for beyond what may appear as a picturesque pattern of allusions, they establish within the work an indigenous sensibility conductive to its reception as a written work. Thus, the oral tradition can be said to function in Achebe's novel in a dual capacity: as both an authentic representation of the culture that serves as the reference of the manifest content, and at the same time, as an integral component of the narrative mode, endowing the fictional discourse with a peculiar resonance. Franco Moretti has called *Things Fall Apart* 'a world text.' [734]

Gadamer appears to relate his hermeneutics with a 'world text' or a common language of understanding as a condition of understanding when he explains that the conversation is not a disposition of one person alone. It involves all the persons in a dialogue. The intercultural aspect of this fusion allows for conversation to take place and the product of this conversation is authentic integrated and intercultural understanding. In this communion through conversation, we are involved with a different and better outlook and better meaning. These are all seen as part of our hermeneutical situation that affects our horizon or our consciousness of reality. Our history influences our historical consciousness.

4.2.5 Gadamer and Achebe: Hermeneutical Situation and Effective Historical Consciousness

Gadamer recognizes the importance of the hermeneutical situation as a principle of hermeneutics and as part of the conditions of understanding. The consciousness of the hermeneutical situation is, according him, important in

---

[733] Janmohamed, *op. cit.*, p. 573.
[734] Irele, "Introduction," *Chinua Achebe Things Fall Apart, op. cit.,* pp. xx- xxi. Irele got Franco Moretti's "a world text" idea from *Modern Epic* (London: Verso, 1996), p. 237.

true understanding of a text or document.[735] The question about the importance of one's 'horizon' and historical consciousness in hermeneutics is sometimes variedly understood. The main thing to remember is that we are always within a hermeneutical situation and cannot stand out of it. It is the situation in which we discover ourselves while considering a tradition. Gadamer analyzes historical consciousness, historical situation and the issue of horizon. He argues:

> Understanding tradition undoubtedly requires a historical horizon, then. But it is not the case that we acquire this horizon by transposing ourselves into a historical situation. Rather, we must always already have a horizon in order to be able to transpose ourselves into a situation. For what do we mean by 'transposing ourselves'? Certainly not just disregarding ourselves. This is necessary, of course, insofar as we must imagine the other situation. But into this other situation we must bring, precisely, ourselves. Only this is the full meaning of 'transposing ourselves'. If we put ourselves in someone else's shoes, for example, then we will understand him—i.e., become aware of the otherness, the indissoluble individuality of the other person—by putting *ourselves* in his position.[736]

When one possesses a horizon, it does not really imply the acquisition of a historical situation. Historical situation does help in the development of a horizon. It is also possible to have both a historical situation and a horizon. These help make the task of hermeneutics a comprehensive endeavor in which the truth of understanding and meaning are achieved. One's worldview is part of one's horizon and the historical situation could be seen as part of the historical experiences of that individual. The nature of the historical experiences is that they are comprehended by way of historical awareness to form a perspective or range of vision of things. Gadamer describes it as a single horizon that involves other things, and as a moving horizon it embraces whatever is part of this historical consciousness or awareness. Our historical consciousness is self-evident to us since we are historically attuned.[737]

---

[735] Gadamer, *Truth and Method*, trans. Joel Weinsheimer and Donald G. Marshall, *op. cit.*, p. 301. Gadamer notes, "Consiousness of being affected by history (wirkungsgeschichtliches Bewußtsein) is primarily consciousness of the hermeneutical *situation*."

[736] *Ibid.*, pp. 303-304.

[737] Gadamer, *The Relevance of the Beautiful and Other Essays, op. cit.*, p. 11.

Effective historical consciousness and the effect of history are interchangeable themes with no philosophical or hermeneutical difficulties when understood as the influence of history. This effective historical awareness could be hermeneutically disclosed in Achebe's African narrative.

Following Gadamer's hermeneutical approach, Achebe's narrative situations or general African historical background present in *Things Fall Apart* (discussed in chapter three above) serves as the form of historical consciousness or awareness of the ethno-philosophy of Igbo Africans and universal aspect of hermeneutics in understanding Africa worldviews. Achebe attempts to create the historical awareness through his narrative literature and reconstructive imagination. *Things Fall Apart* explores and discloses the consciousness of the historical situation of the African experience, views and world in its entirety. It is compelling with a hermeneutical advisory that any attempt to overcome or overlook the historical consciousness of African historical situation, especially by African thinkers, is a hermeneutical impossibility since their historical situation is an essential aspect of their African experience and identity.

The main difficulty for African scholars is in the re-presentation of this African historical situation and experience in a way that does not do justice to the totality of truth of African worldviews and understanding. However, when this happens, it does not necessarily mean that such consequent misunderstanding or misrepresentation is purposely intended by a writer. The reality of African historical situation and its illumination is among the things we make use of in hermeneutics rather than attempt to neglect or overcome it. One cannot overcome that which is an essential structure or constitutive of one's being and the understanding of one's existence. Even one's historical situation could be interpreted as part of human fallen-ness or facticity. It is the context or condition in which we are found, dialogued or conversed with. It is the situation that Achebe's wanted his readers to discover and dialogue in order to fully understand without assumptions. It is the situation of one's encounter with other cultures and worldviews. This encounter with other cultures within our situation that comes in the form of consciousness is nothing but part of our self-reflection on the world and on ourselves.[738] It is part of other people's awareness of our perception of reality in a meaningful way.

---

[738] Gadamer, *Philosophical Hermeneutics*, *op. cit.*, pp. xxvi-xxvii.

Gadamer describes this as that point of encounter with our uniqueness and positive differences seen through the lenses of cultures.[739]

Effective historical consciousness or effective history (*Wirkungsgeschichte*) is part of the general encounter that leads to productive conversations or dialogue.[740] This is really what Achebe's project is all about: the recovery of the history of influences or awareness of history of effects that make it possible for renewed understanding of his African world through ongoing conversation or cultural dialogue. Gadamer's hermeneutical recognition of the value of ongoing conversations is the key to our consideration of social identity issues and intercultural values. In this way, Gadamer and Achebe are already involved in the intercultural exchange or fusion of horizons through their use of the principle of effective historical consciousness. So far, I have tried to lead this discussion in a hermeneutical way so as to bring to light the partial or not so comprehensive intercultural understanding present in Achebe's narrative.

Achebe's goal in this analysis remains clear: to help his society redevelop itself, overcome the negative consequences of this unsuccessful cultural encounter and "put away the complexes... And it is essentially a question of education....I think, my aims and the deepest aspirations of my society meet"[741] Having this as his clear goal, Achebe then presents his narrative as the synthesis of culture and languages with some unanticipated intercultural negative consequences.[742] *Things Fall Apart* does make an excellent presentation of Igbo life-world and make it available for African thought/hermeneutics scholarship.[743] It brings to the consciousness of current generation of Africans the reality of their history as told by one of their kind. The past experiences, being made present within a historical context, determine the future of African self-hermeneutical understanding. The past effectively influences the future of African people. There is an important dialectics of influences and awareness of what these influences are based on the struggles of the past and how that past was made present by those who

---

[739] Gadamer, *The Relevance of the Beautiful and Other Essays, op. cit.*, p. 11.
[740] Gadamer, *Philosophical Hermeneutics, op. cit.*, p. xvii; See Gadamer, *Wahrheit und Methode: Grundzüge einer philosophischen Hermeneutik* (Tübingen: Mohr, 1960), p. 261.
[741] Achebe, *Morning Yet On Creation Day: Essays, op. cit.*, p. 71.
[742] Grifiths, *op. cit.*, p. 70. I read this "a world language" to mean a linguistic world or a world of linguisticality rather than a 'single language for all cultures.'
[743] Irele, "Introduction," *Chinua Achebe Things Fall Apart, op. cit.*, p. xvii.

dictated, in many spheres, the history and fate of a people through their writings.

The historical accomplishments/influences in Achebe's work are clearly known to him, but Achebe himself acknowledges certain limitations in his portrayal of Igbo African community. He emphasizes that his contribution is only an aspect of a desirable totality in the quest for self-identity and self-determination rather than a unilateral presentation of an African society. Achebe accepts that the Igbo past, like any society, is far from perfect but still needs some constructive reappraisal and positive publications of its philosophical thought and values.[744]

The focus for Achebe is on his contributions to African worldviews and interpretation. Achebe's traditional background had a preference for oral form of communication. The encounter with the West provides the opportunity to communicate the historical reality of the Igbo world in a written language to a global world. Achebe has assumed this responsibility to put African narratives in their true hermeneutical contexts. But his choice of English, although it did make *Things Fall Apart* get access to millions of readers outside the Igbo culture, it also unfortunately presents some hermeneutical challenges: Igbo worldviews were not fully and meaningfully reflected in English language. The use of English language reflects an individualistic interpretation of tragedy for Okonkwo. It does appear that Achebe merely presents Igbo culture within the tradition of the European colonial novel.[745] Achebe, in general, has set the pace for an introspective hermeneutical inquiry through his narrative (as Socrates will suggest as self-evaluation.)

Despite his honest and positive views, I argue that he partly failed at accomplishing certain philosophical and hermeneutical goals which he at the beginning set out to address. To achieving these goals I have continued with following Achebe's demanding critical invitation to further interpret African philosophical thought from an intercultural perspective. That means, despite Achebe's goodwill, the process of understanding has to go on; this is why we are taking up this hermeneutical project. It is one thing to express one's intention, and it is another to really get the task done without creating more or

---

[744] *Ibid.*, p. xvi.
[745] Ogede, *Chinua Achebe and the Politics of Representation, op. cit.*, pp. 17-18.

less other problems. My critique is not to negate all that Achebe accomplished, but to recommend that Gadamer helps in furthering the hermeneutical project of self-understanding and understanding in general to a universal dimension— in the universality of hermeneutics.

I think that there is at least one serious criticism that Gadamer helps us with through his style of hermeneutics. That is, Achebe had constraints of colonialism (linguistic colonial effect) to write in the language of the colonial masters. His use of English language is part of welcoming the dictating and dominating cultural views that negatively influenced the representation of African worldviews.[746] This criticism, I think, is what Gadamer forestalls (knowingly or unknowingly) when he considers every language as capable of reflecting every worldview or suitably translates it. Language itself has a universal character to communicate the reality of its world. His views ought to be hermeneutically and ontologically understood. For the African writers who criticized Achebe English language narrative, it is a linguistic and ideological issue. These are surely two different approaches. As philosophy and hermeneutics, Gadamer's view is most appropriate in addressing the intercultural problem of language and hermeneutics from the inner meaning /inner *logos* and universal reason.

In summary, the central place of truth in Gadamer's hermeneutics is evident in focusing on role of the inner meaning and the subject matter in the text (not on the author) while seeking understanding. Without the subject matter in the relationship, then the parties in dialogue will have difficulties in the process of the fusion of horizons between them. The object of communication is language, while the subject matter of communication/conversation is the issue at stake. There are many applications or usages of horizon. For instance, language itself could be considered as the horizon of hermeneutics while understanding of a subject matter in a narrative is equally a horizon. Gadamer's principle of the fusion of horizons as a condition of understanding demands that one integrates the horizons provided by African texts, the language, and the thoughts of different individual interpreters or scholars. The result is a development of new meaning and understanding of the subject matter without distortions.

---

[746] Janmohamed, *op. cit.,* pp. 585-586.

A new meaning implies a new horizon which is constitutive of the nature of understanding and the understanding of hermeneutical situation.[747] Our hermeneutical situations are disclosive because they are part of understanding the world-in-itself. Every worldview as a horizon is a perspective, a disclosure of an experience of the world rather than a relative articulation of the world-in-itself. Gadamer explains that each view of the world is only a positive contribution to understanding the 'world in itself,' and not really about understanding in totality being-in-itself.

The importance of this distinction between the world-in-itself and worldview (view of the world) is to show that each worldview is only a perspective that aims at understanding being through language and the linguisticality of understanding. Again, it is an individual experience of the world. Our worldview is not a perfect or comprehensive experience of the world-in-itself. It is open to other worldviews, especially when confronted by better understanding. It could also come through individual insight in the internal expression of one's understanding.

The application of Gadamer's hermeneutical views helps us develop our own hermeneutical themes to consider Achebe's tragedy narrative in a clearer light. Achebe's notion of *tragedy* is only an experience of 'Tragedy,'[748] a worldview of a people compared to a general notion of tragedy in the world-in-itself. Each notion of tragedy, for instance, does not imply the whole or the totality of the concept of tragedy. As Achebe says about tragedy, the notion of it is not so clearly presented in the different traditions or civilizations.[749] This is the first basis for distinction on the worldviews of each people, especially using the notion of tragedy.

The notion of tragedy leads us to the notion of person. This notion of person is important in light of Achebe's articulation of Okonkwo's personality crisis that leads to tragedy in the novel because of his exaggerated self-image.[750] This highlights the connection between a *communal* tragedy with relational notion of the person in the first instance. An African worldview of

---

[747] McDowell, *op. cit.*, p. 176. The idea of fusion of horizons implies transposing our understanding and overcoming what initially appeared unknown or alien (*Ibid.*, p. 191.)

[748] I choose to use Tragedy (capital) to mean in world-in-itself context, while 'tragedy' describes an individual cultural worldview about tragic event or situation.

[749] Rowell, *op. cit.*, pp. 265-266.

[750] http://web.africa.ufl.edu/asq/v4/v4i3a1.htm (Accessed March 18, 2011.)

tragedy is only an African experience of tragedy, while a European notion of tragedy is also only European's experience of tragedy. However, there may be some similarities between these different horizons/worldviews about tragedy. But is there any place for a distinction in realities that seem alike? For Gadamer, the act of distinguishing goes both ways. Whatever is distinguished is distinguished from something else that is different to it. So there is the one that is different and the one that it is different from. Gadamer's model of hermeneutics requires the application of the act of understanding to literature/texts. The truth of hermeneutics is already present but has to be made intelligible within the context of the history of effects. Truth presents itself primarily as a disclosure.[751]

Gadamer's succeeds through hermeneutical circle—dialoguing with the text; good prejudices; effective historical consciousness or effect of history and the fusion of horizons in analyzing intercultural implications of hermeneutics and language. Understanding the other is one of the challenges of our time. [752] These hermeneutical principles are part of universality of hermeneutics that can be used across cultures in the quest for true meanings. Every cultural world has its own experience of the world-in-itself and not any one of these worldviews is a totality of reality itself. There are fundamental conceptual differences between the cultures of the world. No one culture solely possesses the key to the totality of truth through understanding. For meaning, understanding and interculturality purposes, there is an essential relation between effective historical consciousness and the fusion of horizons. The fusion of horizons justifies the position that every historical experience has "truth" that could be altered because of better information is accessed or understood in time. There is no worldview or range of visions that captures an all-time truth. [753] Openness is part of the progress of history. [754] As we acquire more historical experience we are open to the fact of choosing between defensible beliefs. [755] In the process of this fusion or encounter, the rationality

---

[751] Kertscher, *op. cit.,* p. 149.

[752] Taylor, *op. cit.*, p. 279.

[753] Warnke, *op. cit.,* p. 171.

[754] Gadamer, "The Heritage of Hegel," Gadamer, *Reason in the Age of Science*, trans. Frederick Lawrence (Cambridge: MIT Press, 1981), p. 40. See Gadamer's view on Hegel's Philosophy of History.

[755] Warnke, *op. cit.,* p. 171. Warnke argues that "the lesion of historical experience is that no "truth" is unalterable and that no account of nature, society or art is valid for all time.... For Gadamer, however, experience remains a form of justification: precisely through an openness to the implications of our experience we acquire both more warranted beliefs and

of a tradition is recognized through the information provided by other traditions that have the resources to help "identify and to understand the limitations of our own tradition."[756]

It is only an enlightened culture that is able to understand its place within a whole world-community. Through this intercultural encounter we learn from others and through this form a clearer understanding.[757] The ultimate relevance of this task in hermeneutics is that we understand the universality of language and learn to be open-minded, acquire sensitivity and the taste for good judgment. The worldview of each community is only an aspect of the world-community or global community.

4.3 Conclusion

Achebe's narrative literature presents us with a difficult problem. I focused on two main aspects of a problem: a) the intercultural problem of language, and b) the intercultural problem of hermeneutics, with specific application to African notion of tragedy.

On the first aspect (the language part), I highlighted on what was lost or the negative implication of African narrative in English language following the arguments of African scholars that African language ought to be used *first* in communicating African experience. However, Gadamer's solution strictly addresses the intercultural problem of language through the inner meaning of language (not the native language.) Everything could be said through language and in its inner unity is the *interpersonal and intercultural* dialogue deeply present. His approach is ontologically and hermeneutically based. For Gadamer, written language through literature provides us with the most reliable form of hermeneutics. The quality of hermeneutics is dependent upon the language of dialogue: a written language or an oral language. As gain or advantage, written language has more consistency, reliability and un-changeability that is important in hermeneutics or the understanding of

---

an increased capacity to discriminate between what is warranted and was is not." (*Ibid.*, p. 171.)

[756] MacIntyre, "Relativism, Power and Philosophy," *op. cit.*, p. 19.

[757] Warnke, *op. cit.*, pp. 173-174. Warnke explains that through fusion of horizons which is the basis for intercultural encounter, we learn from others differentiated views, we learn to be open to new tact and ways of interpreting reality. (*Ibid.*, pp. 173-174.)

meanings. It has also helped in the communication of new meanings present in Achebe's narrative.

The second aspect (the hermeneutical part) of this thesis is on African notion of tragedy which is complicated because of Achebe's use of English rather than Igbo language. Somehow the English language hinders the ability to effectively communicate the subtle uniqueness present in African notion of tragedy. I directly interpreted some helpful African proverbs, including the *Chi proverbs* and *notion of Chi*. The hermeneutical and philosophical role of *Chi* is important in understanding Okonkwo's tragedy in Achebe. There is the presence of fate and personal decisions approved by one's *Chi*.[758] One needs the support of his god to succeed in one's task. The *Chi* also acts as a mediator. These are my conclusions in using the hermeneutical themes like the notion of *Chi* and notion of *Person* etc., by getting their true meanings through applying the hermeneutical circle, questioning the text (chapter and passages of the text, proverbs and metaphors) or the whole and part approach, and vice versa; good prejudices principle; fusion of horizons; hermeneutical situation and considering the influences of history in the narrative. The role of *Chi* or fate or destiny is important in understanding the communal African notion of tragedy instead of a personal tragedy as easily thought in Achebe's Okonkwo. We recall our two hermeneutical conclusions using the hermeneutical principles and claim of the universality of hermeneutics of Gadamer: **a**) The *Chi* proverbs and notion of *Chi*: Okonkwo has shown fidelity to his *Chi* and the Oracle; His success and fortune was from his *Chi* (fate) - it affirms a communal notion of African tragedy, and **b**) The notion of Person: Heroic cultural personage leading to tragedy related to African notion of person: "I am because we are..." also points to a communitarian personhood and communal tragedy. Thus, the communal tragedy is about what Umuofia people lost as cultural heritage/fortune (philosophical, epistemological, ideological, cultural, linguistic etc.,) during their encounter with Western culture (colonial District Commissioner, missionaries etc.,) rather than Okonkwo's personal tragedy. Based on our use of Gadamer's universality of hermeneutics and other principles of hermeneutics, it is conclusive to say that African notion of tragedy is a communal tragedy in Achebe's text.

---

[758] Madu, *op. cit.,* p. 183.

When one reads a book like Achebe's, it is important to ask such authors (through their texts) what their words exactly mean as Gadamer recommends. This is one of the ways that my thesis takes in order to truly understand Achebe's contributions. It is easy to believe that Achebe should best know and understand what he has written in the narrative. However, an author's comments may not really represent his/her exact thoughts.[759] There is the possibility of understanding an author better than he understands himself. We also need to see if there could be new interpretations or new meanings because of our changing interests, generations and situations.[760] As Gadamer says that every interpretation should be "transparent to the text, so that the meaning of the text can speak to ever new situations. The task does not exclude but absolutely *requires* the translation of what is transmitted."[761]

Language is the horizon of hermeneutics and an important medium of understanding.[762] Gadamer's ontology of language remains the message and an essential condition of hermeneutics: 'Being that can be understood is language' or "being is language."[763] He does not argue against using a foreign language to communicate the truth of another language.

Gadamer's hermeneutics provides a philosophical framework and an optimistic platform that I need for the interpretation of African thought, with specific reference to the notion of tragedy in a narrative discourse like Achebe's. It helps us to see the limitations in Achebe's narrative and how to improve its understanding through the application of hermeneutic principles of Gadamer. It also helps in understanding African philosophical thought experience and comprehension of their inner meanings in general. Our research moves from particular understanding of hermeneutics to the universality of hermeneutics and how that claim of universality addresses the intercultural problem of language and hermeneutics in a contemporary world of cultural diversity. Certainly not everything in Gadamer's hermeneutics is applicable to our specific African situation. In the end, it is about the universality of hermeneutics and its applicability to texts of every culture and the inner meanings. It is about cultural identity and recognition; mutual

---

[759] Kertscher, *op. cit.*, pp. 144-145.
[760] Gadamer, *Philosophical Hermeneutics, op. cit.*, p. xxvi.
[761] *Ibid.*, p. xxvi.
[762] Kertscher, *op. cit.*, p. 143.
[763] Gadamer, *Truth and Method*, trans. Joel Weinsheimer and Donald G. Marshall, *op. cit.*, p. 481.

understanding and meaningfulness; and dialogic hermeneutics. Hermeneutics is not an abstract theory; it associates with understanding our life experiences and our life-world in an intercultural world.

CHAPTER 5
General Conclusion

5.1 Conclusion

The history of the development of hermeneutics has shown a common perspective about hermeneutics in general, especially the central role of language and *inner* word or meaning in hermeneutics. Hermeneutics involved the preservation of true meaning through the art of understanding.[764] The meaning and understanding of ideas have been communicated through the 'theater' of tragedy from the ancient to the modern time. The drama or 'theater' of tragedy serves a didactic purpose and for the purification of the spectators through the experience of fear and pity which leads to a better understanding of the meaning of life. Theater is like a form of 'language' that communicates inner meaning. Gadamer's philosophical hermeneutics developed through the influence of the ancient, medieval and the modern periods' understanding of texts, works of arts and oral communication. He acknowledged at various times the influence of Plato, Aristotle, Schleiermacher, Dilthey, Heidegger etc to his view on hermeneutics. I emphasized Gadamer's particular consideration of Schleiermacher's influence in his philosophical hermeneutics because it is central to my hermeneutical discourse on contemporary African thought and developing written African language. Schleiermacher saw hermeneutics as the art of understanding and also the art of avoiding misunderstanding.

Gadamer's critique and adaption of some of the hermeneutical views of earlier philosophers, including Schleiermacher, gave rise to his 'Philosophical hermeneutics' and the claim to the universality of hermeneutics. For him hermeneutics simply put is the art of understanding. Understanding gives us access to clear meaning and highlight the conditions of understanding. The conditions of understanding are the linguisticality of understanding, our fundamental mode of being, the historicality of human situation, the universality of hermeneutic experience, hermeneutical circle, good prejudices, temporal distance, the fusion of horizons, dialogue and conversation etc., which are essential aspects of the universality of hermeneutics. We need to

---

[764] Grondin, *Sources of Hermeneutics, op. cit.*, p. 33.

understand the structure of human thought and the process of arriving at true meaning. The main task of hermeneutics is the understanding of texts by dialoguing with them. A written language is preferred to an oral language because of the reliable nature and the intellectual quality of texts in a written tradition. Gadamer extended hermeneutics to concern itself not only with dialoguing with the texts, but also with dialoguing with other people in their cultural world—as the intercultural aspect of hermeneutics (intercultural dialog.) This dialogic nature of hermeneutics makes it suitable as part of the human sciences.

Philosophical hermeneutics falls within the human sciences and social sciences rather than within the natural sciences. Hermeneutics is not confined within the method of the natural sciences. Philosophical hermeneutics required a hermeneutical rather than a logical approach. Logic is bi-valent in its approach and is after truth and falsity. In Gadamer's hermeneutics, it is not about one truth and use of one specific method. It requires using different lenses which demand dialogue, a fusion of horizons or understandings to come to a better understanding. Our horizon moves with us as we progress in understanding. Gadamer's hermeneutical framework does not correspond to given rules but according to lived experience. Understanding demands that the task of hermeneutics required openness to clear meaning. His hermeneutics is a content-oriented rather than author-oriented project. To generate meaning, we need to use the conditions of understanding mentioned above or the hermeneutical principles, like the fusion of horizons, hermeneutical circle, to move from the whole to the part, and back again etc. The 'whole' could be the language in which a text is written.

These main hermeneutical principles are better used in the interpretation of texts or narrative literature. Considering Gadamer's focus on literature as work of art through language, I chose a classic African narrative-Achebe's *Things Fall Apart* as the text for my hermeneutical application. I considered a hermeneutical and expository approach and specific application of hermeneutics to the African notion of tragedy because Gadamer himself briefly discussed the hermeneutical relevance of Aristotle's notion of tragedy as aesthetics in narrative literature. Achebe's classic narrative presented us with the problem of hermeneutics and the problem of language as the two sides of one problem of understanding in an emerging hermeneutical and intercultural world.[765]

Following Achebe's text, the problem of understanding centered around the problem of language (applied to the problem of writing an African novel in foreign languages when African language could first describe her reality) and the problem of hermeneutics (applied to the notion of tragedy.) Achebe's English narrative somehow hindered the indigenous linguistic community from developing a written language. It also failed to portray the Igbo African narrative of tragedy through a linguistic aesthetic. If Achebe had 'first' written his narrative in Igbo language he would have truly expressed the communal aspect of tragedy in light of African thought and language. Achebe's use of English is disadvantageous to the development of African linguistic and philosophical narrative, especially in a post-colonial world and a philosophical world of an emerging dialogical civilization that seeks to engage with all, including with non-Western perspectives.

Achebe's use of English language seemed to him adequate to express the truth of the reality of the Igbo (African) people in his work. He understood the importance of hermeneutics since he used it in reconstructing the story of his people for the purpose of their "education."[766] The important role of language came with the suggested possibility of a *continental African language* or simply any African language for African philosophical literature through the fusion of understandings or horizons. In the immediate absence of a continental African language, there is still need to recognize that any language is for communication because each language is dialogic, disclosive and has the intellectual quality to communicate any meaning. The philosophical world of each culture is expressed through language and each language is capable of communicating its people's worldviews.

Gadamer's answer to Achebe's intercultural problem of language is the use of ontological argument based on the *inner* word or *inner* meaning and the

---

[765] This is related to the idea of "Hermeneutical Orientations" in African philosophy that Samuel Oluoch Imbo, Tsenay Serequeberhan, Marcien Towa and Okonda Okolo have been associated with. The essential advancement of African philosophy is through hermeneutics. See Samuel Oluoch Imbo, *An Introduction to African Philosophy* (Maryland: Rowman and Littlefield Publishers, Inc., 1998), p. 27ff; See also Serequeberhan, *The Hermeneutics of African Philosophy: Horizon and Discourse, op. cit.*
[766] Achebe, *Morning Yet On Creation Day, op. cit.*, p. 71.

justification that every language has the capacity to communicate meaning through adequate translation. I did pursue the argument on translation in a different way since Achebe's text is not *first* a translation from a local (indigenous) African language. Gadamer's approach helped us to answer the intercultural hermeneutical aspect of understanding the *communal* notion of tragedy through the application of the notion of *Chi* (proverbs) and the notion of *person* as new horizons and good prejudices to facilitate understanding of true meaning. This is distinctive (through hermeneutics) because of the *communal* perspective of tragedy traced from the African ideas of *Chi* or fate and the *Person* as a relational being (I am because we are.)

In other words, Gadamer's philosophical hermeneutics sufficiently addressed and justified the understanding of African worldviews as part of a linguistic community. Language is not a means or a tool but "a life process."[767] Every language is capable of expressing reality and is always part of the 'world'--that is disclosed. Gadamer's hermeneutical task is about the truth in the world in which we live and "to which we are opened."[768] His philosophical hermeneutics is a "new critical consciousness [that] must now accompany all responsible philosophizing which takes the habits of thought and language."[769] Gadamer's ontology is 'Being can be understood is language'-language is an essential aspect of the being that we quest to understand. Every understanding is the understanding of being itself.

Finally, I conclude with Gadamer that the claim of the universality of hermeneutics is on the ontological linguistic constitution of understanding. Like Gadamer, language is the horizon of hermeneutics and the medium of understanding.[770] Although Gadamer sets out to discuss hermeneutics as a form of dialoguing with the text, he also succeeded in advancing the idea that hermeneutics involves dialoguing with other peoples and cultures. He addressed the intercultural problem of language and hermeneutics in a unique way, through his understanding of the universality of hermeneutics. Within interculturality, language and hermeneutics are the two faces of the art of understanding. Gadamer successfully addressed this intercultural problem of

---

[767] Gadamer, *Truth and Method,* trans. Joel Weinsheimer and Donald G. Marshall, *op. cit.,* p. 443; Gadamer, *Truth and Method* (New York: The Seabury Press), 1975, p. 404.
[768] *Ibid.,* p. xxiii; Gadamer, *Truth and Method* (New York: The Seabury Press), 1975, p. xiv.
[769] *Ibid.,* p. xxiv; Gadamer, *Truth and Method* (New York: The Seabury Press), 1975, p. xv.
[770] Kertscher, *op. cit.,* p. 143.

language and hermeneutics as a unique contribution to general knowledge and to the newly developing discipline on African philosophy, *African Hermeneutic Philosophy* or African philosophico-hermeneutical thought, especially in a global hermeneutical world of fusing/merging cultural worlds. The modest novelty of my research requires a hermeneutical, expository approach and to gradually/effectively encourage this African philosophical aspect of hermeneutic scholarship within the global intellectual community. It is an invitation to further study Gadamer's claim of the universality of hermeneutics or the applicability of the general/universality of hermeneutics to all texts: classical or not; cultural or not. Hermeneutics is not just an academic discipline but also understanding the mode of human existence (being in the world) and experience of meaning as constitutive in every human world.

BIBLIOGRAPHY

Primary sources

Achebe, Chinua. *Things Fall Apart*. London: Heinemann, 1958.

    .*Things Fall Apart*. Greenwich: Fawcett, 1959.

    .*Things Fall Apart*. New York: Anchor, 1959.

    .*Things Fall Apart*. Portsmouth: Heinemann, 1996.

    .*The Trouble with Nigeria*. Enugu: Fourth Dimension Publishing Co. Ltd, 1983.

    .*A Man of the People*. Garden City, New York: Doubleday Anchor Books, 1967.

    .*Morning Yet On Creation Day: Essays*. London: Heinemann, 1975.

    .*African Short Stories*. London: Heinemann Educational Books, 1984.

    .*No Longer at Ease*. Greenwich: Fawcett Books, 1985.

    .*Anthills of the Savannah*. Garden City, New York: Doubleday Books, 1988.

    .*Hopes and Impediments*: *Selected Essays*. New York: Anchor Books, 1989.

    .*Hopes and Impediments: Selected Essays*. Garden City, New York: Anchor Books, 1990.

    .*Home and Exile*. Oxford: Oxford University Press, 2000.

    .*The Education of a British-Protected Child*. Canada: Doubleday Canada, 2009.

Achebe, Chinwe. *The World of the Ogbanje*. Enugu: Fourth Dimension, 1986.

Adichie, Chimamanda, Ngozi. *Half of a Yellow Sun*. Toronto: Vintage Canada, 2007.

    .*The Thing Around Your Neck*. Toronto: Alfred A. Knopf, 2009.

Aligwekwe, P. *Continuity of Traditional Values in the African Society the Igbo of Nigeria*. Owerri: 1991.

Altizer, Thomas J. J., ed. *Truth, Myth and Symbol*. Englewood Cliffs, New Jersey: Prentice Hall, 1962.

Anieke, Christian. *Problems of Intercultural Communication and Understanding in Achebe's Representation of the Igbo and their Culture*. Enugu: Mbaeze Printing Press, 2008.

Aristotle. *Poetics*, trans. W.H. Fyfe. London, William Heinemann Ltd. 1932.

.*The Basic Works of Aristotle*. New York: Random House, 1941.

.*Categories and De Interpretatione*, translated with notes by J. L. Ackrill. Oxford: Clarendon Aristotle Series, 1963.

Armour, Leslie. *The Idea of Canada and The Crisis of Community*. Ottawa: Steel Rail Publishing, 1981.

Audi, Robert, ed. *The Cambridge Dictionary of Philosophy*. Cambridge: Cambridge University Press, 2nd ed., 1999.

Ayandele, E. A. *The Missionary Impact on Modern Nigeria, 1842-1914: A Political and Social Analysis*. New York: Humanities Press, 1967.

Barthes, Roland. *Le Degre zero de l'ecriture*. Paris: Editions de Seuil, 1953.

Beier, Ulli, ed. *The Origin of Life and Death: African Creation Myths*. London: 1966.

Benedict, Ruth. *Patterns of Culture*. London: Routledge, 1971.

Booker, Keith, M., ed. *Critical Insights: Things Fall Apart*. Pasadena, California: Salem Press, 2011.

Bujo, Benezet. *The Ethical Dimension of Community: The African Model and The Dialogue Between North and South*. Nairobi: Paulines Publication Africa, 1998.

Cassirer, Ernst. *An Essay on Man*. New Haven and London: Yale University Press, 1967, (1st ed., 1944).

. *Philosophy of Symbolic Forms*.Yale 1953. 7th ed., 1968.

Catan, John, R., ed. Aristotle*: The Collected Papers of Joseph Owens*. Albany: State University of New York, 1981.

Coates, J. B. *The Crisis of The Human Person: Some Personalist Interpretations*. London: Longmans, Green and Co, 1949.

Coltman, Rod. *The Language of Hermeneutics: Gadamer and Heidegger in   Dialogue*. New York: State University of New York Press, 1998.

Dawson, David. *Allegorical Readers and Cultural Revision in Ancient Alexandria.* California: University of California Press, 1992.

Dilthey, Wilhelm. *Gesammelte Schriften 5.* Göttingen, 1966.

.*Dilthey's Philosophy of Existence: Introduction to Weltanschauungslehre,* translation of an Essay with Introduction by William Kluback and Martin Weinbaum. Westport, Connecticut: Greenwood Press, Publishers, 1978.

.*Jahrbuch 3,* 1985.

.*Jahrbuch 6,* 1989.

.*Selected Works, Volume IV: Hermeneutics and the Study of History,* edited, with an introduction, by Rudolf A. Makkreel and Frithjof Rodi. New Jersey: Princeton University Press, 1996.

Donceel, J. F. *Philosophical Anthropology.* New York: Sheed and Ward, 1967.

Dostal, Robert, J., ed. *The Cambridge Companion to Gadamer.* New York: Cambridge University Press, 2002.

Echeruo, Michael, J. *Joyce Cary and the Novel of Africa.* London: Longman, 1973.

Edel, Abraham. *Aristotle and His Philosophy.* Chapel Hill: The University of North Carolina Press, 1982.

Egar, Emmanuel, Edame. *The Rhetorical Implications of Chinua Achebe's Things Fall Apart.* USA: University Press of America, 2006.

Eliade, Mircea. *The Sacred and the Profane.* New York: Brace and World, 1959.

.*Myth and Reality,* trans. W. R. Trask. New York: Harper and Row, 1963.

Emenyonu, Ernest, N., ed. *Emerging Perspectives on Chinua Achebe.* Trenton, New Jersey: Africa World Press, Inc., 2004.

Emonet, Pierre-Marie. *The Greatest Marvel of Nature: An Introduction to The Philosophy of the Human Person,* trans. Robert R. Barr. New York: The Crossroad Publishing Company, 2000.

Falola, Toyin. *The History of Nigeria.* Westport, Connecticut: Greenwood, 1999.

Ferraris, Maurizio. *History of Hermeneutics,* trans by Luca Somigli. New Jersey: Humanities Press International, Inc., 1996.

Forde, Cyril Daryll. *African Worlds: Studies in the Cosmological Ideas and Social Values of African Peoples*. Oxford: Oxford University Press, 1954.

Gadamer, Hans-Georg. *Wahrheit und Methode: Grundzüge einer philosophischen Hermeneutik*. Tübingen: Mohr, 1960.

.*Wahrheit und Methode. Gesammelte Werk I*. Tübingen: J. C. B. Mohr (Paul Siebeck), 1986.

. *Hermeneutik und Ideologie*. Frankfurt: Suhrkamp, 1970.

.*Truth and Method*. London: Sheed and Ward, 1975.

.*Truth and Method*, trans. revised Joel Weinsheimer and Donald G. Marshall. New York: Crossroad, 2nd rev. ed., 1991.

.*Truth and Method*, trans. Joel Weinsheimer and Donald G. Marshall. New York: Continuum, 2nd rev. ed., 1998.

.*Truth and Method*, trans. Joel Weinsheimer and Donald G. Marshall. London: Continuum, 2nd rev. ed., 2004.

.*Truth and Method*. Harrisburg: Continuum. 2004.

.*Philosophical Hermeneutics*, trans. David E. Linge. Los Angeles: University of California Press, 1976.

.*"The Problem of Historical Consciousness" Interpretive Social Science: A Reader,* eds. Paul Rabinow and William M. Sullivan. Berkeley: University of California Press. 1979.

.*Dialogue and Dialectic: Eight Hermetical Studies on Plato*, trans. Christopher Smith. New Haven: Yale University Press, 1980.

.*Reason in the Age of Science*, trans. Frederick G. Lawrence. Cambridge: MIT Press, 1981.

.*The Relevance of the Beautiful and Other Essays*, ed. Robert Bernasconi. Cambridge: Cambridge University Press, 1986.

.*Gesammelte Werke*. Tübingen: J.C.B. Mohr [Paul Siebeck], 1986.

.*"Text to Interpretation," Dialogue and Deconstruction: The Gadamer-Derrida Encounter*. Albany: SUNY Press, 1989.

.Plato's Dialectical Ethics: Phenomenological Interpretations Relating to the Philebus, trans. Robert M. Wallace, London: Yale University Press, 1991.

.Gadamer on Education, Poetry, and History: Applied Hermeneutics, trans. Lawrence Schmidt and Monica Reuss, Albany: SUNY Press, 1992.

.Heidegger's Way. Albany: State University of New York Press, 1994.

.Philosophical Apprenticeships, Cambridge: MIT Press, 1995.

.The Philosophy of Hans-Georg Gadamer, ed. Lewis Edwin Hahn, LaSalle: Open Court, 1997.

.Hermeneutics, Religion, & Ethics, trans. Joel Weinsheimer, New Haven and London: Yale University Press, 1999.

.Language and Linguisticality in Gadamer's Hermeneutics, ed, Lawrence K. Schmidt. Maryland: The Lexington Books, 2000.

.The Gadamer Reader: A Bouquet of the Later Writings, ed. Richard E. Palmer. Evanston, Illinois: Northwestern University Press, 2007.

Garver, Eugene. *Aristotle's Rhetoric: An Art of Character*. Chicago: The University of Chicago Press, 1994.

Gikandi, Simon. *Reading Chinua Achebe: Language and Ideology in Fiction*. London: James Currey, 1991.

Githae-Mugo, Micere. *Visions of Africa: The Fiction of Chinua Achebe, Margaret Laurence, Elspeth Huxley, and Ngugi wa Thiong'o*. Nairobi: Kenya Literature Bureau, 1978.

Grondin, Jean. *Introduction to Philosophical Hermeneutics*, trans. Joel Weinsheimer .New Haven: Yale University Press, 1994.

.Sources of Hermeneutics. Albany, New York: State University of New York Press, 1995.

Gross, Alan G and Arthur E. Walzer, ed. *Rereading Aristotle's Rhetoric*. Illinois: Southern Illinois University Press, 2000.

Gutmann, Amy, ed. *Multiculturalism*. Princeton, New Jersey: Princeton University Press, 1994.

Halliwell, Stephen. *Aristotle's Poetics*. North Carolina: The University of North   Carolina Press, 1986.

Havelock, E. A. *The Literate Revolution and its Cultural Consequences*. Princeton: Princeton University Press, 1982.

Hegel, G. F. *Reason in History*, trans. Robert S. Hartman. Englewoods Cliffs, New Jersey: Prentice Hall, 1953.

.*The Philosophy of History*, trans. J. Sibree. New York: Dover, 1956.

Heidegger, Martin. *An Introduction to Metaphysics*, trans. Ralph Manheim. New Haven: Yale University Press, 1959.

.*Being and Time*, trans. John Macquarrie and Edward Robinson. New York, 1962.

.*Being and Time*, trans. by Joan Stambaugh. Albany, New York: State University of New York, 1996.

.*On the Way to Language*, trans. Peter D. Hertz. New York, 1971.

.*Platon: Sophistes, Gesamtausgabe* vol. 19. Frankfurt: V. Klostermann, 1992.

.*Plato's Sophist*, trans. Richard Rojcewicz and Andre Schuwer. Bloomington: Indiana University Press, 1997.

Herskovits, M. J. *Dahomean Narrative*. Evanston, 1958.

Höffe, Otfried. *Aristotle*, trans. Christine Salazar. New York: State University of New York Press, 2003.

Husserl, Edmund. *Ideas: General Introduction to Pure Phenomenology*, trans. W. R. Boyce Gibson. London: George Allen and Unwin, 1976.

.*Briefwechsel*. Dordrecht: Kluwer, vol. 5, 1993.

Innes, C. L and Bernth Lindfors, eds. *Critical Perspectives on Chinua Achebe*. Washington DC: Three Continents Press, 1978.

Irele, Francis, Abiola, ed. *Things Fall Apart Chinua Achebe: A Norton Critical Edition*. New York: W. W. Norton and Co, Inc, 2009.

Iroegbu, Panteleon. *Appropriate Ecclesiology* (*Through Narrative Theology to an African Church*). Owerri: International Universities Press, 1996.

Isichei, Elizabeth. *A History of the Igbo People*. London: The Macmillan Press, 1976.

Ker, David, I. *The African Novel and the Modernist Tradition*. New York: Peter Lang, 1997.

Killiam, G. D. *The Novels of Chinua Achebe*. London: Heinemann, 1969.

Kiros, Tedros. *Moral Philosophy and Development: The Condition in Africa*. Ohio University Center for International Studies-Monographs in International Studies Africa Series Number 61, Athens, Ohio 1992.

Kymlicka, Will. *Multicultural Citizenship*. Oxford: Clarendon Press, 1995.

Lavers, Ann and Colin Smith. *Writing Degree Zero*. New York: Hill and Wang, 1968.

Lukacs, Georg. *The Theory of the Novel*. Cambridge, Massachusetts: Harvard University Press, 1977.

Lukes, Steven. *Essays in Social Theory*. New York: Columbia University Press, 1977.

Madu, Okechukwu Raphael. *African Symbols, Proverbs and Myths: The Hermeneutics of Destiny*. New York: Peter Lang, 1996.

Malpas, Jeff, Ulrich Arnswald and Jens Kertscher, eds. *Gadamer's Century: Essays in Honor of Hans-Georg Gadamer*. Cambridge, Massachusetts: The MIT Press, 2002.

Maritain, Jacques. *The Social and Political Philosophy of Jacques Maritain,* ed. by Joseph W. Evans and Leo R. Ward. New York: Image Books, 1965.

Marrou, H. I. A *History of Education in Antiquity*, trans. George Lamb. New York: Mentor, 1964.

Mbiti, John S. *African Religions and Philosophy*. London, 1969.

Merleau-Ponty, Maurice. *Signs*. Evanston, Illinois: Northwestern University Press, 1964.

Misgeld Dieter and Graeme Nicholson, eds. *Hans-Georg Gadamer on Education, Poetry, and History: Applied Hermeneutics*, trans by Lawrence Schmidt and Monica Reuss. New York: State University of New York Press, 1992.

Msiska, Mpalive-Hangson, and David, Whittaker. *Chinua Achebe's Things Fall Apart: A Routledge Study Guide*. New York: Routledge, 2007.

Mueller-Vollmer, K., ed. *The Hermeneutics Reader*. Oxford: Continuum, 1985.

Njoku, John. E. Eberegbulam. *The Igbos of Nigeria: Ancient Rites, Changes, and Survival*. Lewiston, New York: Mellen, 1990.

Njoku, Francis, O. C. *Development and African Philosophy: A Theoretical Reconstruction of African Socio-Political Economy*. New York: iUniverse, Inc., 2004.

Nwala, Uzodimma. *Igbo Philosophy*. Lagos: Lantan Books, 1985.

Obiechina, Emmanuel. *Culture, Tradition and Society in the West African Novel*. London: Cambridge University Press, 1975.

Ogbaa, Kalu. *Understanding Things Fall Apart: A Student Casebook to Issues, Sources, and Historical Documents*. Westport, Connecticut: The Greenwood Press, 1999.

Ogbalu, Chidozu, and Emenanjo, Nolue., eds. *Igbo Language and Culture*. Ibadan: University Press Ltd, 1982.

Ogden, C. K., and Richards, I. A. *Meaning of Meaning*. London: Routledge and Kegan Paul, 1948.

Ogede, Ode. *Chinua Achebe and the Politics of Representation*. Trenton: NJ: Africa World Press, 2001.

   .Achebe's Things Fall Apart: A Reader's Guide. London: Continuum International Publishing Group, 2007.

Oguejiofor, Obi, J., ed. *Philosophy, Democracy and Responsible Governance in Africa*. Munster: Lit Verlag, 2003.

Ohaeto, Ezenwa. *Chinua Achebe: A Biography*. Oxford: James Currey Ltd, 1997.

Okere, Theophilus. *African Philosophy*. New York: University Press of America, 1983.

Okoli, Anayochukwu. *A Sojourner in Her Own Tribe*. Enugu: Mekanand Publications, 1998.

Okpewho, Isidore, ed. *Chinua Achebe's Things Fall Apart: A Casebook*, Oxford: Oxford University Press, 2003.

Olakunle, George. *Relocating Agency: Modernity and African Letters*. Albany: State University of New York Press, 2003.

Onyema, Anozie. *The Igbo Culture and the Formation of Conscience*. Owerri: Assumpta Press, 1999.

Page, T. E., Edward Capps, William Henry Denham Rouse, eds. *The Loeb Classical Library ---Philo*. London: William Heinemann Ltd, MCMXXIX, Vol. 1.

Palmer, Richard E. *Hermeneutics*. Evanston: Northwestern University Press, 1969.

Panikkar, Raimundo. *Myth, Faith and Hermeneutics*. New York: Paulist Press, 1979.

Parker, Michael and Roger Starkey, eds. *Postcolonial Literatures: Achebe, Ngugi, Desai, Walcott*. Houndmills, Basingstoke: Macmillan, 1995.

Pepin, Jean. *Myth et Allegorie*. Paris, 1958.

Philo, *Allegorical Interpretation*, trans. F. H. Colson and G.H. Whitaker. London: William Heinemann Ltd, MCMXXIX, Vol. 1.

.*The Works of Philo*, trans. Charles Duke Yonge. Massachusetts: Hendrickson Publishers, 1993.

Placide, Tempels. *Bantu Philosophy*. Paris: Presence Africains, 1959.

Plato, *The Collected Dialogues of Plato*, ed. Edith Hamilton and Huntington Cairns. Princeton, New Jersey, 1961.

.*Phaedrus and Letters VII and VIII*, trans. Walter Hamilton. London: Penguin, 1973.

Ravenscroft, Arthur. *Chinua Achebe*. London: Longmans, Green and co Ltd, 1969.

Ricoeur, Paul. *History and Truth*. Evanston, Illinois: Northwestern University Press, 1965.

.*The Conflict of Interpretations: Essays in Hermeneutics,* trans. Don Ihde. Evanston: Northwestern University Press, 1974.

.*Interpretation Theory: Discourse and the Surplus of Meaning*. Texas Christian University Press, 1976.

.*The Rule of Metaphor: Multi-Disciplinary Studies of the Creation of Meaning in Language,* trans. R. Czerny. Toronto: University of Toronto Press, 1977.

.*Main Trends in Philosophy*. New York: Holmes and Meier, 1979.

.*Time and Narrative*, trans. Kathleen McLaughlin and David Pellauer, Chicago: The University of Chicago Press, Volumes 1-3, 1983.

.*Text to Action: Essays in Hermeneutics*, trans. Kathleen Blamey and John B. Thompson. Evansto: Northwestern University Press, 1991.

.*Hermeneutics and the Human Sciences,* trans. John B. Thompson. Cambridge: Cambridge University Press, 1994.

Schleiermacher, Friedrich. *Hermeneutik,* trans. H. Kimmerle, Heidelberg: Karl Winter, 1959.

.*Hermeneutics: The Handwritten Manuscripts*, ed. Heinz Himmerle. Missoula, Montana: Scholars Press, 1977.

.*Hermeneutik und Kritik*. Frankfurt am Maim: Suhrkamp, 1977.

Serequeberhan, Tsenay, ed. *African Philosophy: The Essential Readings*. New York: Paragon House, 1991.

.*The Hermeneutics of African Philosophy: Horizon and Discourse*. New York: Routledge, 1994.

Secondary sources

Bellinger, Martha Fletcher. *A Short History of the Drama*. New York: Henry Holt and Company, 1927.

Boal, Augusto. *Theater of the Oppressed*, trans. C.A. and M.O.L McBride. New York: Urizen Book Inc., 1979, original work published in 1974.

Eliade, Mircea, ed. *The Encyclopedia of Religion*. New York: Macmillan Publication Co, 1987, Vol. 11.

English, Edward, D. *Reading and Wisdom of the De Doctrina Christiana of Augustine in the Middle Ages*. Notre Dame and London: University of Notre Dame Press, 1995.

Goodenough, Erwin Ramsdell. *By Light, Light: The Mystical Gospel of Hellenistic Judaism*. London: H. Milford, Oxford University Press, 1935.

Lovelace, Alice. "A Brief History of Theater Forms." *Motion Magazine*, February 15, 1996.

Lucas Basil Mitchell, et al. *An Engagement with Plato's Republic: A Companion to the Republic*. England: Ashgate Publishing Limited, 2003.

Montague, George. T. *The Living Though of St. Paul*. Milwaukee: Bruce Publishing Co., 1966.

Nasr, Seyyed Hossein. *Islam: Religion, History, and Civilization*. New York: HarperSanFrancisco, 2003.

Pappas, Nicholas. *Plato and the Republic*. New York: Routledge Taylor & Francis Group, 2003, Second edition.

Picirilli, Robert. *Paul the Apostle*. Chicago: Moody Press, 1986.

Pollock, John. *The Apostle*. Wheaton, III: Victor Publishing, 1972.

Robb, Kevin, ed. *Language and Thought in Early Greek Philosophy*. LaSalle: Hegeler Institute, 1983.

Ross, W. D. *Aristotle*. London: Methuen & Co. LTD, Third Edition, 1937.

Ruch, E. A and K. C. Anyanwu. *African Philosophy: An Introduction to the Main Philosophical Trends in Contemporary Africa*. Rome: Catholic Book Agency, 1981.

Schmidt, Lawrence, K., ed. *Language and Linguisticality in Gadamer's Hermeneutics*. Maryland: The Lexington Books, 2000.

Senghor, Leopold, S. *On African Socialism*, trans. Mercer Cook. New York: Praeger, 1964.

Simonetti, Manlio. *Biblical Interpretation*, trans. John A. Hughes. Edinburgh: T&T Clark Ltd, 1994.

Smith, Christopher, P. *The Hermeneutics of Original Argument*. Evanston, Illinois: Northwestern University, 1997.

Southern, Richard. *The Seven Ages of the Theater*. New York: Hill and Wang, 1961.

Soyinka, Wole. *The Interpreter*. Britain: Northumberland Press Ltd, 1965.

   .*Myth, Literature and the African World*. Cambridge: Cambridge University Press, 1976.

Spiegelberg, H. *The Phenomenological Movement: A Historical Introduction*. TheHague: Martinus Nijhoff, 3rd Edition, 1982.

Sumner, Claude, ed. *African Philosophy*. Addis Ababa: Addis Ababa University Press, second edition, 1998.

Sweet, William, ed. *Philosophy, Culture, and Pluralism*. Quebec: Editions du Scribe, 2002.

Taran, L. *Academia: Plato, Philip of Opus, and the Pseudo-Platonic Epinomis.* American Philosophical Society, Philadelphia, 1975.

Taylor, Charles. *Hegel.* Cambridge: Cambridge University Press, 1975.

.*Sources of the Self: The Making of the Modern Identity.* Cambridge: Harvard University Press, 1989.

Thiong'o, Ngugi wa. *Decolonising the Mind: The Politics of Language in African Literature.* London: Heinemann, 1986.

Thiselton, Anthony, C. *New Horizons in Hermeneutics: The Theory and Practice of Transforming Biblical Reading.* Grand Rapids, Michigan: Zondervan Publishing House, 1992.

Thompson, John. B. *Critical Hermeneutics: A Study in the Thoughts of Paul Ricoeur and Jürgen Habermas.* Cambridge: Cambridge University Press, 1981.

Turkington, Kate. *Chinua Achebe*: "Things Fall Apart". London: Edward Arnold, 1977.

Warnke, Georgia. *Gadamer: Hermeneutics, Tradition and Reason.* Oxford: Polity Press, 1987.

White, Hayden. *The Content of the Form: Narrative Discourse and Historical Representation.* Baltimore: Johns Hopkins University Press, 1987.

Whitman, Jon. *Interpretation and Allegory: Antiquity to the Modern Period*, ed. with introductory essay by Jon Whitman. Leiden: Koninklijke Brill NV, 2000.

Wiredu, Kwasi and Kwame Gyekye, eds. *Person and Community.* Washington, D. C.: The Council for Research in Values and Philosophy, Vol. 1, 1992.

Woo, Hoon, B. "Augustine's Hermeneutics and Homiletics in De doctrina Christiana Humiliation, Love, Sign, and Discipline." *Journal of Christian Philosophy 17,* 2013.

Wright, Ernest G. *Great People of the Bible and How They Lived.* Pleasantville, New York: The Reader's Digest Association, Inc., 1974.

Wright, Richard, A. *African Philosophy: An Introduction.* New York: University Press of America, 1984.

Articles on Gadamer

Adkins, Arthur. "Orality and Philosophy." *Language and Thought in Early Greek Philosophy*, ed. Kevin Robb. LaSalle: Hegeler Institute, 1983.

Gadamer, Hans-Georg."Hermeneutik." *Historisches Wörterbuch der Philosophie*, ed. J. Ritter, 3 vols. Basel-Stuttgart: Schwabe, 1974.

Gaines, Robert, N. 'Aristotle's Rhetoric and the Contemporary Arts of Practical Discourse.' *Rereading Aristotle's Rhetoric*, ed. Alan G. Gross and Arthur E. Walzer, Illinois: Southern Illinois University Press, 2000.

Grant, Frederick Clifton. "St. Paul and Stoicism." *The Biblical World*, Vol. 45, No. 5. Chicago: The University of Chicago Press, May, 1915.

Gross, Alan, G. "What Aristotle Meant by Rhetoric." *Rereading Aristotle's Rhetoric*. eds. Alan G. Gross and Arthur E. Walzer. Illinois: Southern Illinois University Press, 2000.

Guignon, Charles, B. "Martin Heidegger." *The Cambridge Dictionary of Philosophy*, ed. Robert Audi. Cambridge: Cambridge University Press, second edition, 1999.

Kertscher, Jens. "Gadamer's Ontology of Language Reconsidered." *Gadamer's Century: Essays in Honor of Hans-Georg Gadamer,* eds. Jeff Malpas, Ulrich Arnswald and Jens Kertscher. Cambridge, Massachusetts: The MIT Press, 2002.

MacIntyre, Alasdair. "Relativism, Power and Philosophy," *Proceedings and Addresses of the American Philosophical Association.* APA, Newark, Daleware, 1985.

."On Not Having the Last Word: Thought on Our Debt to Gadamer." *Gadamer's Century: Essays in Honor of Hans-Georg Gadamer,* eds. Jeff Malpas, Ulrich Arnswald and Jens Kertscher. Cambridge, Massachusetts: The MIT Press, 2002.

McDowell, John. "Gadamer and Davidson on Understanding and Relativism." *Gadamer's Century: Essays in Honor of Hans-Georg Gadamer,* eds. Jeff Malpas, Ulrich Arnswald and Jens Kertscher. Cambridge, Massachusetts: The MIT Press, 2002.

Rabinow, Paul and William M. Sullivan, eds. *Interpretive Social Science: A Reader.* Berkeley: University of California Press. 1979.

Segrave, Daniel, L. Gadamer's Hermeneutical Circle, Canonical-Composition Hermeneutics and Paul's "Mystery of Christ" Paper presented at the Annual

Symposium Urshan Graduate School of Theology, Florissant Mo. November 6-7, 2008.

Taylor, Charles. "Understanding the Other: A Gadamerian View on Conceptual Schemes." *Gadamer's Century: Essays in Honor of Hans-Georg Gadamer,* eds. Jeff Malpas, Ulrich Arnswald and Jens Kertscher. Cambridge, Massachusetts: The MIT Press, 2002.

Wachterhauser, Brice. "Getting it Right: Relativism, Realism and Truth." *The Cambridge Companion to Gadamer,* ed. Robert J. Dostal. New York: Cambridge University Press, 2002.

Warnke, Georgia. "Hermeneutics, Ethics, and Politics." The *Cambridge Companion to Gadamer*, ed. Robert J. Dostal. New York: Cambridge University Press, 2002.

Articles on Achebe and African Thought

Achebe, Chinua. "The Role of the Writer in a New Nation." *Nigeria Magazine*, No. 81. June 1964.

."What Has Literature Got to Do with It?" Chinua Achebe, *Hopes and Impediments*, *Selected Essays*. New York: Anchor Books, 1989.

Anozie, Stanley Uche. "Human Rights and Terrorism: The Niger Delta Oil War." *Morality and Terrorism*, ed. Mahmoud Masaeli. California: Nortia Press, 2012.

Begam, Richard. "Achebe's Sense of an Ending: History and Tragedy in *Things Fall Apart*." *Critical Insights: Things Fall Apart*, ed. M. Keith Booker. Pasadena, California: Salem Press, 2011.

Friesen, Alan. R. "Okonkwo's Suicide as an Affirmative Act: Do Things Really Fall Apart?" *Critical Insights: Things Fall Apart*, ed. M. Keith Booker. Pasadena, California: Salem Press, 2011.

Grifiths, Gareth. "Language and Action in the Novels of Achebe." *Critical Perspectives on Chinua Achebe*, ed. C. L. Innes and Bernth Lindfors. Washingston D.C.: Three Continents Press, 1978.

Gyekye, Kwame."Person and Community in African Thought." *Person and Community*, ed. Kwasi Wiredu and Kwame Gyekye.Washington, D.C: The Council for Research in Values and Philosophy, Vol. 1, 1992.

Hallen, Barry. "Phenomenology and the Exposition of African Traditional Thought."
African Philosophy, ed. Claude Sumner. Addis Ababa: Addis Ababa
University Press, second edition, 1998.

Hoegberg, David. "Principle and Practice: The Logic of Cultural Violence in Achebe's
Things Fall Apart." Critical Insights: Things Fall Apart, ed. M. Keith Booker.
Pasadena, California: Salem Press, 2011.

Imbo, Samuel Oluoch. *An Introduction to African Philosophy.* Maryland: Rowman and
Littlefield Publishers, Inc., 1998.

Irele, Francis Abiola. "The Tragic Conflict in the Novels of Chinua Achebe." Critical
Perspectives on Chinua Achebe, ed. C. L. Innes and Bernth Lindfors. Washington
D.C: Three Continents Press, 1978.

        ."Introduction." *Things Fall Apart Chinua Achebe: A Norton
Critical Edition*, ed. Francis Abiola Irele. New York: W. W. Norton and Co, Inc.,
2009.

Janmohamed, Abdul. "Sophisticated Primitivism: The Syncretism of Oral and Literate
Modes in Achebe's *Things Fall Apart." Chinua Achebe Things Fall Apart
(Authoritative Text, Contexts and Criticism),* ed. Francis Abiola Irele. New York:
W. W. Norton & Company, 2009.

Jones, Eldred. "Language and Theme in *'Things Fall Apart'." Review of English
Literature*, Vol. 4. 1964.

Kortenaar, Neil Ten. "How the Centre is Made to Hold in *Things Fall Apart."
Postcolonial Literatures: Achebe, Ngugi, Desai, Walcott,* eds. Michael Parker
and Roger Starkey. Houndmills, Basingstoke: Macmillan, 1995.

        ."The Question of Modern African Tragedy." *Chinua Achebe Things Fall Apart
(Authoritative Text, Contexts and Criticism)*, ed. Francis Abiola Irele. New York: W.
W. Norton & Company, 2009.

Lindfors, Bernth. "The Palm Oil with which Words are Eaten." *African Literature
Today*, 1968.

        "The Palm-oil with which Achebe's Words are Eaten." *Chinua Achebe Things Fall
Apart (Authoritative Text, Contexts and Criticism)*, ed. Francis Abiola Irele. New
York: W. W. Norton & Company, 2009.

Lovesey, Oliver. "Making Use of the Past in *Things Fall Apart." Chinua Achebe's Things
Fall Apart*, ed. Harold Bloom. New York: Infobase Publishers, 2010.

McLaren, Joseph. "Things Fall Apart: Cultural and Historical Contexts." *Critical Insights: Things Fall Apart*, ed. M. Keith Booker. Pasadena, California: Salem Press, 2011.

Menkiti, Ifeanyi, A. "Person and Community in African Traditional Thought." *African Philosophy: An Introduction,* ed. Richard A. Wright. New York: University Press of America (Third Edition), 1984.

Mkhize, D. N. "The Portrayal of Igbo Culture in Zulu." *Chinua Achebe's Things Fall Apart*, ed. Harold Bloom. New York: Infobase Publishers, 2010.

Mphahlele, Ezekiel. "The Language of African Literature." *Harvard Educational Review*, 34. Spring 1964.

Njoku, O. C. Francis, "An African Philosophy of Right: Basis for Leadership and Governance." *Philosophy, Democracy and Responsible Governance in Africa*, ed. Obi J. Oguejiofor. Munster: Lit Verlag, 2003.

Nnoromele, Patrick, C. "The Plight of a Hero in Achebe's Things Fall Apart." *Critical Insights: Things Fall Apart*, ed. M. Keith Booker. Pasadena, California: Salem Press, 2011.

Okpala, Jude Chudi. "Igbo Metaphysics in Chinua Achebe's *Things Fall Apart.*" *Callaloo* 25, 2002.

Okpewho, Isidore. "On the Concept: "Commonwealth Literature." *Meditations on African Literature*, ed. Dubem Okafor. Connecticut: Greenwood Press, 2001.

Onwuanibe, Richard, C. "The Human Person and Immortality in Ibo (African) Metaphysics." *African Philosophy: An Introduction*, ed. Richard A. Wright. New York: University Press of America, 1984.

Onyemelukwe, Ifeoma. "Search for Lost Identity in Achebe's *Things Fall Apart.*" *Emerging Perspectives on Chinua Achebe*, ed. Ernest N. Emenyonu. Trenton, New Jersey: Africa World Press, Inc., 2004.

Pandurang, Mala. "Chinua Achebe and the 'African Experience'." *Chinua Achebe Things Fall Apart (Authoritative Text, Contexts and Criticism)*, ed. Francis Abiola Irele .New York: W. W. Norton & Company, 2009.

Paul Rabinow and William M. Sullivan., eds. *Interpretive Social Science: A Reader,* Berkeley: University of California Press. 1979.

Rowell, Charles H. "An Interview with Chinua Achebe." *Chinua Achebe's Things Fall Apart: a casebook*, ed. Isidore Okpewho. Oxford: Oxford University Press, 2003.

Sarr, Ndiawar. "The Center Holds: The Resilience of Ibo Culture in *Things Fall Apart*." *Global Perspectives on Teaching Literature*, ed. Sandra Ward Lott, Maureen S.   G. Hawkins, et al. Illinois: National Council of Teachers of English, 1993.

Senghor, Léopold Sédar. "Negritude: A Humanism of the Twentieth Century (1966)." *I am Because We Are: Readings in Black Philosophy*, eds. Fred Lee Hord (Mzee Lasana Okpara) and Jonathan Scott Lee. Amherst: University of Massachusetts Press, 1995.

Shelton, Austin, J. "The 'Palm Oil' of Language: Proverbs in Chinua Achebe's Novels." *Modern Language Quarterly*, 30, No. 1. 1969.
Tylor, Edward Burnett, *Primitive Culture*. London: John Murray, 1871.

Uzukwu, Elochukwu, E. "Inculturation of Eucharistic Celebration in Africa." *African Christian Studies*, Vol. 1, 1983.

.*Church and Inculturation*. Nigeria: Pacific College Press Ltd., 1985.

Williams, Raymond. "Culture and Civilization." *The Encyclopedia of Philosophy, ed.* Paul Edward. New York: Macmillian Publishing Co, Inc., & The Free Press: Vol. 11, 1967.

Unpublished Works

Anozie, Stanley Uche. "Authentic Integration Process in Canada and the Contemporary African Concept of the Human Person: Martin Buber's I-Thou Socio philosophy." Unpublished Philosophy Master's Thesis, Dominican University College, Ottawa, August, 2009.

."Fate and Morality in J. R. R. Tolkien's *The Lord of the Rings* and Plato's *Ring of Gyges*." Unpublished Seminar Paper, Saint Paul University, Ottawa, June, 2010.

."Human Rights and Nigeria Niger-Delta Oil Crisis: Alan Gewirth –The Community of Rights." Unpublished Public Ethics Master's Research Paper, Saint Paul University, Ottawa, August, 2010.

CPSIA information can be obtained
at www.ICGtesting.com
Printed in the USA
LVHW051025310121
677942LV00011B/1276